The Clash of Moral Nations

The Clash of Moral Nations

Cultural Politics in Piłsudski's Poland, 1926–1935

Eva Plach

OHIO UNIVERSITY PRESS

ATHENS

Ohio University Press, Athens, Ohio 45701
www.ohio.edu/oupress
© 2006 by Ohio University Press

Ohio University Press books are printed on acid-free paper ∞ ™

First paperback printing in 2014
Paperback ISBN 978-0-8214-2080-5

HARDCOVER   14 12 11 10 09 08 07 06   5 4 3 2 1
PAPERBACK   21 20 19 18 17 16 15 14   5 4 3 2 1

Cover: Detail from *Pytia* (1917) by Jacek Malczewski. Reproduced by permission of the Muzeum Nawdowe Krakowie

Library of Congress Cataloging-in-Publication Data
Plach, Eva, 1969–
   The clash of moral nations : cultural politics in Pilsudski's Poland, 1926–1935 / Eva Plach.
      p. cm. — (Ohio University Press Polish and Polish-American studies series)
   Includes bibliographical references and index.
   ISBN-13: 978-0-8214-1695-2 (alk. paper)
   ISBN-10: 0-8214-1695-2 (alk. paper)
   1. Poland—Politics and government—1918–1945. 2. Poland—Intellectual life—1918–1945. 3. Politics and culture—Poland. 4. Political culture—Poland. 5. Pilsudski, Józef, 1867–1935.
   I. Title. II. Series.

DK4409.5.P58 2006
943.8'04—dc22

                                        2006045334

Publication of books in the Polish and Polish-American Studies Series has been made possible in part by the generous support of the following organizations:

Polish American Historical Association, New Britain, Connecticut

Stanislaus A. Blejwas Endowed Chair in Polish and Polish American Studies, Central Connecticut State University, New Britain, Connecticut

The Polish Institute of Arts and Sciences of America, Inc., New York, New York

The Piast Institute: An Institute for Polish and Polish American Affairs, Detroit, Michigan

*For my mother, Aniela (Ćwik) Plach, and in
memory of my father, Józef Plach (1922–1994)*

It would be lethal if I, taking after many Poles, delighted in
the period of independence (1918–1939); if I did not dare to
look it straight in the eyes with the coldest lack of cere-
mony. I ask that you not consider my coolness a cheap
striving for effect. The air of freedom was given to us so
that we could begin to come to terms with an enemy more
tormenting than the taskmasters we have had up to now:
ourselves. After our struggles with Russia, with Germany,
a struggle with Poland awaited us. It is not surprising,
therefore, that independence turned out to be more bur-
densome and humiliating than bondage. As long as we
were absorbed with the revolt against a foreign power,
questions such as "Who are we?" "What are we to make of
ourselves?" lie dormant, but independence awakened the
riddle that was slumbering within us.

—Witold Gombrowicz (1904–69), diary

Contents

Series Editor's Preface

The interwar era is one of the most underresearched periods in modern Polish history. Nonetheless, it could be argued that during these years, when the country was reconstituted as a nation-state by the terms of the Treaty of Versailles, when the stability of Central Europe loomed as a huge and open question, and when the rise of totalitarianism threatened the post–World War I geopolitical order, events in Poland exerted a determinative influence on the next five decades of European and world history. The failures of the Piłsudski regime and the post-Piłsudski era doomed visions of a Central Europe stabilized and defended through federalist collective security arrangements and left in their wake a power vacuum that was filled forcibly in September 1939 by Nazi and Soviet armies.

In *The Clash of Moral Nations: Cultural Politics in Piłsudski's Poland, 1926–1935,* Professor Eva Plach of Wilfrid Laurier University tackles the intricacies of this underresearched, yet crucial, period. But instead of examining—or, rather, reexamining—the institutional and structural roots of the growing crisis that led first to the fall of Polish democracy and then to the rise of the soft dictatorship of Marshal Piłsudski, Plach investigates the underlying crisis in Polish ideology, culture, values, and world view through which Polish political events and social and economic conditions were filtered and understood and which gave rise to Piłsudski as the would-be moral defender of the nation.

Plach presents here a fresh approach and a highly original take on the period, its fissures and conflicts, and its principal actors. *The Clash of Moral Nations* promises to make an important new contribution to the historiography of these critical years, particularly in its examination of gender issues in interwar Polish political life, a hitherto unexplored topic, but one that Plach argues, quite persuasively, is central to the political and ideological discourse of the period. The book enriches our understanding of the cultural and social themes that marked the road that led to general war in Europe in 1939 but also, ironically, may help to illuminate the rightist currents in contemporary Polish society and political life in the early twenty-first century.

Publication of the Ohio University Press Polish and Polish-American Studies Series marks a milestone in the maturation of the Polish studies field and stands as a fitting tribute to the scholars and organizations whose efforts have brought it to fruition. Supported by a series advisory board of accomplished Polonists and Polish-Americanists, the Polish and Polish-American Studies Series has been made possible through generous financial assistance from the Polish American Historical Association, the Polish Institute of Arts and Sciences of America, the Stanislaus A. Blejwas Endowed Chair in Polish and Polish American Studies at Central Connecticut State University, and the Piast Institute and through institutional support from Wayne State University and Ohio University Press. The series meanwhile has benefited from the warm encouragement of a number of other persons, including Gillian Berchowitz, M. B. B. Biskupski, the late Stanislaus A. Blejwas, Mary Erdmans, Thaddeus Gromada, James S. Pula, Thaddeus Radzilowski, and David Sanders. The moral and material support from all of these institutions and individuals is gratefully acknowledged.

John J. Bukowczyk

Acknowledgments

Many institutions and individuals contributed to this book, and it is a pleasure to acknowledge them here. For their financial support, I would like to thank the Social Sciences and Humanities Research Council of Canada, the University of Toronto, and the Wilfrid Laurier University Research Office. I owe the largest debt of gratitude to Piotr Wróbel, Konstanty Reynert Chair of Polish History at the University of Toronto, for his tremendous personal and intellectual generosity. I consider it a great privilege to know so fine a historian. From the University of Toronto, I would also like to thank Michael Marrus, Andrew Rossos, and Modris Eksteins, each of whom shared time and expertise most unselfishly. In addition, I am enormously grateful to Antony Polonsky of Brandeis University for his comments on an earlier version of this work as well as for his ongoing support. I would also like to thank John Bukowczyk, editor of the Polish and Polish-American Studies Series, as well as Gillian Berchowitz and Rick Huard at Ohio University Press.

I would also like to thank my colleagues and friends at Wilfrid Laurier University; I could not imagine a better place to be a historian than Laurier. In particular, Erich Haberer, John Laband, Joyce Lorimer, Susan Neylan, and George Urbaniak have been gracious and reliable mentors. I have been fortunate, in fact, to have had other superb mentors over the years: Barbara Todd of the University of Toronto, as well as Deborah Gorham and Pamela Walker of Carleton University in Ottawa, are among the best historians I know, and they remain an inspiration.

For the Polish context, I would like to thank Anna Żarnowska for her assistance during my stay in Warsaw and Andrzej Chojnowski for entertaining my earliest ideas on this topic. The librarians and archivists at the National Library in Warsaw and at Warsaw's Archive of Recent Documents were terribly kind and patient, as were the archivists at the Manuscript Division of the National Library and at the University of Warsaw Library Archives.

Thanks go to the following historians, my friends, for their input at different stages of this project: Hilary Earl, Joseph Kadezabek, Tracy McDonald, Aleksander Panev, and Alexander Prusin. For their support, I also thank Gillian Burnett, Peter Copeland, Ken Hogue, and Ina Puchala, as well as the various branches of the Wallwork family. Robert Wallwork has been with me, and therefore with this project, since its inception. He has been the most loving and generous husband and friend, and simply the finest intellectual companion.

My father, Józef Plach, was born in Poland in 1922, the year that the Second Republic's first president, Gabriel Narutowicz, was assassinated. My mother, Aniela (Ćwik) Plach, was born in 1935, the year that Józef Piłsudski died. Coincidentally, these dates form the temporal boundaries of this project. My parents have given me a life that has made so very much possible, and I dedicate this effort to them.

Abbreviations

BBWR	Bezpartyjny Blok Współpracy z Rządem (Nonpartisan Bloc for Cooperation with the Government)
PPS	Polska Partia Socjalistyczna (Polish Socialist Party)
PSL-Piast	Polskie Stronnictwo Ludowe–Piast (Polish People's Union–Piast)
SN	Stronnictwo Narodowe (National Party)
ZLN	Związek Ludowo-Narodowy (People's National Union)

Guide to Pronunciation

The following key provides a guide to the pronunciation of Polish words and names.

a is pronounced as in *father*

c as ts in *cats*

ch like a guttural h

cz as hard ch in *church*

g always hard, as in *get*

i as ee

j as y in *yellow*

rz like French j in *jardin*

sz as sh in *ship*

szcz as shch, enunciating both sounds, as in *fresh cheese*

u as oo in *boot*

w as v

ć as soft ch

ś as sh

ż, ź both as zh, the latter higher in pitch than the former

ó as oo in boot

ą as French *on*

ę as French *en*

ł as w

ń changes the combinations -in to -ine, -en to -ene, and -on to -oyne

The accent in Polish words always falls on the penultimate syllable.

Three Days That Shook the Republic, May 12–15, 1926

WHEN WINCENTY WITOS (1874–1945), the leader of the right-wing branch of the Polish peasant movement, the Polish People's Union–Piast (Polskie Stronnictwo Ludowe–Piast, PSL-Piast), entered into a coalition government with other right-nationalist parties on May 10, 1926, riots broke out across Warsaw, Poland's capital.[1] The formation of another "Chjena-Piast"[2] government, as its detractors referred to the coalition, recalled the devastating inflation, unemployment, and worker unrest that had marked Witos's earlier coalition government of 1923. The sense of desperation in a population already dealing with serious economic and political crisis in the Polish Second Republic was raised to dramatic heights.[3] As it happens, the new Witos government would last only five days before it crumbled in the face of a military coup launched by renowned political leader Józef Piłsudski (1867–1935).

By the mid-1920s, Piłsudski had already devoted himself to Poland in a variety of remarkable ways: he had been an antitsarist socialist revolutionary in the Russian partition during the late nineteenth century, a founding member of the pro-independence Polish Socialist Party (PPS), and an early editor of the influential underground socialist newspaper the *Worker (Robotnik)*.[4] Piłsudski had served as the Second Republic's head of state from 1918 to 1922, Poland's first marshal since 1920, and chief of the general staff from 1918 to 1923. He was a resolute patriot and an indefatigable proponent of Polish independence.

In his vitriol against the new Witos government and the right-nationalists, Piłsudski was supported by a loosely linked assortment of men and women drawn from Poland's intelligentsia, many of whom shared past experiences first in the Socialist Party and later in the wartime struggle for independence. Linked primarily by their loyalty to the charismatic Piłsudski, the Piłsudski-ites (Piłsudczycy), or the Belvedere Camp,[5] as they were also known, formed one of the most important political forces in the new state. Even though the Piłsudskiites did not have a definable political structure or party until after the coup of May 1926, their ideology and political goals had been taking shape since independence. Notably, the Piłsudskiites shared an attachment to nineteenth-century Polish romanticism and to the idea of a brotherhood of nations and were steadfastly committed to maintaining the multiethnic heritage of the old Polish-Lithuanian Commonwealth.[6] These views made the Piłsudskiites the sworn enemies of the right-nationalist camp, best represented by the National Democrats. National Democracy's cofounder, elder statesman, theoretician, and symbolic leader throughout the interwar period was Roman Dmowski (1864–1939). Dmowski subscribed to an integral Polish nationalism and be-lieved that ethnic and national bonds were the highest forms of social cohe-sion; he envisioned a Poland that was ethnically homogenous, Catholic, and morally and socially conservative.[7] The National Democrats' political party, the People's National Union (Związek Ludowo-Narodowy, ZLN), was the strongest and largest party of the right. The National Union was included in the May 1926 Witos coalition.[8]

The formation of this right-nationalist coalition in May 1926 greatly an-gered Piłsudski and his supporters and served as an occasion for them both to rage against the nationalist right generally and to condemn the whole state of political life in the new Poland. From the Piłsudskiite perspective, the course of postpartition Polish history—that is, the history of Poland since indepen-dence in 1918—had yielded few glorious moments, and in this regard, the Pił-sudskiites claimed, the nationalists had much to answer for.[9] Since the very inception of the Second Republic, one political crisis after another emerged to shake citizens' confidence in the ability of the government, indeed of the democratic process generally, to address adequately the many pressing social and economic challenges that the new state faced. Most notably, there was the assassination by a National Democracy supporter of the Second Repub-lic's first regularly elected president, Gabriel Narutowicz (1865–1922), in 1922. Narutowicz had won the presidency with the votes of a significant portion of the country's ethnic minority population, which accounted for about 30 per-cent of the whole.[10] That Narutowicz had been Piłsudski's favored candidate for the job further discredited him in the eyes of the nationalist right, and his victory sparked a series of violent street riots. His assassination shortly after the election widened the gulf between, on the one hand, the Poland of the nationalist camp and, on the other, the Poland of the Piłsudskiites, the political left, and the progressive liberal-democrats—grouped, at least for a time, into a single polarity.[11] This tension between the two positions became even more pointed when, in certain right-nationalist circles, Narutowicz's assassin was hailed as a hero.[12] The assassination of the first president of the newly independent nation marked an early turning point in the republic's short history and further poisoned an already tense political and social environment. Independence was fast becoming, as Witold Gombrowicz had suggested, "more humiliating than bondage."[13]

A total of fourteen governments had attempted to govern Poland from 1918 to May 1926, and by the mid-1920s political polarizations had reached a fever pitch; there were almost one hundred political parties in Poland, close to a third of them represented in the Sejm, the lower house of the Polish parliament.[14] The basic point on which even people of wildly opposed political views agreed was that there existed a pressing need to "fix" the Second Republic. Many blamed the unfortunate political situation on the March 1921 constitution, which had provided for a weak presidency and a strong Sejm. The critics argued that this arrangement made successful majorities difficult to maintain and necessitated a reliance on coalition governments—which were themselves difficult to achieve in a highly polarized political environment— and had laid the groundwork for the impractical and ultimately disastrous "Sejmocracy" (parliamentocracy) that had emerged in Poland.[15] So it was that politics in the Second Republic, until those fated days in May 1926, was defined by a succession of short-lived and unstable governments. The Witos government of 1926 appeared as yet another in a long line of uninspired and ineffective coalition governments.

As the Witos government was forming, the Piłsudskiites spread a rumor that the new coalition was prepared to act decisively against the constitution and that it was orchestrating a coup to assure long-term political preeminence for the nationalist right. From the Piłsudskiite perspective, there was some real cause for alarm: in a short political statement published earlier in 1926, *The Times and the People (Czasy i ludzie)*, Witos had raised the ire of Piłsudskiites by advocating radical changes to Poland's parliamentary democracy. He had warned that the already "catastrophic" situation in Poland could deteriorate even further, and he implied the need for a "strong hand" to take charge of the situation.[16] In these early days of May, Witos's words underscored the foreboding that many felt.[17]

The events that unfolded during the coming days should not have come as much of a surprise to any astute observer of the Second Republic. As journalist Konrad Olchowicz stated in his memoirs, no one could have predicted what exactly would happen during these early days of May, but many were able to sense change in the air: "One could have expected anything."[18] Demonstrations, some spontaneous and some planned, in opposition to the Witos government and in support of Piłsudski erupted across the capital on May 11.[19] Piłsudskiites paraded around Warsaw shouting, "Long live Piłsudski" and "Down with Witos." In an effort to recall the Polish Legions, which had been organized to spearhead the fight for an independent Polish state during the Great War and in which Piłsudski had been a dominating personality, Piłsudskiites forced people to sing the march of the First Brigade. Piłsudski himself had commanded the First Brigade, and several years after Polish independence had been achieved, the march continued to function as a Piłsudskiite national anthem. The tension was further heightened when rumors spread that gunshots had been fired on Sulejówek, a villa on the outskirts of Warsaw to which Piłsudski, disgusted by a political system burdened with what he had called "the moral responsibility" for the assassination of President Narutowicz, had ostensibly retired in 1923. The rumors did much to provide Piłsudski with a moral justification for what happened next.[20]

On May 12, Piłsudski and his army of about two thousand men advanced toward Warsaw.[21] Piłsudski's aim was to organize a nonviolent show of force and to mount an impressive political demonstration that would prove to everyone that only Piłsudski could save a nation plagued by social, economic, political, and ethnic tensions and that, accordingly, he should be handed executive power peacefully.[22] Confronted with resistance from the government, however, Piłsudski was forced to consider other options, and so it was that the May coup d'état unfolded. By the end of the three-day civil war, as many referred to the events, close to four hundred people would be dead and about one thousand injured.[23]

Late on the fourteenth and into the morning of the fifteenth, the government forces asked for a cease-fire in order to prevent the escalation of violence across Poland.[24] The president resigned, as did Prime Minister Witos and his government. Piłsudski became minister of military affairs (from May 15) and inspector general of the Polish armed forces (from August 28).[25] On Piłsudski's instruction, Kazimierz Bartel (1882–1941) became prime minister on May 15. A short while later, the Sejm and the Senate elected Piłsudski president of the republic, but Piłsudski refused the position. On Piłsudski's recommendation, scholar and former socialist Ignacy Mościcki (1867–1946) was elected president in June 1926; he held the post until 1939.[26]

The coup of May 12–15, 1926, expressed frustration with the profound failures of each successive government of newly independent Poland, with the deep polarization of political life, and with the quality of independence generally. The young republic had been experiencing what the Piłsudski faction referred to as a "moral breakdown" of its public life.[27] Supporters of Piłsudski emphasized that the coup had been waged for the "moral good" of the nation and with the intention of effecting a Poland-wide spiritual rebirth. The Polish Socialist Party, of which Piłsudski had been a founding member but with which he had long ago broken, hailed Piłsudski's actions as a revolution against the Chjeno-Piast coalition, which threatened to ruin the nation "politically and morally," and they welcomed the "better future" that lay ahead.[28] Warsaw's liberal *Morning Courier* (*Kurier poranny*) similarly hailed the "moral rebirth of the nation" that the coup promised to introduce and proclaimed that the event formed a necessary precursor to wider economic and political reform.[29]

Piłsudski himself had remarked just weeks after the coup, "In the reborn country, there did not emerge a rebirth of spirit . . . rather, scoundrels and rogues and blackguards held sway. The nation has been reborn in only one area, that is, in terms of individual boldness and service to the state in times of battle. Thanks to this I was able to take the war to its successful end. In all other areas I have found no rebirth."[30] It was Piłsudski, moreover, who had issued a nationwide call on the night of May 12, just as the events were getting under way, to focus on what he called *imponderabilia*—"like honor, virtue, courage, and generally, all the internal strengths of a person."[31] It was this appeal to widen the scope of what was considered political and to embrace imponderables that resonated powerfully and in a wide variety of unexpected ways with the populace of the Second Republic. This resonance forms the backbone of the present study. Piłsudski's coup of 1926 gave birth to what became known as the *sanacja,* a word derived from the Latin *sanatio,* meaning healing, rejuvenation, cleansing, or reform. The sanacja period lasted, in various permutations, right to the outbreak of the Second World War and to the last days of the Second Republic, in 1939.

Historians have traditionally interpreted the coup as the product of a profoundly sick postpartition political culture. They have understood the sanacja as a period devoted to effecting fundamental reforms in the state's political structures and practices, especially to rewriting the March constitution and securing a stronger executive branch of government. The sanacja was an era dominated by appeals to a new, modern, and more productive citizenship, to the primacy of collective over individual interests, to "clean hands," "the state above all else," and "work as the highest calling." Studies emphasizing these aspects of the question have been numerous and important.[32] The present study, rather than offering a broad overview of the post-May regime and in contrast to traditional approaches to the period, is interested in the wider cultural significance of the sanacja and in the ways in which its language of purification, health, and rebirth resonated outside the very public and strictly political and military contexts in which the event is customarily considered. This is a study of the incredibly powerful yet underexplored subtext of the period, of the ways in which the sanacja was imbued with a fantastically wide range of meaning after 1926, and of the way in which it was used, misused, and manipulated in the cultural and political discourses of the Second Republic; it is a study of the sanacja as symbol and potential. As such, it understands sanacja broadly, as a particularly flexible and reverberant idea that could move between and speak simultaneously to both the political and the cultural realms.

The May coup and the sanacja it proclaimed initiated a fascinating national forum on what the new state had become, and it provided a focus for the ideas about national and moral identities that had been circulating in Polish society ever since the inception of the Second Republic. By popularizing a vocabulary of rebirth and change, of moral responsibility, civic duty, and citizen accountability, work and collective action, the sanacja sparked a widespread debate about the meaning of Poland and Polish national identity in the modern era. Both as a concrete political mandate and as an idea, the sanacja was astonishingly imprecise: it favored a rousing rhetorical appeal to imponderables—abstract invocations of morality, virtue, action, and civic courage—over practical reform measures. The utopian open-endedness of the sanacja, the very malleability and mobility of its language, made it available to opponents and proponents alike as a set of ideas with which to critique contemporary social, political, and moral ills. It was in the malleability of the term *sanacja* and in its applicability to a varied range of problems that potential lay.

Maria Dąbrowska (1889–1965), one of the most successful and well-respected writers associated with the progressive leftist interwar intelligentsia and for some time a proponent of Piłsudski's actions, wrote in her diary, on May 17, 1926, just days after the coup: "There happened in Warsaw a thing at once terrifying and wondrous, like a chapter from Greek history. A military revolution with a moral ideal. . . . Two moral nations have clashed in Poland. One a nation of action and perfection, of getting to the heart of questions, and the second a nation of lies and convention. The values for new life have been formed. But what will we, society, do with them? Piłsudski cannot do everything for us."[33]

Dąbrowska's words reveal the tremendous anticipation that she and many like her placed in the May coup; it would be the start of something positively momentous and of a revolution unlike any other. This idea that Piłsudski had rescued the nation from a dreadful future and had laid the basis for positive change was perpetuated by the press as well as in personal attitudes and commentary; it was also reflected in the emergence of organizations devoted to specific aspects of the sanacja's potential. Those who supported Piłsudski and the coup—men and women drawn mainly, though not exclusively, from the left-liberal intelligentsia—claimed a morally just position for themselves. Theirs was the nation of "action and perfection"; these were people who embraced the modern age and the new intellectual currents and cultural shifts that came with it, and they saw in the sanacja the opportunity for secularism and for a severing of the seemingly inviolable connection between Catholicism, Polishness, and patriotism. Their positions could not be reconciled with the nation of "lies and convention," associated so clearly in the minds of the Piłsudskiites with their archenemies, National Democracy and the right-nationalist-Catholic camp generally. For right-nationalist-Catholic opponents of the coup, the sanacja, supported as it was by agents of secular reform, was itself irrefutable evidence of the lingering ill effects of the partitions and of the deep moral rot that had infested the Polish national body. The May coup reflected these polarized political allegiances in the republic, but it also exacerbated them by creating even more obviously divergent camps and transforming them into irreconcilable moral categories.

At the most reductive level, the clash of Poland's moral nations was between left and right. But at a more essential level, the struggle was over "who" would shape and ultimately control definitions of everything from models of femininity and definitions of the nation to ideas about citizen activism and service to the state. The fight was over symbols and definitions of Polishness and of Poland, over who and what would determine and control the postpartition future. The political caesura of 1926 forced people to take sides, declare allegiances, and articulate visions of the ideal future. This study will explore how the moral nations took shape after the coup; it will probe the political and cultural landscape that was formed in Poland after May 1926 with the proclamation of a very powerful—and very flexible—notion of moral reform.

The Imponderables

Individuals and groups imbued Piłsudski's sanacja with varied and creative meaning. Each chapter begins with the May coup itself and studies a particular reading of the event and the ensuing sanacja; each focuses, that is, on a different rendering of Piłsudski's imponderables. I begin by examining the preoccupation with moral crisis evident in the Warsaw-based press immediately before and after the May coup. Though they had existed since the start of independence, debates about culture and morality escalated in the right-nationalist press as a result of the proclamation of a sanacja and generally, as a result of the Piłsudskiites' dominance over the political life of the state. Right-nationalist opponents of Piłsudski used the sanacja as a springboard from which to launch wholesale condemnations of the moral and cultural state of the nation. Already we see a persistent tendency in post-May Poland for public discussions of the sanacja to refer back continually to themes related to gender, sexuality, and moral degeneration and regeneration. This focus on sexual and moral questions, as reflected in the debates studied throughout this work, is an important element in the broader political culture of the Second Republic.

Letters written to Piłsudski during the sanacja from segments of the public —some from the margins of society— show that a wide range of individuals believed they had something important to say about the sanacja and that Piłsudski himself should listen to their opinions. After all, had Piłsudski not invited precisely this sort of active citizen involvement in shaping discourses about the moral fabric of the nation? These letter writers adopted much of the same language about national and moral cleansing that appeared in more formal and important renderings of the sanacja project, but each added his or her own unique twist to the basic sanacja concept. The simple fact that these letters were written in the first place encourages us to understand the sanacja in its widest possible incarnation and in terms of its broadest potential. While people differed over what kind of a sanacja was necessary, few would have denied that some sort of a serious reflection on the state of Poland was necessary.

The left-liberal intellectuals who formed the little-known Warsaw-based Society for the Moral Rebirth of the Nation (Towarzystwo Odrodzenia Moralnego Ojczyzny) (1926–32) embraced Piłsudski's coup as an important catalyst for moral and national rebirth. While it is fair to say that the society remained ineffective for the duration of its existence (if one measures effectiveness in terms of membership numbers and projects completed) it nevertheless saw a number of prominent sanacja politicians—like Walery Sławek and Janusz Jędrzejewicz—pass through its ranks. Though the group achieved little, its statements of intent and its analyses of the meaning of sanacja and of the state of Polish independence reveal much about the mood, expectations, and hopes of the period.

A wave of women's activism was also sparked by the coup, resulting in the formation of groups like the Women's Democratic Election Committee (Demokratyczny Komitet Wyborczy Kobiet) (1928) and the Women's Union for Citizenship Work (Związek Pracy Obywatelskiej Kobiet) (1928–39). Some women of the pro-Piłsudski, left-liberal intelligentsia, with Zofia Moraczewska in the lead, argued that, as women, they had a special role of fulfill in the sanacja project. The sanacja, after all, had declared the importance of moral health and of achieving a national cleansing, and according to such women, the moral realm was women's preserve. If the formal political sanacja were serious about moral reform, then women needed to be brought in on the project; in the process, women would themselves be transformed into fully engaged female citizens of the new state.

Returning to the ideas about gender roles and sexual morality raised at the beginning of this study, I introduce Tadeusz Boy Żeleński—cabaret writer, publicist, exponent of women's rights over their bodies, medical doctor, and prolific translator of classic French literature—as the most powerful symbol of what critics identified as the pernicious cultural sanacja that had raged within Poland since May 1926. Right-nationalist-Catholic critics created the term *Boy's sanacja* to register a link between the political sanacja, on the one hand, and, on the other, liberal attitudes toward modern and Western cultural trends and values. This coupling represents perhaps one of the most creative and telling manipulations of the sanacja word and idea. Right-nationalist critics argued that the sanacja had authorized flagrant violations of Polish history, religious beliefs, and appropriate gender roles and had licensed a private (im)morality that was inconsistent with political stability and good citizenship. "Boyshevism," Bolshevism, a Judeo-Masonic conspiracy, and the sanacja, critics maintained, were all expressions of a single threat.

Through these five different sites of analysis, I examine sanacja-era Poland's preoccupation with the idea of impending moral collapse. Each section explores contemporary discourses about the moral health of the nation—discourses fueled by anxiety about Poland's postpartition cohesion and stability, its identity, cultural autonomy, and encounters with European modernity. This book, then, is as much about the forms that debates about collective national identities took during Poland's interwar period and about the struggles inherent in reconciling competing visions of the nation, as it is about the sanacja specifically.

In all these renderings of the imponderables, moreover, this study focuses (though not exclusively) on the so-called elites of the Second Republic, on the intellectual stratum of society.[34] The majority of the population in the new Polish state was composed of peasants and agricultural laborers, and the divide between social groups was wide; this was, arguably, one of the defining features of the new Poland. The intelligentsia, in contrast, formed a very small group: in 1921 it constituted about 3.5 percent of the economically engaged population (out of a total population of about 27 million) and by 1931 it had grown by just over one percent.[35] The Polish interwar intelligentsia included not only those who had professional qualifications from institutes of higher education but also all those who made a living from nonmanual labor—writers, scholars, artists, office workers, civil servants—whether or not they had been formally educated.[36] The Polish intelligentsia, like the eastern European intelligentsia more broadly, was not typically part of a traditional middle class, as it was in western Europe.[37] It was, rather, part of an economically in-secure group. Yet the intelligentsia in eastern Europe, and in Poland especially, was a culturally, politically, and socially central group. Its centrality derived from the singularly important role it had played during the nineteenth-century partition period, when it was engaged in what historians have called a rule of souls.[38] During this period, members of the intelligentsia played an almost sacred role in the nation, serving as political leaders and as the unofficial am-bassadors of the Polish nation and its independence cause. [39]

Confronted with independence, the intelligentsia was forced to renego-tiate its role in and its relationship to the nation. Indeed, a self-reflexive inter-est in what role the intelligentsia played or should play in the nation was a key feature of postwar debates not just in Poland but across Europe. In con-trast to western Europe, the intelligentsia in Poland after the war could for the first time "abandon" the nation and what had hitherto constituted the defining imperative of its existence. Independence allowed some members of the intelligentsia to rethink their moral responsibility to the nation and to es-chew, for example, the tendency to use literature as a way of furthering the Polish national cause; members of the intelligentsia could act instead to de-velop new terms of interaction between themselves and the nation. Individu-als might have chosen to remain committed popularizers of patriotic ideas, or conversely, they might have opted to ignore the national question com-pletely. The very recognition of that choice was anathema to certain cultural commentators, and the question produced intensely polarized views.[40]

As we shall see, ideas regarding the role of the intelligentsia in indepen-dent Poland were linked, in turn, to debates about what the sanacja was or should be. It was the intelligentsia that was most engaged with questions about the nation's moral health and potential and that found in the sanacja's call to defend the nation's imponderables a focus and inspiration. Through the debates that the intelligentsia generated and in which it was involved, it en-gaged some of the most fundamental ideas about what it meant to be Polish.

This exposition, moreover, is focused on personalities who were based in Warsaw and on the cultural products and trends that emanated from the Sec-ond Republic's capital city. Warsaw's population in 1918 was 758,400 (down from 884,500 in 1914); it reached 936,700 by 1921. The city enjoyed a compara-tively diversified work force, including a high percentage of blue-collar work-ers. Its population also included a significant percentage of self-employed artisans and merchants. The population was composed mainly of Polish Catholics and Jews; Germans and Ukrainians existed only in small numbers in the capital city.[41]

Emphasis on a single city, surely, cannot accommodate the various regional divisions and peculiarities evident in the Second Republic. The need for caution, then, in drawing certain generalizations from a study based on Warsaw, is acknowledged. At the same time, and as some contemporaries themselves argued, Warsaw functioned as the undisputed cultural and intellectual center that shaped nationwide patterns.[42] The intelligentsia, whose ideas underpin this study, was either physically present in Warsaw or was engaged with the ideas that emanated from that city. In addition, Warsaw was by far the most important center of publishing in the Second Republic, and most of the major periodicals of the period, some of which are used in this study, were published there.[43]

Warsaw was also invested with great symbolic meaning. As the capital city, it was the seat of the government and the locus of the many important political happenings that were central to the way that contemporaries thought about the trajectory of independence. Piłsudski's May coup, moreover, did much to cast Warsaw into the spotlight. The fighting between Piłsudski's forces and the government troops had actually taken place in Warsaw, and it was there that men had died fighting during those fateful days in May. Piłsudski's ensuing sanacja government was based in Warsaw; it was, for better or worse, the seat of the moral revolution.[44]

Narrating the Event

From the beginning, the coup d'état provided fertile terrain for political, social, and cultural analysis. Contemporary reporters, writers, politicians, and intellectuals all wrote about some aspect of the event, pondered its causes and its ramifications, and declared their allegiances.[45] Historians have also shown great interest in the coup and are agreed that the event was the single most important political caesura of the interwar period.[46] The earliest communist scholarship tended to depict the Piłsudski coup and the Second Republic generally as a socially, economically, and politically reactionary period that stymied the real potential of socialism.[47] Beginning with the late

1970s and early 1980s, the coup and the sanacja became the subject of several important works in political history.[48] This interest in the sanacja, and in the Second Republic generally, has blossomed during the postcommunist period, as historians of the Third Republic draw parallels between Poland's most recent period of independence and the Second Republic.[49]

In the whole of this scholarship on the coup and the sanacja era, a number of specific emphases emerge. One of the most richly studied topics concerns whether the coup was planned or whether it was a more improvised affair. There is some evidence to suggest that Piłsudskiite conspiratorial groups, especially within the army, had worked assiduously for a few years before May 1926 to position the ostensibly retired Piłsudski for a future return to public life. That the portion of the army loyal to Piłsudski encouraged Piłsudski's return to public life is beyond doubt, and that Piłsudski had used his semiretirement to rally support for himself and to arouse hostility toward the center-right coalitions is also clear.[50] But it is fair to say, too, that the coup d'état, as it actually occurred, was a blend of both meticulous planning and spontaneous and intrepid action. Piłsudski did not expect to spark a civil war in Poland, though he was prepared in May 1926 for a number of developments and was willing to consider a wide range of actions.[51] But whether the actual May events were planned or not is beside the point of this exposition. What is important is that during those days in May, Piłsudski unleashed forces and ideas that he did not and would not control. The unpredictability of the sanacja and its ability to seduce different individuals and groups in unanticipated ways reveal much about Polish conceptions of independence and national identity.

Historians have also been interested in the extent to which we can understand the affront to democracy in May 1926 as a uniquely Polish affair, or conversely, as symptomatic and reflective of a Europe-wide postwar phenomenon marked by frequent assaults on democratic institutions and a profound crisis of faith in democratic potential. Clearly there were many similarities between what was happening in the Polish context and what was occurring throughout Europe at this time. In the eastern European context, this question of democracy in the interwar period has been a particularly vexing one: all the states in the region, with the exception of Czechoslovakia, succumbed quickly and thoroughly to varying forms of authoritarianism.[52] Historians of Poland tend to regard the government from 1926 to 1930 as a "guided democracy." During this period, certain structures and forms of the parliamentary system were retained. At the same time, however, Piłsudski himself appointed the cabinets, played a preponderant role in decision making, and assumed some of the postures of a dictator.[53] Typically, 1930 is taken as the end of guided democracy and the end of the first, comparatively mild, period in the sanacja's history. In September 1930, Piłsudski imprisoned at the fortress of Brześć (Brest Litovsk) members of the sanacja political opposition, grouped together in a bloc of center-left parties called Centrolew.[54] The sanacja camp defended its actions in this matter by arguing that the opposition activists were preparing a coup against the government and that time was limited; in this reading of the event, the continued assaults on democracy become a purely defensive attempt to prevent the spread of anarchy.

After Brześć, the regime turned increasingly authoritarian and lost much of the support on which it had relied since 1926. According to Maria Dąbrowska, Brześć represented the final severing of the moral links between the people and Piłsudski.[55] By 1930 the sanacja was viewed by many former supporters as an immoral, spent idea. Many condemned the political regime that the sanacja had created as authoritarian and cursed the regime's promoters as fallen moral beacons who had failed to make good on the sanacja's promises of national rebirth. The present study does not fundamentally overturn either this sensible periodization or characterization of sanacja phases. It does place the emphasis, however, on the continuity of the utopian or neo-romanticist elements of the sanacja and on the willingness of people to keep imagining and reimagining how they might reach the imponderables and effect the wholesale rebirth of Polish society.

Things changed with the death of Piłsudski, in 1935. This was the moment that the actual sanacja regime lost its uniting force and inspiration. By this time, too, any claims that the sanacja represented higher morality and that it worked for the greater good could scarcely be made. Finally, by this time (the early to mid-1930s) pressing social and economic concerns eclipsed arguably intangible questions about moral health and national renaissance. At the moment of Piłsudski's death, the sanacja camp had largely disintegrated (though its successors ruled to the outbreak of World War II), and it became impossible to imbue the sanacja with virtue and positive potential.[56]

A great deal of scholarly attention has also been accorded the fact that a significant segment of the political left, most notably the Polish Socialists, and the Communists, initially supported the military coup and saw in it the hope and potential for a real socialist revolution.[57] The figure of Piłsudski himself was instrumental in this.[58] There were a number of compelling reasons for the socialists to place their faith in Piłsudski, their old comrade from the prewar socialist movement. Piłsudski had the real support and confidence of a number of prominent socialist men and of a large part of the left-liberal progressive intelligentsia. Piłsudski, moreover, was a far better option than that represented by the nationalist camp. Furthermore, Piłsudski's language about the need for fundamental transformation and dramatic revolution, for a purge and cleansing, was easily absorbed into and accommodated by a socialist worldview. The contention of this study is that the language of the sanacja was so broad and open-ended as to make a daunting variety of interpretations possible.

And yet the reality was that the Piłsudski of the Second Republic was not a socialist; historians have often repeated Piłsudski's alleged statement that he had stepped off the socialist train at the stop marked independence.[59] The results of the coup, as Polish Socialists of the period would quickly see, hardly approximated a left-wing agenda. Shortly after the coup, Piłsudski issued a press interview in which he attempted to clarify his intentions and to dispel any thoughts that the coup d'état had been waged to effect fundamental changes to the status quo. The interview was published in Warsaw's *Morning Courier* on May 27, 1926. His would be "a revolution without revolutionary consequences," Piłsudski stated, and he cautiously but deliberately distanced himself from the left.[60] In the months following the coup, Piłsudski would build political support not on the left, as many had hoped he would. Rather, he reached out to the political and economic conservatives (not to be confused with National Democrats and nationalists generally) on the right.[61] It became clear that the coup was intended to preserve and protect the status quo rather than overturn it.[62]

The sanacja, as previous scholarship has emphasized, possessed no real program beyond the open-ended avowals of cleansing, reform, and strengthening the state.[63] My own treatment of the sanacja does not construct a political program for the regime nor does it attempt to bring narrative coherence to official sanacja policy decisions and programs. Instead, I argue that it was precisely in the post-May camp's lack of clear goals, purpose, and ideology that possibilities existed. This open-endedness meant that the sanacja could successfully attract a variety of different groups—large and small, central and marginal—to its fold and incorporate many different tendencies. It meant, too, that opportunity existed to mold the sanacja idea in many imaginative ways. My interest is in the forms of these manipulations; it is in understanding why so many people reacted so strongly—either in support of or in opposition to the sanacja—and in why the idea of sanacja proved to be so compelling. As such, this project introduces a new way of understanding the period generally and the sanacja specifically. It builds on the many and very good studies that have understood the coup as an extraordinary political event. Instead of retracing the fortunes and failings of the political sanacja and of the Piłsudskiite camp as a government and regime, however, I begin from the premise that the sanacja must be understood, first and foremost, as a potential and as a tantalizing idea infused with neoromanticist and even utopian assumptions. I understand the sanacja not as a political force (in the narrow sense of *political*), but as a forum through which different actors in the young state could talk about moral disintegration and moral renewal, about nation and identity, about gender and politics. Independence, as Gombrowicz stated, had "awakened the riddle that was slumbering within us";[64] the very idea of a sanacja encapsulated this process of awakening, while it also acted as a catalyst for even more pronounced reflection on what Poland had become and what it should be.

1 ⦙⦙⦙ Poland's Postwar Moral Panic

Stanisław Kozicki (1876–1958), a prominent politician of the nationalist-right camp, reflected in 1932 on the numerous challenges that contemporary Poland faced and offered the following summation: "In addition to everything that is going on there [in western Europe after the Great War], we are undergoing a transition from slavery to freedom and are exerting a great effort to organize our own state. Can one really be surprised that the transitional period is lasting longer and is more complicated?"[1] Though it was unpleasant and troubling, it was natural enough, Kozicki reasoned, for the Second Republic to confront monumental problems on all fronts and at all levels. Commentators like Kozicki moved effortlessly from blaming the lingering effects of the partitions for the problems evident in the Second Republic, to blaming the Great War and the subsequent border wars, the political structures of the new state, the ethnic minorities, the international situation and geopolitics. But commentators also impugned something far less tangible and potentially far more explosive: the moral health of the nation. A vocabulary of infestation and filth, of healing, good ethics, and moral rigor, was heard frequently in the press of the early independence period as many looked to the moral realm as possessing great explanatory power. In an atmosphere of economic uncertainty, social tension, and political animosity, cultural and moral visions of newly independent Poland were bound to clash. Bit by bit, the contours of a discursive moral panic developed alongside the political crises, the social unrest and the economic ruin. Within intellectual circles of the Second Republic, debates raged about the quality of the nation's moral fabric.

Just as they did in western Europe, debates about Poland's moral health developed with a ferocious intensity right from the start of the postwar period. Evident in the Second Republic before the May coup of 1926, these debates were instrumental in laying the groundwork for an intensification of interest in moral themes after May 1926. If the May coup could capitalize on a feeling of disaffection and malaise, as I argue it did, then this was possible only because the foundations for a nationwide forum on moral health had been laid earlier. Piłsudski's coup and the proclamation of a sanacja would provide a resonant focus for discussions about morality—political, social, and sexual—that had been circulating in the Second Republic ever since independence. The sanacja could and did function rhetorically as a moment of rebirth precisely because many people had become accustomed to thinking about the need for a dramatic cultural and social transformation and had become comfortable with a language of crisis, moral degeneration, spiritual renewal, and moral rejuvenation. The sanacja grew out of and reflected a deep-seated moral crisis, while it also acted as a catalyst for an invigorated focus on moral questions.

Moral Crisis in Postwar Europe

In the aftermath of the Great War, and with the profound and all-encompassing transformations that the war occasioned in Europe, anxiety about culture and the vitality of nations was raised to unprecedented heights. Historians have described the postwar era as one replete with moral anxiety, as a time of cultural and moral crisis. These terms designate periods in which analysis of the forms of social and national organization, purpose, and potential develop a widespread appeal. Moral crises are sparked when the structures of a given community change dramatically and, consequently, when visions of the world and conceptions of right and wrong clash, as can happen during and in the aftermath of war. As people search for explanations and subject their environments, both local and national, to intense scrutiny, they typically identify scapegoats to blame for ushering in changes they perceive as threatening.[2]

The term *moral panic* was coined by British sociologist Jock Young, who used it to describe quite a different context: the public reaction to forms of supposedly threatening youth behavior, especially drug use, in Britain in the 1960s. But the term has since been used to describe any period that provokes concerted and widespread scrutiny of the meaning and structures of social organization, of moral beliefs, and of the ties that bind people together. When the members of a given society disagree fundamentally about how to create categories, norms, and models to evaluate action and perception, and when they disagree over what values the society should promote, the result is a moral crisis, or a pervasive feeling that something is not quite as it should be.[3]

Feminist scholars have further suggested that in times of acute political or moral chaos, social disorder, and perceived danger, ideas about gender difference acquire an especially powerful resonance and are easily linked to more general national preoccupations. Though certain levels of anxiety over gender roles are arguably always present to some degree, changes in the intensity of this anxiety and variations in its expression during particular historical moments can be quite revealing. During chaotic times, the disorder of social life is represented by and reflected in the perceived perversion of what is assumed to be a natural order between the sexes: men are portrayed as ineffectual and unable to fulfill their obligations, while women are depicted as replacing men in their public roles, as strong and assertive as well as careless in their attitudes toward family and nation. What are understood to be immutable gender norms and relationships are depicted as having been overturned and violated.[4] The overall impression is of a broken-down social order that only dramatic intervention can fix.

Historians of the postwar western European context have argued that the Great War, in part because it was an experience so exceptional and devastating, produced a profound and long-lasting moral and cultural crisis.[5] Many analyses have focused specifically on the gendered aspects of this crisis. In postwar France, for example, anxiety about women's new status, choices, and opportunities was discursively linked to nervousness about sluggish population growth and to the effects that this was expected to have on military potential, national prosperity, and security. A violation of "proper" gender norms and the emergence of a "civilization without sexes" (to quote the title of a monograph on the subject) portended the ruin of France itself.[6] Similarly, postwar Britain nurtured its own anxieties about how the war had opened new possibilities for women and had altered gender relations, and how, in turn, both private and public morality were affected adversely, to the detriment of the nation as a whole.[7] In Germany contemporary sources reveal a heightened anxiety about women's perceived embrace of sexual liberation and a commitment to all manner of "modern" ideas, from the latest fashions to paid employment.[8] Critics, especially during the National Socialist period, argued that the "New Woman" of the Weimar era had brazenly abandoned her womanly duties and forsaken family and nation, putting Germany itself in peril.[9]

Historians of western Europe, and of North America,[10] have produced many interesting analyses of the deliberations about moral and national health that erupted after the war and have paid special attention to the ways in which an emphasis on gender identity and gender relations became a part of these debates. A discursive focus on women and their newfound rights, their supposedly modern styles of dress and comportment and their daring new behavioral choices, emerges in such times of turmoil.

Historians of eastern Europe, in contrast, have been slow to offer specific analyses of the postwar moral trauma that might have accompanied the numerous political and economic crises after the war. They have tended to prioritize instead the strictly political aspects of nation and state building that the war occasioned. There are many reasons for this. In the Polish case, the independent Second Republic, which represented the realization of long-held Polish patriotic dreams, was hardly a favorite topic of the post–World War II Communist regime. Moreover, historians of Poland or other Soviet Bloc countries could not often indulge in the luxury of studying topics that did not suit the ideological imperatives of the moment and that did not promote a desired narrative about one's national history.[11]

And yet the Polish context provides an especially fruitful terrain for the study of a postwar moral crisis; the language and preoccupations of the period show this very clearly.[12] The Second Republic had to contend with more than just the effects of the Great War, as other countries did; it also had to come to terms with the end of a partition period that had lasted well over a century. This was the transition "from slavery to freedom" to which nationalist-right politician Stanisław Kozicki referred. It was hardly surprising, given this double burden, that so much discursive attention was devoted to Poland's moral health in the post-1918 years. The fact that political life was not functioning smoothly, that economic problems were fierce, and that social and ethnic tensions were dangerously high, suggested, many contemporaries argued, that Poland's "moral health" was also in need of serious attention and reform. "Something," people said, was not right. It is to the specific Polish context that we now turn.

Moral Citizenship in the Second Republic

That the partitions had imprinted many undesirable features on the Second Republic was beyond dispute: the long partition era had deprived Poles of the experience of state administration and political organization and of opportunities for social cooperation and growth. Thereafter it became standard fare for commentators to invoke the partitions when trying to explain the political, social, and economic problems that plagued the Second Republic. At the same time, some commentators in the Second Republic noted that certain aspects of partition-era patriotism had been passionate and ideal, and that the Second Republic needed to emulate the best features of this national devotion if it were to survive the challenges of the modern period. A fantastic legend about consummate partition-era commitment to the nation developed in independent Poland (although only a very small elite actually expressed this unwavering national devotion during the partition period) and became a measure by which to gauge contemporary patriotism. Citizenship in the Second Republic was recast as much more than a constitutionally regulated designation; it acquired the status of a moral category,[13] a duty to the nation and to Polish history that, if ignored, would result in a tragedy on the scale of the late-eighteenth-century partitions.

In the postwar era of national soul-searching about what it meant to be a Pole living in a resurrected Poland, certain expressions of partition-era Polish womanhood became for some an especially revealing marker of national commitment and, it follows, of the health of the nation generally. With the partitions, the men of the nobility and the political institutions they had dominated in the Polish-Lithuanian Commonwealth lost their special and publicly recognized status. And while men went off to fight for Polish independence, women dominated the private sphere and turned it into a site of sedition and hope; the home became a repository of Polishness, a vital center of political and national mobilization in a patriotic spirit. Commentators from across the political spectrum in the Second Republic heralded women of the partition era for fulfilling their "natural" roles as bearers of national culture as well as for having played an indispensable role in the national struggle, for protecting national virtues, for passing along language and tradition, and thus, at the most basic level, for ensuring the very existence of the Polish nation.[14]

Women of the Second Republic could not but fail to measure up to the models of femininity and citizenship that had arisen out of the partition period. Some commentators in the Second Republic were quick to observe that independence-era women had too quickly become satisfied with mere formal territorial independence and with their newly won political rights, including suffrage rights; women of the Second Republic were accused of having become so enamored with the concept of rights that they forgot what responsibilities to the nation they, as women and as mothers, "naturally" possessed. Many critics emphasized that independence-era women had been lured away from husbands and children by the temptations of modern life. The effects of women's supposed disregard for national imperatives were evident in the depth of the problems the Second Republic confronted; as a result of women's choices, the family suffered, and the nation suffered, too.

As early as the border wars of 1919 to 1921, but after the formal declaration of Polish independence in 1918, women were already singled out for threatening to eschew their responsibilities to the nation. Contemporary women needed to be reminded of the sacrifices their foremothers had made and which they, as good and moral citizens of an independent Poland, should also make. An army poster from the border wars urged, "Be like Polish women from the past, who, without a tear, sent their most beloved to their deaths. . . . Away with rags and fashions, trite phrases and fox-trots, and that whole hideousness of a low and impoverished life. Your dance hall is an army hospital, your fashions, a headband with a cross."[15] If women needed to be reminded even during the wars over Poland's borders that they were morally obliged to fulfill the dictates of citizenship, then it could come as a surprise to no one, the reasoning went, that during a time of formal peace after 1921, when the threats to Poland were less tangible, women continued to act with callous indifference toward the nation. Far from being unimportant, women's behavior went to the very core of definitions of citizenship and symbolized what some believed was the lamentable state of national commitment in the independence era.[16]

References to the dangerous "savage mores" of the postpartition period, to the dire effects private immorality exerted on the nation as a whole, and to the need for women to take seriously their citizenship duties resonated with a dire urgency as the political and economic problems mounted in the Second Republic. The discursive attention given to gender and morality—a focus that conveyed, in turn, an anxiety about the nation generally—was especially marked in the press of the period, which, owing to its numbers and influence, came to occupy a central role in the political and cultural life of the nation.[17] Almost all political groupings in the Second Republic had their own periodicals, such that reading a particular publication revealed a great deal about one's political affiliations and ideological underpinnings.[18] Divisions were based on seemingly simple left and right categories; left and right were, however, incredibly complicated and imprecise designators. These, as we shall see, became even more tangled in the post-May period, when divisions between left and right gave way at least in part to pro- and antisanacja and were replaced by moral precepts and values.[19] Nevertheless, the press of the Second Republic became an especially useful instrument of politics with a vital role in shaping public opinion, popularizing ideas, and expressing profound frustrations with contemporary life.[20]

One typical supplication to the republic's women appeared in a conservative and highly moralistic magazine entitled *World and Truth* (*Świat i prawda*) in 1925: "The whole nation watches you. . . . The Fatherland calls out to you with every pain and every sadness."[21] Another appeal from the same publication stated that women, quite simply, were "on the front lines" of the nation's future, and would have to answer for their actions "before God and history." The author stated: "One could reproach today's mothers for many, very many, things," and he pointed to women's short hairstyles, knee-length skirts, low-cut dresses, and to the fact that the modern woman's household was more likely to have rum for the guest's tea than something for the children's bread. Nothing less than Poland's future was at stake.[22] Yet another author, referring to the way in which the yearly "springtime of peoples" effected changes in women's fashions, concluded, "Women's summer dresses really most clearly reveal the state of the spirit and of culture."[23]

Models of femininity and expressions of gender identities reached to the very heart of morality, and morality, in turn, reflected both on the quality of citizenship in Poland and on the very essence and vitality of the nation. As another writer in *World and Truth* stated, the penalty for turning a blind eye to the "moral gangrene" would be "a complete turn to savagery of our mores, and with this . . . the worst political consequences"; the allusion here to the partitions served as a painful reminder and warning.[24] Another author in the rightnationalist *Current* (*Prąd*) argued that while the Polish political nation had been reborn in 1918, the moral nation had not, and women in particular were betraying Polish history and tradition during the postpartition era. "A *non-Polish* type [of woman] is a wife whose only ambition is fashion and flirtation, . . . a 'mother' who supports neo-Malthusianism, which leads to the dying of the race and the nation." The nation always ended up paying for women's experimentation: "The nation needs for a woman to be a mother not only in the flesh, but also of the spirit." Only a woman whose sense of her duty is based on "faith and morality" would guarantee the strength and longevity of the nation.[25]

Here, in the midst of staggering inflation, social unrest, and political instability, women's "fashions and flirtation" made it to the forefront of at least some commentators' editorials on the state of the nation. These debates reached an especially interesting note in the months immediately preceding the coup—months of extremely tense political wrangling—on the pages of a journal called *National Thought* (*Myśl narodowa*).

Writing the Moral Crisis

National Thought was established in Warsaw in 1920.[26] Its mandate, as its editors proclaimed, was to develop "a nationalist ideology—in an emotional, intellectual, and practical sense—for the generations" and to encourage productive thinking "in a nationalist spirit."[27] The journal was the de facto political-theoretical mouthpiece of the People's National Union, the political party of Dmowski's National Democrats. Through its association with National Democracy, *National Thought* formed part of one of the most powerful press networks in Poland. By the mid-1920s, *National Thought* had become a leading journal of the urban right-nationalist intelligentsia generally, and during the post-May period, this segment of the intelligentsia included some of the sanacja's bitterest opponents.[28] Moreover, *National Thought* reached a wide audience, as it often allowed its own articles to be reprinted in other publications, just as it reprinted pieces first published elsewhere. As such, *National Thought* shared views and at least portions of an audience with the National Democrats' main daily newspaper, the *Warsaw Gazette* (*Gazeta warszawska*), as well as with the *Morning Gazette* (*Gazeta poranna*), and the *Warsaw Courier* (*Kurier warszawski*), for example.

In general terms, *National Thought* echoed the attitudes toward morality, sex, and respectability that were generally associated with the National

Democrats and their founder, Roman Dmowski. "A society in which morality declines, in which shamelessness [and] brutal or subtle immorality flourishes, in which a person loses respect even for himself," Dmowski wrote, was one in which a person lost his or her ability to aspire to noble goals and one in which the slide toward moral—and therefore national—ruin was assured.[29] For Dmowski, declining morals were at least in part the product of contemporary challenges to what he regarded as a natural hierarchical order between men and women. Dmowski was known to despise "feminists," who, he believed, placed their individual needs above those of their families and the nation. According to his very traditional view of women's roles, all aspects of political life constituted a man's preserve, and women held the important job of raising children and creating for their men a happy and comfortable haven away from the hustle and bustle of the public world.[30]

Given its connection to the nationalist right, *National Thought* constitutes an especially valuable lens through which to explore the relationship between morality, culture, and politics. During the period immediately preceding the May coup, when political tensions were at their peak and the mood was one of anticipation and frustration, the contours of a discursive moral crisis, not coincidentally, followed, reflected, and exacerbated political anxieties. In the first months of 1926, *National Thought* published a number of articles that assessed the moral health of the nation. Some of them were written by Aleksander Świętochowski (1849–1938). Świętochowski had been a leading ideologist of late-nineteenth-century Warsaw positivism. He was an eminent and controversial publicist and National Democratic ideologue throughout the Second Republic, and he contributed regularly to *National Thought*.[31] On the subject of Poland's pressing political and moral problems, Świętochowski—or the Parliamentarian of Truth,[32] as he was sometimes dubbed sarcastically—had much to say.

Świętochowski's regular column in *National Thought* was entitled "Liberum veto." This bold title recalled the Polish-Lithuanian Commonwealth. The late-nineteenth-century Kraków school of historians had argued that the Polish-Lithuanian Commonwealth fell precisely because of a weak, self-absorbed nobility that thought little about national interests. The nobility's irresponsibility and recklessness were best represented by the *liberum veto,* the right of an individual noble to veto any legislation passed during a session of Parliament. Once the veto was invoked against a specific piece of legislation, all other legislation brought forward during that session was also considered null and void, rendering the work of governing extremely difficult. As the strength of the Polish-Lithuanian Commonwealth weakened perceptibly in the late seventeenth century, and especially into the eighteenth, nobles were known to sell their right of veto to the highest bidder, often a Russian. Ever since the partitions of the Polish-Lithuanian Commonwealth, many commentators thus used the infamous term *liberum veto* as a shorthand to describe the shortcomings of the ill-fated state and the positively abominable conception of citizenship that its abuse implied.

Świętochowski used "Liberum veto" as a painful reminder to his readers in the Second Republic that political institutions and cultural practices could and would demoralize the population and threaten the very existence of the state, as was shown to have been the case with the Polish-Lithuanian Commonwealth. Świętochowski used the veto as a symbol of desperate opposition, and he used his column as a forum for issuing acerbic and incisive criticisms of the state of independence. He employed the right of veto as a powerful and symbolically rich jumping-off point to rail against the cultural, social, and sexual frivolity of his own day.[33]

In February 1926, Świętochowski wrote in his regular "Liberum veto" column about the economic and political crises in Poland. But he asked his readers to consider these problems from a very peculiar perspective. Though he certainly recognized the international aspects of the adverse economic situation, Świętochowski assailed women—from all social classes—for having mismanaged household budgets and for carelessly embracing the trappings of modernity. He objected to women's elaborate hats, their fine hose and delicate shoes, and expressed fear that Poles were again living beyond their means and without due regard for the paramount needs of the nation. "I saw workers digging potatoes while wearing gloves and silk blouses," he said. This was all the more objectionable in the context of financial crisis. For Świętochowski, women's profligate ways functioned as an omen of something worse to come. He wrote: "During the time of slavery [the partitions] she [the Polish woman] was a heroine, a priestess, a teacher of virtue and modesty; in independent Poland she is again like she was in the period of her passage into slavery over one hundred years ago."[34] Świętochowski read the general state of national morality through women's actions and attitudes and in the mid-1920s was loathe to find that women were showing a wanton disregard for "Poland."[35] Behind Świętochowski's statements was the sense that Polish independence was not yet secure and that the legacy of the partitions had not yet been overcome completely. Świętochowski feared that the nation would again be hurled into an abyss, as in the late eighteenth century. He revealed a belief that true independence could only be achieved through displays of moral fortitude and rigor. Further, he understood women to play a central role in shaping not just a private and individual morality but a wider public and national morality as well. According to Świętochowski, moral chaos reinforced and reflected political chaos and vice versa.

While parliamentary politics in the republic became especially unstable in early 1926, Świętochowski, one of the most notable personalities of the day, writing in a very prominent journal of the nationalist right, focused his attention specifically on Poland's moral health and drew his readers' attention to women's delicate shoes. So precarious and strained was the situation that Świętochowski observed that he felt compelled to introduce into the discussion the most frightening specter possible: the demise of the political state. In the same breath, Świętochowski implicated women directly in what he viewed as the dreadful condition of political, economic, moral, and national life, suggesting that the formal realm of politics was linked irrevocably to what was understood to be the private sphere.

National Thought columnist Zygmunt Wasilewski (1865–1948), writing not long after Świętochowski, addressed some of these same themes and probed openly the relationship between rigorous moral codes and effective political systems. Wasilewski was a key National Democratic ideologue. At one time he had served on the editorial board of the National Democrats' main publication, the daily *Warsaw Gazette* (*Gazeta warszawska*), and since 1925, he had worked as editor of *National Thought* and had become very influential in National Democratic publishing circles.[36] He outlined his views plainly: "The loosening of morals lays the foundation for the disintegration of responsibility to society and the nation—and vice versa. . . . A person must battle the weakness of his nature, and society has to help in this . . . so that the nation can live in a civilized fashion."[37] At the top of the list of dangerous moral trends, Wasilewski, not unlike Świętochowski, placed women's changing positions in society and, following from this, a disruptive individualism. He pointed to the dire effects that women's changing styles and scope for action were having on the institution of the family, and thus, on the nation itself. The culture of "everything goes" disturbed Wasilewski a great deal. He singled out all forms of "pornography"—art, literature, theater, dance halls, film, and women's fashions—as constituting what he called "the elementary school of moral, social, and political breakdown." This produced a situation in which everything that "the church and the family" had built over the centuries was threatened with wholesale destruction.[38] For Wasilewski, these issues went to the heart of Polish nationalism: "The Polish spirit is creative only when it is clean, when it does not indulge, when it is inspired by the social psyche and by its own strong ethical standard."[39]

What concerned commentators like Świętochowski and Wasilewski was that citizens of the Second Republic generally, and women specifically, seemed to have become satisfied with official independence and believed naively that the formal recognition of a Polish state somehow guaranteed its long-term existence. Instead, the argument these men wished to make was that territorial independence was simply one aspect of real independence, and indeed, that the moral rebirth that had to accompany physical rebirth was still lacking. As suggested above, these emphases were rather typical for the nationalist-right camp generally, which understood that the nation was based on the family and that the Polish-Catholic modest and moral woman played a vital role in maintaining the family, and therefore the nation.[40]

Provocative dance styles and revealing fashions had not caused the problem, and "modernity" would have arrived on the Polish scene whether or not the parliamentary system of the Second Republic was functioning smoothly and whether the economy was strong or weak. But given the significant political and economic problems in Poland, the examples of "immorality" that the critics revealed served to emphasize just how very sick the new republic was and how far it was from solving some basic problems. Women's new fashions and forms of behavior became such an issue for men like Wasilewski and Świętochowski precisely because women's ostensibly private behavior was seen as contravening basic conceptions of Polishness at a time when Poland continued to show signs of weakness and instability.

Behind these ideas rested the assumption that the so-called public and the private realms reflected and influenced one another. It made sense, then, to turn the fox-trot or women's new fashions into pressing national issues. Zygmunt Wasilewski articulated the connection well when he warned his readers in another *National Thought* piece not to believe that political problems were merely skin-deep: "To heal life, one must reach beyond politics into morality, . . . which is the foundation of public life."[41] Wasilewski submerged public and private life into a single category, and suggested that together, the private and the public realms imprinted themselves on the nation. This is one of the key ideas that is later taken up after the coup and that underpins many of the sanacja-era discourses about the nation.

The Crisis Mounts: The National Forum on Morality

Precisely because the Second Republic faced so many monumental problems, a reliance on a language of crisis and doom came easily, and a vocabulary that emphasized moral culpability and imminent demise was widespread even before the official political sanacja emerged. The idea of sanacja was able to take hold after the coup in part because the foundations for a national forum on morality had been laid before the coup; the idea of sanacja, that is, had been invented long before May 1926. What critics like those examined above were calling for when they railed against women's fashions, changing gender roles, and the general state of moral life in the newly independent nation was a sanacja, a cleansing and purge, albeit of a very different kind from the one advocated by the Piłsudskiites. Precisely because some people had grown accustomed to thinking about moral health and to employing language that teased moral implications from any event or trend, they were that much more receptive in May 1926 to the idea of a nationwide project of cleansing and moral reform and were that much more eager to accept in principle the need for a sanacja. From the start of independence, Poles had been experiencing what historian Jerzy Jedlicki calls a "moral hangover," and they were engaged in a very difficult process of learning how to reconcile expectations with contemporary realities. "On top of this feeling of a moral hangover," Jedlicki writes, "there appeared later the sanacja."[42] The sanacja drew attention to these disappointed dreams and false expectations and provided a focus for debate.

The year 1926 constituted a moment of reckoning. It is to the May coup and to the ensuing period of sanacja that we must look in order to really understand the nature of interwar Poland's moral crisis. The coup unleashed an

ever more focused and consistent emphasis on questions of moral degeneration and regeneration and sparked what we may call a profoundly divisive
and serious moral crisis. The postcoup period marked the moment when
questions about national identity raged strong, when disputes about culture
and nation building asserted themselves with ferocity; it was the moment at
which varying interpretations of public, national, and private morality confronted each other. The May events, in part because they brought to the sur-
face the formidable political divisions within the Second Republic, unleashed
a deep and painful period of national reflection that turned on definitions of
morality.

How and why could the coup work in this fashion and how could the
sanacja acquire such potent meaning? Piłsudski's primary aim in May 1926
was to prevent the ascension to power of the political right, to put a decisive
stop to political malfeasance and corruption, to guarantee himself a prominent role in the affairs of the state, and to protect the army from what he believed was fatal political interference. The Piłsudskiites had spoken about the
coup as marking a political turning point, as initiating a cleansing of Poland's
public life and a reform of its malfunctioning political system. They had also
spoken about the coup as launching a collective effort on behalf of the nation,
as an opportunity for the beleaguered new state to devote attention to much-
neglected "imponderables" and to launch an impressive and unprecedented
national sanacja.

The word *sanacja* seemed ideally suited to characterizing this national
agenda. The word had been used in Polish society for a few years before May
1926 to describe reform in various areas of life, from political and economic to
social. Piłsudskiite ideologue Adam Skwarczyński (who will be discussed in
greater detail in chapter 3), first applied the word to Poland's political problems when he used the phrase "sanacja of the state" in 1923.[43] *Sanacja* had also
been used repeatedly in the press to refer to the efforts of Prime Minister
Władysław Grabski (1874–1938) to propose solutions to the nation's crippling
financial crisis of 1923 and 1924.[44]

But when Piłsudski used the word after he launched his successful military coup, it reverberated with the public in a way it had never done before. In
not defining what exactly the future would entail, in failing to provide a clear
vision of what the Piłsudskiite sanacja would look like, and in emphasizing
only the desire to "strengthen the state above all else," the idea of a sanacja be-

came available to anyone and everyone to use as they saw fit. After the coup, *sanacja, healing, rebirth, reform, cleansing,* and *the imponderables* became terribly popular terms, as various constituencies attempted to make sense of the great political events of May 1926. Once they were unleashed, the Piłsudskiites were unable to contain how they were used and to what effect, or by whom.

Troubadours of Rebirth

That there had been an official and dramatic proclamation of the need for national rebirth and moral revolution in May 1926 surprised few; indeed, immediately after the coup many rushed in to assert that, in fact, they had been communicating this need for some time. "Everyone" believed in the need for a sanacja, though everyone also differed on just what kind of rebirth was necessary and for what end.

The goals of rebirth, the language of moral healing, and the need to emerge on the other side of moral crisis were, of course, most evident in that part of the press that was tied openly to the sanacja camp. One article in mid-May in the pro-Piłsudski *Voice of Truth* (*Głos prawdy*) stated what many people, from all positions along the political spectrum, accepted to be true: that Poland had been physically reborn in November 1918, but that this "had not been a complete moral rebirth of society." The author described how he understood the May coup: "His [Piłsudski's] name has become a symbol of renaissance. . . . Around him has gathered an unorganized group of all the best yearnings and possibilities."[45] With his coup in the spring of 1926, Piłsudski had occasioned a springtime like no other, and the event was nothing short of a national renaissance. The coup itself was the "first act" in a far larger process of reform and rebirth and had given Poland the opportunity to dispossess itself (to use a concept drawn from Polish partition-era history) of the winter covering of mulch (*chochoł*) that had for too long stifled its creative potential.[46]

Similarly, the *Helm of Zagłębia* (*Ster Zagłębia*), the organ of the Józef Piłsudski Social-Political Club (Organ Klubu Polityczno-Społecznego im. Józefa Piłsudskiego), defined the reigning motto in post-May Poland as, simply, "sanacja," and the group declared its unqualified support for the idea of building a better Poland.[47] One author suggested that the sanacja resembled the period of national reform launched between the first partition of the Polish-Lithuanian Commonwealth in 1772 and the subsequent partitions in 1793 and 1795. The first partition had sparked great reform efforts in all areas of life and these had produced the famous 1791 constitution; the period is remembered as the Polish Enlightenment. The *Helm of Zagłębia* hoped that May 1926 would mark the start of a similarly illustrious period in Polish history.[48]

A certain marginal group of interwar spiritualists grouped in the Brotherhood of Spiritual Rebirth (Bractwo Odrodzenia Duchowego) expressed no surprise that all of a sudden, after the coup, "everyone" was using the word *rebirth*, talking about morality and claiming a need for some kind of nationwide catharsis. One Brother was anxious to point out, though, that the concept of "moral revolution" predated the coup: "That which we are looking at today is the fruit of the seeds sown in the Polish soul by the greatest thinkers of the nation" many years ago.[49] The fact could not be denied, however, that a "psychosis of rebirth," as the Brother referred to it, raged in post-May Poland; the word *rebirth* appeared in the press, in public opinion, in literature, theater, and even in business with an amazing frequency, he noted.[50] Polish society would do well to "throw some cold water" on what the Brother referred to as the "journalistic troubadours of moral rebirth." He warned that any word and concept that gets used as much as rebirth has since the May coup would ultimately become meaningless. He joked that soon Poles would be buying "reborn cigarettes" (*papierosy odrodzone*) and would be lighting them with "reborn matches" (*zapałki odrodzone*).[51]

Similarly, a poem entitled "The Newest Illness" appeared in the right-nationalist satirical magazine the *Fly* (*Mucha*), just a month after the coup, in June 1926. The poem referred to the various maladies that were appearing across Poland in the post-1918 period and also to "the new illness that has now arisen." This unspecified new illness, of course, could only be taken as a reference to the recent May coup. This new malady was spreading quickly, through town and country, "entering homes through keyholes," infiltrating the Sejm, saturating literature and private life. There was no hiding from "the rotten illness," and it would soon affect everyone. The problem, however, was that no one was certain what its effects would be.[52]

A similar embrace of a language of transformation, uncertainty, and rebirth was evident in a Warsaw journal called the *Helm* (*Ster*), which was billed as a nonparty journal for and by the intelligentsia. Independent Poland, the first issue proclaimed, lacked a true appreciation of the crisis that was at hand. The journal had been established, therefore, to awaken people, to inculcate high civic virtues in the populace, and "to effect a collective rebirth of the Polish spirit."[53] With the May coup waged and won, the *Helm* found a focus and inspiration for its ideas. It explained that the coup had been caused by political factors, certainly, but that it had also evolved out of "deep moral causes." Though associates of the *Helm* generally had reservations about the May coup, they nevertheless understood why the civil war had happened and they agreed that the coup was a symbol of profound problems in Poland. These revolved primarily around the ways in which people were (or were not) expressing their responsibilities as citizens.[54] One contributor asked readers "to look into their hearts" and to determine whether they were doing enough to build honor, to foster decency, and to define the great imponderables, or whether, conversely, their commitment was to the frivolous worship of "wine, women, and song." [55] The *Helm* hoped that the coup would awaken people to the bitter reality that reigned in Poland and that it would motivate them to work for change.

The potential for collective action on behalf of Poland that the coup had popularized was further reflected in the morally conservative *World and Truth*. The journal's associates saw the coup as "a removal of the cancer" in Polish life, and they were prepared to wait and see what kind of change would follow. Their analyses of contemporary life in post-May Poland were infused with references to health, cleansing, and rebirth, and, as we have seen in a number of previous examples, their assessments included a criticism of contemporary femininity.[56] One author, for example, published a story in the summer of 1926 about the increased incidence of drunkenness among "beautiful, elegant, charming" young women, "most often from the best families." While their parents were out on the town, shirking both parental and national obligations, these "daughters of the citizenry" followed suit and got drunk. Such lapses in moral judgment were all the more offensive, the author stated, during a period of "national rebirth." Women in particular, he continued, had a special role to fulfill in ensuring that the good of the collective was protected: "The work of the mother-educator, mother-Pole . . . is as necessary as life itself. . . . Polish woman! History calls you to do right by your nation." Women's responsibility was to God and nation, and at no time was this more apparent than the present moment.[57]

A vocabulary of healing and rebirth was ubiquitous and powerful after the coup. Regardless of what people felt about the Piłsudskiites and about the coup specifically, the notion of sanacja had wide appeal and was applicable to a broad range of topics. The idea of moral revolution permeated the contemporary discourses of the post-May period. And as soon as the Piłsudskiites released the term *sanacja,* the idea acquired a life of its own; contemporaries used it to refer to much more than the strictly formal realms of politics and state administration.[58]

The idea and language of spiritual and moral rebirth were especially prevalent within Catholic circles, which were often tied to the parties of the nationalist right. However, before the war Roman Dmowski and his National Democrats had had an ambiguous and sometimes strained relationship with the Catholic Church; National Democratic nationalism had been a decidedly secular nationalism. But by the first decade of independence, Dmowski embraced Catholicism as an integral component of Polish national identity. Dmowski articulated this point unambiguously when he wrote in 1927: "Catholicism is not an appendage to Polishness . . . . [I]t is embedded in its essence, and in a large measure it *is* its essence." To remove Catholicism from Polishness, Dmowski continued, was to destroy the nation itself.[59]

The fusion of Catholicism with right-nationalism is perhaps best represented in the Camp of Great Poland (Obóz Wielkiej Polski). The camp was established by Dmowski in Poznań in December 1926 as a supraparty far-right political and social movement. Its goal was to rejuvenate the nationalist right, especially in light of the existence of the sanacja political camp, and to effect a kind of rebirth within National Democracy. The camp described itself as "an organization of the conscious strengths of the nation" and affirmed its commitment to the Roman Catholic faith, to fighting Jewish influences on Poland, as well as to maintaining "a high level of morality and moral discipline." It operated outside the Sejm, was extremely hierarchical, and incorporated elements of Italian Fascism into its structure and ideas. The camp served as a radical right-nationalist counterweight to the sanacja vision of moral rebirth and as such offered an altogether different kind of rebirth for the Polish nation.[60]

In addition to the Camp of Great Poland, we can point to many other examples of Catholics embracing after the coup a vocabulary that emphasized the need for moral regeneration. The relationship between mass Catholic organizations and the sanacja regime, or between the Polish Catholic hierarchy and the sanacja, is outside the scope of this study, but it is nevertheless appropriate to note here that the early sanacja era was one of peaceful relations between the regime, the Vatican, and the Polish Catholic Church hierarchy. This obliged the Church hierarchy in Poland to tread carefully when it came to criticizing the sanacja.[61] Yet when it came to "moral" issues, to questions of private morality, the Church (and Catholics generally) had far more in common with the National Democratic camp than with the sanacja.

In an opening address to a Catholic meeting in Poznań in early November 1926, Poland's primate, August Hlond, referred to the "crisis of spirit" in the eight-year-old independent state and to the "deep fissures" that thus far Poland had been unable to heal. At the end of 1926, Poland stood at a critical crossroads and was engaged in full-scale soul-searching. That Poland was occupied with this process was hopeful, but the moment required sustained vigilance, according to Hlond. In one breath, he railed against petty party wrangling and against divorce and broken homes. He called on all Poles "to rest the entirety of our private and public lives on a Christian base" and work toward rebirth. Hlond emphasized the need for a spiritual cleansing to accompany the purification of public life, for fear that neither would succeed alone.[62] In his exhortations, made just months after the coup, during a time when it was not yet absolutely clear which way the political sanacja would go, Hlond kept a safe distance from commenting directly on politics, and he underscored that the role of the Church was located outside the formal political realm. At the same time, Hlond spoke about the paramount need for traditional values to prevail, for people to remember that politics and private morality were intertwined, and that together they determined the future of the state: "We call in vain for the healing of public life if we do not heal our individual souls with Christ." Hlond referred a number of times throughout his address to rebirth and to the need to effect a cleansing of the Polish soul.[63] He recognized the potential power of the idea of moral rebirth that the Piłsudskiites had popularized and attempted to stake a Catholic claim to the idea.

A Catholic monthly entitled the *Knight of the Immaculate (Rycerz niepokalanej)*, one of the best-selling periodicals in the country, also accepted the need for rebirth.[64] The *Knight,* however, was openly hostile to the sanacja and believed that the new regime portended a morally spent and physically prostrate Poland. Shortly after the coup, the *Knight* reprinted a speech given by

Andrzej Strug, "a prominent Mason," to illustrate the bases for its trepidation. Strug praised the May events, called them a "victory of decency," and looked forward to building the new Poland. The *Knight* responded by condemning Masons as "backward pagans" and as a threat to the moral health of schools, art, theater, film, and literature.[65] Implicit in this condemnation of the Masons was a criticism of the very sanacja behind which Strug had thrown his support. According to the *Knight,* the connections between the post-May camp and international Masonry were all too clear. Articles in the *Knight* appearing in the months following the coup continued to refer obliquely yet assuredly to "the danger hanging over Poland" and to "the assaults on the Church and faith" that had recently emerged.[66] Piłsudski's coup, in depriving the nationalist right of political power, also shut out the *Knight*'s supporters from the government.[67] As a result, it became all the more important for the *Knight* to defend and to promote Catholic-nationalist virtues; the coup and the ensuing sanacja provided the paper with a concrete event around which to mobilize. The *Knight* became a forceful disseminator of the view that the moral and cultural qualities of the state affected directly its political well-being as well as its international potential and security. Its position was that the sanacja would deprave the nation's moral health and would thus jeopardize the very existence of the state. As one author in the *Knight* stated, "The times when it was sufficient to be a Catholic in private life have passed. Today one must be [a Catholic] everywhere."[68] The rebirth the *Knight* hoped for in Poland would not find support among Piłsudskiites.

After the coup the right-Catholic-nationalist *Current* was quick to outline its views on what had occurred in Poland in the spring of 1926. The editors agreed that Poland needed to be rebuilt from its very foundations and stated that for the last seven years Poles had been talking about just this need. It was only with the May coup, however, and the rise to preeminence "of those who are furthest from us" that the calls for rebirth became louder and more focused. And this state of affairs, the journal's associates agreed, was troubling. Sanacja-era Poland would witness a very different kind of "moral rebirth," one inconsistent with the *Current*'s basic approaches to private and public life: "Without a doubt, more than ever before, religious, moral, and national values are threatened in Poland."[69]

Together, these examples show that the coup and the official public declaration of the need for a nationwide sanacja resonated with journalists and, to some extent, we can presume, with at least some of their readers; many in the Second Republic were prepared to believe in the need for some kind of rebirth, and many believed that there were extraparliamentary problems that needed attention in Poland. The type of rebirth that was favored, and how it would be achieved, however, were the source of much disagreement. It was the critics of the sanacja who proved especially adept at appropriating the idea of rebirth and wielding it to advance their own visions of the "moral nation" that independent Poland should become: a Catholic-nationalist Poland. Political opponents of the sanacja created a fascinating rhetorical link between, on the one hand, the political crisis that the May coup and the sanacja represented and, on the other, the strictly moral and cultural crises they identified everywhere around them. They used the coup as a convenient crisis around which to organize their ideas about morality and their assessments of national life.

As the theoretical mouthpiece of the strongest branch of right-wing nationalism, *National Thought* columnists were vehemently opposed to Piłsudski and to the sanacja. Many of the personalities associated with *National Thought*, as stated earlier, were prominent public figures—writers, journalists, politicians—whose names and opinions were well known and gained wide currency through the press of the period. On the whole, they believed that some kind of rebirth was necessary in the Second Republic and, further, that Piłsudski and his entourage would not effect the right kind of rebirth. Opponents of the political sanacja got in on the game, fastened onto the event, and used it as the starting point for their own analyses of what was wrong with the republic.

In doing so, these sanacja opponents engaged, ironically, in the nationwide discussion about what Poland was and how it should rebuild itself for the future. In a partial and peculiar way, they fulfilled one of the coup's mandates: to stimulate a national forum on Poland. The coup was, at one level, about shaping an active citizen body that would work for the good of the collective and that would place the needs of the state first. Even those who bitterly opposed Piłsudski and the coup and all that it represented were mobilized to think, talk, and write about the moral health of the newly independent nation. In devoting a great deal of attention to moral issues and to gender problems, and in admitting that more than just the structures of Parliament or the nature of the constitution needed fixing in Poland, they embraced, after a fashion, the idea of effecting a sanacja of Poland's political, moral, and cultural life.

National Voices against Immorality

National Thought's first published response to the events that had so fundamentally shaken Polish society came on 22 May 1926, about one week after the coup. The piece was written by *National Thought* coeditor Jan Rembieliński (1897–1948)[70] and was entitled, quite simply, "After the Coup d'État." Rembieliński began cautiously by saying that it would be imprudent to pronounce judgment just yet as to precisely what effects the coup and the fierce civil war had exerted on the structures of the state and on its political organization. But, he stated, "the moral atmosphere of the coup, the moral disintegration that is occurring under its influence, we can already describe today."[71]

Rembieliński conceded to his Piłsudskiite opponents that Polish society was in dire need of a full-scale "moral rebirth" and that some extraordinary shake-up might well have been expected sooner or later. But Rembieliński, a National Democrat, doubted whether Piłsudski and his supporters would be capable of effecting the right kind of moral rebirth. He referred to Piłsudski's statement about having waged the coup in order to protect certain imponderables—like honor, virtue, and courage—and wondered openly about whether an (illegal) military coup could ever constitute a moral good. Rembieliński predicted that the effects of the coup would be just the opposite of moral and just and that the post-May camp would in fact breed licentiousness and immorality.[72] By excluding specifics from his warnings, Rembieliński left much to the imagination of his readers.

In his statement about the coup made just weeks after the events, *National Thought* coeditor Zygmunt Wasilewski similarly expressed skepticism about the Piłsudski camp's ability to lead the nation away from moral crisis.[73] Nevertheless, Wasilewski feared that people might in fact be swept away by the rhetoric and the excitement created by what he referred to as the "apostles of morality" and might be fooled into believing that their best interests lay with the sanacja camp: "The Warsaw street gawked at this tragic battle just as one gawks at wrestlers. . . . Duped by a press ambush of pornography and sensation, the Warsaw street has allowed its thinking to become insane and has lost the sense of whether and where truth exists, of where the interest of the state lies."[74] Wasilewski did not trust individuals to make right decisions about the sanacja, and he felt that the sanacja, for its part, had mounted a dangerously effective advertising campaign designed to appeal to people's basest instincts.

Wasilewski and Rembieliński presented analyses of the coup that were very much consistent with the criticisms that the right-nationalist camp generally offered of the May events. Piłsudski had long been the nationalist right's sworn enemy, and the fact that he had seized power so audaciously in the young state further raised the nationalist camp's antipathy toward him and all those who rushed to declare their allegiance to the sanacja project. Accordingly, the People's National Union, National Democracy's political party, initiated a poster campaign within days of the coup with the aim of countering Piłsudskiite propaganda that affirmed the marvelous quality of the May events. One such poster stated plainly the nationalist right's objections: "Everything that constitutes the moral fabric of the nation and the state—guarantees of the strength and solidarity of the army, faith and confidence, honor and brotherhood of arms, law and allegiance—were sullied and quashed."[75]

The key concern of the nationalist right, and especially of men like Wasilewski and Rembieliński, was that the Piłsudski forces would divide the nation into two camps—into Dąbrowska's "moral nations"—and would take Poland down a dangerous political path. Wasilewski also believed that this division would exert highly noxious effects on the morality of the nation, and he further warned that people underestimated the importance of morality to a nation's political survival: "A lack of moral vigor. That is where Poland's fall will be."[76] In another piece written in the autumn of 1926, Wasilewski reaffirmed these points and added that the price Poland had to pay for addressing specific imponderables was already showing itself to be too high: "That which apparently . . . began because of the need to reorganize the army, and later took on the character of a parliamentary crisis, is slowly becoming a clear attack on the life of Polish civilization."[77] Earlier, he had defined civilization as "the whole person—the matters of his or her psyche," and posited a direct link between Polish ethnicity, Catholic religion, western European civilization, and commitment to nation.[78] Roman Dmowski echoed this sentiment that the May coup portended something rotten for Polish civilization and that it threatened Poland with an ever-swelling "eastern wave."[79] Many Piłsudskiites, after all, were former socialists, some were in fact Masons, some were of Jewish background, and many were generally associated with left-liberalism, secularism, and progressivism.[80] They had a comparatively more inclusive sense of what it meant to be a Pole and failed to enforce the view, at least at this early stage of the sanacja, that a Pole was a Catholic, and only a Catholic. According to the nationalist right, this apparent leniency constituted an affront to Polish history and a betrayal of Poland. The "war over culture" and civilization (and not just a war over politics and parliamentary power), the demoralizing of the Polish nation, occurred on this plain and over these issues.[81] The model citizenry that each side wanted to create—the "moral nations" that each extolled—were different in important ways. Critics of the sanacja, grouped as they were around *National Thought* and other publications associated with the nationalist right, believed that the attributes of the public sphere could not but be reflected on the private level. As in other postwar contexts, the Second Republic's moral panic expressed itself at least in part in a battle over the ideal relationship between the private and public spheres; the nationalist right beseeched people not to forget the inherent politicization of the private sphere.[82]

Columnists in *National Thought* explored the links between the political and moral realms and made the point time and again, as one critic stated, that every (political) revolution, like the May coup, is caused by a "moral crisis."[83] *National Thought* editors elaborated on this basic association and made it a constituent feature of the journal's analyses of the contemporary state of affairs: "Everything in the life of the nation is organically linked. . . . We see from experience of public life how economic life is linked with internal politics, how the domestic side of politics is linked with external politics, and how all politics is linked with moral life."[84]

Aleksander Świętochowski, too, used *sanacja* not only to describe the political regime of the Piłsudskiites but to characterize pervasive moral decay and cultural crisis. His position was unambiguous: sanacja-era Poland was "a swamp."[85] He understood that the right kind of morality formed the basis for the right kind of nationalist commitment: "decency" and "clean character" were the key determinants of "national culture," and a healthy national culture, in turn, determined the state's viability and potential. Świętochowski compared Poland's current situation to the Teutonic threat of the medieval period before jumping rhetorically to the early modern era to remind his readers that the penalty last time for mismanagement and arrogance was the partitions. "Maybe Poland has never been so morally sick as it is today," he concluded.[86]

Did the sanacja really represent such a threat, and was sanacja Poland really so very "morally sick"? Star *National Thought* contributor Adolf Nowaczyński (1876–1944) certainly thought so. Nowaczyński was a playwright of some distinction, a journalist of acerbic wit, and generally a public figure of considerable, and controversial, stature in the Second Republic.[87] Though he had dabbled in anarchism in his youth, Nowaczyński lived much of the interwar period as a committed right nationalist and viperous antisemite.[88] He reveled in his reputation as a bold and arrogant writer of clear right-nationalist political affiliations. During the period that interests us here, stretching from the mid- and late 1920s to the early 1930s, Nowaczyński maintained a regular column entitled "Offensive" (*Ofensywa*) (1921–34) in *National Thought*.[89]

Nowaczyński believed that indeed the political sanacja could be linked clearly and directly to a generalized moral fall in Poland. He argued that the sanacja coincided with the unleashing of a wave of moral extravagance in Poland and that this could only affect adversely the state of Polish independence: "Every countryperson can inform him- or herself how, beginning with the year 1926 and the seizure of power by the Imperatrice of the sanacja . . . we are wearing seven-league boots and are running in pursuit of a growth of criminality in Poland and, among other things, in the number of offenses against sexual morality."[90] Nowaczyński reinforced the point again when he added that this rise in immorality and criminality was attributable directly to the growth of a "sensationalist, gutter, martial [*marszałkowskiej*, an oblique reference to Marshal Piłsudski], pornographic-criminal press."[91] As did some other observers, and as we have seen in other examples, Nowaczyński linked his criticism of the sanacja political era to a rebuke of contemporary sexual morality. The specific form of Nowaczyński's criticism of the sanacja found its most powerful voice in condemning a broadly conceived moral and cultural realm.

Nowaczyński's assertions are difficult to prove and to quantify because the supposed instances of sexual immorality that the journalist identified around him did not often constitute real crimes. What Nowaczyński described was a mood and a feeling, a reaction to change, and he assumed his readers would share and understand these views. He further gambled on being able to link this supposed growth in sexual impropriety with the political sanacja and on his readers being able to understand the subtle connections he drew between the political and the cultural realms.

Nowaczyński's observations, moreover, were made at the start of an increasingly tense political atmosphere in sanacja Poland. As the sanacja entered its more repressive phase, beginning in the late 1920s, the regime's opponents advanced the point repeatedly that the political caesura had occasioned a cultural one and that each reinforced the other. The political environment of the era was marked by an end to the so-called period of *bartelowanie*. Bartelowanie took its name from Kazimierz Bartel (1882–1941), Poland's premier under a number of sanacja governments until 1930. Bartel's governments were defined by some conciliation, moderation, and compromise, but Piłsudski replaced Bartel whenever he needed a more ruthless and determined premier; the end of the first decade of independence was just such a time.[92] In the fall of 1929 the Polish Socialist Party, PSL-Piast, PSL-Liberation, the National Workers' Party, and Christian Democracy formed a potentially powerful left-of-center opposition bloc called Centrolew. This opposition coalition wanted to reinstate real democracy in Poland and to alleviate the suffering that the working people were experiencing as a result of the Great Depression. The government's response to the growing opposition was categorical. When Centrolew organized a thirty-thousand-strong Congress for the Defense of the Law and the Freedom of the People in Kraków in the summer of 1930 and demanded the resignation of the Piłsudski regime and its replacement by a real democratic government, it had gone too far. To prevent further demonstrations, which were already scheduled for the coming months, and to stamp out this and any future efforts to oppose the regime, the sanacja authorities arrested close to one hundred Centrolew leaders as well as thousands of the opposition activists. They were all detained in the fortress of Brześć. The message was clear: political opposition would not be tolerated in sanacja Poland.[93]

Nowaczyński learned this lesson the hard way. In May 1931 a politically motivated assault left one of his eyes seriously damaged. His other eye had sustained serious and irreparable injury in a previous attack in 1928 on Warsaw's Złota Street.[94] The first sanacja bandits were never caught by the authorities. According to the *National Thought* columnist who reported on the more recent assault case in 1931, the aim of both assaults was clear: to blind the man regarded as one of the sanacja's most incisive critics so that he would be unable to continue his campaign of exposing the sanacja as the sham that all right-thinking Poles supposedly knew it to be. The situation in Poland was dire, the *National Thought* columnist concluded, and the latest attack on Nowaczyński only underscored just how low Polish life had sunk. The state of affairs, the reporter concluded, was "unfit for a European nation."[95]

Poland's contemporary crisis, Nowaczyński offered in the autumn of 1931, had reached epidemic proportions. As Nowaczyński stated in his regular column, "In sanacja Poland, in Poland of the First Brigade, it is bad and most monstrous. . . . [i]t's no longer a crisis or a slump, but a slow dying of the whole culture."[96] The attitude that Piłsudski's sanacja had stimulated and continued to license a cultural decline alongside a political decline existed right from the start of Piłsudski's coup. This assertion remained rhetorically powerful even five years after the event, as the sanacja tightened its grip on the political process and extended its preserve into a greater number of areas. After Brześć, the sanacja camp was the undisputed master of Polish political life, and opposition to the regime had been quashed harshly and unmistakably. Critics like Nowaczyński underlined this fact by referring not to Poland or to the Second Republic generally but by referring specifically to "sanacja Poland" or to "Poland of the First Brigade."[97]

The First Brigade, of course, was the elite branch within the wartime Polish Legions, which Piłsudski had commanded and which, many believed, had been decisive in securing Polish independence. The First Brigade was composed overwhelmingly of men drawn from the intelligentsia, men who had formed the core of Piłsudski's political support since the earliest independence struggles and who would go on to support him through the coup and the sanacja period; these were the Piłsudskiites. Contemporaries made clear discursive links between the sanacja as a political event and reality, and the sanacja as something so big and pervasive, sinister and ubiquitous that it came to define the period itself.

The Sanacja and the Manipulation of Morality

It was possible to reinterpret a military coup waged by an ex-Socialist hero and Polish national patriot as an assault on Polish culture and good morality because of the fantastically broad definition and wide potential of the sanacja concept. The Piłsudskiite political sanacja lacked clear and specific policy goals, just as it lacked a tangible program, other than references to the primacy of the state and the need to change the constitution to provide for a strong executive. Appeals to work, unity, and "moral rebirth" were similarly broad and flexible.[98]

A warning about the open-ended nature of the sanacja came, for instance, in a late May 1926 issue of the *Paths of Reform* (*Drogi naprawy*), which had declared a "cautious" attitude toward Piłsudski's coup and the sanacja. One author stated succinctly that mottoes like "raising the moral standard" and "battling inequality" were dangerously pliant and ambiguous. The ideas associated with these terms, rightly or wrongly, would explode in a variety of directions as everyone rushed to offer a different interpretation of what proper national morality entailed and required.[99]

One *National Thought* commentator stated that he remained uncertain, even on the third anniversary of the coup in 1929, as to what the much-lauded sanacja was all about. Something was still clearly missing from the sanacja project: "We have already had three years of the new epoch, the renaissance, the Sanacja. . . . Versions or diversions on the subject of the moral mission have been spreading like smoke, and yet an uncomfortable question remains: what, really, is the goal? We know the means, but what is the goal? Who knows the goal?"[100] To further make his point, this columnist lined up segments from various pro-Piłsudski proclamations issued immediately after the coup. Each excerpt was chosen to show that at the time of the coup pro-sanacja papers and columnists had extolled the virtues of the May event and heralded the coming of a "moral renaissance." Other excerpts revealed a vocabulary that emphasized hope and renewal, the "sunny days of May 1926," and the wondrous nature of an event that "history will remember fondly."[101] This columnist made the point that the Piłsudski faction itself believed that morality was a central component of the sanacja.

Another columnist expressed his frustration with the sanacja's imprecise goals: "The Sanacja understands contemporary Poland as the seat of the worst physical and moral illnesses. We hear constantly about the ulcers and the gangrene, about cowardliness, and about other horrors that were devouring Poland. They, the resuscitators, thus threw themselves into the task of saving Poland . . . and they began to heal her. . . . For three years they have been healing her."[102] And yet nothing, no aspect of political or cultural life, of social or economic life, was ever declared to have been fixed in sanacja Poland. Though the coup happened to coincide with a bit of an economic upturn, it subsided by the late 1920s, and the reemergent economic problems worked to further exacerbate the political and social turmoil and increased the sense that a profound moral crisis raged in Poland.[103] The rhetoric simply continued to offer the same empty assertions that a sanacja was somehow essential to the health of the state.

Commentators opposed to the sanacja political grouping soon adopted a comical attitude toward this question of what precisely the agenda of the sanacja was, and they mocked the empty promises of and vague references to moral rebirth that the sanacja politicians continued to offer. The sanacja, apparently, was a well-kept national secret. One cartoon from the period depicted the ambiguity well. It showed a man looking at the night sky through a gigantic telescope. The man's associate turned to a third man and stated, "Please, Sir, tell the citizens of the republic that neither on earth nor in the heavens can we find a moral sanacja."[104]

In a climate of general political turbulence marked by assaults on sanacja critics, it was dangerous and imprudent to criticize the sanacja openly. Brześć was definitive proof of this. Instead of launching clear and direct assaults on the political sanacja camp, commentators wrote about the immorality of the era and extended the political sanacja symbolically into the realm of morality and culture. It was resourceful and prudent to suggest that in the sanacja's appeals to unity and work lurked an insidious cultural agenda that would see Poland become a den of sin and vice, of sexual promiscuity and abandoned children. The sanacja was an elastic and mobile symbol in the Second Republic that could be manipulated easily and to great effect.

This tactic was especially useful, given that censorship existed in the Second Republic. Criticizing specific individuals from within the sanacja fold, or impugning the particular governments of the sanacja era, virtually guaranteed the intervention of the censor in the publishing life of a paper. Although the 1921 constitution had guaranteed freedom of thought and freedom of the press, that freedom depended on the implementation of other pieces of legislation. The short-term nature of successive Polish cabinets meant that legislators had been unable to devote sustained attention to issues of press freedom, and the constitutional guarantees of press freedom were therefore not realized in full. In the fall of 1926, only a half year after the May coup, the sanacja government issued a presidential decree that spreading "untrue" information about the government and denouncing representatives of the government and the state was punishable with a considerable fine, of between one hundred and ten thousand zlotys, or by imprisonment from ten days to three months. This censorship decree was presented by the government as part of an effort to maintain the respectability and honor of the state and its servants and, ostensibly, to protect the public interest. The law applied to the author of the offending article but also potentially to associates of the periodical in which it appeared as well as to the editor or editors.[105]

Opposition to this decree was fierce, especially from journalists themselves, and many supporters of Piłsudski argued that this order, which had emerged from within the ranks of the sanacja government, constituted a sure move away from anything approximating a moral sanacja.[106] This 1926 press law was never ratified.[107] In the spring of 1927 two new ordinances regarding the press were considered by the cabinet. The new and unified law that resulted from these deliberations increased the number of potential violations that qualified as an infringement of the laws relating to free speech and increased the penalties that could be meted out for violations.[108] The Sejm voted down this new press law, but Piłsudski forced it through nevertheless.[109] As the sanacja regime grew increasingly authoritarian into the 1930s, censorship followed in the same direction.

This, then, was the atmosphere in which publicists operated in the Second Republic. If a paper ran a piece that impugned the person of Piłsudski directly, boldly condemned the way that he had seized power in May 1926, suggested the basic illegitimacy of the sanacja camp, or implied that the assumption of power by Piłsudski had ushered in few sustained improvements to the Polish economic and social situation, then it was guaranteed to draw unwelcome attention from the censors. Daring declarations like "the cause of Poland's unhappiness is Józef Piłsudski" formed the most clear-cut case.[110] Disparaging any of the key Piłsudskiite figures was also certain to draw the censors' attention, as was making a mockery of the very concept of a moral sanacja and suggesting that the Piłsudskiite version was a poor imitation of a real moral revolution.[111]

Most publications, from the left and right, were subject to some degree of censorship during the sanacja period. At the same time, censorship was often executed in a sporadic and selective manner. Once censored, newspapers would often leave telling blank spots in the distributed versions of their papers in order to remind one and all that freedom of speech did not exist in Piłsudski's Poland. Many others engaged in "voluntary preventative censorship" as a way to avoid the heavy costs associated with pulling an entire edition from print.[112]

As a vocal critic of the regime and a supporter of the political sanacja's National Democratic opponents, *National Thought* felt the power of the censor with some frequency.[113] In a sarcastic *National Thought* column on confiscations, Świętochowski proposed a simple solution: the sanacja should ban outright all publication on permanent surfaces, such as paper or fabric, of anything by the sanacja opposition. In this fashion, they could rest confident that only their own viewpoints would be recorded for posterity.[114] Świętochowski also added that perhaps the sanacja should publish its own catechism in which all the commandments would be clearly outlined for all to read and obey. The only commandment, he suggested, that need not have been changed from the original Ten Commandments was: "Thou shalt have no other gods before me."[115]

|||

The end of the partitions and the proclamation of independence introduced many serious political, social, and economic problems to the Second Republic. As one way of coping with and understanding these problems, people subjected all manner of behavior, possibility, and expectation to intense scrutiny. The moral panic that emerged alongside the political crisis of the presanacja era prepared the way for a full-blown, nationwide forum on morality in the period following Piłsudski's coup of May 1926. Contemporaries were quick to posit links between the political caesura that the coup had occasioned and what some referred to as the cultural caesura that it had also inaugurated. After the coup public discourses about what the event meant and what a sanacja was were creative and rich and emanated from a wide variety of different constituencies. In the postcoup period ideas about nationalism, citizenship, political participation, and moral accountability came to be hotly contested. The sanacja became such a resonant focus because, in part, the political sanacja was itself a wonderfully malleable idea and its political incarnation lacked clear policy initiatives; it thus became available to be used in a variety of creative and unpredictable ways, in ways that Piłsudski and the Piłsudskiites could not predict or control.

2 ⫿ Poland Writes to Piłsudski

IN THE PREVIOUS chapter, we saw that the notion of a moral catharsis had widespread appeal but that there was little agreement on what the moral revolution should look like or who should lead it. This chapter studies the ways in which letter-writers to Piłsudski used the coup as a springboard for launching their own creative analyses of what ailed the young state and of what remedy would best suit the times. Their letters, written between 1926 and the mid-1930s, reveal a great deal about what the sanacja was, what it could have been, and what, in the opinions of some, it should have been.

In writing these letters, individuals inserted themselves into the emerging national forum on Poland and expressed themselves as citizens. The sanacja, after all, had called for fundamental changes in the conception of citizenship as it tried to encourage a broad notion of activism in the life and development of the state. The very act of putting pen to paper, signing one's name, and asking the nation's senior statesperson to take action on a particular issue and on behalf of a specific individual represented, ironically, precisely the sort of citizen activism that the Piłsudskiite sanacja had encouraged. The many letters about the moral health of the nation suggest that the sanacja's message about the need to create an engaged citizenry and to organize a national forum on the state of Poland was reaching a wide audience. These letters support an implicit acknowledgment that "anyone" was equipped to comment on what was happening and what should happen in Poland, and that "everyone" was constituted by the political realities, divisions, and language of the period.

There is little that is inherently unusual about writing to famous and powerful political and social leaders, asking them for advice or assistance, or simply sharing with them one's own views on any number of pressing national issues, and the literature which examines the meaning of such letters is rich. Much of that literature, though, has focused on the letters, petitions, and denunciations addressed to state institutions and high-ranking public figures in totalitarian societies, especially Nazi Germany and Soviet Russia. In these cases, the letters are read for what they can reveal about the extent of control exercised by the regime, about the potential for dissent, and about the willingness of the citizenry to adopt the administration's language and methods, or conversely, to challenge them. In such cases, writing a certain kind of letter was simply a risky business.[1] While the Second Republic of the sanacja period had certainly betrayed important democratic principles, the post-May regime, rather than discouraging public debate, strangely, had in fact licensed citizens to speak up and be heard.

Those who actually participated in the national debate by writing to Piłsudski were a peculiar lot. The views of the letter writers examined here were not representative of the population at large. But the atypicality of these individuals does not condemn them to irrelevance; quite the contrary. As literary critics Peter Stallybrass and Allon White have argued in their influential work, *The Politics and Poetics of Transgression* (1986), the specific content of any individual's observations, even if and when that individual is far removed from the mainstream, nevertheless reflects some of the same cultural and social cues that shape the wider discourses in society. The adoption of specific ideas, symbols, and language to describe the social world is never arbitrary but instead reflects the mood of the times and shows the extent to which individuals, even marginal ones, are constituted by the general events, anxieties, and ways of apprehending the world that are current at a given moment.[2]

At any rate, making a case for representativeness is beside the point of this analysis; instead, this chapter uses these letters to test the pliability of the sanacja concept and to trace its fortunes and failings in unusual places. It does so, in the first place, by embracing the unrepresentative qualities of the letter writers. The authors in this sampling were economically, socially, or culturally marginal people. Their ideas for change were frequently far-fetched or simply laughable. Many were obviously lonely, desperate attention seekers; a number suffered from delusions of grandeur. Others were just naïve or so passionate about Poland, Piłsudski, and the sanacja that they felt an irresistible compulsion to share their views.

What I present here is a curious assortment of unknown men and women who actively and confidently appropriated the grand terms, tropes, and symbols unleashed by the official political sanacja in describing their own troubles and reform ideas. To be sure, these individuals often manipulated and misrepresented the regime's language. But it is precisely the letter writers' active and imaginative appropriations of the sanacja, and their application of the sanacja's rhetoric of cleansing and reform to their own unique and very personal analyses of different aspects of Polish life, that are so revealing of the sanacja's potential, reach, and power.

The intention here is not to present a comprehensive review of all the various subjects with which people approached Piłsudski, nor is it to evaluate the actual viability of people's suggestions, nor to propose that one can make unqualified generalizations, based on this small sampling of letters, regarding the postwar cultural and social mood in Poland as it was experienced by ordinary Poles. Instead, these letters are used to show that at least some individuals were receptive to a language of cleansing and moral reform; they felt compelled to contribute to the nationwide discussion regarding what ailed newly independent Poland and to propose their own ideas for a sanacja of the nation. Here we have several examples of the way in which the imposing narrative of the sanacja, a narrative focused around a formidable rhetoric of cleansing and moral regeneration, played itself out on minor sites of analysis; at least some people had mastered the Piłsudskiite lexicon.

We begin with Kazimiera Iłłakowiczówna (1892–1983), a well-regarded and successful interwar and postwar poet.[3] From 1926 until Piłsudski's death in 1935, Iłłakowiczówna also worked as Piłsudski's personal secretary at the Ministry of War, where she was in charge of answering the unsolicited mail addressed to Piłsudski from the general public. Piłsudski had moved swiftly in the wake of the coup to establish this separate and formal office for dealing with the flood of correspondence he expected to receive from the people of Poland; it is this mail that the current chapter examines. There is no evidence that Piłsudski ever saw any of the letters addressed to him, but that, in any event, is not our main interest. The very fact that Piłsudski established this office suggests that he had prepared for and was willing to accommodate some kind of a dialogue with Poland. That the office was busy shows that at least some people in Poland had much to say about the dramatic and controversial directions in which sanacja-era Poland was moving and that they felt comfortable expressing their opinions within one of the frameworks Piłsudski had offered.

The specific letters were chosen from among the hundreds of available examples because their authors engaged in various speculations about what the coup and the sanacja meant for moral and national health. These letters reflect that at least some people had thought about what sanacja could mean for the country and that they understood it as being about much more than political reform. Just as private opinions were made public through newspapers in Poland, here we see how private opinions were expressed in a context that was neither exclusively private nor completely public. The exploration intended here requires that we step away momentarily from the Warsaw intellectuals who form the backbone of this exposition. It requires, however, that we remain committed to thinking of the sanacja both as an actual political event and as a potential, an idea that was twisted and pulled in a variety of directions.

Secretary Kazimiera Iłłakowiczówna

Though Kazimiera Iłłakowiczówna is best remembered as a poet of considerable distinction and as a frequent contributor to the interwar press on a wide variety of issues, she preferred to describe herself as a "civil servant" working for her country.[4] This reflected both an emotional commitment to Poland and an economic need to supplement the meager earnings of a writer with employment in the civil service.[5] The fate of the Polish nation forms one of the most persistent themes in Iłłakowiczówna's poetry, and her verses are infused with great national pride; Piłsudski himself is the subject of a number of her poems.[6] In one poem she describes the tremendous impact that Piłsudski had on her sense of responsibility to the national cause: "as if in a shadow of a great sycamore . . . / I am growing in the shadow of a giant." In the poem, Iłłakowiczówna goes on to identify herself so closely with Piłsudski that she, in effect, becomes him:

> When I try on his armour,
> a tide of miraculous power flows into me,
> by another's is my arm victorious,
> My eyes become a flash of the spirit,
> in my heartbeat beats a might star![7]

Iłłakowiczówna first met Piłsudski in 1911 while she was pursuing studies at the Jagiellonian University in Kraków (she had earlier studied in Warsaw,

St. Petersburg, and Oxford). At that time she was also preparing her first volume of poetry for publication. Like many other future Piłsudskiites, even before the war Iłłakowiczówna had given up her previous ties to the Polish Socialist Party.[8] Just before the outbreak of the Great War, Iłłakowiczówna found herself in London, and there she became involved in the suffrage movement, selling feminist pamphlets on the streets. Later, she joined those London Poles who were organizing military aid to Piłsudski in expectation, as she says, of the coming great "uprising."[9] It was during this period that she wrote her first letter to this man she had long admired. She declared her support for Piłsudski's wartime military activities and let him know she was learning how to shoot; she asked that he make her his aide-de-camp. To her letter she attached a copy of an army hymn, "Three Chords," that she had written expressly for Piłsudski.[10]

Piłsudski's response to Iłłakowiczówna consisted of a long letter in which he made it clear he did not support women's involvement in the army. Instead, he outlined the "support roles" to which, in his estimation, women were better suited. Iłłakowiczówna was both pleased that such a great person would write to her and annoyed that he did not offer more—especially that he did not comment on the hymn she had sent; she tore up Piłsudski's response.[11] From 1915 to 1917, Iłłakowiczówna was involved in the war, mainly as a nurse.[12] Her active participation in the war, she later stated, "consolidated in me, in a manner not understandable, in a manner irrational, complete, arduous, and unappeasable, a belief in Józef Piłsudski."[13]

Despite her apparently busy involvement in patriotic work during the war and into the Second Republic, Iłłakowiczówna continually berated herself for not devoting more time and energy to social and political activism. In a manner typical for her time, generation, and social circle, Iłłakowiczówna was self-critical of what she regarded as her own, and society's more generally, half-hearted embrace of citizenship in the reborn Polish state: "Life passed totally by me, great life, that which roars and thunders and expels pearls and monsters."[14] The one common thread throughout her life became a burning desire to work for the betterment of Poland and to support Piłsudski more directly, even if this meant giving up those friends who were to become detractors of Piłsudski.[15]

Iłłakowiczówna later noted that it was only during Piłsudski's period of self-imposed political and social isolation in Sulejówek (1923–26) that she had trouble accepting the marshal's choices. Piłsudski was, after all, Poland's master of the house, and according to Iłłakowiczówna, it was inconceivable that he had chosen to abandon his nation in such a fashion.[16] Yet when Iłłakowiczówna received an unexpected call in November 1925 from [Helena] Sujkowska of Piłsudski's office and was told to prepare herself for the time when Piłsudski would need her services, she realized, with great relief, that he might well have been planning something very important during his apparent retirement from public life.[17]

Just days after the May coup, Iłłakowiczówna received the long-awaited second call from Sujkowska and was summoned to work for Piłsudski. Iłłakowiczówna, who lived at the time in the center of Warsaw, had found herself in the thick of the disturbances, and she described a chaotic and busy atmosphere in the city.[18] She could not believe that Piłsudski and President Wojciechowski could not arrive at a mutually satisfactory agreement during those May days of 1926: "Only men can organize things in this way, and so organize things for everyone," Iłłakowiczówna stated ironically.[19] Nevertheless, the news Sujkowska delivered to Iłłakowiczówna that day was simple: "The commander wishes that you become his personal secretary."[20] After some deliberation and initial reluctance (which contemporary critics of Iłłakowiczówna regarded as wholly insincere),[21] Iłłakowiczówna decided to leave her position at the Ministry of Foreign Affairs, where she had been employed since 1918.[22] Thus in mid-1926, Iłłakowiczówna began a term in the Ministry of Military Affairs as secretary to the minister, Piłsudski; she would remain there until Piłsudski's death, in 1935. Though her first days at her new job involved, as Iłłakowiczówna remembers, simply pouring tea for Piłsudski ("who despised it when a man poured tea"), the next nine years would become, she stated, some of the busiest and most rewarding of her life.[23]

Iłłakowiczówna wrote her reminiscences about her tenure as Piłsudski's secretary in *The Path by the Road* (*Ścieżka obok drogi*), first published in 1939.[24] This is a memoir of Iłłakowiczówna's personal and professional relationship with Piłsudski, written with a sense that one day it would be published and would be read by the public, though it is formally dedicated to and intended for her nieces. The book caused quite a media storm: surprisingly, *The Path by the Road*, written by an unwavering Piłsudski supporter, was attacked by Piłsudskiites and praised by his opponents.[25] One critic, Piłsudskiite author Maria Jehanne Wielopolska, dismissed Iłłakowiczówna's *Path by the Road* in a sarcastic and vitriolic book and mocked the way she interpreted all major historic events through her own life. Wielopolska called *The Path by the Road* unbelievably naïve, wildly arrogant, mean-spirited, and self-serving—an immodest walk—via "the dark, dirty kitchen stairs"—toward Piłsudski, that "largest and most sacred of personages."[26]

Iłłakowiczówna was clear throughout *The Path by the Road* that she admired and respected Piłsudski, and she credited him and the May coup with bringing Poland "out of the house of slavery."[27] At the same time, she depicted Piłsudski as a moody, bossy, arrogant individual accustomed to getting his way. She included in her text amusing anecdotes that her critics argued would be taken the wrong way by Piłsudski's opponents. For example, Iłłakowiczówna relayed that during one particular conversation with Piłsudski, he admitted to waging the May coup just so he could assume the position of minister of military affairs and could move into the beautiful Belvedere Palace, where he would be entitled to drink out of the fine large china cups that were reserved specifically for the minister.[28]

Before the May coup and Iłłakowiczówna's becoming Piłsudski's personal secretary in charge of mail, there did not exist a single office responsible specifically and solely for receiving and answering letters addressed to Piłsudski from the general public. For many years before 1926, Michał (Miś) Galiński, an officer who, it was said, frequently lost attachments and important documents that people sent along with their requests, was charged with handling the mail, but this was not a formalized or regularized process. As an author in her own right, Iłłakowiczówna seemed ideally suited for the job. And as Wielopolska speculated, the general view prevailed that a woman would be "naturally" better suited to answering a particular kind of correspondence in a sensitive manner.[29]

Piłsudski hired Iłłakowiczówna as secretary in charge of correspondence immediately upon his reemergence into political life, and thus quickly following the coup. This suggests both that Piłsudski was preparing himself for increased exposure to the public and that he expected a flurry of reaction to his decisions and to the path down which he was taking Poland. Piłsudski's *sanacja*, moreover, rested on the idea of an active and engaged citizenry. In this sense, the establishment of a bureaucracy that would ostensibly welcome people's opinions cemented the idea of citizen participation in nation building. Writing letters constituted a crude form of political engagement.

Mail addressed to Piłsudski first reached the cabinet office of the Ministry of Military Affairs, where it was sorted into categories: requests for assistance (either material or moral), complaints, political opinion pieces, and simple fan mail. From this point the mail was forwarded on, if there was a need, to the particular ministry best equipped to respond.[30] Iłłakowiczówna stated that each letter was read and catalogued and received a response; the amount of work required of the secretary was therefore tremendous.[31] From June to October 1926 there were twenty to forty requests daily, and from October the number of letters increased steadily. In February and March 1928, the letter count reached two hundred daily.[32] By the end of Iłłakowiczówna's nine-year term as Piłsudski's secretary, Iłłakowiczówna estimated that she had responded to a quarter million pieces of mail.[33] This figure, however, does not include the "Madeira post," mail that Piłsudski received while he vacationed on that island from December 15, 1930, to April 29, 1931. The Madeira post, the bulk of which consisted of simple greetings and well wishes, totaled approximately 1,400,000 pieces of mail, or two and a half metric tons.[34] Most of the letters Piłsudski received, according to Iłłakowiczówna, came from the "uneducated masses, or from pseudo-intellectuals."[35]

One of the most common types of letter consisted of a direct request for aid.[36] Anyone who could claim a noble patriotic or military background foregrounded it in their letter, to suggest entitlement to special consideration. Piłsudski, people felt, would listen to them because they had shared with him an intense experience of war and because he was similarly motivated by a burning love for Poland. Much of the mail that Piłsudski received immediately after the war came from veterans who, having fallen on hard times, appealed to shared experiences in battle to solicit sympathy and material aid.[37]

This tendency to appeal to one's own patriotic service became especially popular after the May coup. For admirers of Piłsudski, the coup functioned as a bold symbol of commitment to Poland, as the most recent and dramatic example of action undertaken with the good of Poland in mind. The coup had been waged, in part, to address many wrongs. One of these surely was that individuals who had fought for an independent Poland were now, in the Second Republic, in desperate straits. In an unsigned report written in 1928 on the subject of the mail sent to Piłsudski, the author stated that from the summer of 1926 to the autumn of 1927, people tended to appeal more forcefully to their national service records and were quick to emphasize that they had long been committed supporters of Piłsudski: "the tone [of the letters] was more emotional, lofty, familiar, warmer."[38] In her memoirs of the period, Iłłakowiczówna noted that in the middle of May 1926, when she had just taken up her position as Piłsudski's secretary, Piłsudski had specifically asked her to give special consideration to Legionnaires' requests for assistance. It was important to Piłsudski to maintain his identity as a soldier and to honor the sacrifices others had made for Poland.[39]

According to Iłłakowiczówna, the letters that specified the type of assistance sought described a wide variety of unfortunate circumstances. Many writers sought help in securing a divorce, especially where the Catholic Church had already refused to grant one. Complaints about unfair arrests and police violence were common, as were protests against unjust court decisions. Requests for Piłsudski's presence at an infant's baptism were similarly frequently made, and many writers also invited Piłsudski to become a child's godfather. (He became the godfather to, among others, the daughter of a known thief sought by the police!) In those cases where he had agreed to serve as godfather, it was made clear he would fulfill his responsibilities from a distance and that he was essentially only granting permission that his name be entered in the Church registry. Someone else would hold the child during the baptism, and no material benefits would accrue to Piłsudski's godchildren.[40]

Iłłakowiczówna described the great sense of despair she felt upon hearing people's sad stories and complaints, aware she could do little to help them.[41] Often illiterate, penniless, and desperate, these individuals, she knew, had even sold their winter coats in order to pay someone to write a letter for them, so important was the act of writing to Piłsudski. In her memoir Iłłakowiczówna told of a man who, instead of writing, made his way to Piłsudski's office, hoping to be granted a meeting with him. He had walked to Warsaw from a town called Łuck, in eastern Poland, and arrived hungry and destitute. The guard at the ministry gave the man his own lunch, and Iłłakowiczówna gave him a small amount of money, but that was all they could do for him. The man's story was familiar. He arrived, she remembered, sometime during the last five years of Piłsudski's life, when the minister seldom saw anyone, including Iłłakowiczówna.[42] Consequently, decisions about how to respond to such visits were exclusively in the hands of Iłłakowiczówna, just as the form and content of the responses to letters addressed to Piłsudski was left exclusively to her discretion.[43] Of the many pathetic entreaties she had heard over the years, Iłłakowiczówna commented, "My conscience would absolutely not allow me to leave these requests without a response."[44]

Iłłakowiczówna understood the desire to write to Piłsudski as a holdover from the partition period, when going to the top was well regarded, even by the lower authorities, as a sign of loyalty to that authority. And although a new generation had experiences in a Polish state and in Polish schools, this tendency to turn to the highest state authority remained. Not to have responded to these letters or to have returned a package, for example, would have amounted to a slap in the face and an affront to this loyalty.[45] Significantly, what the correspondence to Piłsudski also showed, according to Iłłakowiczówna, was that there existed "an incredible bond between the leader and the nation," and this, in turn, stood as a testament to the strong sense of community Piłsudski had created since the May coup.[46]

Entering the World of Imponderables

Iłłakowiczówna herself stated that, along with countless others, she was initially disturbed by the May events, and she confessed to having focused only on the deaths and the violence that had accompanied the coup. In retrospect, however, she believed that the events had "brought the country out of political and moral disorder, and were thus extraordinarily salutary in their effects."[47] Iłłakowiczówna trusted in Piłsudski and in his ability to deliver on the fantastic claims that a sanacja of the nation implied: "I live in an epoch when the terms 'sanacja' and 'beautiful work' are often used in a derogatory sense. But 'sanacja' means healing, and 'beautiful work' is nothing other than working in a good mood."[48]

Iłłakowiczówna reflected that in the months immediately following the May coup, there were few positive letters to Piłsudski, and indeed there were many angry and brutal letters that frightened her.[49] The event had licensed and encouraged vociferous debate about the direction in which Piłsudski was taking Poland, and many people were willing to contribute to that debate by writing to Piłsudski directly. People wrote about how the event itself unfolded as well as its merits or demerits, and they very often couched these opinions in general analyses of the Second Republic. These letters speak to the bond between leader and people, and they show the ways in which some people were absorbed by the language that the coup had popularized.

One letter exemplifies those that offered general praise for Piłsudski and the coup and that articulated clear political positions. It came from a Warsaw man just days after the coup ended. He wrote simply that he believed the coup d'état had been a positive step in cleansing Poland of the "insects" that had infested its body. To have allowed the situation to continue as it was would have been an affront to the thousands of soldiers who had died over the centuries fighting for Poland. The man wrote: "It was faith in you which allowed me to know that the days of a new era of moral rebirth and cleansing of the Nation . . . have begun."[50] The author used a vocabulary of health and duty, history and responsibility to describe what had happened. He assumed that rebirth was both necessary and possible, and he did not express great concern that the specific features of this rebirth had not yet been publicly announced in a detailed platform. Likewise many others were prepared to trust in Piłsudski, who after the coup, more than ever before, was cast in the role of savior of the nation. People reacted as much to the fact that it was Piłsudski himself who had launched the May action as they did to the action itself; the coup, the sanacja, and the post-May future could not be separated from the person of Piłsudski. As one contemporary observer stated, Piłsudski became "not just a reformer and conqueror, but an educator—a creator of the future. Not just a blacksmith of accidents and happenings thrown down from above, but also a sculptor of souls."[51]

Another letter to Piłsudski came from one Jan Wiśniowski in 1930 and was typical in presenting only a general opinion on the new regime in Poland. Like many letter writers, Wiśniowski established his loyalty to the sanacja up front; he described himself as a "sympathizer with the ideology of the First Marshal of Poland, a great admirer of his." He also shared that he was a member of the well-known Piłsudskiite political group called the Union for the Reform of the Republic (Związek Naprawy Rzeczypospolitej) and that he was "an exponent of the motto of partylessness," as the Piłsudskiites generally were known to be. Wiśniowski then moved to outlining his long list of patriotic credentials, as letter writers typically did, and emphasized that he had spent six years as a "slave" in Russia. The specific reason for posting the letter is never spelled out (as it was not in many of the letters); the purpose seems to have been located in the act of identifying himself to Piłsudski and of participating in this dialogue on Poland. The impetus to write seems to have come, moreover, from Wiśniowski's sense of having been "wronged both materially and morally" in the Second Republic and of wanting the reality of independence to live up to the dreams. The implicit assumption was that Piłsudski was uniquely able, in the post-May period, to effect the desired changes.[52]

Sometimes, letters to Piłsudski were far more specific about what and how the healing process should be organized. The post-May governments had themselves been slow to offer clear and tangible policy positions but relied, instead, on imprecise appeals to life's imponderables, on the need to strengthen the state and purge immoral influences from its public face, and on the value of citizen participation in the larger process of political reform. This open-ended quality of the sanacja left citizens free to propose a wide range of possibilities, and propose they did. For example, "A Plan for Our Nation" was sent in a thick notebook to Piłsudski from Stanisław Przybysz, of Łódź, just a month after the coup. Przybysz set out to answer what he regarded as the most pressing question in the Second Republic: "What can be done to save the nation?" Taking up themes popularized by the proclamation of the sanacja, Przybysz reached confidently to a vocabulary of moral crisis, salvation, healing, and reform. He expressed particular concern about the wave of fraud and thievery that had been plaguing Poland and about the public immorality to which, ostensibly, the sanacja would put a stop.[53]

Przybysz's ideas were radical and betray what was undoubtedly an unsound mind. His writing style—repetitive, rambling, at times hostile, lacking in punctuation, and with a number of spelling and grammatical errors—suggests further that Przybysz was not well educated and that he did not exist in the mainstream of society. Most notably, Przybysz proposed that each individual (especially individuals working in the public service) caught breaking the law and offending public morality be branded on the forehead and let out into the streets to suffer public censure. A second infraction against public morality would warrant a brand on the cheek, while the third would justify sending the transgressor promptly to the electric chair without any opportunity to mount a defense.[54] The author hoped these rules would ensure that all public servants would be "of good moral character." Przybysz concluded, as a matter of course, that "the female sex" could not be hired for positions within the public service. Here he was picking up on postwar debates about the nature, extent, and effects (perceived and otherwise) of women's employment on men's employment, on the family, on gender identities, and on national identity. As it stood, and based on legislation passed in 1922, women could and did work in the civil service; women formed about 8 percent of public employees according to 1931 statistics. Married women wishing to work in certain positions, however, were first required to secure the permission of their husbands.[55]

On first reflection, one may be tempted to dismiss Przybysz's graduated system of punishment as the irrelevant ravings of an insignificant figure. However, Przybysz's letter is oddly typical in its embrace of the idea of the need for imminent change and for the right of individual citizens to act as partners with the state in stamping out corruption; the spirit of his ideas (rather than his specific proposals for reform) reflect core sanacja themes about citizen activism and responsibility for the shape of Poland. Piłsudski had himself remarked that the coup was launched in order to put a decisive end to governmental abuse of power, and calls to stamp out corruption reached a fevered pitch at this time.

The exclusive and elitist Piłsudskiite paper *Imperatives of the Moment* (*Nakazy chwili*), formed just after the coup by prominent Piłsudskiite Adam Skwarczyński, executed a plan that was far gentler and saner, but not altogether dissimilar to Przybysz's proposal. *Imperatives of the Moment* was established in part to expose the kind of corruption and nepotism that the sanacja had proclaimed it would destroy. The first issue of the paper presented what its editors referred to as a "black list" and a "gray list" on which the names of particularly "immoral" and unworthy public figures appeared. PSL-Piast leader Wincenty Witos, who led the May 1926 cabinet against which Piłsudski acted, made the black list in the first issue, while Gen. Władysław Sikorski, known to oppose Piłsudski's sanacja, made it in the second issue.[56]

As the Piłsudskiites would find, however, and as historians have also shown, the sanacja political grouping was able to uncover very few cases of corruption in previous governments. In this sense, its frequent references to mass corruption and its appeals to public servants to reach for a higher morality were not supported by concrete evidence, but constituted, instead, forms of "primitive propaganda," to quote historian Andrzej Garlicki.[57] It would in fact be the Piłsudskiites that would be implicated in what would become a very public and messy scandal involving election budgets and known as the Czechowicz affair.[58] Nevertheless, the Piłsudskiites cleverly and successfully, at least for a time, maintained an image of demanding and personifying a higher public morality. That image had great appeal in the wider society, and Przybysz's letter is one example of the ways in which Piłsudskiite rhetoric reached different constituencies and resonated forcefully with them. Przybysz recognized the coup as a call for radical changes in the way social and political life were organized in Poland. He worked with some conception of what morality meant or should mean in the state, and he recognized that the coup included an important moral component. Through Przybysz's letter one develops a sense of the degree to which people were engaged with and absorbed the new language and ideas that the era had produced. It is this fact of engagement as well as the forms of expression that are of interest, rather than the viability of the proposals themselves. In the new Polish state, individuals like Przybysz created their own openings for political participation by writing to the most senior statesman. Przybysz inserted himself into the political discourse and participated, admittedly in a crude form, in the fledgling democratic process.

Another response to the May coup came from Jan Popławski, of Białystok Province. Popławski began his letter to Piłsudski, dated June 21, 1926, with a literary reference; he reached to the dire words of Wernyhora from Stanisław Wyspiański's famous national drama, *The Wedding* (*Wesele*) (1901): "You had the golden horn and the hat made of peacock's feathers, you boor . . . you lost them."[59] Wyspiański's play was widely read among a certain segment of the literate public. One of its main points—that the Polish nation had to rise from its slumber and act decisively to create a better future for itself—was often cited in analyses of Poland's contemporary situation. Popławski was concerned about what was happening all over Europe at this time, but especially in Poland, and he could not forget Wernyhora's mocking warning. Popławski was critical of what he referred to as petty party wrangling, given that there were far more pressing economic and social issues in the new state. He praised Piłsudski for having fulfilled "Poland's Providence" but feared that unless all the politicians, administrators, and statespeople of the nation were to find a "common language" with which to work to "save Poland," the nation would again be doomed and would experience another tragedy on the scale of the late-eighteenth-century partitions.[60] Popławski spoke directly to the divisiveness of Polish politics and to the impotence people felt. Behind his statement, indeed behind much of the era's own analyses of national problems, lay a sense that tragedy was always lurking and that history could not be forgotten. Memories of the fall of the Polish state and of the long period of partitions shaped responses to Polish independence and to reform strategies within the Second Republic.

Yet another letter to Piłsudski was written just half a year after the coup by Andrzej Komorowski, a waiter in a dessert shop in Warsaw.[61] The letter bears the heading, "Praise Jesus Christ." Komorowski supported Piłsudski and thanked him for "waking up" the people of Poland, for renewing the nation and bringing order to the state. He even suggested that Piłsudski should become king of Poland (not an uncommon suggestion).[62] Komorowski outlined the many specific areas in which he believed the Second Republic had gone wrong. He pointed to the political divisions and social unrest in the state and to the pervasive sense that corruption was everywhere in the republic. To this rather standard list, Komorowski added another aspect of life that was in desperate need of healing: Warsaw, during the forty years that he had lived in the city, had become "Sodom and Gomorrah." Komorowski hoped that Piłsudski would use his authority "to renew" Poland, "to bring the country to order," and, ultimately, to improve Catholic morality in the city.[63] In this ostensibly private letter, we see again that in sanacja Poland it was but a short step from articulating a critique of the political system to offering a critique of the nation's sexual-moral culture; newspaper commentary published shortly after the coup also reflected this (chapter 1). At least some people, even the socially marginal Komorowski, understood the potential inherent in the sanacja in its widest possible sense and made explicit links between political, social, and moral phenomena. That his ideas are suffused with religious fervor and an apocalyptic reading of the sanacja further shows the variety of manipulations that the sanacja underwent. That Komorowski's letter is bizarre and at times downright confusing does not undermine the basic point that it had emerged as a direct response to Piłsudski's coup. Many different constituencies approached the coup in this way, as the impetus for a massive transformation of society, one that went far beyond the political and military arenas that were so important to Piłsudski himself. The sanacja was expansive and malleable enough to suit a variety of interpretations, and this was one key source of its appeal.

The Piłsudskiites had been clear about stating that public morality needed to be raised, for the good of the state. They had never stated openly that the sanacja should be directed at private morality and said nothing at all about sexual morality. People like Komorowski nevertheless applied the sanacja language about moral reform and spiritual cleansing to the private sphere and defined "cleansing" widely. At the time that Komorowski wrote his letter, late in 1926, it was not yet clear in which direction Piłsudski would move the sanacja, and Komorowski took this as an opportunity to offer his own expectations of and hopes for the future. Komorowski used the coup as a starting point for his own analysis of what ailed Poland, and he interpreted private morality and public morality as two sides of the same coin.

Women Write to Piłsudski

Though most letters to Piłsudski came from men, Iłłakowiczówna stated that the number of letters from women steadily increased, such that by 1928 they constituted one-quarter of all letters. Women and girls wrote mainly to ask for assistance in finding employment or generally for aid in improving an adverse economic situation.[64] Many women presented themselves foremost as mothers, to lend greater legitimacy to their positions. It may well have been that women, especially mothers, felt the burden of dire economic constraints more acutely. But women also wrote letters that engaged directly with the sanacja idea and expressed unambiguous opinions of the path down which Piłsudski was leading the nation. In inserting themselves into the national debates, women were also expressing themselves as citizens, albeit in this tentative, informal, and even somewhat strangely private fashion. One could suggest that the sanacja generally appealed to women in a way that earlier political configurations had not and that women felt especially welcome to participate in a sanacja that had popularized notions of the need for a higher public morality, for improved national health, and for more active community involvement in national affairs. The sanacja celebrated the idea of morality as the highest virtue, and some women extrapolated from this that they, as women, and as the ostensibly more moral and caring sex, possessed real power to shape all levels of society. Women had special obligations to fulfill, as citizens, and they could do so, for example, by joining a group committed to public activism, or they could write to Piłsudski directly. In Piłsudski, some women found a great national figure who seemed to value precisely what they, as women, were seen as being best able to provide in terms of maintaining the national family.

One particularly interesting letter came from Helena Sokołowska, of Warsaw. She wrote her "quiet request" to her "beloved" Piłsudski on September 26, 1930, in the hope that he might grant her an audience.[65] Failing that, her letter was simply an attempt to gain from Piłsudski the much-needed courage to fight what she called the "most difficult battle of all": a moral battle. She began her letter with superlatives about Piłsudski's heroic acts on behalf of the Polish nation and affirmed her commitment to working for the betterment of the whole.[66] As did most letter writers, male and female, Sokołowska outlined her record of service to the nation, which was indeed impressive. Since 1912, she explained, she had had Piłsudski's image and inspiration in her heart and had been propagating his good work through participation in various social and professional organizations as well as through her daily family rituals. In addition, she had fought "energetically and with moral satisfaction" on Piłsudski's side during the Great War. But the reborn state had not turned out as she had hoped, and she had begun to despair.[67]

Sokołowska railed against those who were nominally on Piłsudski's side but who nevertheless did not possess his ideals in their hearts and souls. These skeptics were uncertain of which side would ultimately be victorious, and they were choosing carefully and slowly. "Small and ignorant, they must be enlightened," she suggested, "otherwise they will become troublemakers."[68] She reserved particular venom for women who had come out against Piłsudski and suggested that they were rejecting their responsibilities as women and neglecting their obligations to the nation.[69]

In contrast to those women who had rejected the sanacja, Sokołowska embodied the ideal of sanacja-era femininity. Inspired by having been part of a delegation that had been granted an audience with Aleksandra Piłsudska at Belvedere, Sokołowska made the decision to commit herself more formally to the Piłsudski camp. Sokołowska chose the Pomorze as the region in which to begin social agitation, as she was concerned about the influence of the long-standing German presence there. In Toruń she organized several successful conferences, with the assistance of the provincial governor and the district prefect; later, she organized conferences in other parts of Poland. The public response to her activities was positive, she wrote. Sokołowska understood herself to be motivating others, just as she was motivated by Piłsudski.[70] This was the "work" on which she believed the success of the sanacja project depended. She embraced proudly the epithet her detractors applied to her: she was a "gendarme" for the Piłsudski cause.[71] Sokołowska became, and she called on other women to become, "honorary soldiers" in the war that was being waged in sanacja Poland.

Sokołowska's emphases are interesting for a number of reasons. She clearly understood the sanacja as a larger project, difficult to define yet crucial because it reached to some of the fundamentals of Polish life; the sanacja was nothing less than a war that had forced people to choose sides. She also expressed absolute devotion to Piłsudski himself and held him up as a national savior; in Sokołowska's understanding, Piłsudski was absolutely inseparable from the sanacja. Further, she believed women possessed a special role within the sanacja project and took it upon herself to begin a massive mobilization campaign. The kind of activism Sokołowska participated in and encouraged will be explored in greater detail in chapter 4.

Another letter to Piłsudski came from a woman who identified herself only as residing in Wilno (Vilnius) and as "a common worker" and "mother." It was signed, "With deep and sincere respect, I wish you good health, Marshal. I am the echo of millions."[72] The author stated that she had never before written to Piłsudski, but that the present situation commanded her response: "The heart sings from joy as a result of your having reached to the depths of the filth in Poland."[73] What seems to have prompted the letter was the flurry of criticism directed at Piłsudski during the Brześć affair. "I pity you as though you were my own son," she wrote.[74]

The common worker from Wilno realized that Piłsudski himself might never read the letter but hoped that if he did, the words of a "small person" would be a comfort to him. She wanted him to know that there existed in Poland those "who believe completely in your integrity, and who, with complete sincerity and without ulterior motives, love you." She tried to comfort Piłsudski by suggesting that, if things sometimes failed to go as he had planned or hoped, he should not despair, for he could not accomplish everything alone. She reminded him, and hoped she was not being blasphemous by doing so, that even the Lord could not possibly cope entirely well with the world, as evil exerted such a monumentally powerful force.[75] She wished that people would more eagerly embrace the "Józef Piłsudski cause" and that they would work hard for the good of the collective. She remembered her days of working for the Polish Military Organization (Polska Organizacja Wojskowa) and of giving away her last supplies to others who needed them more. She further recalled the time that her husband, now a sixty-six-year-old former prisoner of war, was interned at Havelberg. She expressed pride about how she had raised her children. At fourteen, her son ran off to the Polish Military Organization, and by the age of sixteen he was a cadet and "helped kill Germans." She raised her daughter to be a nurse to soldiers.[76]

The woman underscored in her letter that she and her family had never been "parasites" on Poland. Instead, according to their strength and ability, they had "cleansed" Poland: "with my entire family, I work for Poland."[77] She worshiped Piłsudski "to the point of ecstasy" and was grateful for all he had done for Poland. Interestingly, this common worker also stated that she wrote to Piłsudski specifically in the capacity of "a Polish woman," and she included the following message: "Polish women, you who are susceptible to [negative] influences but who are decent, control your Polish men so that they shun trouble, vanity and greed, and so that they work as the marshal has worked."[78]

Poland would not survive if it were treated as a full and rich trough which its people polluted at will. And the great Marshal Piłsudski could not exist simply to clean up after others. She reminded Polish women that they had nothing under the Russians, the Germans, and the Austrians, and that whatever ills might have befallen independent Poland, and whatever other trials it would face in the future, Poland was independent, and thanks to Piłsudski, no Pole would ever again have to tolerate "a kick from a Prussian boot." The woman concluded her letter by appealing to everyone to trust Piłsudski and to let him do his work. To be successful and effective, she concluded, Piłsudski needed to know that the people of Poland stood behind him: "Write, talk and shout—you, the small people, so that the Marshal knows about this."[79]

Dziadek Piłsudski

As we see from this last letter, as well as from the previous ones, Piłsudski was at the very center of people's understandings of the sanacja, and his legend extended deeply into the discourses of the Second Republic after 1926.

Perhaps this is no more clearly revealed than in the correspondence that developed between Secretary Iłłakowiczówna and two girls named Jola and Marysia. Jola Knothe, a student in the fourth grade at St. Casimir's school in Poznań, began her letter to Józef Piłsudski with the salutation, "My dearest and beloved Grandfather [*Dziadek*]." On the heels of the girl's compliments for Piłsudski and her praise for all that he had done for Poland, Jola offered an unequivocal expression of her disdain for the sanacja camp's committed opponents: the right-wing National Democrats or, as they were pejoratively referred to, the Endeks: "It makes me so angry that some bad people don't love you and that they also teach their children not to love you these sorts of people are called abominable Endeks why don't you Grandfather do something about them. Take away everything from all those Endeks who have houses, fortunes, stores, take it all away from them. When they are not good Poles why should they have it good in a Poland for which you fought so long for such dirty swine."[80]

Jola quickly moved from berating Piłsudski's opposition to bragging about herself and how diligently she had defended Piłsudski's honor on the school playground. Luckily, her teacher favored Jola's position: "Ms. Rozmuska always told us and at home we were also told that every decent person and good Pole should love you. Wash the dirty linen—that's what the Endeks are, my dear Grandfather."[81] Jola's friend, Marysia Konopkówna, attached her own note to Jola's letter: "And me too, my dear Grandfather, I love you and I won't allow the Endeks to say anything bad about you, but Jola is like a boy and strikes fast."[82] Awed by Jola's boldness and determination, Marysia confessed that initially she was somewhat reticent and was afraid of getting written up in the school daybook. After a particularly insightful conversation with her aunt, however, Marysia realized that, when it came to Piłsudski, the girls had permission to "strike and strike at these raging Endeks." Marysia's aunt, as it turned out, believed that, "with children it is best to get to the soul through the body." Buoyed by a sense of license, Marysia declared, "I am happy and first thing tomorrow I will settle things with one of my wild Endek friends."[83]

Two weeks after mailing their letters to Piłsudski, Jola and Marysia received a response from Iłłakowiczówna. In her response, she thanked the girls for their kind words about Piłsudski and told them that Piłsudski sometimes selected letters he received from children to share with his wife and his own daughters, so that together they could be happy that "Polish children love the one who defends the honor and wholeness of their Fatherland." But Iłłakowiczówna was clear that the girls' letters would not bring joy to Piłsudski or his family. She clearly condemned the physical violence in which the girls claimed to engage, and scolded them for the delight they took in stamping out opposition to Piłsudski on the school playground. Iłłakowiczówna informed Marysia and Jola that her job was to help others understand Piłsudski's message of compassion and love for all the different people who made Poland their home. She exhorted the girls to stop their assaults on the National Democrats and instead to pray for Piłsudski and for his continued ability to work for Poland. She also sent them a book.[84]

The correspondence does not end here, however. Jola wrote back to thank Iłłakowiczówna for the gift and took the opportunity to clarify a few apparent misperceptions. Most important to Jola was to explain who it was that actually started the fights; it was, of course, always the Endeks. Just recently, Jola stated, Endek hooligans threw trash on her family's steps because the balcony had been decorated for Piłsudski's name day. Jola summarized that she "punche[d] them [the Endeks] in the face" only when it was absolutely necessary and warranted; Jola's priority had to be defending herself and her Dziadek. She did finally concede that if it was so important to Piłsudski that she show compassion for the Endeks, "then I will try to be quiet."[85]

In contrast, the originally more reticent Marysia, who again attached a note to Jola's letter, stubbornly stated that she and her friend were simply obliged to continue fighting Piłsudski's opposition. Nevertheless, Marysia remained polite and also thanked the secretary for the book, whose arrival had incited her dying uncle to recover from a long illness. Marysia also made a rather strange request: she asked Iłłakowiczówna not to write back. It seems that Marysia's aunt—the same one who believed that children's souls were best reached through their bodies—felt rather too harshly judged by the tone of Iłłakowiczówna's letter: "Aunt cried about this shame that we brought upon [our home]." Another letter might make matters worse, Marysia reasoned, and she was anxious to prevent that. The correspondence does appear to have ended there.[86]

The letters of Marysia and Jola, both of whom were too young to have a deep understanding of Polish history or politics, reveal much about the marked political polarization in the postcoup era and about how the very notion of a *sanacja*, of the need for a nationwide debate about Poland's moral nations and the quality of independence, permeated deep into the language and cultural discourses of the period. First, it is striking that the girls' letters to Piłsudski were (very neatly) handwritten but were later typed out by Iłłakowiczówna's office. In contrast, many other letters to the office were simply stamped as having been received and answered and were left in their original forms. Speculation about the purpose of this copying has obvious limits, but these letters' special treatment suggests something about their importance to Iłłakowiczówna.

By 1932 the *sanacja* needed all the positive publicity it could get. The Brześć affair—the imprisonment and detention of members of the *sanacja* opposition—had exploded in 1930 and had caused many staunch Piłsudskiites to forsake the *sanacja* as a brutal and authoritarian regime that in no way fulfilled the hopes they had originally placed in it. These letters spoke to the tendency at the time to separate Piłsudski from some of the more unpleasant charges leveled against the *sanacja* regime. Throughout the many challenging periods the regime faced, Piłsudski himself remained popular among large sections of the population. Letters like Marysia's and Jola's would have played into this tendency to portray Piłsudski as somehow above the political process. And the letters were all the more rhetorically powerful because they came from children.

The pro-Piłsudski press was always anxious to show that the marshal had a special rapport with children—a testament, it was argued, to his general kindness. Piłsudski's relationship with his own daughters, Wanda and Jadwiga, was often held up as a model for all Polish fathers. One instance the press delighted in popularizing concerned a document written by Piłsudski, "Protocol of Lived Experience." Addressed to "all Polish children," the protocol emerged as a result of Piłsudski's young daughters' request that on his 1928 trip to Romania, he determine whether the water in the Black Sea was actually black and whether it would color black anything that was dropped into it. The protocol stated that a blue ribbon left hanging in the waters of the Black Sea for one hour did indeed darken. The protocol also noted, however, that the ribbon returned to its original color after it dried, proving, of course, that the water in the Black Sea was not black after all. The results of this little experiment were written up formally and signed by Maj. S. G. Ludwig, a military attaché, as well as by the marshal himself.[87]

Note also that Jola and Marysia lived in Poznań, a region in the northwest of Poland not known to be a stronghold of support for Piłsudski. Poznań was in the heart of the former Prussian partition and was the most economically and culturally developed section of nineteenth-century partitioned Poland.[88] Some people in this region had even viewed with trepidation their inclusion into the Second Republic and regarded people from the Austrian and the Russian areas as backward and uncultured, as unfortunate and embarrassing poor cousins.[89]

During the Second Republic, Poznań cemented its reputation for political conservatism and a tradition of strong Catholicism blended with intense Polish nationalism.[90] Voting patterns in the region reflected these attitudes. When the daughter of Emil Zegadłowicz mentioned to a friend that her parents were voting for the Number One ticket—for Piłsudski and his Nonpartisan Bloc for Cooperation with the Government, the BBWR—in the upcoming elections, she became a social pariah.[91] In most voting regions during the 1928 elections, for example, at least some voters from the political right moved to the BBWR. In the Poznań and Pomorze regions, however, the BBWR failed to attract the right-wing vote and moreover, center votes in the region moved not to the left (as they did elsewhere in Poland), but to the right. That is, Poznań voted en masse for the sanacja opposition, and as a result, the BBWR made the worst showing in western Poland. Poznań was the heart of National Democratic territory.[92]

Interwar opponents of the sanacja were proud of this fact and believed that it only underscored Poznań's status as the most civilized city in Poland. In his memoirs, National Democracy's cofounder, Roman Dmowski, described interwar Poznań: "It was a healthy, strong part of a living Poland . . . possessing a most strongly developed collective will. . . . It didn't simply wish to be in the Polish state; it had something to say in that state. And that's why . . . it was viewed with reluctance by the degenerate type of Poles. In our quest to wrestle this land from German hands, we were not only the representatives of Polish thought in general—the only kind that had a right to call itself Polish—we were also the creators of a strong active spirit on this land of the Polish nation.[93]

The writers from the National Democrats' theoretical journal, *National Thought,* raised Poznań to the position of Poland's "moral capital."[94] Poznań was heralded as the city that had most successfully overcome the political, economic, social, and especially moral crises of the partition period. "The Polish soul" had been able to flourish in interwar Poznań, and, *National Thought* columnist Zygmunt Wasilewski affirmed, the city had successfully created "a clean atmosphere of work." Even after the supposedly dark days that followed the May 1926 coup, Poznań had managed to hold steadfastly to its Catholic and nationalist principles and to resist the onslaught of depravity that the coup, in the opinion of Wasilewski and others associated with the right-nationalist camp, had unleashed.[95]

From the perspective of conservative Poznań, Poland's capital city constituted an "orgy," a site of license and perversion of proper Catholic mores and Polish national traditions.[96] Reaching to the all-too-familiar tactic of ascribing Jewishness to any supposedly immoral trend or idea, noted commentator Mieczysław Piszczkowski stated plainly in *National Thought* that because Warsaw was home to all the various "channels of Jewish propaganda," it unquestionably formed the heart of the demoralized nation.[97] Whatever Warsaw was or was thought to be, Poznań represented the opposite.

The letters of Marysia and Jola to Piłsudski further suggest the degree to which politics in sanacja-era Poland had descended to the same low level as before the coup. The most significant lesson the girls seemed to absorb was that Piłsudski and the post-May camp were good and that the Endeks were not. Even these young girls understood that Poland's two "nations"—the Piłsudskiites and the nationalist right—were at war.

Piłsudski, Archetypal Pole

In the several cases examined above, we see the central role that Piłsudski played in writers' understanding of and relationship to the sanacja. In the minds of contemporaries, the sanacja could not be separated from Piłsudski himself; he was the architect of the political sanacja and the master of the house, like it or not. Given that the formal sanacja lacked a very specific policy agenda, other than a commitment to strengthening the executive and reforming the constitution, Piłsudski represented the single most important unifying element of the regime and of the potential implied in sanacja.

For many supporters in the Second Republic, the name of Piłsudski—with his unqualified patriotic commitment to Poland, his physical prowess, and his self-assurance—was synonymous with selfless and proper Polish manliness.[98] Piłsudski's army uniform, which he always wore, was unadorned by medals and functioned to remind people, subtly but confidently, that without his Legions and his Miracle on the Vistula, there would be no Poland.[99] Supporters emphasized how devoted Piłsudski was to his children, how modestly he lived, and how little he valued material comforts and money. Time and again, contemporaries reproduced images of Piłsudski's bedroom in Sulejówek to show that it contained only functional furniture and little ornamentation, showing that Piłsudski was an everyman all Poles might relate to and many would admire.[100] A portrait of Napoleon hung over Piłsudski's bed, along with a photograph of Piłsudski's brother, who had died in 1918, and a painted view of Wilno, the city of his youth and devotion. Beside the bed rested a photograph of Piłsudski's mother.[101]

The Legionnaires' Union (Związek Legionistów) called Piłsudski an incarnation of "the holy victory of the Polish noble soul," and his name a symbol of a great new era in Polish history.[102] Newspapers that supported the sanacja regularly ran articles in praise of Piłsudski. On his name day, the Feast of St. Joseph on March 19, many papers published glowing retrospectives of the man and his work for Poland. Often mentioned was the May coup of 1926, for having rejuvenated the nation and having sparked concerted action on behalf of independence.[103]

Members of Poland's left-liberal intelligentsia also praised Piłsudski. Skamander poet and *Literary News* (*Wiadomości literackie*) publicist Antoni Słonimski (1895–1976), for example, was known to have kept three photos on his desk: one of the great Polish romantic poet Adam Mickiewicz, another of novelist Stefan Żeromski, and a third of Piłsudski.[104] Dr. Hanna Pohoska (1895–1953), a prominent exponent of the sanacja camp's education policies and wife of parliamentarian and Society for Moral Rebirth member Jan Pohoski (1889–1944), held Piłsudski up as "a living symbol of citizenship." Pohoska emphasized that Piłsudski had given Poland so much more than just territorial independence; he had handed Poland the opportunity to pursue spiritual independence. The latter he had achieved by impressing upon people the need to build a deep understanding of the imponderables.[105] Piłsudski was regarded by many in the postindependence period as embodying distinctively Nietzschean qualities, as "a sort of superman, a new incarnation of the King-Spirit."[106]

Piłsudski, however, certainly had many interwar critics. His opponents cited unmitigated egoism and a lust for power, a willful disregard for procedure and rules, and an irrational and misplaced eagerness; he was Poland's scourge and villain.[107] According to this way of thinking, Piłsudski had allowed the Jewish-Bolshevik-liberal forces to gain a foothold in the republic and to pervert the Polish soul in frighteningly unrecognizable ways, as witnessed by the severe moral crisis many opponents saw in the young Republic. Some called Piłsudski "the first Piłsudskiite," to reinforce the point that Piłsudski nursed an arrogant belief that he was Poland's most important citizen and that he regarded himself as spearheading a veritable movement of reform. Along these same lines, Piłsudski was understood by others to be nothing short of a Mafia boss; his army boys (*chłopcy*) were fanatically devoted to their charismatic and powerful Grandfather and would do anything for him.[108] Still others emphasized that Piłsudski was single-handedly responsible for putting an abrupt stop to Poland's democracy and for dragging Poland toward authoritarianism: Piłsudski was a dictator, plain and simple.[109] The epithet *dyktatuś* emerged among his critics as a blend of the words for dictator (*dyktator*) and daddy (*tatuś*). *Primo de Brigada* referred simultaneously to the Spanish general and dictator Miguel Primo de Rivera and the First Brigade.[110]

Few people would disagree that sanacja-era Poland conformed to the definitions of an authoritarian state, especially after the Brześć affair broke in 1930 and just as the sanacja adopted a comparatively harsh approach to opposition generally. In the Second Republic of the sanacja period, parliamentary democracy was curtailed severely; freedoms of press, speech, and association were limited; and the interests of the almighty state—though no one was clear on what these were—were heralded as the most important determinants of policy and action. Piłsudski was the spectacular leader around whom conspirators and the people at large gathered. It was no secret that Piłsudski had been a keen admirer of Mussolini and his 1922 March on Rome. Both men were understood, by some, to have saved their nations from catastrophe and anarchy and to have launched a vibrant movement of reform.[111]

Poles themselves were aware, of course, of the growing cult status of Piłsudski from the earliest days of independence. Jan Lipecki (pseudonym of Irena Pannenkowa, 1879–1969), railed against Piłsudski in *The Legend of Piłsudski* (*Legenda Piłsudskiego*) (1922). *Legend* became a best seller (several thousand copies in six weeks) and caused a media sensation, partly because it was written by someone who, during the war, had worked with Piłsudski and had considered herself a Piłsudskiite. Pannenkowa moved away from the Piłsudski camp in the early independence period and changed her political orientation, building her reputation as a National Democratic supporter and publicist. She later contributed to several journals, including *Republic* (*Rzeczpospolita*) and *ABC,* where she attacked women's rights activist Tadeusz Boy Żeleński (see chapter 5) and his ideas of sexual and moral reform.[112]

People mistakenly regarded Piłsudski, Pannenkowa argued, as a national hero, as a moral beacon, and as the only and best possible symbol of commitment to the nation. Instead, the author highlighted his egoism and megalomania and emphasized that he had been part of a larger movement in the partition and wartime periods, which surely would have produced another leader had Piłsudski not stepped into the limelight.[113] Pannenkowa maintained it was her responsibility to expose the falsehood surrounding Piłsudski. She offered up these criticisms of his cult so that the all-important rebirth of Polish society, which she did not deny needed to take place, could do so in an atmosphere of honesty and sober thinking.[114] This tone suited the National Democrats quite well. In richly gendered language, *National Thought* described Pannenkowa's text as a "fundamental, essential, measured, tactful, manly, bold, documented demasking of a commercial orgy."[115]

At the same time, one would do well to emphasize the differences between the status of Piłsudski as a cult figure and the cult status that other European leaders attained during the interwar period. Piłsudski was a different kind of dictator. For the last several years of his life, he shunned public appearances, including the parades and festivals that had become standard fare in building cult status. This was partly because by the late 1920s, and certainly into the 1930s, when Piłsudski was the undisputed master of the state, he was already seriously ill. In addition, the image that he valued and strove to create—one of frugality, honesty, and integrity—worked to the sanacja's advantage; the sanacja would not have easily supported an ostentatious leader. The message behind this image of modesty was central to the very idea of the sanacja and to the concepts of national unity, good citizenship, and honest work as the highest calling; people needed to put aside their selfish and partisan or personal interests and to come together to work actively for something bigger than them all: for Poland.

|||

The letters we have examined show not only that Piłsudski was essential to the idea of the sanacja but that his coup sparked a flurry of unexpected and sometimes unusual reactions. The letters written to Piłsudski after the coup have been used here to suggest the many ways in which certain people understood Polish independence generally and the sanacja specifically. The letters reveal much about the political and cultural mood of the period and about the preoccupations and anxieties of at least some people in the state. They suggest not only that the political events of the day registered in important circles and in high places but that they resonated, too, with individuals at the margins of society; even they were shaped by the language that the sanacja had popularized and even they formed their own ideas about what the sanacja portended.

But the imponderables to which the sanacja was devoted, quite simply, were difficult to define and constituted poor markers for charting a consistent or coordinated course for future action. And yet it was precisely in this open-endedness that the potential contained in sanacja lay. The ideas presented by the letter writers considered here underscore the susceptibility of sanacja to diverse appropriations. As the letters further suggest, people showed remarkable confidence in defining the sanacja in their own unique ways and in articulating their creative manipulations directly to Piłsudski himself. In the next chapters, we will study specific organizations that people built after the coup with the intention of answering the imponderables to which Piłsudski had referred. What these random letter writers were only able to hint at, organizations like those discussed in the next two chapters were able to synthesize into more coherent political, cultural, and social agendas.

3 ⫼ Building the Army of Moral Action

On April 29, 1926, a conference entitled "The Moral Obligations of the Present Day" was held at the Warsaw public library. Four individuals from this conference—Aniela Samotyhowa, Helena Sujkowska, Walery Sławek, and Jerzy Radomski—went on to form the Commission for Moral Rebirth (Komitet Odrodzenia Moralnego). In forging this new organization, they agreed that the Second Republic was frightfully sick and that in addition to the political, social, and economic problems it faced, Poland was beset by a wide-reaching cultural and moral crisis. Some eight years after independence, it was increasingly clear that Polish society had not been emotionally, morally, or spiritually prepared to be independent. If citizens' complacency and spiritual listlessness were to continue unabated, members of the commission predicted, Poland would face certain ruin. The failure, this time, would come exclusively from within and as a result would be all the more contemptible. Commission members agreed to work to eliminate the proclivity in Polish public life toward lying and indecency as well as to confront what they regarded as a national tendency toward "cowardliness" and a "lack of sobriety." Aniela Samotyhowa identified the overarching mandate of the commission as simply "a battle with evil."[1]

Just a couple of weeks after this inaugural meeting of the Commission for Moral Rebirth, Piłsudski launched his coup d'état, in mid-May 1926. The commission greeted the coup with great anticipation and interpreted the event as the ideal catalyst for national rebirth and moral rejuvenation; it pledged its full support for the coup, for Piłsudski, and for the idea of sanacja. It renamed itself the Society for the Moral Rebirth of the Nation, and later in 1926 it became the Edward Abramowski Society for Moral Rebirth (Towarzystwo Odrodzenia Moralnego im. Edwarda Abramowskiego).[2]

I use this small Warsaw-based group as another example of the way the *sanacja* stimulated a critical reassessment of the quality of independence. The intellectuals associated with the Society for Moral Rebirth heard Piłsudski's call to define the imponderables and they were quick to act on it. Even before the May events, the society embraced an evocative language of health, illness, morality, healing, work, and community—a language that circulated with terrific frequency in the new state (see chapter 1). After the May events, the society seized on the idea of *sanacja* as a rallying point for its cause, heralded the coming moral rebirth of the nation, and committed itself fully to realizing the goals of national renaissance and fundamental change.

Study of the Society for Moral Rebirth provides a window onto an important segment of the pro-Piłsudski leftist intelligentsia centered in Warsaw. The individuals who were involved in this group were longtime Piłsudskiites. Many had worked alongside Piłsudski in the prewar socialist movement (though like Piłsudski many had long ago left socialist politics behind), and some had been a part of the wartime Legions. This was a generation that knew well the period of partition slavery, having been born in the 1870s and 1880s, and that had exhibited great determination in working to reestablish an independent Polish state. It was this group that formed the core support for Piłsudski's coup and for the so-called post-May camp, and it was this group that was so devoted to discussing ideas about national morality and moral reform. The Society for Moral Rebirth represents an attempt by a small group of Piłsudskiites to take stock of independence and to work toward shaping one vision of the moral revolution that the May coup had proclaimed.

The Piłsudskiites associated with the society, moreover, included especially well known and influential people in the Second Republic. Col. Walery Sławek (1879–1939), who was present at the initial meeting of the Commission for Moral Rebirth, remained a part of the group for a short time during 1926. Sławek was president of the *sanacja*'s mass and supraparty political organization, the Nonpartisan Bloc for Cooperation with the Government (BBWR) from 1928 to 1935, a parliamentarian from 1928 to 1938, and premier from 1930 to 1931 and again in 1935. He was widely regarded as Poland's "second in command," as Piłsudski's most trusted adviser and friend, and as an uncommonly honest and decent politician.[3] Janusz Jędrzejewicz (1885–1951) also showed a brief interest in the group. He was a prominent Piłsudskiite politician, a parliamentarian from 1928 to 1930 and from 1930 to 1935, the minister of religious affairs and public education from 1931 to 1934, and a senator from 1935 to 1938 and again from 1938 to 1939.[4] Antoni Anusz (1884–1935) was a longer-term member of the society and a well-known career politician, associated first with the pro-independence socialists of the prewar period and later with the left-wing peasant party, PSL-Liberation, from which he was elected to the Sejm from 1919 to 1922 and again from 1922 to 1927.[5]

Aniela (Miłkowska Jełowicka) Samotyhowa (1876–1966) was the most active member of the Society for Moral Rebirth, serving alternately as its president and vice-president from the moment of inception in 1926 to the moment of demise in 1932. At various times throughout her life, Samotyhowa worked as a teacher, art critic, writer, and social activist. She had earlier given up doctoral studies in botany at the University of Geneva. In her personal life, Samotyhowa experimented with the radical cultural ideas of her age and was a passionate advocate of free love.[6] The society clearly bears her stamp. Samotyhowa's personal writings (which are voluminous), together with the society's official records (many of which are in Samotyhowa's handwriting), offer an extraordinarily rich insight into the discourses that nourished the intellectual mood in pre-May 1926 Poland and that gave rise to the sanacja.

Despite the affiliation of these prominent individuals with the Society for Moral Rebirth, the group remained small and relatively unknown throughout its six-year existence; its membership never exceeded more than a few dozen people. The society failed to make an indelible impression on the Polish political or cultural scene, and it failed utterly to attain its rather fantastic goal of a complete cultural and moral transformation of Poland. As such, its existence is hardly ever mentioned in the standard political narratives of the period, and it has not been the subject of a single study.[7] Despite the group's failures as an activist organization, the society offers a revealing case study. Its very existence, its ambitions and rhetoric, show just how deeply the grand narrative produced by the coup— the sanacja—penetrated different parts of Polish society, even this one modest corner inhabited by a small segment of the Piłsudskiite leftist intelligentsia.

Organizing for Rebirth

In a diary entry dated May 14, 1926, a day of heavy fighting in the capital, Samotyhowa began chronicling the circumstances that were unfolding before her eyes as Piłsudski and his forces confronted President Wojciechowski and those army contingents that had remained loyal to the government. Samotyhowa wrote about what she observed from the windows in her central Warsaw home and what she experienced during her brief and uneasy excursions into the streets of the city. She described crowds gathering in excitement and fear to watch circumstances unfold. She spent her own sleepless nights, wondering what would befall the nation poised on the brink of civil war.[8]

Like many others, Samotyhowa characterized Piłsudski's actions as having launched a national catharsis: "The removal of heavy boulders, the pushing down of the scarecrow with the straw violin playing a somnambulant song of yesterday's life, a life without a future. It is possible that this will become the prologue to a real Polish renaissance."[9] On Saturday, May 15, Samotyhowa was thrilled to read in the *New Polish Courier* (*Nowy kurier polski*) a description of the events as "a battle over ethical postulates" and as the first such revolution in history. Piłsudski, she wrote, "had achieved a monumental, heroic, herculean act."[10] In June she wrote, "I am most entirely, completely, and absolutely a supporter of Piłsudski and what has happened [the coup]."[11]

Samotyhowa described the reaction that Piłsudski's coup had occasioned, not just in herself but within the larger left-liberal social and cultural milieu of which she formed a part. She expressed a sentiment that would be repeated time and again: "After the May coup, the feeling of a need to form some strong 'moral front' increased."[12] Those men and women who had come together at Warsaw's public library to form the Commission for Moral Rebirth approached news of Piłsudski's coup with eager anticipation, and they were quick to identify themselves with what they perceived as the ideals that had inspired Piłsudski's actions. The coup provided the impetus to organize formally and quickly and to develop a clear statement of influences, goals, and intentions. And thus, the Society for Moral Rebirth was born.[13]

The first line of the group's declaration, drafted during the spring and early summer of 1926, called the May events a "symbol of the rebirth of Poland."[14] With the coup, the declaration read, Piłsudski had elevated "everything that constitute[d] strength, valor, courage, and dignity," while he had dealt a death blow to everything that was "weak, criminal, low."[15] The Society for Moral Rebirth seized on the coup as a nationwide wake-up call, as a plea made to every individual citizen to fulfill his or her "obligations to the fatherland."[16] It was time, as Walery Sławek stated at a June 1926 society meeting, for Poland to build its independence actively and creatively.[17] Now that the Piłsudskiites were in power and their political opponents—the much-despised right-nationalists—relegated to secondary status, this might at last be possible.

But what did it mean to build independence? How did one go about realizing a sanacja? These were the most important (and most difficult) questions to which the society, and indeed the Piłsudski camp generally, committed itself. Society members believed that independent Poland suffered from a weak sense of individual "ethical responsibility" and a poorly developed sense of collective culture. These shortcomings needed to be confronted if the much-dreamed-of renaissance were to be achieved. The goal was to make citizens of the Second Republic understand that they were in fact citizens and that they possessed obligations to the state and duties to fulfill. The society's declaration continued: "At issue is the raising of the value of an idea, of the value of heroism and greatness."[18] The society regarded it as its duty, and the duty of every citizen of Poland, to seize the initiative of the coup, to go forth with Marshal Piłsudski and create what members described as an "army of moral action" that would work to transform citizenship in Poland.[19]

The society's focus on stimulating "good citizenship" echoed concerns expressed in interwar Europe generally, where difficult postwar economic and social circumstances exacerbated political problems and led to numerous creative proposals for reform. But the society's approach to the question of independence and reform, while reflecting these Europe-wide trends, was also rooted firmly in the Piłsudskiite intellectual fold. The society's declaration is peppered with a vocabulary typical of the Piłsudski faction, turning as it did on references to profound change and imminent rebirth and emphasizing collective will and action, heroism, citizen responsibility, the "new person," the primacy of the state, and "work as the highest religious act."[20] It is to this Piłsudskiite ideological fold that we now turn.

The *Way* and Piłsudskiite Neoromanticism

A group of the most prominent Piłsudskiite ideologists and activists was centered around a journal called the *Way* (*Droga*). The *Way* had been established in 1922 by Adam Skwarczyński, Adam Koc, Janusz Jędrzejewicz, Jan Pohoski, and Tadeusz Hołówko, among others.[21] With the *Way*, these Piłsudskiites had created an important forum in which to experiment with, shape, and debate approaches to independence.[22] The fact that some associates of the *Way*, like Pohoski, Jędrzejewicz, Walery Sławek, and Antoni Anusz, were also members (at least briefly) of the Society for Moral Rebirth reveals much about the intellectual status and underpinnings of the group.[23]

The *Way* was edited until 1927 by Adam Skwarczyński (1886–1934), who became one of the best-known exponents of a modern Piłsudskiite romanticist vision that emphasized such broad concepts as the need to develop unity and purpose in a chaotic postwar world.[24] If the sanacja had a primary ideologue and exponent of its position, it was Skwarczyński. Dubbed "the angel of the sanacja camp," Skwarczyński was a committed and longtime supporter of Piłsudski and had fought under him in the First Brigade.[25] Skwarczyński argued that newly independent Poland needed to shape a new "citizen-person," but that that could only be achieved once a "new morality," marked by the embrace of public responsibility and accountability, developed. In pursuit of these goals, the Piłsudskiite neoromanticists rejected political parties and programs and parliamentarism generally; they believed instead that the new morality would emerge only once people were organized into and working through focused and purposeful social groups.[26]

Skwarczyński and his associates believed that productive social and political engagement, or "work," constituted a patriotic and moral imperative to which all citizens were subject; through work one fulfilled a duty to history, to the collective society of which one formed a part, and to the future. As Skwarczyński wrote in the *Way*, "He who wants the nation to create, for the nation to rise to the top, to fulfill a mission—must look into his heart, change, raise his soul, reform the whole of human life. This will not be done through philosophy, words, [and] mottoes. This can be accomplished only through work. It is the only sacrament . . . that forms people's moral sense, forms their character, establishes between them collective desires, aspirations and collective action."[27] This focus on work and on a committed and active citizenship was typical of the Piłsudskiites of the sanacja era, as it was for the Society for Moral Rebirth. One author in the Piłsudskiite paper *Voice of Truth* (*Głos prawdy*), writing to commemorate the tenth anniversary of Polish independence, referred to work, quite simply, as the highest and most noble virtue citizens possessed.[28]

This prevalence of a language of work represents an interesting return to some of the themes that defined the period of "organic work" of the positivist era in the mid- to late nineteenth century in the Russian partition. The period following the defeat of the 1863–64 national insurrection in Russian Poland is traditionally regarded as having precipitated an end to romanticist and idealist approaches to nation building, which had been marked by an overriding belief in the cosmic injustice of the partitions and on winning independence through force of arms. The failure of the January uprising sparked what has come to be known, in contrast to the romanticist era, as a period of positivism or political realism. In this latter period national leaders tried to accept the fact of the partitions, work within the limits imposed by the partitioning powers, and focus on building the social, economic, and cultural strength of the nation before taking up arms. The goal during the positivist period was, in a sense, to achieve independence on a different level.[29] With territorial independence achieved, elements of this nineteenth-century emphasis on rational and scientific approaches to society, on collective will and action, and on building strong foundations reappeared and formed what some scholars have referred to as a twentieth-century neoromanticism.[30] The May coup of 1926 launched a wholesale embrace of neoromanticist language and attitudes toward independence and nation building.

The May coup, according to Skwarczyński, announced boldly the start of a "moral revolution" in Poland. For Skwarczyński, the May moral revolution that Piłsudski launched ranked with November 11, 1918, as a crucial day in Polish history and the beginning of something new and profound that would transform the nation.[31] In addition to using the *Way* as a forum for his ideas, immediately after the coup Skwarczyński established what would be a short-lived newspaper entitled the *Imperatives of the Moment* (*Nakazy chwili*). The *Voice of Truth*, the *Way*, and *Imperatives of the Moment* were the main organs of the Piłsudskiite moral revolution.[32]

During a May 22, 1926, meeting of the Society for Moral Rebirth, member Jan Pohoski endorsed the establishment of the newest organ of the moral revolution, *Imperatives of the Moment.* He called the paper a powerful testament to the wave of societal enthusiasm for rebirth, and he looked forward to the changes that would flow from the May events.[33] The imperatives of the moment to which the title referred included the assumption of the presidency by Piłsudski, the dismissal of the current parliament and the calling of new elections, a general purge and healing of Poland's political system, and a vigilance in stamping out corruption and abuse of power in the government.[34] But the imperatives of the moment also referred to far less precise goals. It was on the pages of these three papers that the Piłsudskiites tried to establish their neoromanticist approach to Polish independence and to encourage people to understand "moral revolution" in the broadest possible sense.

Janusz Jędrzejewicz, society member and *Imperatives* contributor, described the new publication as "an aggressive organ of the moral revolution." Though Piłsudski had made it possible to begin a new life in Poland, the success of the May coup, Jędrzejewicz stressed, depended on the public at large and on the will of the whole society to act.[35] It depended, in fact, on people like those grouped around the Society for Moral Rebirth; members of the society represented ideal Polish citizens, those who took the initiative and prepared themselves to work—albeit in small ways—for the good of the whole. But the task would be a fantastically difficult one. Society member Jerzy Radomski (1892–1943), an army bureaucrat with the rank of captain, was clear about just how trying this whole process of self-examination and of building a new moral citizen would be. The situation in Poland was dire, and a frightening amount of work needed to be done. Captain Radomski stated, "Polish life has entered the swamp, at the bottom of which lies deceit."[36] Radomski pointed to a lack of cooperation as well as to a poor sense of responsibility and public honor in the young state. The transformation of Polish society would not be accomplished easily or quickly.[37]

Further, Radomski echoed a belief that had been popular in Piłsudskiite circles for some time and that had been especially evident on the pages of the *Way:* that modern political parties exerted a detrimental influence on parliamentary life and thus on the state generally. Political parties, Radomski offered, did not even themselves believe in their abilities to develop effective programs for political and cultural transformation.[38] For his part, Sławek underscored that Poland was not alone on the Continent in having nurtured a sense that formal politics and political parties were "something dirty" from which decent people ran far and fast. A number of organizations had formed in Europe during this period and had built their identities around this idea of rejecting traditional political groupings, questioning contemporary practices of democracy, or simply rejecting outright the very concept of democracy.[39]

The Society for Moral Rebirth believed that the May events existed as a testament to political parties' impotence. Members of the society proclaimed loudly that they stood, intellectually and in principle, "beyond politics" and above the party wrangling that they believed had been destroying the republic. At the same time, they believed that the May events functioned as a call to nonpolitical bodies to organize themselves and work for change.[40] Following the views expressed by the Piłsudskiites in the *Way*, the society believed that smaller social organizations rather than mass political parties constituted the wave of the future. Only nonparliamentary organizations could be relied on to create the kind of moral citizen that the new state so desperately needed. Participation in carefully constructed and useful organizations would help citizens feel connected to the state and would build the kind of civic responsibility that was vitally important to its longevity.[41] The society hoped that their group would be just one of the many organizations born of the May events.

Above all, as society members emphasized clearly, the people who committed themselves to working for the sanacja through small local organizations would have to be "absolutely decent" and, as Captain Radomski stated, would have to want to "create good."[42] The society was focused on attracting individuals, rather than already existing organizations, for membership in the group, though in the end existing groups did also qualify for membership.[43] And right from the start, the society's organizers repeated that it was better to have just a few people who were willing to devote themselves selflessly to the cause than to have numerous members who were only half-hearted in their commitment: "It is better to go for depth rather than for width," member Marian Godecki (1888–1939) affirmed. Sławek echoed this view and at this juncture, in mid-1926, he, and the society generally, eschewed the idea of a single large organization that would support the sanacja. Sławek, who in 1928 went on to form the BBWR, the sanacja's mass political body, added that in Poland it had always been, and would likely continue to be, a small number of very influential and committed people—an elite—that ultimately made the difference.[44]

There was no time to waste in pursuing the Polish renaissance. Piłsudski's coup had handed Poland the opportunity to transform a mood that people had discerned since the start of independence but had not named. Samotyhowa offered her own analysis of this atmosphere that prevailed in Poland: "It is suffocating, terrifyingly suffocating . . . an intellectual and spiritual narrowness . . . a heavy boot is extinguishing in Poland the sparks of enlightenment, culture, [and] thought."[45] Just as some right-nationalist commentators used the coup's proclamation of moral sanacja to launch wholesale criticisms of the state of moral and cultural life in the young republic (as we saw in chapter 1), so others used the moral sanacja to embrace the future and to focus on the positive potential they discerned in the notion of a sanacja. By remaining in what Samotyhowa referred to as her own private "cloister"—an internal space free of the "tumult, brutality, and ugliness of daily life"[46]—Samotyhowa realized that she and others like her were shirking their responsibilities and preventing their growth as citizens. Worst of all, they were jeopardizing Poland's growth as a nation.

The sanacja offered Poland the chance to break out of the cloister once and for all and to shake off the continuing vestiges of partition slavery. According to the Society for Moral Rebirth, Piłsudski's coup had ushered in "the new era."[47] The key, Samotyhowa argued, was not to squander the energy engendered by the event and not to waste the momentum. She was troubled that so many stubbornly narrow individuals failed to see beyond the lives lost in the "civil war."[48] If the positive energy that had come out of the events was not maintained, things would fall again "into the hands of little people," and the "bird's wings" would not be allowed to grow.[49]

Abramowski and the Moral Revolution

Instead of looking to politicians in the traditional sense of the word, the Society for Moral Rebirth looked for guidance and inspiration to philosophers and spiritual guides, to figures drawn from Polish history, such as romantic poet Juliusz Słowacki,[50] one of the three Polish bards, or to Piłsudski himself. For Samotyhowa, Piłsudski was a "loved, dear, great Grandfather. A good, intelligent person." She wrote in her diary about having listened to Piłsudski's radio broadcast delivered on November 1, 1926, the eighth anniversary of Polish independence. She remarked on the aura that surrounded Piłsudski, on his "melodious voice, beautiful, strong, hot" and his "very pantheistic existence."[51] Piłsudski shared with his listeners a fairy tale about a maiden and a frog, and Samotyhowa expressed her sense of awe at how magnificent his simple story was. Poland was lucky, according to Samotyhowa, to possess a man as noble and selfless as Piłsudski, a man to lead Poland through this diffi-cult period of work and growth and to teach its citizens how to confront the evil that had plagued the country for the last century. Piłsudski ended his an-niversary address, Samotyhowa recalled, by wishing his radio listeners a "re-born soul" for the year.[52]

That Samotyhowa and the society more generally regarded Piłsudski as the ideal model of a citizen and as the inspiration behind the moral revolution is clear. But the declared spiritual and intellectual father of the Society for Moral Rebirth was Edward Abramowski (1868–1918).[53] The society did not formally add "in the name of Edward Abramowski" to its title until October 1926, and it is important to remember this when assessing the relative impor-tance of Abramowski in terms of shaping the goals and motivations of mem-bers. As late as 1931, Samotyhowa herself expressed confusion about the specific role that Abramowski occupied in the group and wondered out loud whether he was just a symbol and an inspiration, or whether he represented something more.[54] Ultimately, the society kept Abramowski at arm's length and looked to him for motivation rather than concrete policy ideas.

The parallels between Abramowski's ideas about moral revolution and a change in consciousness as a precursor of far-reaching political, economic, social, and cultural change, on the one hand, and the sanacja's own call for moral reform, on the other, undoubtedly resonated powerfully for mem-bers of the society. Adam Skwarczyński was himself known to be a great ad-mirer of Abramowski, and Abramowski generally was well known to the Piłsudskiite intelligentsia.[55] For all these reasons, it was both tempting and logical to articulate an Abramowskian analysis of the sanacja and to incor-porate Abramowski's ideas into the plans for future action.

Edward Abramowski was a highly regarded philosopher and psycholo-gist conversant with the dominant trends within western European thought before and during World War I, and is widely recognized as one of the founding fathers of modern Polish sociology. He was associated, from his early days, with the workers' and socialist movements. At the beginning of the twentieth century he was already actively contemplating the relationship between ethical living and political life and was pondering the place of eco-nomics in what he believed was the coming revolution. Abramowski is also regarded as the main theoretician and promoter of the cooperative movement in Poland; for him cooperativism formed the cornerstone of what he called the "third way to socialism." Early in the twentieth century, Abramowski moved away from scientific socialism and instead extolled contemplative life, arguing that the psyche and human consciousness, ethics and morality, constituted the sources of historical change. During the Great War, when Abramowski was already very ill, he was associated with the Polish Military Organization and with Piłsudski's Legions.[56]

Abramowski suited the Society for Moral Rebirth for a number of reasons. First, there was a personal connection between Abramowski and Samotyhowa: the two knew each other in Geneva, where Samotyhowa had pursued her studies.[57] Moreover, as a philosopher and thinker, Abramowski enjoyed a general resurgence in popularity in the Second Republic.[58] As such, for the society to have incorporated Abramowski into its name may well have lent the group social credibility. Abramowski's ideas about ethics as the driving force of change were especially appealing in a new state plagued by political, social, and economic problems (problems which were compounded by some basic postpartition integration challenges.)[59] The appeal of Abramowski grew after Piłsudski's coup and the proclamation of sanacja. Abramowski's belief that people needed to take an active role in improving their societies echoed sanacja discourse about the need to foster an engaged citizenry in order to build a stronger and more viable state.

The Piłsudskiite neoromanticists popularized a rhetoric that provoked some people to think about Poland's problems as symptoms of much deeper and far more noxious ailments that reached to the very core of Polishness. The real problem was located within the people themselves and within some elusive notion of the Polish national character. Samotyhowa herself devoted a fair bit of attention to defining those aspects of the Polish national character that she believed needed serious redress. These included a tendency to complain, a propensity for malcontentism, and a predisposition toward looking for someone else to blame and waiting for someone else to lead. These qualities, she argued, had produced a culture where the few led and the majority followed and accepted listlessly whatever was handed to them. The citizenry of the Second Republic, Samotyhowa believed, exhibited a "sick will."[60] This was in no small part a result of Poland's partition experience. Too many people were content simply to "have Poland," and as a result they failed "to reflect on their relations with her or on the need to build her."[61] Poland needed to break out of these habits and to raise new generations, generations that would not be mired in a partition-era psychology.[62] Samotyhowa liked Piłsudski's views on this matter: "A couple of generations must first pass before a Polish state culture will again form."[63] Piłsudski's sanacja had introduced a certain new energy into the air, Samotyhowa believed, and represented the opportunity to break out of partition-era patterns—"the cloister" —and to work for Poland in a more meaningful way.[64]

The coup and the introduction of the idea of nationwide cleansing and reform offered an opportunity to focus these ideas. Sanacja rhetoric about the need for fundamental transformation resonated so forcefully precisely because so many people agreed on the need for basic change. The Society for Moral Rebirth constitutes one example of how the coup and the sanacja were used by specific individuals or groups to organize their ideas about healing Poland. The sanacja wielded a vocabulary of basic change and deep moral reform. The society embraced this language and linked it to Abramowski's key belief that without moral revolution, formal political independence might well be virtually meaningless.[65]

The society saw in the coup the potential to achieve the kind of moral transformation about which Abramowski had written and which would lead to wholesale social and political transformation. Samotyhowa believed, following Abramowski, that this transformation would come when the individual citizen was educated "for the collective."[66] The sentiment that social transformation and moral transformation had to proceed together was articulated repeatedly in Society meetings.[67] The results of political revolutions, like the May coup, could only go as far as the moral revolution that accompanied it. The Society devoted itself to fashioning the moral revolution, defined by broad references to social harmony, peaceful coexistence and cooperation, that would accompany the political one.

The Inactive Army

How precisely did the Society for Moral Rebirth go about realizing these fantastically monumental goals? Few of the various projects the society planned or initiated in its pursuit of moral reform were successful. Its criticisms of contemporary society and its speculations about moral rebirth remained, for the most part, in the planning stages. But it is precisely in the group's ideas about Poland's moral state that we find an interesting elaboration of a Piłsudskiite vision of the relationship between formal politics, culture, and morality.

The society was well aware that it had to move beyond these unrestrained avowals of a need for change. The group thus outlined six broad areas on which it would focus. These areas were identified in the declaration statement under the following headings: upbringing, education, administration, economic questions, matters of justice, and social issues. The society planned to organize conferences and discussion sessions, to establish libraries and reading rooms, and generally to spread the idea that people could achieve great personal satisfaction from participating in the state in a more direct and meaningful way. This sense of fulfillment would derive from the simple fact that people's efforts would form part of a great collective effort to build a better Poland.[68]

To facilitate this work on the six areas outlined above, the society divided itself into three branches: ideology-education, politics, and propaganda. The ideology-education branch was broadly concerned with eliminating dishonesty in public life, with educating people on issues of national importance, and with "building honor." The influence of Piłsudski's postcoup statements is clearly evident in the society's language and in members' assessments of what ailed Poland. The political branch worked on national minority issues and was an advocate for schools for minorities (a cause for which many Piłsudskiites had a fair degree of sympathy, at least during the early stage of the sanacja). This branch also devoted attention to what the group referred to as cleanliness, propriety, and professionalism in the administration of the state. The third and last branch outlined the need to work on shaping public opinion through meetings and discussion evenings, and through influencing the press, theater, and film production.[69] The group considered it within its scope and interest to consider all sorts of topics, ranging from forms of democratic participation, to morality in the modern world, women's issues, and the death penalty.[70]

Educational initiatives, broadly conceived, were central to the society's strategy of reform. Among the Second Republic's decisive steps to address the shortcomings of partition-era education, a 1919 decree made elementary education compulsory, universal, and free in Poland for a period of seven years, for girls and boys between the ages of seven and fourteen.[71] Realizing educational goals was another matter, however. Many society members, like Jan Pohoski, had devoted their careers to education. Pohoski argued that in addition to school reform and to laws handed down by the state, private societies had to take an active role in education and intervene to foster the right kind of citizenship.[72] Pohoski, moreover, was married to Dr. Hanna Pohoska, the author of key position papers on sanacja education policies. Pohoska, incidentally, had also been a member of the Women's Union for Citizenship Work since 1934.[73] Samotyhowa had herself worked as a teacher, was involved in the Polish Teachers' Union, and openly believed that teachers were uniquely placed to lead a moral rebirth. Samotyhowa believed that schools needed to organize in such a way that they would harness the creative energy of students and would battle "spiritual inactivity, stagnation."[74]

As a proponent of education reform, the society added its support to the general sanacja approaches to education. Janusz Jędrzejewicz had been involved briefly with the society during its earliest phases and had been instrumental in shaping sanacja-era school reforms.[75] Sanacja pedagogical doctrines emphasized the importance of political or state education (*wychowanie państwowe*) and active citizenship.[76] These approaches to education were well reflected in sanacja journals like the *Way* (*Droga*), *Standard* (*Pion*), *Frame* (*Zrąb*),[77] even the *Epoch* (*Epoka*) and the *Polish Gazette* (*Gazeta polska*).

For her part, Samotyhowa was sometimes overwhelmed by the difficulty of educating a new citizen, and her personal journals and diaries are filled with pessimistic assessments of Poland's future. She focused in particular on the cultural and intellectual distance between the people of the Polish countryside and Poland itself, a Poland "that should be new, strong, independent, free."[78] In addition, Samotyhowa and the society generally were concerned that the emerging proletarian class, with newly minted rights and responsibilities, formed a significant part of the of the state's population yet was ill equipped to contribute to the development of the state. The society thus intended to focus its educational efforts on that stratum. Samotyhowa looked ahead to the day when the proletariat would come into its own and be ready to devote itself to the nation.[79] For the time being, she saw the Second Republic in a transitional period, defined by the "clash of two worlds, two epochs."[80]

Like the Piłsudskiites generally, Samotyhowa and the Society for Moral Rebirth believed that the nation would be led toward rebirth by the Piłsudskiite-sanacja elite. The very structure of the society reflected this typical Polish gentry vision of society, in which the intellectuals were the moral and political leaders of the nation.[81] As Samotyhowa stated at the inaugural conference of the Commission for Moral Rebirth in April 1926, it was imperative to turn for assistance to "artists, literati, theater directors, as representatives of the world of ideas."[82] The society planned explicitly to orchestrate its contribution to the national *sanacja* project "from above."

The society's one concrete effort in the area of education reform remained almost entirely in the planning stages. The intention was for society members to travel out to provincial areas, where people from "the world of work"[83] resided in great numbers. Members would function as missionaries, exposing Poland's youth to ethical models of work and citizenship and enlightening them about the centrality of the May coup to Poland's moral rebirth, in order to nip moral decay in the bud.[84] Samotyhowa referred sarcastically to the Marian sodalities that were rapidly growing in popularity in the provinces, sapping the energy of people who might otherwise have given themselves over to the independence fight.[85] The society's members, all part of the intellectual and cultural elite of the nation, reached to what were, for them, very comfortable and established forms for intervention into the life of the lower classes.

The society's other ostensibly significant attempt to establish real contact with people outside its membership came in the form of a plan to carry out a survey of Polish youth. Through this survey, the society hoped to acquaint its members with what young people valued; this would, in turn, help the society establish future meaningful contact with youth. The group planned to ask young people in the seventh and eighth grades about school courses, family situations, levels of and views on happiness, preferred extracurricular activities, and ideal role models. The idea was to forgo abstract theorizing when approaching youth and to provide them instead with actual practical suggestions about how to live ethically and responsibly. Though survey questions were completed in 1928, there is no evidence that the survey was ever carried out.[86]

The Society for Moral Rebirth also expressed passionate support for ideas of religious tolerance. Emphasizing as it did general "human" moral principles, the society was committed to nonsectarianism and rejected overt and exclusionary displays of nationalism or religious chauvinism, such as those expressed and valued by the National Democrats. As such, the fight for secular education became an important cause to the society.[87] The society formally opposed a decree that came from the sanacja government's Ministry of Religious Affairs, dated December 9, 1926, that essentially confirmed the 1925 concordat between the Polish state and the Vatican. The concordat required that religion be taught in public schools at the elementary and the secondary levels, and it accorded Catholicism a special status.[88] The society objected that the decree gave state sanction to religious authorities in the schools, that it privileged Catholicism and created a "Catholic mood" in the schools, and that, consequently, it limited interest in secular approaches to questions of ethics and morality. These secular approaches were, after all, at the core of the group's mandate. Moreover, the society objected that the decree took from students the ability to choose when and how they would participate in spiritual events, and that it "opened the door to a further and general clericalization of society and culture."[89]

The society wrote a formal protest to the government decree and Samotyhowa presented it to the membership at a meeting held on March 23, 1927. Samotyhowa stated plainly that the ministry decree "has its roots in the imprudent ratification of the concordat by the Sejm, an action that gives Poland up to spiritual dependence on the Vatican."[90] The society thus called for a revision of the concordat by the Sejm and for the government to annul the decree.[91] The last line of what appears to be the penultimate draft of the protest states that the group believed the decree to constitute "an unfortunate mistake made by the government of the moral sanacja."[92]

Significantly, this explicit criticism of the sanacja government was removed from the final text. Members agreed that direct attacks on the government would also hurt Piłsudski and might consequently harm the greater agenda, an agenda that overall was noble and deserved to be protected. The reference was replaced with a simple criticism of the concordat ratified between Poland and the Vatican.[93] In defense of Piłsudski, the society suggested that the decree had been originally formulated by Władysław Grabski and moreover that it was Premier Kazimierz Bartel's name, and not Piłsudski's, that appeared on the decree, making Bartel the most culpable party. In issuing this public statement, the society was also cautious of the image that it portrayed of itself. Just as official society pronouncements were always careful to veil any socialist commitment they may have harbored, so here they were careful not to offend Catholics. The society chose to downplay a bald appeal for separation between church and state, as it feared that such a statement would make it easier for opponents to call the Society for Moral Rebirth a Masonic organization.[94] Issues like the place of Catholicism in the reborn Poland generated intense debate and vitriol on all sides.

In addition to these matters of religious freedom and education that occupied the society's time during the first few years after its formation, a great deal of its energy was devoted simply to debating what the group's priorities were and what name it should bear. The various suggestions for the name change offer interesting glimpses into what the members themselves thought about their society's purpose and public presence. The first suggestion to change the name was made not long after the group's formation, during a meeting held on October 22, 1926. Some members argued that the Society for Moral Rebirth was a vulgar name, that it was pretentious and mocked by others, and that it could too easily be misused. Helena Sujkowska (1873–1944),[95] a leading force in the campaign to have the name changed, suggested that the Democratic Society might be preferable. At a meeting a week later, this suggestion was deemed inappropriate on account of its overly "political character." Other suggestions that were ultimately rejected included the Edward Abramowski Society of Social Work, the Society of Social Service, and the Society of Ethical Work. All were dismissed because they were no better than the current name. A new name was not adopted until the general meeting held at the end of 1928, when the executive provided the general membership with a choice of two names: the Edward Abramowski Ethical Society or the Edward Abramowski Society. The first name was chosen by five members, rejected by four. One member abstained from the vote.[96]

Part and parcel of this discussion about changing the society's name was a parallel debate about whether the society was altogether superfluous. Dr. Justyna Budzińska-Tylicka (1867–1936), a longtime socialist activist prominent in various women's groups and causes, advocated, for instance, that there was simply no need for the society, given that the Polish Society for Freedom (Polska Organizacja Wolności) already existed to work "for the defense of the victory of democracy" and to foster the spirit of 1926.[97] In the autumn of 1926 two members of the Society for Moral Rebirth, Jadwiga Baranowska and Stanisław Małkowski, had actually proposed that the group should disband and simply become a section of the Freedom Society, given the similarities in their goals.[98]

In fact only a small coterie of individuals believed there was a need for a group like the Society for Moral Rebirth. No more than a handful of members were present at any given meeting, the staple participants being Aniela Samotyhowa and Helena Sujkowska, and less frequently Jadwiga Baranowska, Halina Loretowa and Jan Pohoski.[99] But despite the small number of members, the society's executive met quite often. For example, from June 30 to December 14, 1927, twenty-five meetings were held, an average of at least one a week.[100] During these meetings, participants often bemoaned the fact that the group had not risen to greater popularity. Pohoski said simply, "A title and projects but no concrete results."[101]

Members were aware of the society's shortcomings all too well, and many meetings revolved around discussing ways to make the group more popular and effective. One woman, a disappointed and lapsed member, wrote to the society in 1929, outlined her commitment to the moral sanacja, and offered a number of suggestions she hoped would help the society's executive do something concrete and useful. One of these suggestions included the opening of a counseling and advice center to which honest people could turn to report dishonest and immoral behavior. She also hoped that the group would run general-interest lectures, such as on the subject of working effectively in societies and functioning more productively in places of employment.[102] The woman, who described herself as a pedagogue, left the society in 1930 because "I had nothing to do there." She continued, "Without the rebirth of the members themselves, without a deep and heartfelt understanding of the needs of our existence, there can be no further interest [in the group]."[103]

In an attempt to understand why their membership numbers had become so disappointing, the society devised a plan to ask inactive members why they had stopped attending meetings.[104] An interesting response came in early 1930 from Jadwiga Jahołkowska (1863–1931), a prominent women's activist associated with peasant politics. Though Jahołkowska informed the group that she had stopped participating because of a lack of time, she nevertheless offered her opinion on why the society was so ineffective: though it evolved from the best of intentions, it might have been too quick and imprudent when it established itself and outlined its goals. The "moral rebirth of the Polish nation," she suggested, might well have been too bold and large a mission. She further argued that people in such an organization needed a framework within which to work as well as concrete and manageable goals.[105] While the society emphasized activism and wholehearted involvement in a project, it failed to provide small, tangible, realizable goals for individual members.

In contemplating the group's apparent unpopularity and in digesting the varied criticisms and failures of the society, the executive decided in March 1930 to develop a new declaration that would better reflect both the group's priorities and those of the culture around them. "A Declaration of the Ideas of the Society for Ethical Culture" was read and accepted unanimously by all members in February 1930.[106] The statement began not with a reference to the May coup as a symbol for the rebirth of Poland, as the 1926 declaration had, but with the following: "After a three-year existence, we want to outline our physiognomy and tasks for the new today. We believe that the psychological, moral, and intellectual fabric of the nation determines its essential vitality."[107] The statement identified the group's main interest as "ethics," defined broadly as the relationship between individuals, between an individual and society, and between the nation and humanity. Ethics, according to the society, was the basis of "everything else." The declaration continued, "Today, in the midst of being overwhelmed by the world of material culture, the dawn of a new ethics is beginning."[108] "Despite the slavery of capitalism, clericalism, chauvinism, and party narrowness, the never-dying voice of a free person, seeking truth, is being drawn out." The group understood itself to be a pioneer builder of the nation, a tireless opponent of spiritual laziness, dishonesty, and hypocrisy and thus was working to raise the ethical level in "private and social life" and to spread ideas about love and tolerance. Their work was being carried out in a context of Poland's larger internal struggle: "a struggle of basic forces . . . occurring under the guise of politics."[109] Echoing an earlier criticism of contemporary politics, the new declaration suggested that politics had tried to encompass too much and that the term thus had become meaningless, a mask behind which people and trends could hide.

The Society for Moral Rebirth ended its new declaration with the plea that "knowledge about the value of all imponderables penetrates as deeply as possible into our society."[110] By using the word *imponderables,* the group reached, quietly but confidently, to Piłsudski, to the sanacja, and to the goal of moral rebirth as expressed by and associated with the Piłsudski camp. On the one hand, the society realized that the goal of moral rebirth was a fantastically monumental (and perhaps unrealistic) one. On the other, they were unwilling to forgo this goal entirely and offered a subtle but sure reference to Piłsudski.[111]

By 1930, four years after its formation, the society had replaced appeals for moral rebirth with arguably less dramatic references to "raising" the ethical level of Polish society, *ethical* having become preferred over *moral*. Article 3 of the group's constitution, for example, was changed from "The Society for Moral Rebirth strives to maintain constant service to the matter of the rebirth of Poland in all areas of social life," to "The Society for Ethical Culture strives to raise the ethical culture of all areas of Polish social life."[112]

Aware of the need to project a more positive image of itself and to attract greater numbers, the executive undertook in early 1930 to market itself more effectively. It discussed publishing a magazine, for example, but not unexpectedly the project never got under way.[113] The executive also decided to issue a public statement in which it appealed for information about other individuals or groups who were working toward similarly noble ideals. The society hoped to introduce these groups to the wider public and to thereby popularize the ideals of the sanacja itself.[114]

The society's small burst of energy and its shift in focus did not, however, yield many positive results. Though the Brześć affair, the imprisonment by the sanacja government of political opposition members, did not explode until late 1930, the political sanacja had begun to lose some credibility and popularity even before then. The economic situation deteriorated markedly at this time too, and the Piłsudski camp failed to make good on its promise of making life in the Second Republic better. Overt and direct associations with the May coup and with the increasingly authoritarian sanacja government were seen as potentially causing more harm than good.

Despite all its efforts to increase its popularity and to boost membership, membership remained low. A membership list from 1930 shows a total of thirty-three members. There were no honorary or partial members, as the society was based on the idea of work and active participation in nourishing the moral revolution.[115] It had tried to persuade influential intellectuals to join, but to no avail. Maria Dąbrowska came to only one meeting.[116] Helena Ceysingerówna, a prominent activist best known for her journalism and for her work in the Women's Union for Citizenship Work, never joined, nor did writer Paweł Hulka-Laskowski, despite the society's attempts to pique their interest.[117] By 1930 the arguably best known personalities involved in the society—Walery Sławek, Janusz Jędrzejewicz, and even Dr. Budzińska-Tylicka—were long gone. The BBWR undoubtedly took most of Sławek's time, as it must have Jędrzejewicz's, and neither could have felt compelled to devote precious energy to such a small and ineffective group. It remains surprising that they were associated in any way with the Society for Moral Rebirth. Member Marian Godecki, a teacher by profession, became head of continuing education with the Ministry of Religious Affairs in 1928 and was very active in adult education and in efforts to overcome illiteracy, leaving little time for commitments to the society.[118] Jerzy Radomski, who participated only in a couple of early society meetings in the spring of 1926, became very active as a civil servant, first in Warsaw, then from 1928 in the municipal government of Radom.[119]

Much of the intelligentsia, society member Kruszewska concluded, "is busy, it doesn't have time."[120] Another member suggested that Poland was simply too infatuated with material comforts to care much about morals and ethics. If a larger segment of the intelligentsia was not interested, and if the masses were turned off by what Kruszewska referred to as the group's "aristocratism,"[121] then the society was left with no constituency to whom it could appeal.

A Women's Army

Interestingly, the membership of the society was always predominantly female, even though the group never openly described itself as a women's organization and never indicated it would have preferred female members. Of the thirty-three members listed in 1930, only seven were men: Antoni Anusz, Stefan Boguszewski, Marian Godecki, Ludwik Hryniewiecki, Eugeniusz Moszczyński, Janusz Pierzchalski, and Jan Pohoski.[122] The fact that women, especially Samotyhowa and Helena Sujkowska, had established themselves in leadership positions from the group's inception may well have attracted women to the cause, just as it may have discouraged men from joining.

Samotyhowa and Sujkowska rotated themselves through the executive positions for the duration of the group's existence. Both women were committed "women's activists." After 1928, Samotyhowa was herself involved with Poland's largest and most influential prosanacja women's group, the Women's Union for Citizenship Work, and even published an article in the inaugural issue of the union's internal paper, *Citizenship Work (Praca obywatelska)*.[123]

Sujkowska had been active in the Women's Democratic Election Committee, out of which the Women's Union evolved (see chapter 4).[124] Furthermore, the Commission for Moral Rebirth, from which the Society for Moral Rebirth evolved, had contemplated working with the women's section of the Polish Socialist Party. This suggests that at least some of the members believed themselves to be participating in a women's organization. This makes Walery Sławek's presence at the inaugural meeting of the commission all the more curious.[125]

The society's selection of lecture and discussion material further suggests how much the group catered to and was dominated by women. From their interest in child development and childhood education, to women's employment, women's place in the modern world, divorce, unwed motherhood, the legalization of abortion, temperance work, and the Women's Morality Police, the group's choices reflect an agenda with a decidedly feminized appeal.[126] The society's links to the popular middle-class women's magazine *Contemporary Woman* (*Kobieta współczesna*) underscores this too.[127] Samotyhowa herself may have exerted a dominating influence when it came to choosing subjects for society discussion sessions and lecture evenings and thus to shaping the group's identity and focus. Samotyhowa's personal life choices exemplified those of a small and peculiar branch of the left-wing, liberal-minded intelligentsia of the day that experimented with many of the culturally radical ideas of the age. For example, though she had used the surname Samotyhowa since 1914, she did not legally become the wife of Erazm Samotyha until April 1926. Once married, Erazm and Aniela continued to have an atypical union for the time: they often lived far apart from each other and mainly pursued their own careers.[128]

Samotyhowa supported divorce in the case of unhappy marriages, approved of birth control, and rejected the cultural convention that women should be virgins until they marry. She also followed international literature on these topics, and was influenced in particular by Bertrand Russell's writings on questions of sexual morality and marriage; Russell's writings were extremely popular with a segment of Poland's left-liberal intelligentsia of the day. Samotyhowa also monitored with great interest the evolution of the Second Republic's marriage law debates. She even kept a separate journal that she titled "About Love, Marriage, Family, and Personal Freedom," in which she explored her own evolving ideas about sex and love and relationships.[129]

Samotyhowa believed that by changing society's approaches to these so-called moral issues, other social, cultural, and political problems could be better addressed; this is what the society aimed to accomplish.[130] Only once a society could learn to speak openly and honestly about gender roles, Samotyhowa stated openly, could life become truly free and healthy. She criticized the Church and hitherto dominant codes of morality and falsity in marriage as attempts to control and dictate rather than truly educate. She objected to what she believed were parochial moral codes dominant in Poland and argued that these codes required that all ideas inconsistent with Church doctrine be quickly and neatly pushed into a dark corner, never to be seriously considered or discussed.[131] Though these moral topics did not become main subjects within the Society for Moral Rebirth, the fact that one of its main activists was devoted so passionately to them cannot go unnoticed. What this reinforces, in fact, is a pattern that we have seen elsewhere. Individual and collective readings of the sanacja persistently referred back to themes related to gender and sexuality. The political sanacja was tied to the possibility of a real moral-sexual revolution that these left-liberals eagerly awaited.

The Last Days

One can point to many causes of the apparent failure of the Society for Moral Rebirth, and some of them have been addressed above. The nail in the society's coffin, however, was its position on the Brześć affair.[132] The society ultimately condemned the sanacja government's handling of Brześć, arguing that, at bottom, the question was a moral rather than a political one.[133] At the end of 1930 the society wrote a formal letter of protest against Brześć and published it in the *Morning Courier* (*Kurier poranny*), the *Polish Newspaper* (*Gazeta polska*), *Dawn* (*Świt*), the *Worker* (*Robotnik*), the *Polish Courier* (*Kurier polski*), and *Contemporary Woman* (*Kobieta współczesna*). The letter protested the treatment of the political prisoners at Brześć and constituted a defense of all people in Poland, regardless of social, religious, or political views, and regardless of nationality.[134]

Yet some individuals continued to perceive the society's reaction to Brześć as too slow and tentative, and this cost it much support. Citing this reason in a 1931 letter, Stanisław Małkowski (1889–1962) asked that he and his wife be removed from the society's membership registers. Małkowski had been a member since the group's inception in 1926. There could exist no goals, he argued, for which moral laws could be broken justifiably, and he reminded the society that it had arisen under the banner of the "moral sanacja." The society was duty-bound to fulfill its role as the conscience of the ruling coalition and to be honest in front of those to whom it preached moral rebirth. The society had shown itself to be blind to what was really happening, and he regarded the continued existence of the Society for Moral Rebirth as harmful to Polish social morality and an insult to Edward Abramowski, whom he had considered a close friend.[135] Małkowski reminded the society that it had in fact been his idea to add "in the name of Edward Abramowski" to the group's title in October 1926.[136] He argued that the society had an obligation to Poland, to Edward Abramowski, and to "the one-time beautiful legend of Piłsudski."[137]

One of the last general meetings of the Society for Moral Rebirth took place on February 13, 1931. The executive elected at this time went on to hold seventeen meetings until the group's formal liquidation, on June 17, 1932.[138] The formal liquidation was anticlimactic, as the various arguments in favor of and against disbanding were familiar to everyone and had been made continually almost since the society's inception. Eight members voted for liquidation and one against. Members resolved to collect the remaining dues, to pay a debt of 226 zlotys, and to donate the remainder.[139]

After the disbanding of the society, Samotyhowa continued her own social involvement. By 1930 she had already begun working in the art section of the Women's Union for Citizenship Work, which published a brochure that she wrote, "About the Need for Culture and Beauty in Contemporary Polish Life."[140] Like her approach to the Society for Moral Rebirth, her attitude was shaped by Abramowski's views of the social value of art, and she hoped that one day, when Poland was a mature society, art would allow people to engage in deep contemplation and to look for the essence of matters.[141] Perhaps it was precisely this kind of ambition, so evident in the society's rhetoric, that ultimately contributed to the failure of Samotyhowa's effort at moral reform in a primarily agricultural state with severe economic and social problems.

III

As Samotyhowa was fond of saying, people in independent Poland had retreated into their cloisters and had eschewed public responsibility. As a result, the Second Republic was characterized by political instability and parliamentary ineffectiveness, fierce social tension, and economic instability. No group of citizens had been carrying out their responsibilities particularly well. The subtext of the May coup, and the potency of its promise, rested on this collective recognition of an untapped potential and of a collective desire to effect change. The moral sanacja was in part about expanding existing definitions of citizenship and fundamentally transforming political, cultural, and moral life. Notions of citizenship and national virtue, of forms of private and public activism, were catapulted to the forefront of public debate by the May coup and the ensuing period of sanacja. The sanacja had offered an opportunity to assess how well men and women both had been performing their duties as citizens, and it also offered the promise of a much-needed solution.

In the conception of the Society for Moral Rebirth, the sanacja constituted a call to women and men to participate more actively in the nation, to reject a parceling of interests, and to embrace a holistic approach to society and politics and culture. Yet it was never clear exactly how the society planned to tackle the imponderables or how it defined them; indeed, this lack of definition and direction characterized the group. In terms of achieving specific and concrete goals, the group undeniably failed.

But what the Society for Moral Rebirth did manage to do successfully—and the reason why it is a relevant and important group to study—was to proclaim the need to reinvent and expand "Polish politics" in such a way that politics would speak to and incorporate more than what was traditionally regarded as political. Politics, in the group's definition, existed as a tremendously broad concept that by necessity and definition included a sense of moral purpose and potential. In stressing moral reform and raw emotion, instinct and intuition over reason, the society embraced morality as a constituent part of politics. In so doing, it reflected a neoromanticist approach to independence, and it further popularized a discourse that the sanacja had made more widely available about the pressing need for moral health and reform. The sanacja had expanded the discursive public sphere in interwar Poland by proclaiming, loudly and clearly, that all citizens were vital participants in the process of rebirth and that this was a noble goal.

4 ⫶ Women's Activism during the Sanacja Period

Zofia Gostowska Moraczewska (1873–1958), a prominent women's activist and politician in the Second Republic, wrote an anxious letter to her sister on May 16, 1926, just days after Piłsudski launched his coup against the government of Poland:

> Hela, my dear, what we have again lived through! . . . What will come of all this? No one knows. The dance of the straw man or rather the night of the Valkyries, full of apparitions and monstrosities.[1]

In attempting to impress upon her sister the momentous nature of what was happening in Poland's capital city, Moraczewska turned to Stanisław Wyspiański's great turn-of-the-century drama, *The Wedding* (*Wesele*) (1901). She summoned Wyspiański's famous straw man—the *chochoł*—which suddenly came to life one day and shook partitioned Poland from its lethargic approach to the independence struggle. Twenty-five years later, in independent Poland, Moraczewska invoked the metaphor to herald yet another uncertain awakening of the slumbering nation, a nation about to enter the period of sanacja inaugurated by Piłsudski's coup.[2]

Moraczewska regarded Piłsudski's 1926 coup as a nationwide call to rescue newly independent Poland from what she felt was a slow-brewing civil war.[3] The Second Republic, as was clear to everyone, had not had an auspicious start: political life was unstable, the economic situation left much to be desired, and, perhaps most distressingly, the nation's moral life had reached a crisis. Moraczewska feared that modern-day Poles threatened to repeat all the "mistakes and sins, faults and wars of our fathers," as a result of which the

Polish-Lithuanian Commonwealth had fallen in the late eighteenth century.[4] Though in a follow-up letter to her sister Moraczewska expressed some trepidation at the way in which the Polish Sejm "had lost the battle with the commander," she was nevertheless prepared to trust in Piłsudski and to wait for his plan to be revealed.[5] Moraczewska focused on the positive potential of the coup, on the promise it contained to "begin a new life" in Poland.[6] She embraced the motto "the good of the Republic—the highest law" and welcomed the period of cleansing begun in 1926.[7]

In her enthusiasm for change and in the inspiration that she drew from the coup, Moraczewska was certainly not alone; these emotions formed part of the standard Piłsudskiite response to the event. But where Moraczewska differed is in her understanding of the coup as also offering an unprecedented opportunity for women to finally become full and active citizens of the new state. For women like Moraczewska, drawn from the left-liberal Piłsudskiite intelligentsia, the May coup functioned as an inspiration, focus, and opportunity and catapulted them into deeper public activism on behalf of the nation. Finally, after years of a brutally difficult adjustment to independence, a moral revolution had been proclaimed. Women embraced this notion and gave their own meaning to the concept of moral revolution. They believed that women were uniquely and "naturally" capable of "*extracting* selfishness, egoism, laziness, and recklessness from the Polish soul, of *build[ing] national pride*, and reviv[ing] and inflam[ing] a desire for collective work."[8] As a collectivity, Piłsudskiite women proposed a marriage between moral and political purity. They understood the sanacja's language of political decency and productive citizenship as speaking particularly clearly to them, as women and as the supposedly more moral sex.

With Piłsudski's coup and the call to cleanse the nation, women in Poland were handed an opportunity to realize the basic tenets of a maternal feminism that understood as inseparable the national struggle and the fight to realize women's full potential as citizens.[9] Thanks to women's innate difference, the maternal feminist argument ran, women's participation in public life, including their active participation in government, would exert a valuable influence on the nation as a whole.

These ideas about women's obligation to serve the nation drew on Poland's nineteenth-century partition heritage. It was during that period, particularly in the years following the failed January uprising against the Russian

Empire, that the Mother-Pole (Matka-Polka) trope emerged to describe a nationally committed and Polish Catholic woman of the gentry or intelligentsia who was charged with preserving Polishness in the face of the adversity that the partitions presented.[10] That Matka-Polka had fulfilled her patriotic duties admirably during the era of political servitude was recognized in the full suffrage rights accorded to Polish women in the March constitution of 1921.[11] The first years of independence witnessed a steady stream of women's activism and some degree of women's direct involvement in formal politics. It was not until the great caesura of May 1926 and Piłsudski's challenge to put the nation's house in order, however, that Matka-Polka (whose image continued to influence conceptions of women's roles in the reborn nation) was handed a real opportunity to show just what a useful citizen of the new state she could be. The Mother-Pole was handed a special challenge and opportunity to seize the moment and work for the rebirth of the nation. The call for sanacja resonated so powerfully with women like Moraczewska precisely because it used long-standing tropes and ideas, nursed during the long period of partitions, about what a nationally conscious and committed Polish woman should do for her nation. I argue that the May coup and the women's activism that developed as a direct response to it, laid the foundations for the emergence of a new model for Polish femininity, a sanacja-era Mother-Pole. The sanacja-era Mother-Pole described a woman-citizen who, like Moraczewska, believed that *all* women had a duty—an essential obligation—to eschew a narrowly conceived private sphere and to participate actively in building the better tomorrow to which the sanacja had ostensibly committed itself.

The discourse generated around the sanacja and the concept of moral revolution emphasized precisely those skills that women were said to possess in great measure, and so a moral rebirth of the republic, according to the sanacja-era Mother-Pole, was simply unthinkable without the committed participation of the "moral sex." It was women who were uniquely capable, as Moraczewska stated, of "cleaning the moral atmosphere, healing the wounds inflicted by postwar circumstances, battling . . . egoism, greed, corruption, theft, darkness, filth, and poverty of every variety."[12] Piłsudskiite women manipulated the flexible goals of the sanacja and reinterpreted the "imponderables" to which Piłsudski himself had referred, using the whole sanacja project as a catalyst to propel other like-minded women into intense forms of public activism. Their intentions were at once in line with and a departure from the official sanacja agenda. Like all Piłsudskiites, Piłsudskiite women saw in the sanacja, and in Piłsudski, Poland's best hope for a bright future. But they also detected in the sanacja an opportunity for women to come into their own and to stand as full citizens of independent Poland. In inserting themselves into the national agenda, Piłsudskiite women introduced an unexpected dimension to the sanacja. They argued both that women's participation was vital to the realization of a national rebirth and that women, through their involvement in the larger sanacja project, would advance their own status as real citizens of the republic. The sanacja needed women, and women, in turn, needed the sanacja.

Zofia Moraczewska achieved an impressive record of social and political activism,[13] but that record has scarcely been studied in any systematic or detailed fashion, which in turn reflects the underdeveloped state of research into the history of women in Poland.[14] This specific omission is all the more notable given that Moraczewska was especially active and well known in the Second Republic and participated in some of the key events and debates of the era, ones that extended far beyond a narrow understanding of "women's issues." Including Moraczewska's role in the larger story of the activism that the sanacja inspired, while important in its own right, also helps us construct a new narrative of the sanacja, one that forces us to probe what it was about the idea of sanacja that appealed to certain women and mobilized them in tremendous numbers and in ways that previous events or projects had not.

Moraczewska played a key role in two sanacja-era women's organizations. One was the Women's Democratic Election Committee (Demokratyczny Komitet Wyborczy Kobiet), established in Warsaw in 1927 to agitate for the Piłsudski electoral ticket in the 1928 elections. Piłsudski did not establish a full-fledged dictatorship after assuming power in 1926, as we have seen, and instead he left in place the preexisting parliament until November 1927, when its term expired. The March 1928 elections were the first held after the coup, and Piłsudski was eager for the results to impart a degree of legitimacy (moral, if not strictly constitutional) to his actions. Moraczewska, for one, was eager to be a part of the process, and she threw her weight, and that of the Election Committee, behind the Piłsudskiite Nonpartisan Bloc for Cooperation with the Government (BBWR). She believed, clearly, that the goals of moral rejuvenation were within reach. The organization she led, the Women's Democratic Election Committee, tells us much about how a certain group of women, with Moraczewska at the center, understood the coup and its promises to the nation.

The second group was the Women's Union for Citizenship Work (Związek Pracy Obywatelskiej Kobiet). The Women's Union was a large all-national women's organization that was established in Warsaw in 1928 as a kind of successor to the Women's Democratic Election Committee. The Women's Union declared its unequivocal support for Piłsudski and the May coup and grew to become a large and influential prosanacja organization that drew together women from across Poland. The Women's Union developed interesting links between itself, as a women's activist organization, and the sanacja government. The specifics of its tenure and of its relationship with the BBWR yield important perspectives on what the sanacja could and did mean—and what it failed to achieve—in the Second Republic. It is arguably the culmination and the most forceful illustration of women's sanacja-era activism. The women grouped therein advocated a broad definition of the May revolution and popularized the idea that women, as a group, constituted the untapped resource of the Polish nation that, during the momentous spring of 1926, had been called upon directly. In the union's estimation, the sanacja heralded an era in which women would begin making the transition from potential citizens or half-citizens into full and active ones; Poland as a whole would benefit.

An analysis of these two prosanacja women's organizations sharpens our understanding of just how widely the vocabulary of rebirth, public activism, and citizen responsibility circulated in postcoup Polish society. It shows that the sanacja concept was expansive and malleable enough to accommodate concerns that extended far beyond the formal political contexts through which many of the women's (male) contemporaries—and most subsequent historians—have understood it. By seizing a role within the national agenda, Moraczewska and the women involved in these groups encouraged a redefinition of the very meaning of politics, the public sphere, and female citizenship in the Second Republic.

Zofia Moraczewska

Zofia Moraczewska was ready and eager to take up Piłsudski's call to work for Poland. Like Piłsudski himself, Moraczewska was part of a generation born into the conspiratorial atmosphere that marked the period following the failed January uprising against the Russians in 1863–64. This was the generation that had played a pivotal role in the partition-era Polish independence struggles and that was accustomed to devoting their personal and public lives to the national good. Before the war, for example, Moraczewska had served as a key organizer of the small women's section of the Riflemen's Association (Związek Strzelecki), the paramilitary and patriotic group Piłsudski had established in Galicia in 1912. Later, with the outbreak of the Great War, Moraczewska set about mobilizing women to participate actively in the fight for Polish independence. She was instrumental in establishing the Women's League (Liga Kobiet) of Galicia and Cieszyn Silesia in 1915, a group that put women to work as nurses or as couriers or in any other way appropriate for the war effort.[15] At the end of 1918 the Women's League became the first significant women's organization in independent Poland.[16]

Moraczewska and the women with whom she worked during these years formed part of a small social and cultural (though not necessarily economic) elite.[17] Many had been involved with the Polish Socialist Party (PPS) before the war.[18] Most existed in especially close proximity to the centers of power in the newly created Poland of 1918. Moraczewska's husband, for example, was Jędrzej Moraczewski (1870–1944), prime minister of Poland from late 1918 to early 1919 and, until he resigned from its ranks in 1927, one of the most prominent members of the powerful PPS.[19] In addition, from 1920 the Moraczewski family lived in an old villa in Sulejówek, and thus Zofia and Jędrzej were neighbors to none other than Piłsudski himself, who had made his home there since 1923. Moraczewska's elite social and political connections were characteristic of many of the women who dominated the executive ranks of prosanacja women's groups, but of course their experiences and views were not typical of the vast majority of Polish women.

Soon after independence, Moraczewska was part of the small group of women who, newly enfranchised, exercised their rights to full political participation and ran for positions in the new Sejm. Moraczewska won a seat in Poland's first parliament, where she served from 1919 to 1922, as a representative of the PPS from the Kraków region.[20] Moraczewska quickly became disillusioned with formal politics, however, particularly with having to vote along party lines and against her own conscience. She also recalled in her memoirs what she perceived to have been an unarticulated but nevertheless fierce and pervasive sexism in the Sejm. She expressed grave disappointment that in an independent and free Poland—a Poland for which she and other women had worked tirelessly and for which they had sacrificed a great deal—cultural barriers to females' full participation in public life remained. For Moraczewska, one instance in particular, though seemingly minor, resonated with incredible power: a parliamentary debate during which she politely reminded her fellow Sejm members that Poland's population was composed primarily of workers and peasants and that this basic reality could not be overlooked when considering solutions to Poland's economic and social problems. The way eminent socialist parliamentarian Mieczysław Niedziałkowski (1893–1940) dismissed her statement was, she believed, typical of the disrespect male parliamentarians showed to women in politics: "I didn't know that Comrade is such a peasant-lover [*chłopomanka*]." His remark was greeted by great applause in the Sejm.[21]

Frustrated by such attitudes, and because she wanted more time for her family, Moraczewska limited her public and formal political activity from 1922 until 1927. She did not run in the 1922 elections, though nine other women were elected to the Sejm at this time, and three to the Senate.[22] Moraczewska remained active only in the Women's League and in the Political Club of Progressive Women (Klub Polityczny Kobiet Postępowych), which had been formed in Warsaw by influential and socially active women of the intelligentsia in the spring of 1919. The Progressive Women, which maintained branches throughout Poland, had as its goal the nurturing of a strong and capable "woman-citizen," and its mandate included working to guarantee and extend women's rights in all areas of life; these goals would become quite familiar during the sanacja era.[23] Moraczewska stressed in her memoirs that she derived untold satisfaction working with and for women in a setting where women were respected and appreciated.[24] Her enthusiasm for direct, full, committed social activism at the level of formal high politics was reignited with Piłsudski's coup and the call for a nationwide sanacja.

The Women's Democratic Election Committee, 1927–1928

One year after the coup, Moraczewska remained pleased that the spirit of reform inaugurated in May 1926 continued to exist, but she also lamented that many reform initiatives were coming from the top and that the massive citizen activism the coup was supposed to have inspired had not materialized as quickly as she might have liked. Moraczewska also felt that people were simply failing to take on their share of the burden for effecting a sanacja and were only too ready to wait for Piłsudski to "fix everything" himself.[25] For her part, Moraczewska was prepared to act. As president of the Women's League (since 1927), she called into existence the Women's Democratic Election Committee on December 16, 1927.[26] The new Warsaw-based Election Committee, the founding members of which included several prominent female activists in the Second Republic, openly supported Piłsudski, the coup, and the notion of sanacja, and the group was located squarely within the Piłsudski camp.[27]

The Election Committee was composed of two main sections: the presidium and the general committee. The presidium included sixteen elected delegates of those women's organizations that, as a group, had declared their collective wish to join the Women's Democratic Election Committee and work for the sanacja cause.[28] The general committee was composed of individual members from those organizations that had declared their full support for the Election Committee; the numbers in the general committee were unlimited. The committee was funded by voluntary contributions of members as well as by various fund-raising efforts in the community.

The Election Committee openly lent its support to the ostensibly suprapolitical BBWR and hoped that this bloc, if it were to win in the 1928 elections, would function as a real progovernment electoral alliance of all those who, regardless of previous political affiliation, were committed to "fixing Poland."[29] The 1928 elections were regarded as an extremely important public verdict on Piłsudski's actions as well as an attempt to lend an air of legality to a coup that was, of course, technically irreconcilable with the principles of democratic government. Sanacja rhetoric billed the 1928 elections as an opportunity for Poland to "save itself" and to strengthen itself by providing Piłsudski and his associates with a mandate to continue healing the nation. Sanacja propaganda depicted the elections as an opportunity to deal a final blow to the ways of the previous corrupt and volatile parliaments and to megalomaniacal parliamentarians, as well as a chance to inaugurate an era of concerted state building. The BBWR's creator and president, Walery Sławek, himself explained that the BBWR and the upcoming elections presented the hope of reversing the "national moral insanity" that had come to define life in the Second Republic. The "wartime cataclysms" and the general havoc that the previous decades had exerted on the Polish people needed to be counteracted and real democracy built. The BBWR was to be an organization that, by its very structure and purpose, would help restore health to the Polish organism.[30] Only by returning a resounding vote for the Piłsudskiite political grouping, the sanacja camp preached, would these goals be achieved.

The basic stated purpose of the Women's Democratic Election Committee was to help realize these grand ambitions by establishing local branches that would campaign across Poland for Piłsudski's ticket in the 1928 elections.[31] Election Committee women would themselves also run for positions in the new government. Moraczewska explained: "The Fatherland needs us again. . . . There is something in the air that is functioning like a wake-up call—and like a wake-up call—it awakens. And so we are ready, happy, capable of work, full of enthusiasm and will."[32] The committee's founding document contained a total of six postulates. It began with a characteristic Piłsudskiite commitment to "the good of the state, as a whole" and emphasized community interests over the sectarian partisanship of the pre-May days. Poland was conceptualized as an organic entity that required protection at all costs, an entity that necessarily took precedence over sectarian interests of any nature. The second postulate established a clear commitment to a "true democracy" that safeguarded the interests of the whole over the parts and that "guaranteed all citizens equal rights and responsibilities." Piłsudskiite women and men, at least immediately after the coup, operated from a comparatively inclusive definition of Poland and Polishness and regarded the coup as strengthening rather than perverting democratic potential by issuing a resounding defeat of the right-nationalist camp and its extreme Polish chauvinism. The third postulate called for the revision of the constitution of 1921, which, it was well known, the Piłsudskiites had been eager to do since the constitution's inception.[33] The 1921 constitution had created a strong parliament and a comparatively weak executive, or presidency, and was widely blamed by Piłsudskiites for the Sejmocracy (parliamentocracy) that had hamstrung politics before 1926. The first step toward reforming the March 1921 constitution was taken by the sanacja camp shortly after the coup, on August 2, 1926, and the main change this so-called August Amendment introduced was an increase to the powers of the president.[34] The Piłsudskiites believed, and the

Election Committee concurred, that the very process of working on a revised constitutional document would help educate the public in state matters and bring people toward a much-lauded political and social maturity.[35]

The fourth postulate outlined in the Election Committee's declaration affirmed a simple commitment to the "healing of parliamentary life" and an end to the political corruption that had plagued the Polish political process until 1926: "Only people incapable of compromising their honor, both in public life and in private life, can stand on guard for the honor and good of the state."[36] To that end, the propaganda division of the Election Committee took for itself the task of "ideological agitation." The division organized educational courses and lectures and established a "flying women's battalion" to travel around Poland and agitate for the BBWR candidates in the election and to encourage the development of active and useful citizenship in women specifically. This strategy was organized and carried out on a variety of levels across Poland, in large and small urban centers, in rural regions and in urban neighborhoods. The intention was to cover as many electoral districts and to reach as many voters as possible.[37]

The first four of the six postulates outlined by the Election Committee could have applied to a wide variety of pro-Piłsudski groups, referring as they did to the formal political realm, to community, and to national consensus; already here we see the extent to which the women privileged all-national goals over ones that would have served women exclusively. This was a group that conceived of women's activism primarily in terms of how it could benefit the national collective. Only in outlining its final two points did the Election Committee depart from official sanacja policies to focus on women. Points five and six highlighted the need to improve women's social and economic positions in the state and to remove all vestiges of discrimination against women, particularly those evident within civil law and those customs reinforced by the Catholic Church.[38] Such measures were absolutely crucial in the making of good female citizens, the committee argued. But even the fifth point began first by outlining general social welfare concerns to which the committee hoped the subsequent government would pay attention—such as work for the unemployed, affordable housing, a more effective social security net, price controls, and school reform—before going on to call for protection of motherhood, appropriate care for children, and protection for women workers. The last proposal was the only one to focus on women exclusively. It pledged categorical support for women's constitutional equality, as outlined in sections 12, 96, and 102 of the constitution, and called for the removal of all discrimination against married working women (married women were passed over for employment in certain sectors or required their husbands' permission to work), equal pay for equal work, and a minimum wage for women's work. The committee also gave support in point six to improving women's access to education, moving forward with the temperance cause, and increasing resources devoted to eliminating prostitution and all diseases that "degenerate the race."[39]

The tension between feminist goals and national ones is reflected in the very structure of the group's founding document. In its declaration, the committee emphasized that its priority was working for and with the official political sanacja and that it was motivated by the overall good of the state. Within this strategy the committee nevertheless found room to introduce, however carefully, the notion that a real commitment to national reform should include a consideration of women's specific health and welfare needs and should address what it regarded as continued systemic discrimination against women in independent Poland. If the sanacja were really a movement about moral reform, about creating a new kind of committed citizen, then women and the issues that mattered to them could not be left out, the women of the committee argued.[40] Though the official sanacja never referred to "women's issues" as part of its agenda and never articulated an explicit policy choice that would see women become the bearers of national morality, the committee linked these concerns to the sanacja program and suggested, subtly, that the sanacja most certainly did include these kinds of questions; it just needed women to persuade both the wider public and the Piłsudskiite men that this was so. If the sanacja were really a movement about moral reform and about creating a citizen of higher quality, then women and the issues that mattered to them could not be discounted. The Election Committee manipulated the notoriously malleable language of moral revolution and carved out a space for itself within the larger sanacja project.

The March 1928 Elections

The specific approach the Election Committee took in selling itself and the sanacja cause to voters in the 1928 campaign reveals a great deal about how the group negotiated its twin identities, both as a women's group that hoped its activism would benefit women and as a prosanacja and "genderless" patriotic organization. The committee blended these two aspects of its identity in its appeals to the female electorate by making the case that women should take full advantage of their citizenship status and that women's interests would be best served by Piłsudski and a BBWR administration.

According to a poster from the Zakopane Election Committee in southern Poland, the parliament that would come out of the 1928 elections would either make Poland healthy or "push it once again into the abyss of poverty, hatred, and civil war." Women in particular had a responsibility to keep Poland from falling into this abyss by voting for the national consensus represented by the BBWR.[41] While there was little new in this simple patriotic appeal to the Polish Everywoman, to Matka-Polka, the Zakopane committee's message went further. It reminded readers that the independent Polish state had been especially good to women and that Poland was ahead of many western European nations in terms of women's rights. Poland, after all, had granted women voting rights immediately after the Great War, whereas women in France, for example (against which Poles frequently compared themselves), remained disenfranchised until after the Second World War. Readers of the poster would have known, too, that on November 28, 1918, it was Piłsudski, the symbolic leader of sanacja Poland, who had issued the official proclamation of support for women's political equality and suffrage.[42] In this fashion, the Zakopane committee created a powerful association between Piłsudski, independence, women's enfranchisement, the sanacja, and continued support for an expansion of women's citizenship. The implication was that the sanacja was good for women.

In its public declarations, the Election Committee played it safe and made rather traditional appeals to women as Catholic wives and mothers. Committee women did not want to fundamentally transform relations between the sexes, and they did not want to be "liberated from womanhood." Rather, these were women who espoused a maternal feminist justification for their public activism and who believed that, as mothers, wives, and Polish patriots, they had a duty to participate in politics and to transform the political process for the better. Their feminism was inseparable from their nationalism and from their commitment to Piłsudski, the sanacja, and the BBWR.

One election poster created by the Bydgoszcz branch of the committee, for example, affirmed the group's commitment to "fixing the Republic" *and* to "the principles of ethical Christianity in private and in public life."[43] The committee framed its appeals to women voters in terms of a familiar Christian femininity that stood at some distance from the threatening examples of "modern" femininity marked by an apparent renunciation of home, hearth, and God. Another poster, from the Lublin branch, stressed that maternalism was the basis for women's political activism, calling motherhood "women's most sublime calling," and arguing that, therefore, motherhood deserved special government protection. The implication—unproven and unsupported, yet nevertheless forcefully made—was that the sanacja government would offer this protection.[44] A poster from the town of Płock reiterated the importance of a certain expression of women's political participation, stating that "the strength of the fatherland rests on *the family* and the family rests on *the woman.*"[45] This constituted a very safe and traditional rendering of gender roles. Yet another poster, one that was the result of a joint effort by various provincial election committees, simply encouraged women to come out from "the shadows of private life" and to realize how much Poland needed them to work devotedly and publicly for the nation.[46]

While the committee had to be careful to present an image of modest and maternal femininity, it was also forced to invoke the sanacja cautiously and to work assiduously at subverting the negative stereotypes that regularly dogged the Piłsudski camp. The most resonant stereotype was of the sanacja and its supporters as a pernicious group of godless Bolsheviks, Jews, and Masons that threatened the Polish nation at every turn. One opposition election poster described the priorities of the Piłsudskiites in the plainest possible language: "Who wants to join the Masons in the battle with the Catholic religion? Who wants civil marriages, divorces, [and] baptisms without a priest?"[47] Such criticisms of the post-May grouping were made by the nationalist right generally, which was represented in the 1928 elections by the Catholic-nationalist bloc; the bloc would formally adopt the name National Party (Stronnictwo Narodowe, SN) after the 1928 elections.[48] In all respects, postcoup Poland was polarized between the Piłsudskiites and the Catholic-nationalist right; the division described not traditional left-right differences but conflicting ideas about history, about the relationship between ethnicity and Polish nationalism, about the role of the Catholic Church in the state, and about modernity generally.

These divisions extended to women's groups too. While the sanacja inspired a kind of women's activism that pledged allegiance to Piłsudski, as I am arguing it did, it also sparked a reaction against the sanacja. Some women from the right-nationalist camp believed that, "as women," they possessed a moral responsibility to combat what they perceived as the godless sanacja and to reclaim the Matka-Polka trope away from Piłsudskiite women. This was the case, for example, with the National Organization of Women (Narodowa Organizacja Kobiet, NOK), which had been formed immediately after the Great War under the auspices of the right-Catholic National Democratic Party; the group's aim was to build national life according to Christian and nationalist principles. By 1926 the group claimed forty-three thousand members in two hundred branches across Poland and regularly sent its members to Parliament.[49] While Piłsudskiite women argued that Poland's women had a duty to support the sanacja, women of the nationalist right maintained that the responsibility lay with women to support the explicitly Catholic parties against sanacja hegemony.[50] Women had a responsibility to battle what one right-nationalist author stated was a mood that, since the coup, had allowed "eastern influences"—Jews and Masons—to penetrate the ostensibly pure Polish national organism.[51]

The Chełm branch of the National Organization of Women reminded Catholic Polish women of their obligations to the nation and of the need to prevent "the belittling of church and fatherland." From their perspective, every vote for the BBWR ticket in the 1928 elections constituted a vote against the Polish future.[52] An election poster put out by the Catholic-nationalist bloc, with which the National Organization of Women was allied, addressed itself specifically to Polish women and warned them that it was a grievous sin to vote against the Catholic parties. The poster raised the issue of civil marriage and divorce, which the Catholic parties opposed vehemently and which leading figures of the sanacja bloc supported: "A civil marriage means an uncertain tomorrow for a wife, bad luck for a mother, misery for the child, and the break-up of the family."[53] The political sanacja, the BBWR, Piłsudski, and the women's groups that supported the sanacja were thus linked rhetorically to immorality and national decay.

The women of the Democratic Election Committee were eager to confront head-on the allegations made by the nationalist right and to convince voters that such accusations were simply false. Election Committee women were critical of an exclusionary Catholicism which contended that only explicitly Catholic groups were sufficiently committed to Poland. An election poster in Katowice, created by the Silesian branch of the committee, made it clear that sanacja women also stood for a Christian Poland and that, like the National Organization of Women, they valued women's traditional roles in serving their families and their nation. The poster addressed the "Woman-Mother of a Christian family; responsible for the future of the Polish nation and for maintaining clean moral goals."[54] An Election Committee poster in Kalisz addressed the "Polish woman who believes in God and is religious!" and affirmed that the BBWR was full of "decent and practicing Catholics" committed to a moral path in life. The poster went on to remind its audience that Piłsudski had orchestrated the Miracle on the Vistula in 1920, which saw the Bolshevik armies defeated by the Polish forces at Warsaw, and that Piłsudski's anti-Bolshevism was beyond reproach.[55] Another poster issued by the Democratic Election Committee stated that it was an outright lie that the BBWR ticket was "an enemy of the Catholic Church." It also referred to Piłsudski's "pogrom against the Bolsheviks" in 1920 to underscore the Piłsudski camp's long-standing commitment to anticommunism. In using the word pogrom, moreover, the appeal played to the stereotype of Jews' affinity for communism, and conveyed subtly a commitment to a mono-ethnic and Catholic Poland.[56] It was simply a lie, another poster from Kielce stated, that the BBWR was full of godless Masons, for even the pope had blessed Piłsudski, and the Vatican had continued to maintain good relations with post-coup governments.[57] The Lublin branch of the Election Committee went so far as to suggest that to denounce Piłsudski was not altogether different from bucking the authority of the pope and the Polish bishops, with whom Piłsudski had also established good relations.[58] Through these messages, the committee tried to convey that women could in fact be good Poles, Catholics, wives, and mothers and still support the sanacja.

Both the sanacja women and the antisanacja women agreed that the female sex was naturally equipped with special talents that, in the new political era that had begun with the proclamation of a moral revolution, they were under an even greater obligation to use. However, just how to harness women's higher moral potential, for what end, and under the aegis of what specific party, was bitterly contested. Within the confines of a femininity determined by notions of immutable gender difference and women's innate moral superiority, the women of the Election Committee advocated a model of female citizenship that demanded (not simply encouraged) public political activism on the side of the sanacja. After the coup, with their ideological compatriots (and often family members and friends) in power, sanacja women were actually in a position to have the centers of power hear them. Moreover, in blending references to the need for women to be included fully in the sanacja's formal political sphere with calls for "schools, shelters, clinics, hospitals . . . so that goodness and light defeat poverty and darkness," as one election poster from Kowel in Poland's eastern borderlands did, the committee popularized a broadened interpretation of the sanacja agenda.[59]

This is not to argue that the sanacja offered women a whole new world of possibilities, that it "liberated" them, or that the sanacja-era Matka-Polka trope challenged societal conceptions of what roles a woman should adopt. At best, the sanacja provided an elite group of women with an opportunity to claim limited spaces in otherwise restrictive political discourses. In elevating questions of morality and ethics to national importance, the sanacja allowed women to claim a voice in an important national forum. At its most restrictive, the kind of sanacja-era women's activism described here entrenched ideas about the inherent moral superiority of women and both reaffirmed and popularized the notion that Polish women had an obligation, first and foremost, to serve their nation by fulfilling commitments to husbands and children and by acting as moral beacons. The language that committee women used in their election posters to appeal to women voters, drawing as it did on comparatively safe images of Polish Catholicism, family, and nation, could hardly be considered radical. The call for a sanacja resonated so powerfully with some women precisely because it called on Polish tradition and relied on a language of duty, faith, and the greater good that was reminiscent of a vocabulary popularized during the partition period. The women who were actually involved in propagating a sanacja vision did not wish to overturn what they regarded as the most fundamental biologically and culturally prescribed roles for women. They did believe, however, that women should not suffer exclusion from full political participation and from realizing their potential as citizens simply because they were women. Just the opposite was true: they believed that because women were endowed with a higher moral sense, Poland could not afford to exclude them from political life.

Despite the efforts of the Election Committee, the BBWR failed to achieve a landslide in the 1928 elections, winning just over 25 percent of the votes for seats in the Sejm.[60] The election nevertheless functioned as a partial justification of the coup, and in forming the government the BBWR formally became the political incarnation of the sanacja vision.[61] Two women from the Election Committee entered the Sejm: Maria Jaworska (1885–1957), a high-school teacher from Lwów and an active member of the Polish Teachers' Union (Związek Nauczycielstwa Polskiego), and Eugenia Waśniewska, a member of the pro-Piłsudski Party of Work (Partia Pracy).[62] Zofia Daszyńska-Golińska, a historian and longtime socialist and women's activist, was elected to the Senate.[63] Altogether in the Second Republic, thirty-two women held forty-one Sejm mandates, and eighteen women held twenty Senate mandates, but with the exception of Irena Kosmowska, no woman attained the level of minister in any interwar government.[64] The highest rate of women's participation in the formal political structures of the state did come, however, in the post-May period. Moreover, three-quarters of the women in the Sejm and all female senators were born before 1890; they were thus part of the so-called post–January uprising generation, which included Moraczewska and Piłsudski himself. Almost all came from the numerically small intelligentsia elite, precisely the social stratum from which key Piłsudskiites were drawn, and approximately two-thirds of female representatives were university graduates.[65]

The Women's Union for Citizenship Work, 1928–1933

When the Women's Democratic Election Committee disbanded, March 25, 1928, a new group was founded that would function for the remainder of the interwar period as an umbrella body for prosanacja women's organizations: the Women's Union for Citizenship Work.[66] Moraczewska was the group's first president (1928–32), and its founding members included several notable female activists: Maria Jaworska, Halina Chełmicka-Jaroszewiczowa, Wanda Drzewiecka, Zofia Daszyńska-Golińska, Wanda Twardowa, and Dr. Bronisława Dłuska. As with the Election Committee, women in the union's executive were part of a small Polish intellectual elite and had many personal connections to the formal political sanacja. Most had in fact followed Moraczewska into the union from the Election Committee.[67] By 1930, the Women's Union had between thirty and forty thousand members, all women of Polish ethnicity, working in branch organizations across the Second Republic, from Wilno to

Poznań. Though the union established an impressive network of branch organizations across Poland's urban and rural regions, the Warsaw-based central bureau was run by a tiny coterie of elite women, led by Moraczewska.[68] What follows is a discussion based not on the actual impact that the union had on the masses of women throughout the country or the work that the numerous branch organizations undertook, but rather, an exploration of the structure and the inner workings of the union's Warsaw-based executive committee.

While the Women's Democratic Election Committee had been established as a temporary organization to support a specific effort—helping the BBWR win the 1928 elections—the mandate and goals of the Women's Union for Citizenship Work were expressly long-term and arguably more ambitious. At the opening meeting of the union, in March 1928, Moraczewska boldly declared that the women intended to "cleanse the moral atmosphere" in Poland and "heal the wounds inflicted by postwar circumstances" and that they would battle the "egoism, greed, corruption, theft, ignorance, filth, and poverty" that was everywhere around them.[69] The Women's Union, as Moraczewska herself stated, would work to prevent "the fall of moral culture" in Poland.[70] The assumption here, oftentimes stated overtly by the women, was that, in contrast to men, women were *naturally* equipped with the higher moral sense that would enable them to effect this Poland-wide moral revolution. Only by including women in the grand sanacja plans, the women argued, would the future of the state be guaranteed. For the Women's Union, the sanacja and the general spirit of reform launched by the coup functioned as an ideal focal point, "a single banner" around which women could be mobilized to work productively for the collective and transformed into full and real female citizens. The union was steadfastly committed to creating a new type of woman-citizen, "cognizant of the full weight of her rights and responsibilities," and believed that it was only by embracing a broad definition of citizenship that the future of the whole state could be guaranteed.[71] The Women's Union encouraged women's active participation in shaping the terms of the moral rebirth that everyone agreed was absolutely vital. As such, the union stands as the culmination and as one of the most forceful illustrations of women's sanacja-era activism.

Certainly, the Women's Union was not the only women's organization mobilized into existence by the sanacja and not the only group that declared commitment to Piłsudski and to a moral revolution. The Union of Polish

Legion Women (Związek Legionistek Polskich), for example, was formed in Warsaw in 1929 to bring together all those prosanacja women's groups from across Poland that were interested in fostering "collective action, in the spirit of free thinking, on the moral and economic rebirth of the nation."[72] The Organization for Preparing Women for the Defense of the Country (Organizacja Przysposobienia Kobiet do Obrony Kraju) was another prosanacja women's group that advocated the idea that women were warriors fighting for the defense and dignity of their nation.[73] These groups had much in common with the Women's Union for Citizenship Work, and many women were members of all groups simultaneously. As such, the Women's Union formed part of a wave of women's extraparliamentary social organizations that became ubiquitous after the coup and that reflected both a Poland- and a Europe-wide postwar disappointment with traditional political parties. Moraczewska and the women with whom she worked saw themselves as part of this wider trend in society.

Moraczewska herself admitted that the Women's Union, at one level, could be compared to larger, better known, and far more influential groups born of the coup. One such better-known group was the Union for the Reform of the Republic (Związek Naprawy Rzeczypospolitej). This group had been established in June 1926 by a younger and more liberal group within the pro-Piłsudski intelligentsia. Members were typical European postwar critics of parliamentary democracy: they were weary of parliamentary government, had lost faith in the efficacy of political parties, and believed that extraparliamentary organizations were as important as (if not more important than) parliamentary ones.[74] The Women's Union's embrace of the May challenge pinpointed many of the same problems that the Union for the Reform of the Republic raised. But the Women's Union also focused on certain other telling issues and offered its own unique conceptualizations of what the sanacja should entail.

The fact that the Women's Union was designed specifically by and for women as a feminist organization places it within a special category of sanacja-era activism. One union member, speaking about the group generally, spelled it out: "I will say it—We are feminists! Of course, not in . . . a quarrelsome sense, but rather in a contemporary sense, one that recognizes the enormity of the social program [before us]; we understand perfectly our role in the realization of this program. . . . We are feminists because we are initiating a battle with a system that governs us without us."[75] That the union conceptualized women's issues as being integral to the sociopolitical transformations that Poland needed gave it a distinctive character. Moreover, it invited women's active participation in shaping the terms of Poland's moral rebirth. Women were central to the elaboration of a new national vision, and the task of the union was, therefore, "to prepare women for a future, obligatory service to the state, whose boundaries and organization . . . women themselves should elaborate."[76]

Union women argued that the existing deficiencies in Polish national life were the result of, as one member stated, "the one-sidedness of the male psyche." They steadfastly believed that the differences between the sexes were innate and immutable and that, in contrast to men, women were more moral, sensitive, and open to compromise.[77] The sanacja had called for a more moral society. Armed with their expertise in the private domain and with a belief that women would introduce higher values into political life, union women understood that they were answering the sanacja's call to effect a real nationwide moral revolution. They set out to "rationalize the household economy" on a national scale.[78]

One union member, Natalia Greniewska, boasted that the organization taught women how to "live" for their country: "We women, mothers and educators, . . . our souls not poisoned by party politics, will bring to political life new values based on nonpartisan work for the state. We will introduce our instinct for social work, our love for truth and for knowledge, responsibility, and women's intuition."[79]

Across the country, the union branches told their members time and again that women's participation in political life would exert positive influences on national life generally.[80] Women, after all, were especially well suited to introducing ethics into contemporary life and to fostering "decency in public and private life, deep feelings of honor, and civil courage." Women would also ensure that these traits were passed on to future generations.[81]

Union women were always quick to argue that women served the sanacja in a unique and vital way, both because women exhibited a natural higher morality, and because women would draw attention to issues which men ignored. Moraczewska praised the fact that the Women's Union was an organization created by women and for women. Only women were eligible for membership in the Women's Union, and only women were welcome to attend the various lectures hosted by the group and to write for the group's biweekly magazine, *Citizenship Work (Praca obywatelska)*, which circulated, though in small numbers, from 1928. Moraczewska believed that women, quite simply, would feel more comfortable in an all-female setting.[82]

And yet, despite this talk of "all" women working together to create a sense of collective purpose and future, membership in the Women's Union was formally limited to women of Polish ethnicity or to those who were assimilated completely into Polish culture. According to this typical way of thinking, fully assimilated Jews, for example, were simply Poles, and so of course they could participate in the group. For her part, Moraczewska favored the inclusion of nonassimilated Jewish women in the union: "Our alliance is a citizen organization; it talks about the equality of all citizens in terms of rights and responsibilities, it endeavors to win all citizens over to the state, it desires to awaken and consolidate respect and love for Poland in their hearts."[83] In addition, Moraczewska stated, Jewish women's presence in the organization would assist in breaking down the "Chinese wall" that separated Roman Catholic women from women of other faiths.[84] At the same time, she understood full well the general reluctance to accept an influx of Jewish women into the organization, in part so as to protect the group, and the sanacja, from opponents' attacks.[85] She was prepared, nevertheless, to let the issue remain dormant, and the Women's Union remained open to ethnic Poles only. The citizenship that the union aimed to improve in the Second Republic—which counted close to 30 percent of the population as a national minority—was narrowly defined along ethnic lines.

The Women's Union in Action

The ways in which the Women's Union thought of itself and understood its role in sanacja-era Poland are best reflected in its structure, in the projects it undertook, and in the questions to which it devoted its resources. The Women's Union for Citizenship Work was simply organized into various sections defined by specific functions. These included basic divisions for finances, relations with the press, and foreign and municipal affairs. But it also included sections that spoke to women's unique concerns and abilities, and the bulk of the union's energy was invested in citizenship education, schooling, women's issues, care for children, culture, and beauty.[86] The sections overlapped considerably, as each submitted to the overarching goal of making women into active citizens. This general goal was perhaps best summarized by the Section for Citizen Education itself: "Our aspiration and our goal is the rebirth of Poland in the spirit . . . of independence: the harmonious cooperation of a strong government with the Sejm and the Senate, arousing in society high values and citizen virtues."[87]

Moraczewska and the women with whom she worked in the union were always clear that constitutional and political equality were not themselves sufficient conditions for stimulating these higher values and women's noble citizen virtues; they constituted a necessary start, but no more. The union maintained, as did the Election Committee before it, that women could only become complete and fully active citizens once they were protected in their obligations as mothers and wives and once all vestiges of legal, psychological, and cultural discrimination against women were removed. They also emphasized the importance of giving women access to information and material assistance.[88] Accordingly, the Women's Union sponsored various educational and "social work" initiatives, and this, really, formed the core of the group's activities.[89] In addition to organizing information sessions on varied topics, they also ran various charity efforts designed to give women (especially poor women) the resources they needed to make informed and independent decisions about their futures.[90] The Section for Women's Issues, a large and especially active division within the union, educated women in the law and the structure of government, informed them about their rights as employees, and offered courses in public speaking. This section also gave material aid to women and facilitated access to employment training. In addition, it organized libraries and ran a lecture series on such varied topics as the upbringing of the soldier-citizen, women in Polish history, social activism and the contemporary woman, the life of Marshal Piłsudski, Polish foreign policy, the revision of the constitution, and the history of the Women's Union itself.[91]

The Section for Women's Issues was also responsible for keeping women abreast of the evolving work of the Codification Commission, which had been established in 1919 to write unified laws for the republic. One of the most controversial of these concerned changes to marriage laws, especially the right to both civil marriage and divorce. In general, the Women's Union supported liberal changes to marriage legislation, with many union women arguing that this right was already commonplace in the West and that there it had not replaced religious marriage ceremonies and did not constitute an affront to good mores.[92] The Women's Union considered carefully the various aspects of the proposed marriage question and commented in very specific ways on how each section of the new law might affect women. Its views were summarized in a report presented to the Sejm. In this document, the women of the union articulated a commitment to absolute equality between men and "wives and mothers," and they launched objections to any sections of the proposal that failed to recognize that equality. Their demands included allowing women to add their own surnames to those of their husbands, removing a woman's obligation to obey her husband, eliminating all restrictions against married women's employment, guaranteeing women legal entitlement to their own earnings, and making mothers and fathers equally responsible for their children.[93]

In the same vein, the union's Section for Moral Care, another large division of the union, pushed to work more closely with the government-sponsored Sanitary-Moral Commission.[94] The Commission's members—doctors, police, and representatives of various social organizations—recommended state policies on such "moral problems" as prostitution and venereal disease.[95] The Women's Union, moreover, was a vocal advocate of the existing Women's Police Force and worked with it in an advisory capacity. The Women's Police Force was formed in 1925 on the initiative of the Polish Committee for the Elimination of the Trade in Women and Children and with the assistance of the Ministry of Internal Affairs. The female recruits were trained for six months in the general procedures of police service, with emphasis on dealing with prostitution, venereal disease, the white slave trade, and general hygiene. The idea of a women's police proved so popular that by 1936, Poland had 148 female police.[96] The head of the Women's Police was Stanisława Paleolog, and she was also a member of the union's Section for Women's Issues.[97]

In 1929 the Section for Women's Issues proposed the establishment of a family planning clinic that would work to promote, as Moraczewska herself stated, "the defense of the real family, of the human dignity of women, and of the social relations threatened by today's order of things."[98] The proposed clinic would offer medical services to pregnant women and would sell birth control devices. Consultation would cost either one or two zlotys or would be free for women unable to afford the fee. Birth control devices would be sold for what they cost at hospitals.[99] Abortions, however, would not be provided; Moraczewska was clear that the clinic aimed for the "defense of motherhood" and steadfastly condemned abortion.[100] As part of this planned initiative, the Section for Women's Issues also hoped to organize a series of informative lectures by notable speakers and to found a publication. At a November 1933 general meeting of the Women's Union, however, little concrete action had been taken and the entire controversial plan was still being debated.

The Women's Union constitutes but one example of the way in which social organizations broadened the definition of the political in sanacja-era Poland. We see in the union a blend of formal politics and community-level social activism, as well as an articulation of the view that a real national revolution would come about only when all parts of the nation—women included—were involved in its creation. This nexus of interests, far from being fleeting or accidental, the Women's Union maintained, was essential to realizing a true sanacja of the republic. As Halina Jaroszewiczowa, a founding member of the union and a leader of its Section for the Care of Mothers and Children stated, caring for women and giving them the resources they needed to succeed formed a fundamental part of the larger sanacja goal of improving the collective: "as a professional worker, mother, [and] educator bestowed with a remarkable social instinct . . . a woman is capable, most completely and directly, of grasping the totality of work and of social welfare questions."[101] Jaroszewiczowa added that the issues the Women's Union for Citizenship Work raised in its activism were of national importance and that union activities on behalf of women fell under the category not of philanthropy but of valuable "citizen service."[102] According to this way of thinking, fighting for women's workplace rights, supporting the women's police force, or battling prostitution—all of which the union did—constituted precisely the kind of community-based citizen activism the Piłsudskiites were well known to favor—even if the official centers of sanacja power never spoke about these specific so-called women's issues.

The Women's Union and the Political Sanacja

The relationship between the Women's Union and the political sanacja, the BBWR, was not always smooth, however. Although many of the leading members of both groups had personal ties and shared a powerful commitment to Piłsudski, and although the union received some funds from the BBWR and participated in its parliamentary circle, the union was nevertheless a formally separate organization that guarded its own independence.[103] Moraczewska in particular openly opposed the orthodoxy of the time, which stated that all pro-Piłsudski groups had to accede to the final authority of the BBWR.[104]

Conflict between the BBWR and the union erupted over a number of issues, including the new marriage legislation drafted by the Codification Commission. In a letter to her sister, Moraczewska complained that the BBWR was reluctant to accept the more liberal proposals recommended by the commission for fear of "starting a war with the clergy during this difficult time." But, she asked, "Are we going to submit to fanatical clerical backwardness?"[105] Moraczewska further argued that it was especially difficult for a woman to oppose the majority opinion voiced in the BBWR.[106] She resented that the BBWR all too often regarded the Women's Union as merely a ladies' auxiliary group and that it frequently "pushed to the side, disregarded, fought" the union's initiatives.[107] Moraczewska had hoped that the union, working as the partner of the BBWR, would be part of something important: "We wanted to participate in the moral rebirth of a nation poisoned by the venom of slavery . . . we wanted Poland to become a Piedmont for the renaissance of great universal ideas." She lamented that "the values present in women's collective will" were not being adequately harnessed by the political incarnation of the sanacja.[108]

As in the wider society, the confidence of some union women in the abilities of the BBWR to effect the anticipated sanacja began to falter just a few years into the new era. After all, there were no visible signs of moral rebirth, of political and social harmony, or of a vastly increased social welfare state. Perhaps most significant, it remained unclear into the late 1920s and early 1930s what the sanacja stood for, either politically, socially, or economically; the sanacja favored rhetorical appeals to lofty goals over concrete policy initiatives. According to Moraczewska, the BBWR was selling out and was slowly becoming a reactionary rather than a progressive force. Historians of the sanacja have argued that in fact the BBWR was at bottom a conservative grouping and that it became so focused on maintaining its power that it failed to address adequately the many social and economic issues that needed attention.[109]

But perhaps the most serious point of conflict arose over what Moraczewska called the BBWR's "mistaken politics," best reflected in the Brześć (Brest
Litovsk) affair of 1930.[110] The arrest and mistreatment of political opposition
members in the months preceding the elections of November 1930 did more
than anything else to make many in Poland, including many of the women in
the union, question their relationship to the BBWR and the ruling camp. Brześć
caused a major caesura in sanacja-era Poland and cost the sanacja both political
support and moral authority for the remainder of the Second Republic. Not-
withstanding the reservations of Moraczewska and some other union members
about Brześć, however, the organization showed a united, pro-BBWR front for
the so-called Brześć elections of 1930. The Women's Union resurrected the
Women's Democratic Election Committee to form the Women's Organizations' Election Committee (Komitet Wyborczy Organizacji Kobiecych). This
new Election Committee, under the leadership of Moraczewska, was composed
of a number of prosanacja women's groups, including the Women's Union, the
Preparation of Women for the Defense of the Country, the Women's League,
and the Organization of Women with Higher Education; together these organizations campaigned for the BBWR list generally, but especially on behalf of
the women on that list.[111] Some of the committee's main activists included
Halina Jaroszewiczowa, Jadwiga Próchnicka, Jadwiga Maleczewska, Hanna
Hubicka, Maria Garczyńska, and of course, Moraczewska.[112]

By imprisoning the opposition just months before the November 1930
elections, punishing any attempts to mount a sustained opposition to the
BBWR and orchestrating other election "irregularities," the sanacja camp en-
sured that the BBWR would in fact secure a better majority in the government
than it had achieved in 1928. The BBWR won 247 Sejm seats and 76 Senate seats
(out of 444 and 111, respectively). Many commentators agreed that democracy
in Poland had become a complete farce in 1930 and that a Piłsudski dictatorship had been established. The prosanacja Women's Union was implicated in
the unsavory aspects of the 1930 elections, both because of its vocal support
for the Piłsudski camp and because eight women from the Women's Union,
Moraczewska included, were elected to the Sejm, and one was elected to the
Senate in 1930. Together, these elected women formed what became the
Women's Group within the BBWR club.[113]

Moraczewska was reproached by some of her associates, first for her si-
lence over Brześć and later for offering bland condemnations of the excesses

in which the Piłsudski camp had engaged, all the while maintaining an unwavering faith in Piłsudski and in the idea of sanacja. In a piece entitled "Naïveté, Hypocrisy, or Simply Cynicism?" one socialist activist, Stanisława Woszczyńska, commented that it was impossible to reconcile criticism of Brześć with continued support for the sanacja, as Moraczewska had attempted to do. Woszczyńska's views were published on January 13, 1931, in the socialist *Worker* (*Robotnik*), which, as the main voice of the Polish Socialist Party, had adopted a vigorous antisanacja position since shortly after the coup, as soon as it became clear that the May revolution, launched as it was by a former fellow traveler, would not constitute a "real" socialist revolution. Woszczyńska took Moraczewska to task for stopping short of launching a full-scale condemnation of the sanacja and also made it clear that she was addressing herself to all women who continued to support Piłsudski through the recent events.[114] Women, the implication was, had a moral duty to oppose the barbarity of the BBWR.

Moraczewska later wrote to the BBWR's president, Walery Sławek, stating her disapproval and the disapproval of "hundreds like me." She wrote that, as a committed member of "our camp," she had both the right and the responsibility "to call things by name and not to hide from anybody." "Mr. President!" Moraczewska wrote, "Everything that is decent, incorruptible, and independent is beginning to slip away from our camp." She regretted that "a strong hand" had become a popular term and practice supported by people of "weak ideas and moral value," and she lamented that the beautiful rhetoric of national unity "on which we leaned during the first elections to the Sejm in 1928, is melting away."[115] Not surprisingly, however, Moraczewska's complaint did not produce any discernible change in government methods. The BBWR continued to justify its brutality as necessary to proceed with the work of constitutional and political reform.

Brześć also had the effect of compounding certain internal problems that had developed within the Women's Union. The most prominent of these involved a cash deficit issue in the Wilno branch of the Union in the fall of 1930. The Wilno press, from the *Wilno Daily* (*Dziennik wileński*) to the *Wilno Express* (*Express wileński*), was alive with the story of how the local women's sanacja group was mired in a financial scandal.[116] The *Worker* talked about a "civil war" in the Women's Union and about the degree to which the affair had created a great deal of "bad blood" that reached into general sanacja circles.[117]

The details of the case suggest that the president of the Wilno branch, parliamentarian Janina Kirtiklisowa, blamed a 1930 financial shortfall of over three thousand zlotys on one Hanna Jabłońska, an administrative clerk at the union's Wilno office.[118] Feeling unfairly accused of having stolen or mismanaged funds, Jabłońska wrote to the union's main branch in Warsaw and asked it to launch an investigation, which it did. The investigation found no evidence to suggest that Jabłońska had misappropriated the money, and it further argued that Kirtiklisowa, as the president of the Wilno branch, was ultimately accountable for the shortfall in funds. Accusing Kirtiklisowa of having used her position as a parliamentarian (since the 1930 elections) and wife of an important official to create a little fiefdom in Wilno, and describing the Wilno offices as badly disorganized, the Warsaw main branch asked Kirtiklisowa to leave the union in June 1931. It also ordered her to repay the money that Jabłońska had been forced to put up as soon as she had been accused.[119]

In response, Kirtiklisowa demanded that the BBWR itself undertake a formal investigation and informed Jabłońska that she would not repay her the money.[120] The Revision Commission, the BBWR's investigating body, included Senator Evert, Judge F. Gwiżdż, parliamentarian J. Tyszkiewicz, Mrs. Drzewiecka (secretary of the main branch of the Women's Union), and Senator Hanna Hubicka. This commission concluded that there was not enough evidence to make a definitive ruling on the matter. They did note, however, that Kirtiklisowa was a valued servant of the Polish state and that she had faced an especially challenging job at the Wilno branch of the Women's Union. Though they ruled that Jabłońska had to be held responsible for the deficit, they added that it might have occurred from simple carelessness rather than malicious intent, and they concluded that the matter was, at bottom, an unfortunate mistake.[121] Kirtiklisowa, who was, after all, a Sejm member and the wife of a prominent public official, was cleared of all wrongdoing.[122] Moraczewska's loyalties were clear: she arranged for the Women's Union main branch to repay Jabłońska most of the money she had put up when the affair first broke.[123]

And it was in this fiasco that the seeds for Moraczewska's profound disappointment with the way in which women were participating in politics lay. These allegations of corruption, along with the women's continued support for the post-Brześć BBWR, made it difficult for Moraczewska to maintain that women were best able to inject a higher morality into the political landscape.

Moraczewska's confidence in women's abilities was even further undermined by the eruption in the early 1930s of a leadership struggle between herself and Maria Jaworska, another prominent activist and parliamentarian.[124] This conflict, which polarized the union into two rival camps, reflected certain personal tensions but also highlighted opposing views on the ideal relationship between the union and the BBWR. In contrast to Jaworska, Moraczewska was of the opinion that the existing political form of the sanacja was a perversion of Piłsudski's original noble intentions and that women would do best not to be associated with it. Moraczewska explained: "I was always concerned about maintaining the *purity* of the 'sanacja' of society, on whose health and moral vigor the development and future of the state depends."[125] From what she observed, any claims the BBWR made to purity and moral vigor were empty. She condemned the dogmatism of the BBWR and the undemocratic practices in which it had engaged, and she argued that people should be taught rather than forced to become good citizens.[126] For her part, Moraczewska regretted the conflicts that had erupted. She feared that they would tarnish the image of women's activism generally and would further contribute to the sense that women could not handle working together. Most important, she feared the public would conclude that arguments about women's higher morality were simply empty and could in no way be used as a justification for their active participation in the public sphere.[127]

From 1931, after Brześć and just as the new stage of constitutional reform was launched by the BBWR, Moraczewska again had cause to question her commitment to the BBWR and her faith in what the sanacja was achieving. While the BBWR organized debates about proposed changes to the constitution, the Women's Union also planned its own information sessions in which women were encouraged to participate; these generated heated discussions and polarized opinions. For her part, Moraczewska expressed her personal reservations about the direction in which the proposals were moving, and she was clear about objecting to the spirit of the new document. She feared that the position of the citizen in the state was not elaborated richly or clearly enough and that in general the proposals paid too much attention to rights and not enough to responsibilities.[128] Moraczewska slowly became even more convinced of the impossibility of making politics moral.

Moraczewska finally submitted to her conscience and stepped down as president of the Women's Union for Citizenship Work in December 1933.

Along with her most loyal supporters, Moraczewska completely severed her ties with the organization within a couple of years.[129] Under the leadership of Maria Jaworska—Moraczewska's former rival—(from February 1934), the new union had a comparatively problem-free relationship with the BBWR. Though they were occasionally driven to protest certain practices of the sanacja government,[130] in general this new Women's Union was steadfastly pro-government and became a sort of trusteeship of the BBWR.[131]

|||

Moraczewska was immensely disheartened by the Women's Union's lack of success in injecting morality into the political process and in showing that women exacted a higher moral standard. She expressed deep regret over the fact that women, through the Women's Democratic Election Committee, and then the Women's Union for Citizenship Work, had not succeeded in making Polish politics "more moral." And yet Moraczewska abandoned neither social and political activism nor her faith in a utopian conception of sanacja, especially in the sanacja's emphases on moral healing and its talk of inclusivity and community. In May 1935, the year Piłsudski died, Moraczewska formed the Women's Social Self-Help Organization (Samopomoc Społeczna Kobiet). Modeled closely on the Women's Union, Moraczewska's new organization aimed to provide a "school of citizenship for Poland's women."[132]

The Self-Help Organization was cautious about forming real ties to governmental bodies, but it ultimately did establish an affiliation with the successor to the BBWR, the Camp of National Unity (Obóz Zjednoczenia Narodowego). If the relationship of the Women's Union to the BBWR was controversial, the relationship of the Self-Help Organization to the Camp of National Unity was that much more contentious.[133] Moraczewska maintained faith in the idea of Piłsudski and of the call to fight for the imponderabilia.[134] She continued to hope, of course, that the end result of her work would be a better society, and she continued to believe that women's roles in this project were vitally important to its success. But she seemed to realize that the pursuit of these goals would constitute a long and arduous journey, one she might not see completed in her own lifetime. The much-talked-about concept of rebirth required, after all, a fundamental transformation of people themselves: *"The world of women must create new ethical canons, it must base itself . . .*

on a new, strong, and morally reborn person-citizen."[135] Like everything else in the Second Republic, these goals were left unfulfilled at the outbreak of the Second World War.

Did Moraczewska and the women with whom she worked during the sanacja era ever stand a chance of achieving the desired purification of Polish life and of bringing a moral revolution to the young state? The sanacja was a captivating utopian idea with great rhetorical potential, but ultimately its potential fell flat, and this failure is well reflected in the two groups examined here. First, it was difficult for these groups to serve a sanacja idea that was itself poorly defined; how, really, does one transform people, and what exactly would these transformed new citizens look like? Second, despite the union's impressive membership numbers, it was dominated by a small group of elite women who had the leisure to imagine a more ethical polity. In a period defined by economic uncertainty and social discord, these women did not ultimately offer the great masses of women any solace. Lastly, the women's association with the ruling clique was a double-edged sword. On the one hand, it was an entrée into a closed and powerful political circle; on the other, it forced the women to juggle a variety of not always compatible objectives; Moraczewska, for one, was acutely aware of these tensions.

That the Piłsudskiite women did not succeed in actually effecting the moral rebirth of the nation is no more surprising than that none of the mainstream sanacja political groups succeeded in realizing the same goal. Nevertheless, their efforts stand as a forceful illustration of Piłsudskiite women's depth of commitment to grand ideas and of their attempts to carve out a space for themselves within the grandest project of them all: the sanacja. In inserting women's own concerns and priorities into the sanacja landscape, they restyled the very nature of that project—or at least of its potential—and in doing so they encourage us to understand the sanacja in its widest possible scope and for its deepest utopian elements.

5 ⫼ The Play-Boy in the Sanacja Nation

THE LAST CHAPTER brings full circle this study of the ways in which the sanacja resonated in the cultural discourses of the Second Republic. As we saw in the first chapter, during the sanacja period some right-nationalist commentators linked their disdain for the sanacja political system with their abhorrence for so-called modern and anti-Polish cultural and moral expressions. The arguments generated at that time reflected competing visions of the nation and went to the very core of how different constituencies defined the notion of moral citizenship. As the nation's most inflammatory symbol of modernity, immorality, and anti-Polishness, Tadeusz Boy Żeleński (1874–1941) was an absolutely central symbol of the cultural sanacja.[1]

Though a medical doctor by training, Żeleński was a very well-known, engaging, and extremely controversial presence on the Polish cultural scene from the turn of the century through to the Second World War. He first achieved notoriety as a writer for the Green Balloon (Zielony Balonik) cabaret from 1905 to 1910; it was there that he developed his stage and pen name, Boy, and it was by this name that he was generally known to friends and foes alike for the duration of his life.[2] Boy was also a prolific theater critic and an accomplished translator of French literature; his admiration for French culture was well known. But Boy is perhaps best remembered as a gifted feuilleton writer, as an unusually talented and active social commentator or "social doctor" who observed few cultural and national taboos and indeed reveled in violating them.[3] It is Boy's identity as a feuilleton writer that has cemented his lasting reputation as a significant personality of the Second Republic.

The most notable of Boy's feuilleton pieces first appeared in the liberal *Morning Courier* (*Kurier poranny*) and in what many consider to have been the Second Republic's premier literary magazine for the left-liberal intelligentsia, the *Literary News* (*Wiadomości literackie*).[4] The height of Boy's journalistic and social activism and, it follows, the time during which he was vilified as a dangerous moral influence, dates from the late 1920s to the mid-1930s. During this period, Boy led what many called a sexual revolution in the Second Republic by advocating the right to civil marriage and to divorce and by supporting a woman's right to birth control and to safe and legal abortions. Boy was also instrumental in establishing Poland's first family planning clinic, popularly referred to as "Boy's clinic," in 1929,[5] and he was a founding member of a controversial journal called *Planned Life* (*Życie świadome*), which began publishing in 1932 and was devoted to exploring family planning, "free love," and eugenics. In addition, it was on Boy's inspiration that the progressive social reform group, the League for the Reform of Mores (Liga Reformy Obyczajów), was established in Poland in 1933 as a branch of the London-based World League for Sexual Reform.[6] In general, Boy opposed clericalism, condemned narrow nationalist sermonizing, mocked what he regarded as a pervasive Polish provincialism, and proclaimed, in the words of one critic, the "immorality in morality."[7]

For all these reasons, Boy was the bête noire of the Catholic-nationalist far right and was the perfect incarnation of sanacja (im)morality. The term *Boy's sanacja* emerged after the coup to register a link between the political sanacja that began in May 1926 and the so-called sexual revolution of which Boy was the undisputed leader.[8] It was precisely this blend of rhetoric and activism, so evident in Boy's career during the 1920s and 1930s, that singled him out for special opprobrium in certain circles and that elevated him above other foes of the right-nationalists, like the assimilated Jewish poet Julian Tuwim, well known for his satirical wit and for a quick readiness to mock the nationalist elements of Polish culture. By linking Boy to the sanacja, critics created a rhetorically powerful tool to deride simultaneously the actual political sanacja and an invented cultural sanacja that, they argued, the political caesura had occasioned and licensed. What critics perceived the Piłsudskiites to be doing in the formal political realm—threatening the very essence of some notion of Polishness—Boy was perceived to be doing in the realm of culture. Both the political sanacja and the cultural sanacja, according to critics, were reflections of a single threat.

This coupling of Boy and the sanacja is revealing. First, it shows that Boy's impact stretched far beyond a narrow cultural realm. Though Boy has never lacked notoriety, his writings and the causes to which he devoted himself are, strangely, still awaiting a more prominent place in the historical narratives of the Second Republic. Boy was much more than an unusually eloquent troublemaker; the specific forms of the controversies he stimulated, as we shall see, suggest a great deal about the mood of the era.[9] The coupling of Boy and the sanacja also suggests the need to rethink the very existence of separate political and cultural realms; contemporaries themselves were quick to collapse distinctions between these spheres and to argue passionately for the need to acknowledge reciprocity between political events and cultural trends. Given that the formal political sanacja lacked a clearly articulated political program, it was that much easier for critics to link it to a brewing cultural sanacja. The way Boy and the sanacja were manipulated by their opponents went to the core of contemporary ideas about what Poland was and should be and showed just how mobile the concept of "political" was in the Second Republic.

The Curtain Opens on Boy's Sanacja

Karol Koniński, a well-known critic, summarized the noxious effects of Boy's social activism and writings: "Boy says that it is stuffy [in Poland], so he opens the windows. But is he opening them to best advantage? Is he not opening the windows at the back of the house, facing the even stuffier, stinking outhouse?"[10] For Koniński, the changes Boy advocated in Polish society were profound, depraved, and threatening. He condemned Boy as a "hedonist" and asked readers whether it was really worth "diverting the whole direction of our civilization [and] devaluing the entire meaning of Christianity" in order to participate in what he referred to as Boy's sexual revolution. Poland had real political, economic, and social problems to contend with, and yet because of Boy's influence, all anyone wished to talk about, according to Koniński, was sex.[11]

National Thought feuilletonist Adolf Nowaczyński, who regularly offered scathing indictments of Boy, agreed. Nowaczyński complained that instead of devoting his admittedly numerous talents to good causes, Boy focused on topics that ranged from "copulation to problems of pederasty, Freudianism, planned parenthood, onanism, abortion, 'companionate marriages,' gays, prostitution, venereal disease clinics, and eros generally."[12]

Nowaczyński further observed that Boy had undergone a stunning transformation since his move from Kraków to Warsaw in the early 1920s: "Under . . . Belvedere he quickly became a poet of satire, a master of polemic."[13] Nowaczyński's reference to Belvedere invoked Piłsudski's residence in Warsaw and suggested, subtly, that under the sanacja governments, Boy experienced a new license.

Certainly, the trend toward immorality was a constituent feature of the "modern age," and similar complaints resonated across Europe and fed the pervasive moral crisis of the postwar era (see chapter 1). Critics, Nowaczyński included, recognized that Poland's encounters with modernity were not anomalous. But critics were also quick to point out that the sanacja had compounded the typical problems associated with modernity. Nowaczyński asked his readers not to believe that it was a mere coincidence that Boy had become so influential and popular during the sanacja era.[14] The position of Nowaczyński and a number of the writers associated with right-nationalist publications was that post-May or sanacja-era Poland had actively created an atmosphere in which Boy's antinationalism, "free thinking," and anti-Catholicism were possible and even encouraged. Nowaczyński coined the simple Polish-English catch-all *"moral in-sanacy"* to refer to a dangerous ("insane") trend in morality and link it to the sanacja's political presence.[15] In the hands of the sanacja's opponents, the very word *sanacja* became a powerful pejorative, a way of describing perversion, moral decay, and a wholesale attack on Polish culture, history, and religion. The cultural slump in which the Second Republic found itself had been transformed, in sanacja-era Poland, into a bona fide, widespread moral and cultural crisis.

Catholic-nationalist publicist Czesław Lechicki[16] devoted many years to exploring the nature of Boy's sanacja, which he defined as "the desire to replace family life with herd life, and Christian morality with the morality of the public house."[17] According to Lechicki, it was only during the sanacja period that Boy was able to unleash his evil and preach his immoral ideas and ways undeterred. Lechicki believed that May 1926 constituted a momentous date for Poland in more than a strictly political sense: "In the era . . . of the 'moral Sanacja,' Boy completely threw off his disguise and began his offensive."[18] Lechicki used the plainest possible language to link the emergence of the sanacja with Boy and to suggest that the political sanacja had released Boy from the constraints that until that point had bound him.

For Lechicki, the evolution was logical and predictable, as he considered it a basic fact that the political downfall of a nation dates from its moral downfall. Piłsudski was able to seize power simply because Poland was a mess on all fronts. Lechicki compared the effects of the moral depravity he saw everywhere around him—from a mania for the body, pornography, prurient film, and "unhealthy" journalism, to a generalized turning away from religious and national questions—to some powerful poison that caused weakness and ultimately impotence: "Like syphilis for the body, so is immorality for the soul."[19] The sanacja was able to remain in power, according to Lechicki, because Boy and a handful of others had emerged to subvert every last shred of morality and good sense that Poles possessed; Boy eroded the bases for good citizenship. Given what Lechicki believed was the pitiable state of Polish culture, it was all the more important, he contended, for people to speak out in defense of Polish Catholic morality.[20] In one year alone, Lechicki published three works outlining the immorality rampant in sanacja Poland; Boy figured prominently in each. Lechicki offered these published indictments as "manly displays of civil courage" and independent thinking, as "testaments of truth" and "expressions of Christian conscience."[21]

Adolf Nowaczyński would undoubtedly have regarded Lechicki as a second-rate intellectual, as part of the "half-intelligentsia," as the insult went.[22] Nowaczyński's condemnations of Boy displayed a nimble use of language and a clever manipulation of concepts.[23] In comparison, Lechicki's were melodramatic, shrill, and often pathetic in their embrace of simplistic notions of nationalist commitment and literal interpretations of the Bible to buttress any given position. And yet both Lechicki and Nowaczyński reserved special vitriol for Boy and understood him to be a symbol of a dangerous cultural tide that had erupted with the onset of the political sanacja. Both Nowaczyński and Lechicki believed that public opinion had to be organized so as to guarantee that Boy would be discredited successfully, and both waged a press campaign against Boy and immorality—and against the sanacja itself.

Central to understanding these vituperative condemnations of Boy and the claims that he constituted a plague on Polish culture was a wider concern about the role of the intellectual in the nation. Opponents held Boy up as the most egregious example of a perverted Polish intellectual who had forsaken his historic obligation to the nation to lead by example and to serve as Poland's conscience. If ever Poland needed a conscience, it was during what Nowaczyński described as the contemporary era of "political prostitution." Nowaczyński condemned Boy as a "slum intellectual" who turned his back brazenly on the nation and embraced the role of "apologist for sexual prostitution."[24]

Nowaczyński further reminded his readers that moral irresponsibility on the part of Poland's elite had once resulted in the partitions.[25] The specter of the dismemberment of the state was commonly raised to argue that the partition era was the repository of some great moral lesson that the Second Republic had better absorb. Literary critic Dr. Mieczysław Piszczkowski argued that the partitions had created an atmosphere of "moral hypocrisy" that fundamentally perverted people's good judgment. So severe was this perversion that many years later, in an independent Poland, people were still affected by it and embraced what Piszczkowski called Boy's "catechism of pansexualism."[26] The real heart of modernity, Piszczkowski offered, was to be found not in "radio, zeppelins, dances, Americanization, the League of Nations, women's suits, four-times-divorced women, the *Literary News*, free thinking, military dictatorship, and so on" but rather was situated in Catholic and nationalist approaches to culture and politics.[27] Piszczkowski slipped in a reference to Piłsudski's military coup alongside references to standard markers of the modern age and of immorality; in doing so, he underscored for his readers that all the aforementioned evils were part of the same trend. Like Lechicki and Nowaczyński, Piszczkowski believed that in postpartition Poland, Boy had become a potent symbol of the intellectual and moral corruption that could again lead to the state's downfall.[28]

Journalism in the Sanacja's Golden Age

In general terms, these were the charges leveled by the Catholic-nationalist right against Boy. But critics recognized that Boy was just one of many voices that needed to be battled, and they understood that immoral ideas appeared in many different publications. Critics therefore developed a shorthand for describing those publications that subscribed to views that offended them: *sanacja journal*. In the first instance, this term was used to describe publications that showed varying degrees of allegiance to Piłsudski, the coup, and the notion of a sanacja; they included the key organs of the Piłsudskiites, like the *Polish Gazette* (*Gazeta polska*) and the *Way* (*Droga*).[29] The term *sanacja journal* also referred, however, to publications that were not overt mouthpieces for political positions and that seldom even discussed the major political issues of the day. The term referred, that is, to periodicals with which Boy and other intellectuals of a similar left-liberal persuasion were associated.[30] *Sanacja journal* conveyed that the editorial staff, writers, and readers of a given periodical embraced "modern" ideas, which included, as Piszczkowski had suggested, everything from provocative dances and masculine fashions for women to divorce and, apparently, military dictatorships. It conveyed a rejection of the primary association between Polishness and Catholicism and revealed something about a paper's position vis-à-vis the nation, religion, and morality. According to Nowaczyński, sanacja journals, quite simply, "demoralized and depraved the public."[31] On one occasion, Nowaczyński referred to the *Morning Courier*—the journal in which Boy first began publishing on sexual and moral reform, and one generally associated with the liberal, democratic, and progressive wing of the Piłsudski camp—as "the organ of Lucifer."[32] On another, Nowaczyński described the *Republic's Tomorrow* (*Jutro rzeczypospolitej*) as marked by "a hatred of God, but a love of Boy."[33] Father Jan Piwowarczyk, editor of the Christian Democrats' *Voice of the Nation* (*Głos narodu*), referred generally to the "putrefied moral liberalism that seeps out from the government press."[34]

Though much "immoral literature"[35] and many sanacja journals circulated in Poland during this period, arguably the worst offender, the right-nationalist camp agreed, was the *Literary News*. Many of Boy's most controversial feuilletons about civil marriage, divorce, and abortion rights appeared in the *News*. It was without question the leading literary and high-culture journal of the interwar period: it was willfully modern and "Western," and openly modeled itself on the French *Nouvelles littéraires*.[36] The *News* was founded in 1924 by Mieczysław Grydzewski (who also edited the paper for the duration of the interwar period)[37] and by Antoni Borman as a nonpartisan journal devoted to exploring all issues relating to culture, broadly conceived. During its first year, three thousand copies of each issue were published, and this figure reached a height of fifteen thousand in the 1930s. Its readership, however, is estimated to have reached thirty to forty thousand, as a single copy was passed from person to person.[38]

The *News* originally refused formal affiliation with any political party or camp and published authors from all positions along the political spectrum, including the nationalist right. By the late 1920s, however, during a period marked by increasingly tense cultural and political antagonisms, the *News* became ever more associated with left-liberalism. It earned a reputation for propagating a vehement dislike of the right-Catholic-nationalist factions within the Polish political and cultural landscape and for mocking Polish national traditions.[39] The *News* formed, in a sense, the antithesis of the National Democrats' *National Thought* (see chapter 1), with which Nowaczyński, Rembieliński, Wasilewski, and Świętochowski, among other trenchant cultural and political commentators, were associated.[40] With notable Polish and foreign contributors,[41] the *Literary News* was read by everyone who wished to remain alive to the progressive intellectual and cultural trends in Poland and across Europe.[42] Many of the *News*'s contributors had earned a much-prized spot at a special table at Warsaw's exclusive Café Ziemiańska, where the elite writers and poets of the day gathered.[43]

For these reasons, some contemporary commentators argued that the *Literary News* embodied a dangerous anti-Polishness and perverse immorality and, as a result, that it constituted a threat to the integrity and independence of the nation.[44] Nowaczyński called the *Literary News* "the News of the Indifferent," referring to the paper's unwillingness to take the "right" stand on political questions; he warned that nothing less than the fate of the nation was at stake.[45] One Father Charczewski referred to the *News* as the *Literary-Gynecological News* to underline what he believed was the journal's obsession with matters of sex, while Lechicki called it the *Gynecological-Venereal News*.[46] As such, the *News* had cemented a reputation as a disseminator of immorality and as the mouthpiece of Masons, Jews, and Bolsheviks.[47]

Significantly, the *News* was also charged by some opponents with political opportunism and an easy allegiance to the ruling sanacja clique. There was absolutely no ambiguity in post-May Poland that the *Literary News*, despite its avowals of apoliticism and although the journal often published authors associated with all points along the political spectrum, was sympathetic to the Piłsudski camp. A number from the *News* circle had been part of Piłsudski's wartime Legions, and many had participated specifically in the Piłsudski-led First Brigade. Certain individuals like Julian Tuwim and Antoni Słonimski were known to socialize regularly with top-rank Piłsudskiites like General Bolesław Wieniawa-Długoszowski (1881–1942).[48] It was not until the Brześć affair of 1930 that some members of this group, including Boy, severed their ties with the Piłsudski camp.[49] Others remained devoted Piłsudskiites even after Brześć had greatly reduced the credibility of the sanacja camp. Such was the case with Juliusz Kaden-Bandrowski (1885–1944), a notable figure in the interwar literary world and widely regarded to be, as one critic stated, "the little Piłsudski of literature."[50]

By and large, the actual contributors to and associates of the *News,* including Boy, were not part of a group that participated actively in political parties or spin-off political organizations, and members of the *News* circle were not the sort to run for political office. For its part, the *Literary News* spent little time analyzing the political scene directly.[51] From reading the *News,* for instance, one would initially have had no idea that in May 1926 the constitutionally elected government of the Second Republic was defeated by a military coup waged by an ex-socialist military man who had managed to arouse the passions, at least initially, of socialists, centrists, veterans, and much of the left-liberal intelligentsia.[52]

All this did not mean, however, that the *News* circle was apolitical, in a narrow sense of politics, or that those associated with the journal were indifferent or oblivious to politics, the fate of the nation, or the state of culture, as their critics charged. To Boy and his like-minded friends that constituted Poland's left-liberal intelligentsia, Piłsudski represented a preferred alternative to the National Democrats. Boy and many of the others who were associated with the *Literary News* were doubtlessly relieved in May 1926 when Piłsudski seized power from the right-nationalist Chjeno-Piast coalition. They could believe that the assumption of power by a military leader supported by at least part of the army represented, ironically, the victory of a democratic Poland and the best hope for liberal-democratic and secular ideas to flourish. According to this way of thinking, the coup constituted a morally just act waged against the murderers of President Gabriel Narutowicz and against a "clerical-Endek" invasion of Poland.[53]

It is from this perspective that one can understand how and why Boy was able to write, only a month after the coup, to longtime friend and women's rights activist Helena Staniewska, "You have no idea the extent to which, since the May coup, and despite everything that was painful and tragic in the event, the air has become easier to breathe; this must be a sign that something is changing for the better."[54] It was precisely this potential for change that both sides—the Piłsudskiites and the left-liberal intelligentsia on the one hand,

and the National Democratic and right-Catholic-nationalist camp on the other—saw in the political caesura of 1926 and the ensuing sanacja. The former group approached this potential eagerly and with positive anticipation. In contrast, the nationalist right condemned the potential for great change, found it vexing and threatening, and so determined to resist it with all available resources. According to the nationalist right, Boy embodied the worst of sanacja Poland, and his sexual revolution threatened the moral and religious foundations on which they believed the nation to be built; Boy was a brilliant incarnation of the potential of the sanacja. In taking advantage of the opportunities opened up by 1926 and the ensuing disempowerment of the nationalist right, Boy and the left-liberal circle of intellectuals of which he was a part led their own version of a sanacja of Polish culture.

The Play-Boy Betroths Miss Sanacja

The fact that Boy chose to write on a variety of sensitive topics, that he was associated, however loosely and indirectly, with the Piłsudskiites, and that he was an especially visible member of the left-liberal intelligentsia marked him as an easy target for attack. But if Boy's associations and ideas were controversial, so too were the specific literary forms he adopted to elaborate his views. One of the most vulgar symbols of the new position that journalism occupied in independent Poland, according to some observers, was the feuilleton, a short and light collection of observations and impressionistic vignettes appealing to the general reader.[55] Boy was widely regarded as a master of the feuilleton.

The notable historian of literature, Stanisław Pigoń (1885–1968), granted Boy the dubious distinction of being a "feuilleton virtuoso." Pigoń said that in his feuilletons Boy wove together anecdotes, distorted their facts and emphasis, and generally manipulated and misled people.[56] Popular interwar writer Jalu Kurek (1904–83) ascribed Boy's success to the short feuilleton form itself. The lightness of the form added insult to injury, Kurek argued, for it failed to pay adequate respect to the serious and all-important national issues that were treated therein.[57] Lechicki called the feuilleton form Boy's primary weapon in his "game of intellectual golf"[58] and added that in using the form, Boy failed to pay due respect to serious national issues.[59]

Eminent interwar literary critic Karol Irzykowski also condemned Boy in his highly controversial *Little Darling* (1933) for raising the feuilleton and anecdote forms above scientific studies, history, and fact. Irzykowski's work was a wholesale attack on Boy, the "pornographic" content of his writing, and his writing style. Irzykowski condemned Boy categorically as a pernicious influence on national literature generally. He objected to the fact that Boy was popular, that Boy enjoyed his notoriety and, unbefitting to an intellectual, that he advertised his writing and targeted "everyone" as a potential consumer of his ideas.[60]

Modern-day literary critic Theodor Fontane feminizes the feuilleton form as "an ornament, a witty illustration; it is coquettish and wants to please, captivate, and conquer, but it does not at all intend to convince, once and for all."[61] Like the form itself, Boy's writings were derided by certain contemporaries as reflecting the supposedly irrelevant concerns of a woman; they were frivolous and unnecessary and therefore jeopardized the nation. And yet, like a coquettish woman, Boy's feuilletons were dangerous because they flirted with and titillated readers, aroused their curiosity and awakened their base instincts, leaving them eager for more. With his feuilletons, Boy committed "moral prostitution."[62]

Regrettable though it was, the fact nevertheless remained that Boy had captivated a mass following. As Nowaczyński described it, "the Green Balloon appears like a huge zeppelin flying over the ocean of reader-admirers."[63] Throughout the "sanacja nation," as Nowaczyński referred to Poland, Boy enjoyed cultural clout.[64] The *Voice of the Nation*'s Father Piwowarczyk relayed his dismay upon reading in the progovernment *Wilno Courier (Kurier wileński)* that Boy was "a minister of education in partibus."[65] Piwowarczyk further suggested that certain sanacja circles (with the exception of the conservative wing of the BBWR) expressed clear sympathies for Boy's ideas and "defended the affairs of Boy Żeleński as though they were their own, with a great output of energy and passion."[66]

In an effort to undermine Boy as an intellectual and social activist, opponents identified the groups that were most likely to respond positively to Boy's writings. It went without saying that only the "self-educated or uneducated sanacja intelligentsia" liked Boy.[67] But critics offered a further description of who it was that liked Boy: it was women, who lacked "reasonableness" and who by "nature" were flippant, weak willed, and feebleminded, that took

Boy seriously.[68] The Play-Boy, Nowaczyński stated, using the English words, captivated women.[69] Similarly, novelist Kurek emphasized that it was "hysterical women" who were most attracted to Boy's immoral ideas.[70] Lacking men's direction, and with their own minds and spirits "upset by the war," women became especially vulnerable to the influence of one Boy Żeleński, and embraced Boy's preaching that "abortion and divorce are the eighth heaven of Muhammad."[71] Yet another commentator stated that a typical female supporter of Boy (*kobieta boyowska*) "was a bitch and only a bitch. Her purpose was . . . to satisfy sexual appetite."[72]

Christian Democratic publicist and dramatist Stanisław Miłaszewski (1886–1944), writing in the *Republic* in 1929, feminized not just the readers of Boy, but Boy himself. Miłaszewski suggested that Boy self-consciously played the coquette and enjoyed the attention heaped upon him. For his part, Boy played up to the stereotypes: "A friendly commotion has developed around me, like around a young woman about whom there is a rumor that she is promiscuous. Time and again, the city or the town moves closer to me. . . . And me? . . . With a smile . . . I whisper: 'I don't know . . . maybe . . . sometime'—which really means: 'Some more, gentlemen, some more.'"[73] What critics believed Boy advocated, and what they said the sanacja nation licensed, implicitly or explicitly, was feminine immodesty and a conception of womanhood that was removed from, and indeed mocked, nationalist imperatives.

Boy considered it his duty to do precisely this, and he reveled in the controversy he aroused, even referring to himself as "the anti-Christ . . . with the pseudonym Boy."[74] In a letter to one of his critics, Boy stated that he tended to get "nervous" when he failed to arouse passionate reactions (including critical ones) in others: "I begin to fear . . . that I am no longer necessary for the nation. . . . This is my role. To be [an] antidote for your charming lies."[75] Perhaps the most well known and shocking of Boy's views on contemporary women and mothers—and, implicitly, on the state and direction of Polish culture—was revealed in this statement: "I prefer today's mother, who, returning from a dance, wakes her son and tells him how much fun she had. . . . And we can be sure that when this little son finds himself in the citadel [prison] for dabbling in communism, she will be able to save him less often, but also all the more effectively. . . . Good riddance to the prewar mother!"[76]

Statements like this drew vitriolic criticism from many corners. Publicist Izabela Moszczeńska-Rzepecka (1864–1941) wrote a rebuttal to Boy's vision of the ideal postwar mother by reaching, as many did, to the partition days and to examples of women's tremendous national devotion in a time of collective need.[77] In Moszczeńska's estimation, the result of analyzing serious issues "from a cabaret point of view" and of women spending their nights at dances instead of at home with their husbands and children, would be a future in which one generation after another was lost to communism until finally the Polish nation itself would cease to exist.[78]

As suggested in chapter 1, a number of critics made women's roles in the independent state a key component of their analyses of contemporary culture and politics. Aleksander Świętochowski, for example, pointed repeatedly to the ridiculous situation Poland found itself in at the end of the first decade of independence: women in the republic possessed all the rights of full citizenship and yet they continued to act "like women" and thereby threatened the collectivity. Instead of witnessing a process whereby the "emancipationists" were transformed into "persons" in the postwar world, Świętochowski regretted that the opposite had in fact occurred and that women were wasting their newly won freedoms.[79] The result of this would be, as one (female) critic offered (recalling a trope that was so dominant in French culture of the day), a "masculinization of women . . . à la garçonne." Victor Margueritte's novel *La garçonne* (*Chłopczyca*), published in France in 1922, presented the prototype of the new postwar woman: she was young, beautiful, independent, "modern," and willful, and she displayed little concern for getting married and raising children. The concept of la garçonne embodied a new era in which traditional gender roles had lost all meaning.[80] France—"the El Dorado of immorality," according to Lechicki—was already contending with the "moral gangrene" that had gripped its women, and he feared it would be the entire nation that would pay the price.[81] Nowaczyński warned that Boy, "the Polish Margueritte," was helping to fashion a Polish prototype for la garçonne and thus actively threatened Poland's culture, integrity, and, ultimately, its independence.[82] For critics like Lechicki and Nowaczyński, women constituted the weak point in the Polish bulwark against degeneracy and moral decay.

What made the situation in Poland all the more dangerous was the existence of the sanacja. To dramatize the connection between Boy and the political sanacja, Nowaczyński invented a "Miss Sanacja" (he used the English term) and offered her up as the perfectly perverted Polish woman:[83] she valued the latest fashions and ways of apprehending the world, she went to dances and knew the latest steps, she read Boy's feuilletons, and, of course, she rejected tried-and-true Polish-Catholic approaches to life. The way in which women assumed the posture of a Miss Sanacja became so important to these commentators because they believed that women, as mothers, played a vital role in forging a sense of national consciousness and good morality. At the most basic level, Miss Sanacja had forsaken her apparently natural and God-given roles and had rejected her obligations to the Polish nation. This new sanacja-era woman, according to Nowaczyński, took as her model the likes of film star Hanka Ordonówna rather than a true national model in the style of Emilia Plater, a national heroine of the great November uprising of 1830–31 against the Russians. In flaunting her sexual morality, Miss Sanacja thumbed her nose at good and proper citizenship and the ideals of civic virtue.[84] Miss Sanacja was the antithesis of the ideal moral citizen that critics had hoped would emerge in the Second Republic.

With the simple terms Play-Boy and Miss Sanacja, Nowaczyński drew evocative links between private and public morality, between Boy, modern (and hence immoral) women, and the political sanacja that ruled Poland. These links provided convenient and rhetorically effective points of focus. Whereas before the coup critics talked in vague generalities about how the war and the introduction of modern ideas had perverted good tradition, after the coup they could look specifically to the sanacja political camp for having allowed immorality to flourish undeterred. During the height of Boy's sexual revolution, critics could further attach their vitriol to a particular individual and transform him symbolically into a living incarnation of sanacja-era depravity.

Many interesting visual representations of these connections come from satirical cartoons of the period; cartoons are generally useful for representing moods, crystallizing opinions, and offering judgements.[85] The images depicted and the messages offered in cartoons reflect the modes of understanding dominant in society at a given moment. By far the best and the most successful satirical paper of the interwar period was the *Warsaw Barber* (*Cyrulik warszawski*) (1926–34). The *Warsaw Barber* was established as a weekly in Warsaw in June 1926 by individuals in the Skamander literary-artistic circle, many of whom were also involved with the *Literary News*. In particular, Jan Lechoń and Piłsudskiite Col. Adam Koc were instrumental in bringing the *Warsaw Barber* to life. Though it spared no one and nothing from its sharp tongue, it was widely known that those who ran and worked for the magazine were politically and intellectually tied to the sanacja camp and that they received funds from the sanacja government.[86]

In a cartoon by Maja Berezowska, a regular contributor to the *Warsaw Barber* and perhaps the Second Republic's most renowned cartoonist, a police officer issues a ticket to a couple apparently interrupted in a sylvan tryst. The officer seems bored by the routine procedure, the woman ashamed, the man self-satisfied. In the distance we see other lovers who will undoubtedly receive, or have just received, a similar visit from the officer. The caption reads, "Frequent May events," which contemporary readers would have understood as a play on "May events" (*wypadki majowe*), a common name for the 1926 coup.[87] It is instructive to read this cartoon with an eye to the debates about sexual morality that were raging in Poland at the time it was produced, at the height of the press war, in 1932, between Boy and his critics. The cartoon is effective precisely because people recognized that the coup had occasioned, whether in reality or only rhetorically, more than just a political revolution. At the same time, it is tempting to see in this cartoon a reminder of the growing power of the regime and of the sanacja's slide, since 1930, toward authoritarianism. The police officer in Berezowska's cartoon suggests that no area of life could escape the watchful eye of the government.[88]

The link to the political sanacja was never far away. Sometimes it was explicit, as with the direct reference to the May events. In others it was subtler and focused more narrowly on the general state of moral decay that the sanacja government was apparently doing nothing to stop.[89] In a cartoon with the caption "The Diplomatic Body," a sexy modern woman, the quintessence of a woman who supported Boy, is surrounded by three adoring older men, political figures drawn from the Second Republic itself.[90] The implication is that sanacja politicians were themselves benefiting from and participating in the new morality and secretly supported Boy in his sexual revolution. The government was part of the problem in more ways than one. To battle Boy's sexual revolution, therefore, one had also to target the political regime; each sanacja, the political and the cultural, reinforced and supported the other. Nowaczyński summed up the connections clearly when he referred to Boy as being "tightly connected to the sanacja mentality."[91]

The Sanacja, Jews, Boyshevism, and Bolshevism

The nationalist far right in the Second Republic commonly used a very particular string of words—Jewish, Bolshevik, Masonic, socialist, communist, godless, moral relativist—to impugn an idea, trend, person, or political reality. The words condemned anything and everything perceived to be too liberal, modern, and "un-Polish"; together they formed one large and undifferentiated category of perversion and barbarity.[92] The descriptors became even more popular and meaningful during the politically polarized sanacja period. In the post-May period, *sanacja* evolved to occupy its own place alongside Masonic, Jewish, and Bolshevik.

Boy was accused of many different kinds of assaults on Poland, and one of the explanations his opponents offered was that he was a Mason. Freemasonry had existed in Poland since the eighteenth century, and the Masons maintained a presence in the Polish lands throughout the interwar period. Masonry in the Second Republic did include Catholics but was better known to be a base for atheists, liberals, assimilated Jews, and bourgeois intellectuals who supported the Piłsudskiite political grouping and espoused left-liberal views.[93] The Masonic program was based on a belief in republicanism, a secular society, and respect for national minorities.[94] Boy was well aware that the label Mason was regularly applied to him and that his views were considered to be Masonic. In one feuilleton, Boy stated clearly that he was not a Mason and joked that once he had considered joining a Masonic lodge but was discouraged when he could not easily find out where one signed up.[95]

The *Knight of the Immaculate*, a Catholic journal, suggested that all Masons celebrated Piłsudski's coup and enjoyed a close relationship to the post-May political camp. The *Knight* condemned Masons—just as it condemned the sanacja government—as "enemies of morality, enemies of the Immaculate."[96] From the *Knight's* perspective, both threatened to distort traditional Polish-Catholic values and to replace them with secular approaches to all aspects of life.[97]

Secularism and immorality—and thus the sanacja, according to some critics—were perhaps even better associated with the Jews. For their part, Boy's critics were eager to ascribe Jewishness to Boy. Publicist Lechicki, for example, invented a distant Jewishness for Boy (he suggested that Boy's mother, Wanda z Grabowskich Żeleńska, was a descendant of the Frankists)[98] and used this to make sense of the apparent anti-Polishness in Boy's ideas.[99] Dr. Kazimierz Morawski (1884–1944), a publicist associated with the conservative Warsaw-based *Catholic Review* (*Przegląd katolicki*), proposed a distinction between a "born" Jew and an "artificial" Jew.[100] This was akin to the distinction between an actual Jewish presence and a "Jewish influence" in the nation; both were dangerous and constituted, as another critic suggested, nothing short of a "fourth partition of Poland."[101] A writer in the left-liberal *Republic's Tomorrow* explained that the nationalist right wing simply could not reconcile Boy's ideas and actions with Polishness. To buttress their beliefs in certain fundamentals, the nationalists were compelled, therefore, to invent the category of artificial Jew to describe those ethnic Poles who transgressed against the nation.[102] Critics wielded the category with abandon to describe depraved trends, people, and governments. This distinction between real and artificial Jews was central to the way in which the epithet Jew functioned in the Second Republic.

Reaching to Jews to ascribe blame for unwelcome trends and developments possessed a long and ignoble history, not only in Poland but throughout Europe, where Jews had long formed the classic Other. European racism created categories of "inferior races" onto which antinational traits were inscribed; for these purposes, Jews assumed the characteristics of a race. Jews were categorized as sexual degenerates and were said to possess an uncontrollable and selfish sexual lust that could not be reconciled with ideal expressions of national masculinity and femininity.[103] According to some National Democrats, antisemitism was absolutely integral to Polish national survival. Jews, both real and artificial, were a foreign and unwelcome element within Poland that, if not battled assiduously, would put the state in peril.[104] In addition to the sexual perversion and immorality attributed to Jews in general, Jews in Poland had long been associated with exploitation, dishonesty, rivalry, alienness, and, most basically, anti-Polishness.[105]

An interesting visual depiction of these connections appears on the cover of a book entitled *Women's Danger* (*Niebezpieczeństwo kobiece*) (1929). A modern woman, wearing high heels and a miniskirt and sporting short hair, is being led by a ring and rope attached to her nose toward a building called Paradisus. The man leading her is a Jewish soldier. The image is all the more resonant because the woman seems oblivious to her impending fate; she is engrossed in her reflection in the mirror she is carrying.[106] The image would have reinforced to viewers that Jews had perverted good mores and good sense thoroughly and completely, such that even obvious displays of Jewish malfeasance were going unnoticed, allowing ultimately for the eventual takeover of Poland by a Jewish onslaught.

The inauguration of the sanacja regime helped focus and foster this antisemitism. Though Polish antisemitism was at its most virulent in the mid- and late 1930s, references to Jews as a pernicious foreign influence in Poland, calls to boycott Jewish businesses and to purge Jews from Poland, existed throughout the Second Republic. Many notable and well-respected politicians, like Roman Dmowski, and indeed many of the writers associated with *National Thought*, were known to believe passionately in the need to resolve the "Jewish problem" in Poland.[107] The political sanacja, in part because it included a number of assimilated Jews among its ranks and because it failed to actively protect a Catholic Poland, provided its opponents with an opportunity to represent the political sanacja as a "Jewish institution" and as having created a Judeophilic mood in Poland. The way critics represented the sanacja—as a product and a reflection of the Judaization of Polish culture—created yet another basis for antisemitism.

Time and again, critics of the sanacja made the statement that Jews were the sanacja's most eager supporters. The pro–National Democratic and anti-sanacja *Poznań Courier* (*Kurier poznański*) referred to "the Sanacja-Jewish flirt."[108] The English term *moral-in-Semity* emerged as a variation of the oft-used *moral insanity*,[109] but went further and implicated the Jews in the immorality that was acknowledged in right-nationalist circles to be rampant in sanacja Poland.[110] Nowaczyński stated plainly that Boy was popular among the "Jews and the sanacja elite," and he named Jews as being particularly susceptible to the sanacja sham and as lapping up Boy's ideas.[111] The influential National Democratic *Warsaw Gazette* stated that the sanacja's failure to tackle head-on the "Jewish problem" in Poland was one of its most serious shortcomings.[112] Election posters of the sanacja opposition regularly equated a vote for the sanacja camp as a vote against Poles and the Catholic Church, against tradition and history, and a vote for the Jews.[113] One Catholic-nationalist poster created for the 1928 elections warned of the "invasion of Poland by Jews" and stated plainly why citizens should not vote for the BBWR: "The sanacja has given Jews every possibility to realize their efforts to control Polish culture and to cut it off from its essential Polish elements."[114]

Shortly after the May coup, one *National Thought* columnist lamented that the sanacja version of moral rebirth would see the country taken over by a Jewish presence, and this, in turn, portended a time when Poles would be second-class citizens in their own country.[115] Another *National Thought* commentator, Stefan Sacha, stated plainly, "The sanacja is today mostly a force that tears apart existing ties of national, religious, and social life."[116] Central to Sacha's criticism was that the sanacja exhibited clear anti-Catholic and pro-Jewish tendencies.[117] Sacha wondered at the fact that sanacja supporters agreed with the idea of a "Palestine for the Jews," while ironically they rejected the motto, "Poland for the Poles."[118]

Aleksander Świętochowski echoed this way of thinking too, concluding that the situation was now so grave that Poland "received the blessing of only one power: the Palestinian rabbi."[119] Reflecting on the years that had passed since the inception of the sanacja, one writer for the virulently anti-semitic *At-the-Base-of-Wawel Watchword* (*Hasło podwawelskie*) described the sanacja period as one in which once noble ideas like Poland, Pole, and nation had developed negative associations: "We must rehabilitate the Polishness that has been defiled and violated by the Jews."[120]

The journal that best represented the supposed and much-feared Jewish-sanacja takeover of Polish culture was, not surprisingly, the *Literary News*. The *News* was vilified by the nationalist right for propagating immorality and for simultaneously supporting the political sanacja, as argued above. The National Democrats' *Warsaw Gazette* called the *Literary News* a singularly effective promoter of immoral views precisely because the *News* was "published and edited by Jews."[121] Although the popular image of the *News* was that it was "Judeophilic,"[122] and although many assimilated Jews contributed regularly to editions of the *Literary News*, specifically "Jewish issues" seldom appeared on its pages; it was simply not that paper's style to focus on particularistic regional or ethnic questions.[123] What critics referred to when they condemned the *News* as a Jewish paper had more to do with the kinds of questions its writers raised and with its general disinclination to foster a particular vision of Polish nationalism that would have affirmed the connections between Polishness and Catholicism.

One special issue of the *News* reveled in this reputation. The title of this special edition was *Jadą Mośki literackie*, which means *The Literary Jews are Coming*, or *Here Come the Literary Moshes* [Jews].[124] The four-page satirical issue (not mailed to regular subscribers) came out shortly after the May coup and was dated "Sunday, every July, 1926." *Jadą Mośki* sounds like *Wiadomości* (*News*). This reinforced the already well-established and culturally familiar stereotype that linked left-liberal politics (for which the *News* was known) and Jews (as in the phrase "liberal-Judeophilic")[125] and cleverly invoked the much-talked-about "Jewish invasion" of Poland. The editor of this special issue of the *News* was given as Eljasz Zielski from Lwów, though it remains unclear who actually wrote the issue and whether it was created by the *News* circle itself—by Julian Tuwim for instance, on whom speculation has fallen—or whether it was the work of antisemites. At any rate, the issue mocked all the leading poets associated with *News* and transformed itself into all that the critics accused the *News* of being.[126]

Never far behind the designation Jewish was the label Bolshevik.[127] Boy and many of his like-minded colleagues were in fact genuinely intellectually interested in certain cultural and social aspects of the Soviet communist experiment, and the *Literary News* sometimes wrote about aspects of communism on its pages, especially in 1933 and 1934.[128] It was thus extremely easy for critics to deride Boy as a Bolshevik and the *Literary News* as the home base for Bolshevik operations in Poland. But while Bolshevik describes a person and an act, it was also used more generally to convey an attitude toward certain national, moral, and cultural questions.[129] Just as Jews were divided into real Jews and ethical Jews, so Bolsheviks were similarly divided. It therefore mattered little that Boy was not an actual Bolshevik. One columnist defined "de facto Bolsheviks" according to "mores and views on God, the person, the nation, and the state."[130] The columnist further employed the term "ethical Bolshevik" to describe *News* writer, staunch Piłsudskiite, and novelist Juliusz Kaden-Bandrowski: "a lack of moral feeling masks communist ideology."[131]

Nowaczyński defined Bolshevism's counterpart in the realm of culture and morality and, as became his trademark, introduced a neologism into the Polish language of the period.[132] Boyshevism (*Boyszewizm*) suggested a clear association between Boy and Bolsheviks and underscored the fear that the Boy phenomenon was real, dangerous, and spreading quickly. Nowaczyński stated: "Bolshevism is a worldview and an anticipation. Boyshevism is a fad and a narcotic, but one as harmful as 'cocaine.'"[133] Boyshevism provided commentators with a catchy and powerful shorthand with which to deride Boy and the ideas he was associated with. This was a stunningly effective tactic that went a great distance toward planting powerful associations in the minds of contemporaries. According to Nowaczyński, Boy's only "social service" was to pervert and "de-Christianize" Polish morality and to Boy-shevize the Polish intelligentsia.[134]

Czesław Lechicki argued similarly: "The battle with Boy is not a battle with one bad person that will pass us by but a battle with the outpost of Bolshevism, with the conspiratorial mafia that poisons the soul and, with its bacteria of anarchy, poisons the atmosphere of public life."[135] The result of the quick spread of Boyshevism, according to Lechicki, was a perversion of models of femininity and masculinity and a propagation of "gender communism," which no nation could withstand.[136] Another critic summarized simply: "The strength of Boyshevism is the weakness of Poland."[137]

Bolshevism was further linked to the ruling clique. Lechicki repeated to his readers a saying that "a certain witty landowner" had thought up: "Polish politics today is disseminated by the BB [BBWR]; whereas Bolshevism is disseminated by the BBB [*bezkarność, bezczelność, błaznowanie;* impunity, insolence, buffoonery]."[138] Boy commented in one of his feuilletons that indeed, his own views were derided only with the letter *b: "bolszewicki, bezczelny, bezwstydny and bezbożny"* (Bolshevik, insolent, shameless, and godless).[139]

Perhaps the most compelling evidence of Boyshevism and of the absolute decline in Polish moral standards in sanacja-era Poland emerged around the issue of civil marriages and divorces. It was due in large part to Boy's assiduous journalistic activity that the civil marriage and divorce questions garnered as much attention as they did in the late 1920s and that they became the focus of a national debate. Marriage- and divorce-related statutes from each of the partitioning powers still prevailed in the various regions of the Second Republic. Often, these laws contradicted one another, and this situation was further complicated by the confluence of dozens of religious and civil acts.[140] It was generally accepted that "marriage anarchy" prevailed in Poland.[141] The Codification Commission that had been established at the start of independence to standardize laws for the new state presented its highly controversial recommendations for civil marriage and divorce rights in 1929.[142]

In the same year Boy published "The Dissoluble Indissoluble Bond" (*Rozerwalna nierozerwalność*) in the *Morning Courier.* Boy argued that the consistory courts of the Catholic Church frequently dispensed annulments to those who simply had the means to pay for them. This created a whole class of women that Boy referred to ironically as consistory virgins. Boy was clear in his view that the Church acted hypocritically when it dispensed annulments for a fee, while at the same time it campaigned assiduously against divorce and lobbied the Codification Commission to disallow divorces and civil marriages altogether. Boy stated his position in a language reminiscent of Piłsudski's oft-quoted explanation as to why he had launched the coup: "I would also like for there to be less inequality, a little bit less hardship, fewer lies and hypocrisy in the relations between people in reborn Poland."[143]

The commission's final proposals on the civil marriage and divorce questions represented a middle-of-the-road solution. Under the terms of the 1931 project, church weddings were retained, yet civil marriages were also brought in, and both were made equally valid in terms of the law. Civil divorce was formally allowed and yet was restricted to those cases where stipulated conditions were met. The proposals caused a media storm that raised questions about national health, the state of the family, and the quality of independence. Both sides objected to the commission's proposals. The liberal left believed that they were a sell-out to the Catholic hierarchy. For its part, the Church hierarchy quipped that Poland now courted the devil. Cardinal Hlond stated simply that the proposals were "an affront to God and to the Polish nation."[144] The *Knight of the Immaculate* described them as "godless and monstrous" and "Bolshevik."[145]

The proposals of the Codification Commission were linked not just to Boy and other proponents of secularism and modernity but to the larger political sanacja as well. Nowaczyński faulted the sanacja government for failing to stem an apparently immoral tide that saw the number of marriages in Poland decline from 320,000 in 1930 to 280,000 in 1931. The sort of "sexual reform" that Poland tolerated, Nowaczyński offered, was unusual even for the Soviet context. In this fashion, Boyshevism was elevated to the status of a singularly vicious phenomenon.[146] The Polish episcopate referred to the commission's proposals as "sanacja communism."[147] Czesław Lechicki's outburst on this topic constituted a vitriolic attack on "the left and the radical wing of the Nonpartisan Bloc [for Cooperation with the Government; the Piłsudskiite political camp] . . . socialist doctors and actors," as well as against Boy, the *Literary News,* and other sanacja publications like the *Wilno Courier* for allowing the Codification Commission's proposals to come to pass. According to Lechicki, the government displayed an entirely wrongheaded approach with respect to morality and the nation.[148]

The journal *Pole-Catholic* (*Polak-Katolik*) stated that only a tiny fraction of an already small radical social and political circle was pressing for these rights to civil marriage and divorce but added that, regrettably, this circle had been very powerful since the May coup. *Pole-Catholic* further argued that it was the sanacja colonels (the core Piłsudskiites) who, buoyed by the power they had achieved since May 1926, wanted new sex lives to go along with the new political power they enjoyed; they wanted the state to sanction their decisions to leave their wives and families.[149] In her memoirs, Maria Bobrzyńska similarly referred to the inclination shown by former Piłsudskiite Legionnaires to "change wives like they change gloves."[150] Father Piwowarczyk suggested wryly that Brześć, from a sanacja point of view, represented nothing other than the time when "high-living women" proclaimed their desire to be liberated from the bonds of matrimony to pursue lives of sexual and cultural experimentation.[151] The link between supposed immodesty and the post-May government of the sanacja underpinned the discourse about the moral crisis that the Second Republic faced.

The sanacja government's approach to these questions, Father Piwowarczyk continued, was inconsistent with the repressive political system it had built and that it defended so tenaciously.[152] Other authoritarian systems, like that found in Mussolini's Italy, Father Piwowarczyk stated, had introduced legislation and policies clearly intended to promote moral and national discipline in the "right" way. Dance halls were closed, for example, divorces became illegal, and motherhood was raised to a national duty and women's highest calling. A campaign in support of planned parenthood would have been unthinkable in the Italian Fascist context. The opposite was true in sanacja Poland, however: "It is undoubtedly one of the weakest points of the post-May camp in Poland."[153]

Linking the notion of the sanacja as a loathsome political reality with that of a perceived cultural and moral decline also came from the left. Though initially supportive of the coup and the potential of the sanacja to launch a real socialist revolution, the left was quickly disillusioned with Piłsudski and became one of its most bitter critics, as we have already seen. Emil Haecker (1875–1934), editor of the Kraków socialist paper *Forward* (*Naprzód*), and a onetime Piłsudski supporter, referred to the "divorced sanacja men" "for whom changing wives is no less important a dogma than Brześć."[154] Indeed, a few key sanacja men were known to have taken advantage of a loophole in the legislation and to have converted from Catholicism to Protestantism in order to circumvent the Church's prohibition of divorce and remarriage.[155] Haecker further argued that Boy's concern for women was selective, at best, and that Boy seemed to have an interest in the plight of women only when they were seeking divorce or when they were pregnant.[156]

Unlike the open-ended references to "a growth in immorality" in sanacja Poland and to Boy "depraving" the nation with his talk about sex, the civil marriage and divorce question was a tangible and immediate concern. Further, it was easily linked to the political sanacja, given that the Codification Commission, which developed the legislation, was an institution of the republic. The sanacja government, though it ultimately adopted a middle-of-the-road position with respect to these issues, did not, in the opinion of right-nationalist commentators, go far enough. The sanacja could have acted decisively to simply disallow civil marriages and divorce altogether, and it could have confiscated Boy's articles on the subject. Instead, the sanacja revealed its real preferences and "proved" to critics that in fact it was everything they said it was. The cultural sanacja was best revealed in the heated polemics that arose around the civil marriage and divorce issues.

|||

Tadeusz Boy Żeleński was derided by some of his contemporaries as an especially inflammatory symbol of modernity, immorality, and anti-Polishness. But Boy was far from simply an arbitrary symbol of the cultural sanacja and of moral decay. In Boy, critics found a composite character of everything they believed was wrong with post-May Poland: Boy was a symbolic Jew, a symbolic Mason, a symbolic Bolshevik; Boy was the perfect incarnation of sanacja Poland.

Critics of the sexual revolution that Boy created and led invented the notion of Boy's sanacja and used it not just to impugn Boy but also to deride the political camp they had already spent years maligning. To critics, Boy and the Piłsudskiites were part of the same package. Critics argued that Boy was reasonably contained in pre-May Poland but that in sanacja Poland, Boy wrote and acted with a greater sense of entitlement. According to critics, Boy tried to complete the revolution that had been announced in May

1926; Boy's sanacja was the logical accompaniment to and the corollary of the political sanacja. In the hands of right-nationalist commentators, *sanacja* conveyed more than just political authoritarianism and the demise of democratic institutions; it conveyed a sense of moral laxity, promiscuity, and a flagrant violation of nationalist imperatives. The cultural sanacja was a reminder that independence was not yet secure and that in fact it had gone dreadfully wrong.

6 ⫿ Assessing the Spring of Miracles

Piłsudski's coup d'état of May 1926 and the period of sanacja that it inaugurated were the most explosive political events of the Polish interwar period. Historians have typically approached the sanacja period from a strictly political perspective, emphasizing the sanacja camp's visions for changing the constitution and state structures. But there was no single way of understanding the sanacja, of acting on a perceived need for moral rebirth, or of effecting change in the nation. Instead, the May coup both triggered and reflected strident debate about the moral health of the newly independent nation—debate about modernity and the pace of social change, about public and private mores, national identities, and cultural boundaries. This approach to the sanacja introduces a much-needed cultural dimension to our understandings of political discord and of contested visions of national identity in the Second Polish Republic, and in the process it suggests the basic interconnectedness of the political and cultural realms.

Citizens of Poland engaged selectively but eagerly in a process of inventing the terms and the targets of some idealized sanacja. "Everyone" was prepared to accept that Poland needed to be fixed and reformed, but exactly how this would be done was the point of contention and the source of such acerbic polemic. A variety of different constituencies seized on the coup and the ensuing calls for moral and spiritual rebirth—for a sanacja of the Polish nation—and twisted and shaped that concept to reflect their own ideas about what the postpartition nation needed. After 1926 Poles interpreted and reinterpreted what sanacja meant and used the event to focus their criticisms of and views on the nation.

In each of the preceding chapters I have taken some different imponderable as a starting point, as the site on which a particular incarnation of the sanacja concept unfolded. Each chapter describes, that is, what the defining theme of Polish political life from 1926—the sanacja—looked like from a specific perspective. Relying on the press of the period, chapter 1 explored the way in which rhetorical expressions of crisis and of a need for rebirth, moral reform and spiritual renewal, swelled after the coup. The coup and the ensuing sanacja provided convenient focal points for criticisms of contemporary moral and cultural developments. This was especially true of that portion of the press associated with the right-nationalist camp, the National Democrats. To many of the publicists associated with the right-nationalists, it was clear that a pernicious cultural sanacja accompanied the political caesura launched by the May events. Opponents of the political sanacja seized upon the language that the coup introduced—a language of healing, rebirth, and fundamental reform, of citizen activism and work as the highest moral calling—and manipulated it easily and cleverly in order to launch wholesale attacks not just on the ruling clique but on the state of independence generally. In the process, they advanced ideas about what it should mean to be Polish in the early twentieth century.

Chapter 2 focused on the letters written to Piłsudski after the coup. These letters further reveal the degree of creative manipulation that went on with respect to the sanacja in post-May Poland. Individual men and women, many of whom were located well outside the mainstream of society, used the sanacja as an opportunity to inject themselves into some of the most important political and cultural debates of the period and to offer their own analyses of what ailed Poland. Many of the ideas expressed in these letters were hardly representative of those espoused by either mainstream individuals or groups, but the very fact that the letter writers presented concepts and reform proposals that had at their core some notion of moral rebirth underscores the extent to which the powerful sanacja narrative had permeated all corners of society.

Chapters 3 and 4 approached the sanacja from the perspective of organizations. The sanacja fully intended to spark the growth of nonparliamentary, citizen-based associations that would devote themselves fully to the state. Chapter 3 is a study of a small prosanacja group called the Society for Moral Rebirth. A study of this society provides us with a view of how some members of the Piłsudskiite left-liberal intelligentsia understood the coup and the idea of moral renaissance. The men and women grouped in the society regarded Piłsudski's coup as a brilliant symbol of national potential, and they embraced the event accordingly. Yet the society remains a curiosity. It achieved virtually nothing, despite its association with many important Piłsudskiites. Like the political sanacja, the society's goals were perhaps too broad and unrealistic and its activism too unfocused.

Chapter 4 concerns women's understandings of the coup and their organizational responses to the sanacja. This topic has had far too little attention devoted to it, though it is loaded with possibilities. Women within the urban, left-liberal intelligentsia acted swiftly in the wake of the coup to popularize the notion that the event promised a magnificent moral renaissance. The women argued, moreover, that they, as women, had a key role to play within the moral revolution. Through the Women's Democratic Election Committee and the Women's Union for Citizenship Work, these women inserted themselves directly and visibly into political life. They believed that the Polish nation needed them during the sanacja period, just as it had needed them during the partition period. Accordingly, they proposed a marriage between moral purity and political purity and argued that, as women, they were uniquely well equipped to transform the nature of independence-era citizenship.

In doing so, prosanacja women forced a redefinition of the very meaning of politics in the Second Republic, of the public sphere and of female models of citizenship. The sanacja-era model of womanhood that women like Zofia Moraczewska espoused constituted an updated and modernized version of the Matka-Polka (Mother-Pole), one that was prepared to meet the real challenges women faced in the twentieth century. Like the members of the Society for Moral Rebirth, however, many of the women associated with the Women's Democratic Election Committee and the Women's Union for Citizenship Work were disheartened by not being able to effect the kind of broad-reaching change they had hoped for.

In chapter 5 we come full circle and probe the ways in which a small number of critics of the sanacja camp used Tadeusz Boy Żeleński as a focus for their analyses of the sanacja's effects on culture, broadly conceived. As the most vexing incarnation of sanacja-era moral laxity and cultural decay, Boy became an ideal target. With the term *Boy's sanacja,* critics conveyed their understanding that the political sanacja was about much more than just parliamentary affairs and constitutional reform.

Throughout, we have studied the "clash of moral nations," to which Maria Dąbrowska had referred just days after the coup. At the most basic level, the clash was between the left and the right. The struggle was over who would shape and ultimately control definitions of everything from models of femininity, sexual mores, and definitions of the nation to ideas about ideal citizen activism and service to the state. The fight was over symbols and definitions of Polishness and of Poland, over who would determine and control the shape of the postpartition future. The political caesura of 1926 forced people to take sides, declare allegiances, and articulate visions of the ideal future.

This study ends with the early 1930s, after the Brześć affair exploded and undermined definitively the moral integrity of the sanacja. By this time, the discussions about morality and culture that had marked the first years of the sanacja had fizzled out. There were many reasons for this. First, the direction in which the sanacja moved swiftly and assuredly from 1930 was toward authoritarianism. As a result, fewer and fewer constituencies could realistically and honestly support the political sanacja, and in turn, fewer could speak with any sincerity about the noble potential of the sanacja and a sanacja-inspired moral rebirth. It became increasingly clear that the political sanacja had become an authoritarian political machine and a socially and culturally conservative force. As this realization took hold, the potential for inventive manipulations of the sanacja idea diminished.

Moreover, Piłsudski himself had receded from the spotlight by the early 1930s, and certainly by the mid-1930s, as his health continued to fail, his physical and spiritual presence in Poland was noticeably diminished. He died in the spring of 1935, after a long illness. Without Piłsudski, the symbol and heart of the sanacja, the very idea of moral renaissance could not but fade away: Piłsudski had been the strongest unifying element of the sanacja. After his death, and with the power struggles that developed in the ruling camp afterward, the sanacja became simply another authoritarian regime. It became increasingly obvious that the sanacja was about maintaining political power.

The Great Depression, too, exerted a powerful impact on the ways in which contemporaries regarded and wrote about moral revolutions and rebirth. The Depression hit Poland especially hard, and by the early 1930s, as profound economic troubles exacerbated social ones, the mood grew increasingly tense and violent. Even the left-liberal intellectuals, who had devoted so much time to linking the political sanacja with positive cultural transformation, gave this up in favor of pointing out that most Poles were in dire straits and that the government was failing to implement policies and programs that might have alleviated the problems.

This shift in emphasis was most marked in the press and in the literature of the period. What literary critics have called social reportage arrived in the Second Republic of the mid-1930s with a great fury.[1] Neorealism pervaded journalism and literature, and authors exhibited ever-stronger social consciences. Ewa Szelburg-Zarembina's *Ecce Homo* (1932), for example, was a bitter condemnation of the Polish state for its failure to deal adequately with the Depression and for its tendency to look on human suffering with apparent indifference. Irena Krzywicka, a devotee of Boy's sexual revolution and a prominent figure within the *Literary News* circle, embraced what she referred to as the literature of fact. She argued that ordinary people wanted to know basic, day-to-day information about what was going on around them and that journalists had a moral obligation to tell these simple stories.[2] Krzywicka wrote an especially moving account in 1932 of the unemployment and chronic poverty in an industrial town near Warsaw called Żyrardów.[3]

By the mid-1930s basic economic and social needs—needs to which the sanacja governments had devoted too few resources—eclipsed nebulous moral and cultural concerns. In an atmosphere of economic desperation, debating moral questions and talking in abstract terms about rebirth, healing, and national renaissance rang rather hollow. In addition, Poland's increasingly tense and precarious international situation came to preoccupy people's thoughts and efforts. Alongside actual threats to the territorial integrity of the state, no other issue could seem as pressing.

As a regime, the sanacja maintained power from 1926 through to the German invasion of Poland in September 1939. In this sense, the sanacja was successful. After all, it had achieved some of its main aims: the elevation of the state over particularistic interests, the taming of parliamentary democracy, the reform of the constitution, and the strengthening of the executive. Work on a new constitution had begun immediately after the coup and was completed with the April constitution of 1935. The new constitution was antidemocratic, antiparliamentarian, and authoritarian, and it made the president responsible only "before God and the state"; in this regard, it was tailor-made for Piłsudski.[4] Yet Piłsudski died just weeks after the April constitution was passed, and a power vacuum emerged in the sanacja camp.

After the death of Piłsudski, the sanacja camp entered a phase of decomposition, and various interests vied for preeminence. The BBWR was replaced by the Camp of National Unity (Obóz Zjednoczenia Narodowego) in 1937 partly as a response to the growing social influence and political power of the right and of the increasingly radicalized peasant and socialist movements. The sanacja camp itself moved to the right during this period and embraced the nationalism and antisemitism that had been associated previously with the National Democrats; in some respects, the sanacja came to resemble the right-nationalist camp that, at one time, it had fought so determinedly.

The sanacja as an ideal and a potential is far more difficult to evaluate. The sanacja that did exist failed to measure up to the potential that people like Zofia Moraczewska or Aniela Samotyhowa had ascribed to it, and from their perspective it could only have represented a wasted opportunity. The disappointment came in part from the dissonance between the political sanacja and the invented sanacja. It was in part because of the political regime's lack of clear policies and boundaries that the sanacja as an ideal was so easily manipulated. The interest here has not been in the sanacja as a political movement or presence in a strict sense. It has, rather, been in the way in which the sanacja circulated through society and developed a meaning and potential that was quite removed from that which was intended for it by Piłsudski in May 1926, or by the Polish governments after 1926. On the one hand, the idea of a sanacja was a powerful one, and this is revealed in the many unusual ways in which people and groups embraced the term and applied it to all manner of issues. On the other, no one individual or group achieved the much-heralded moral renaissance or revolution, and no one was even certain what exactly this revolution would have entailed or looked like. By studying people's attempts to define and to shape the sanacja, however, we learn much about the preoccupations, hopes, and mood of the period.

This work has tried to do just that: to introduce new ways of reading the most important political caesura of the interwar period and to unpack its potential. The imponderables that form the basis of this study in no way purport to be the only ones, or even the most important. They are, rather, selected examples, and they are intended to spark further interest in studying the subtext of the sanacja; each chapter could easily serve as the basis for a more focused study of the period and mood launched by Piłsudski's coup of 1926.

Would these discursive emphases on the nation, on moral degeneration and regeneration, have circulated in the Second Republic with or without Piłsudski and the sanacja? They more than likely would have, just as some of these conflicts and tensions erupted in the rest of Europe in the postwar period. In a Poland dominated not by the Piłsudskiites but by National Democracy, however, the arguments would have taken a very different shape. But it is also fair to state that these debates would not have reached the pitch they did without the sanacja and the introduction into the Second Republic of a publicly endorsed vocabulary of rebirth and healing, cleansing, and fundamental reform. The sanacja provided an extremely important focus for these discourses, and different individuals—important and eminent individuals in addition to marginal and unknown ones—nourished and discharged them in a variety of fascinating ways.

The May coup was much more than just a simple "event," as contemporary language described it. The coup was not caused only by the political problems in the Second Republic, and its impact cannot be assessed only in relation to how it altered political structures and conceptions of the public sphere. The May coup was really the start of a "spring of miracles," to quote one contemporary commentator.[5] The May coup, I argue, was a revolution *with* revolutionary consequences, not *without* them, as Piłsudski had asserted in the spring of 1926 that it would be. The features and terms of this revolution were articulated by Poles themselves, and they evolved around issues that the Piłsudskiites in power had neither intended nor authorized. The May coup was revolutionary in offering Poles a chance to define and to work on the great imponderables. In the process, the May coup and the ensuing sanacja provided people with a valuable education in political participation, construed in its broadest formulation. As one historian remarked, just a few years after the May coup, "That which Piłsudski has achieved is rather to be read between the lines than in any casual deed; he is not merely the hero of a world of romanticism, but at the same time of a world of imponderabilia."[6]

Notes

Introduction

1. On Witos, see Bernard Singer, *Od Witosa do Sławka* (Paris: Instytut Literacki, 1962); Andrzej Zakrzewski, *Wincenty Witos* (Warsaw: Iskry, 1985). See also Witos's memoir: *Dzieła wybrane,* vol. 2, pt. 2, *Moje wspomnienia (lata 1918–1933),* ed. Eugeniusz Karczewski and Józef Ryszard Szaflik (Warsaw: Ludowa Spółdzielnia Wydawnicza, 1990).

2. On May 17, 1923, the right-nationalist People's National Union and Christian Democracy joined with the Piasts and signed the Lanckorona Pact (Pakt Lanckoroński). The government that emerged from this coalition was called the Christian National Unity Association (Chrześcijański Związek Jedności Narodu). The derogatory name for the new alliance was Chjena, which sounds like the Polish word for hyena (*hiena*). It served under the premiership of the Piast leader, Witos, from May to December 1923. On politics in the Second Republic, see Andrzej Ajnenkiel, *Parlamentaryzm II Rzeczypospolitej* (Warsaw: Wiedza Powszechna, 1975), 106–9; Andrzej Ajnenkiel, *Historia Sejmu polskiego,* vol. 2, pt. 2, *II Rzeczpospolita* (Warsaw: Państwowe Wydawnictwo Naukowe, 1989).

3. On the economic and social tensions of the period, see Antony Polonsky, *Politics in Independent Poland, 1921–1939: The Crisis of Constitutional Government* (Oxford: Clarendon Press, 1972), ch. 3, esp. 116–19; Andrzej Ajnenkiel, *Od "rządów ludowych" do przewrotu majowego: Zarys dziejów politycznych polski, 1918–1926* (Warsaw: Wiedza Powszechna, 1978); Andrzej Friszke, *O kształt niepodległej* (Warsaw: Biblioteka Więzi, 1989); Michał Śliwa, *Polska myśl polityczna w I połowie XX wieku* (Wrocław: Ossolineum, 1993).

4. On the Polish Socialist Party, see Jerzy Holzer, *Polska Partia Socjalistyczna w latach 1917–1919* (Warsaw: Państwowe Wydawnictwo Naukowe, 1962).

5. Piłsudski lived in Warsaw's Belvedere Palace while he was head of state, from 1918 to 1922—hence the designation Belvedere Camp.

6. On the difficulty of defining the ideology of the Piłsudskiites, see Andrzej Garlicki, *U źródeł obozu belwederskiego* (Warsaw: Państwowe Wydawnictwo Naukowe, 1978), 5. See also Władysław T. Kulesza, *Koncepcje ideowo-polityczne obozu rządzącego w Polsce w latach 1926–1935* (Wrocław: Ossolineum, 1985), 34–38.

7. On Dmowski and National Democracy, see Andrzej Micewski, *Roman Dmowski* (Warsaw: Wydawnictwo Verum, 1971); Jerzy Holzer, "The Political Right in Poland, 1918–1939," *Journal of Contemporary History* 12, no. 2 (July 1977): 395–412; Roman Wapiński, *Narodowa Demokracja, 1893–1939* (Wrocław: Ossolineum, 1980), 141–63; Roman Wapiński, *Roman Dmowski* (Lublin: Wydawnictwo Lubelskie, 1988).

8. On the formation of the ZL-N, see Holzer, "Political Right," 398–99. From 1928 the National Democrats' political party was called the National Party (Stronnictwo Narodowe, SN).

9. See Andrzej Garlicki, *Przewrót majowy* (Warsaw: Czytelnik, 1978), 220–22; Garlicki, *Józef Piłsudski, 1867–1935* (Warsaw: Czytelnik, 1989), 326–34. The term *nationalist* is used here to mean right-nationalist; in Polish usage, *nationalist* usually refers to Dmowski and the ideology espoused by the National Democrats and related parties. Piłsudski would best be described as a national hero rather than a nationalist one. On the use of the term *nationalist camp*, see Krzysztof Kawalec, ed., *Roman Dmowski o ustroju politycznym państwa* (Warsaw: Wydawnictwo Sejmowe, 1996), 286.

10. Narutowicz was supported primarily by the Jews and the Germans. The Ukrainians were the most numerous ethnic minority at 15 percent, followed by the Jews at 8 percent; the Germans, Belarusans, and Lithuanians constituted the remainder. On minorities, see Stephan Horak, *Poland and Her National Minorities, 1919–1939: A Case Study* (New York: Vantage Press, 1961).

11. Daria Nałęcz, *Sen o władzy: Inteligencja wobec niepodległości* (Warsaw: Państwowy Instytut Wydawniczy, 1994), 7.

12. On Narutowicz's election and assassination, see Daria Nałęcz, ed., *Nie szablą, lecz piórem: Batalie publicystyczne II Rzeczypospolitej* (Warsaw: Instytut Badań Literackich, 1993), 16–18, 24. On the 1922 presidential elections, see Daria Nałęcz and Tomasz Nałęcz, "Gabriel Narutowicz, prezydent Rzeczypospolitej 14 XII–16 XII 1922," in *Prezydenci i premierzy Drugiej Rzeczypospolitej,* ed. Andrzej Chojnowski and Piotr Wróbel (Wrocław: Ossolineum, 1992), 35–48.

13. Witold Gombrowicz, *Diary: Volume One, 1953–1956,* trans. Lillian Vallee (1957; repr., Evanston, IL: Northwestern University Press, 1988), 151.

14. Sejm deputies were part of parliamentary clubs; by 1922 there were seventeen parliamentary clubs. Deputies could move in and out of clubs as they saw fit, and they often did so with the hope of forming stronger coalitions. See Władysław Pobóg-Malinowski, *Najnowsza historia polityczna polski,* vol. 2, *1914–1939,* 2d ed. (London: B. Świderski, 1967), 178, 186–87; Jerzy Holzer, *Mozaika polityczna Drugiej Rzeczypospolitej* (Warsaw: Książka i Wiedza, 1974), 111–12.

15. On the constitutional question from 1918 to 1921, see Mark Brzezinski, *The Struggle for Constitutionalism in Poland* (Basingstoke, Hampshire: Macmillan, 1998), 50–51; Michael Bernhard, "Institutional Choice and the Failure of Democracy: The Case of Interwar Poland," *East European Politics and Societies* 13, no. 1 (Winter 1999):

34–70. On the specific features of Poland's proportional representation system, see Alexander J. Groth, "Proportional Representation in Prewar Poland," *Slavic Review* 1, no. 23 (March 1964): 104, 106.

16. Wincenty Witos, *Czasy i ludzie* (Tarnów, Poland: Józef Pisza, 1926). For Witos's account of this period, see Wincenty Witos, *Dzieła Wybrane*, vol. 2, pt. 2, 264–97.

17. Marian Romeyko, *Przed i po maju* (Warsaw: Wydawnictwo Ministerstwa Obrony Narodowej, 1967), 209–20; Garlicki, *Józef Piłsudski*, 303–9; Joseph Rothschild, *Piłsudski's Coup d'État* (New York: Columbia University Press, 1966), 38–39.

18. Archiwum Państwowe Miasta Stołecznego i Województwa Warszawskiego w Warszawie, file 273, Konrad Olchowicz, "Wspomnienia i refleksje dziennikarza, 1914–1939," 72. Olchowicz worked with the *Warsaw Courier* (*Kurier warszawski*).

19. Henryk Charlemagne, "Wydarzenia majowe 1926," *Stolica*, no. 20 (May 16, 1971): 4, as quoted in Marian Marek Drozdowski, *Sprawy i ludzie II Rzeczypospolitej: Szkice i polemiki* (Kraków: Wydawnictwo Literackie, 1979), 134–35.

20. Wacław Jędrzejewicz, *Kronika życia Józefa Piłsudskiego, 1867–1935*, vol. 2, *1921–1935* (London: Polska Fundacja Kulturalna, 1977), 103–10; Garlicki, *Przewrót majowy*, 224.

21. For a published collection of archival documents concerning the days of the coup, see Andrzej Garlicki and Piotr Stawecki, "Przewrót wojskowy w Polsce w 1926 r. Wybór dokumentów," *Wojskowy przegląd historyczny* 23, no. 1 (1978): 218–73.

22. Historians have also referred to anecdotal evidence on this point. Piłsudski is alleged to have told his wife on the morning of the twelfth that he would be home in time for lunch. See Aleksandra Piłsudska, *Memoirs of Madame Piłsudski* (London: Hurst and Blackett, 1940), 330. For a detailed description of the events from May 12 to 15, see Garlicki, *Przewrót majowy*, ch. 5.

23. In total, 379 people died (including 164 civilians), and 920 people were injured. See Garlicki, *Przewrót majowy*, 269. The official tally of the dead has been reprinted as "1 czerwca 1926, Warszawa, Zestawienie Komisji Likwidacyjnej Generała Lucjana Żeligowskiego o zabitych i rannych podczas zamachu stanu—w dniach 12–15 maja 1926 r.," in *Józef Piłsudski o państwie i armii w świetle wspomnień i innych dokumentów*, ed. Jan Borkowski (Warsaw: Państwowy Instytut Wydawniczy, 1985), 146.

24. For a description of the situation in the rest of Poland, see Garlicki, *Przewrót majowy*, 257–59.

25. See Garlicki, *Józef Piłsudski*, 334–57; Rothschild, *Piłsudski's Coup*, 125–47; Jerzy Halbersztadt, "Józef Piłsudski a mechanizm podejmowania decyzji wojskowych w latach 1926–1935," *Przegląd historyczny* 74, no. 4 (1983): 677–724.

26. In the June presidential elections, Mościcki received 283 votes, while his opponent, Adolf Bniński (1884–1942), received 200 votes. There were 56 ineligible or

spoiled votes. See Tadeusz Smoliński, *Rządy Józefa Piłsudskiego w latach 1926–1935: Studium prawne*, Seria Prawo, no. 115 (Poznań: Uniwersytet im. Adama Mickiewicza, 1985), 55.

27. Archiwum Akt Nowych (hereafter AAN), Zbiór Druków Ulotnych, file 225, poster addressed to "Citizens of the Republic," May 16, 1926. This poster was signed by Piłsudski, among others.

28. S., "Robotnicy! Obywatele!" *Robotnik*, no. 131 (May 13, 1926): 1. See also "Wielka chwila," *Robotnik*, no. 133 (May 15, 1926); "Sanacja moralna a zwycięstwo demokracji," *Robotnik*, no. 146 (May 29, 1926): 1. On the socialists and the coup, see Adam Pragier, *Czas przeszły dokonany* (London: R. Świderski, 1966), 318–24.

29. F. Bierkiewicz, "Walka o odrodzenie moralne narodu," *Kurier poranny*, no. 137 (May 19, 1926): 1. Another similarly positive evaluation of Piłsudski's actions was delivered in "Rząd legalny—a głównie—rząd uczciwy," *Kurier poranny*, no. 134 (May 16, 1926): 2.

30. Piłsudski's statement is drawn from a speech he made to the Sejm on May 29, 1926; segments of it have been reproduced widely. See, for example, Andrzej Wierzbicki, *Naród-państwo w polskiej myśli historycznej dwudziestolecia między-wojennego* (Wrocław: Polska Akademia Nauk, 1978), 120; Wacław Jędrzejewicz, *Piłsudski: A Life for Poland* (New York: Hippocrene Books, 1982), 236.

31. Józef Piłsudski, "Wywiad udzielony prasie po pierwszym dniu walk ma-jowych," in *Pisma wybrane* (London: M. I. Kolin, 1943), 413. On Piłsudski's "impon-derabilia" speech, see also W. F. Reddaway, *Marshal Piłsudski* (London: Routledge, 1939), 228–29.

32. In terms of historical analyses of the coup, two names stand out: Andrzej Garlicki and Andrzej Chojnowski. Garlicki's *Przewrót majowy* outlines the politi-cal causes of the coup, while his *U źródeł obozu belwederskiego* outlines the very be-ginnings of the formation of the Piłsudskiite political camp. For a discussion of the sanacja camp in power, see Garlicki, *Od maja do Brześcia* (Warsaw: Czytelnik, 1981). See also Andrzej Chojnowski, "Józef Piłsudski przed i po przewrocie majowym," *Przegląd historyczny* 77 (1986): 723–32; Chojnowski, *Piłsudczycy u władzy: Dzieje Bezpartyjnego Bloku Współpracy z Rządem* (Wrocław: Ossolineum, 1986).

33. Maria Dąbrowska, *Dzienniki, 1914–1932*, ed. Tadeusz Drewnowski (Warsaw: Czytelnik, 1988), 179–80. This same quote is used in a variety of texts. See, for ex-ample, Andrzej Chojnowski, "Moralność i polityka: Kobiece lobby w Bezpartyj-nym Bloku Współpracy z Rządem," in *Kobieta i świat polityki w niepodległej Polsce, 1918–1939*, ed. Anna Żarnowska and Andrzej Szwarc (Warsaw: Wydawnictwo Sejmowe, 1996), 161; Nałęcz, *Sen o władzy*, 255; Roman Wapiński, *Pokolenia Drugiej Rzeczypospolitej* (Wrocław: Ossolineum, 1991), 263–64. The Piłsudskiite Adam Skwarczyński had much earlier uttered a similar statement. It was published under Skwarczyński's pseudonym, Adam Płomieńczyk, in the *Way* (*Droga*), nos. 1–2

(1923): 3. See Nałęcz, *Sen o władzy,* 206. Dąbrowska's reference to moral nations clashing is, of course, the inspiration for the title of the present study.

34. See Wapiński, *Pokolenia Drugiej Rzeczypospolitej,* 334, 364; Wapiński, *Świadomość polityczna w Drugiej Rzeczypospolitej* (Łódź: Wydawnictwo Łódzkie, 1989), ch. 1.

35. Żarnowski, as quoted in Polonsky, *Politics in Independent Poland,* 30. The population statistics come from Janusz Żarnowski, *Społeczeństwo Drugiej Rzeczypospolitej, 1918–1939* (Warsaw: Państwowe Wydawnictwo Naukowe, 1973), 19.

36. Janusz Żarnowski, "East-Central European Societies, 1918–1939: The Polish Example," trans. Charles E. Railsback, in *Poland at the 14th International Congress of Historical Sciences in San Francisco: Studies in Comparative History,* ed. Bronisław Geremek and Antoni Mączak (Wrocław: Polish Academy of Sciences, 1975), 250–51. See also Janusz Żarnowski, "Społeczeństwo i kultura II Rzeczypospolitej," in *Z dziejów Drugiej Rzeczypospolitej,* ed. Andrzej Garlicki (Warsaw: Wydawnictwa Szkolne i Pedagogiczne, 1986), 299; Żarnowski, "Państwo polskie, a rozwój społeczeństwa polskiego, 1918–1939," in *Odrodzenie państwowości i przemiany struktur społecznych w Polsce i Czechosłowacji, 1918–1945: Materiały XXVI posiedzenia Komisji Historyków Polskich, Czeskich i Słowackich. Warszawa 20–23 listopada 1988 r,* ed. Maria Bogucka (Warsaw: Polska Akademia Nauk, Instytut Historii, 1991), 79–80. Also on the Polish intelligentsia, see Aleksander Gella, "The Life and Death of the Old Polish Intelligentsia," *Slavic Review* 30, no. 1 (March 1971): 1–27.

37. On western Europe, see Julian Benda, *The Treason of the Intellectuals,* trans. Richard Aldington (1928; repr., New York: Norton, 1969). On the intelligentsia in eastern Europe as a whole, see Alexander Hertz, "The Case of an Eastern European Intelligentsia," *Journal of Central European Affairs* 11, no. 1 (January 1951): 22; Zygmunt Bauman, "Intellectuals in East-Central Europe: Continuity and Change," *East European Politics and Societies* 1, no. 2 (Spring 1987): 168–69.

38. The term appears in Bohdan Cywiński, *Rodowody niepokornych* (Warsaw: Wydawnictwo Krąg, 1984), 135.

39. On Poland's nineteenth-century intelligentsia, see Jerzy Jedlicki, *A Suburb of Europe: Nineteenth-Century Polish Approaches to Western Civilization* (1988; repr. and trans., Budapest: Central European University Press, 1999); Jerzy Jedlicki, "Historia inteligencji polskiej w kontekście europejskim," *Kultura i społeczeństwo* 44, no. 2 (April–June 2000): 141–62.

40. Janina Leszkiewicz, "Jeszcze o polskiej inteligencji XIX w.," *Kwartalnik historyczny* 72, no. 1 (1965): 89–93; Nałęcz, *Sen o władzy,* ch. 1; Alina Kowalczykowa, *Programy i spory literackie w dwudziestoleciu, 1918–1939* (Warsaw: Ludowa Spółdzielnia Wydawnicza, 1978), 9.

41. Edward D. Wynot Jr., *Warsaw between the World Wars: Profile of the Capital City in a Developing Land, 1918–1939* (Boulder, CO: East European Monographs;

New York: Columbia University Press, 1983), 93–95, 98–102. In the 1921 census, approximately 68 percent of the population of Warsaw defined their religion as Roman Catholic, and approximately 33 percent defined their religion as Jewish (due to rounding, percentages do not total 100). Each of these percentages decreased slightly in the second census of the interwar period, conducted in 1931 (107). See also Marian Marek Drozdowski, *Warszawa w latach 1914–1939* (Warsaw: Państwowe Wydawnictwo Naukowe, 1990).

42. Stanisław Rychliński, *Warszawa jako stolica polski* (Warsaw: Wydawnictwo Biura Ekonomicznego Zarządu Miejskiego, 1936), 180.

43. Andrzej Paczkowski, *Prasa codzienna Warszawy w latach 1918–1939* (Warsaw: Państwowy Instytut Wydawniczy, 1983), ch. 8.

44. The term *moral revolution* had wide currency in the Second Republic. It was most firmly located in the writings of Adam Skwarczyński and the Piłsudskiite journal the *Way* (*Droga*). See, for example, Skwarczyński, "Rewolucja moralna," *Droga* (May 5, 1926); reprinted in Daria Nałęcz, ed., *Adam Skwarczyński—od demokracji do autorytaryzmu.* (Warsaw: Wydawnictwo Sejmowe, 1998), 157–60.

45. See Alicja Bełcikowska, *Walki majowe w Warszawie, 11 maj–16 maj 1926* (Warsaw: Nakładem Drukarni W. Maślankiewicz i F. Jabczyński, 1926); Józef Beck, *Final Report* (New York: Robert Speller and Sons, 1957); Eugeniusz Kozłowski, introduction to *O przewrocie majowym 1926. Opinie świadków i uczestników,* ed. Andrzej Wierzbicki (Warsaw: Ministerstwo Obrony Narodowej, 1984); Eugeniusz Kwiatkowski, *Dysproporcje: Rzecz o Polsce przeszłej i obecnej,* ed. Andrzej Garlicki (1931; repr., Warsaw: Czytelnik, 1989), 323–38; Regina Kociowa, *Irena Kosmowska* (Warsaw: Ludowa Spółdzielnia Wydawnicza, 1960), ch. 8; January Grzędziński, *Maj 1926* (Paris: Instytut Literacki, 1965); Olivier, comte d'Etchegoyen, *The Comedy of Poland,* trans. Nora Bickley (1925; repr., London: Allen and Unwin, 1927); Arkadiusz Adamczyk, "Relacja Bogusława Miedzińskiego z wydarzeń majowych 1926 r," *Zeszyty historyczne* 132 (2000): 226–34; Stanisław Strumph-Wojtkiewicz, Wanda Melcer Rutkowska, and Marja Szpyrkówna, *Moment zwrotny* (Warsaw: Towarzystwo Wyd. Rój, 1926).

46. Some of the main general political histories of the Second Republic (which, as a matter of course include analysis of Piłsudski, the coup, and the whole of the sanacja period) are Andrzej Micewski, *W cieniu Marszałka Piłsudskiego: Szkice z dziejów myśli politycznej II Rzeczypospolitej* (Warsaw: Czytelnik, 1969); Micewski, *Z geografii politycznej II Rzeczypospolitej* (Kraków: Znak, 1964); Holzer, *Mozaika polityczna;* Garlicki, *Józef Piłsudski;* Garlicki, *Od maja do Brześcia;* Garlicki, *U źródeł obozu belwederskiego.*

47. For a brief overview of the ways in which historians of the early Polish People's Republic wrote about the interwar period, see Tadeusz Cieślak, "Badania nad historią Polski od 1914 do 1964—w Polsce Ludowej," *Kwartalnik historyczny* 72, no. 1 (1965): 30–38; Andrzej Garlicki, Tomasz Nałęcz, and Wiesław Władyka, "Druga Rzecz-

pospolita w powojennych badaniach historyków polskich," *Przegląd historyczny* 69, no. 3 (1978): 389–404. For a good discussion of the trends evident in historical writing about Poland, see Piotr S. Wandycz, "Historiographies of the Countries of Eastern Europe: Poland," *American Historical Review* 97, no. 4 (October 1992): 1011–25.

48. See, for example, Garlicki, *Józef Piłsudski; Od maja do Brześcia; Przewrót majowy; and U źródeł obozu belwederskiego;* as well as Chojnowski, *Piłsudczycy u władzy.*

49. See, for example: Janusz Faryś, *Piłsudski i Piłsudczycy: Z dziejów koncepcji polityczno-ustrojowej (1918–1939)* (Szczecin: Uniwersytet Szczeciński, 1991); Śliwa, *Polska myśl polityczna.*

50. For the November 15, 1925, meeting between Piłsudskiite army officers and Piłsudski at Sulejówek, see Garlicki, U źródeł *obozu belwederskiego,* 356–66. On the extent to which the coup was planned, see Tomasz Nałęcz, "W służbie Rzeczypospolitej i w dyspozycji Wodza (obóz legionowy od Oleandrów do zamachu majowego)," in *Życie polityczne w Polsce 1918–1939,* ed. Janusz Żarnowski (Wrocław: Ossolineum, 1985), 205–16; Joseph Rothschild, "The Military Background of Piłsudski's Coup d'État," *Slavic Review* 21, no. 2 (June 1962): 257–58.

51. For this view, see Chojnowski, "Józef Piłsudski," 723–32. In this article, Chojnowski has published excerpts from the papers of Kazimierz Świtalski (1886–1962), which have been deposited at both the Archive of Recent Documents and the National Library, Warsaw. The nine excerpts cover the period from December 1925 to June 1926 and pertain to the unfolding of the political situation in Poland.

52. On European authoritarian movements during the interwar period and, generally, on the failure of democracy, see Hans Rogger and Eugen Weber, eds., *The European Right: A Historical Profile* (1965; repr., Berkeley: University of California Press, 1974); Peter F. Sugar, ed., *Native Fascism in the Successor States, 1918–1945* (Santa Barbara, CA: Clio, 1971); Iván T. Berend, *Decades of Crisis: Central and Eastern Europe before World War II* (Berkeley: University of California Press, 1998).

53. Historian Andrzej Garlicki calls Piłsudski a dictator. See Garlicki, *Przewrót majowy,* 271. For Piłsudski's views on dictatorships, see "Wywiad udzielony korespondentowi *Le Matin,*" in Piłsudski, *Pisma wybrane,* 417.

54. On the formation of the sanacja opposition, see Antoni Czubiński, *Centrolew: Kształtowanie się i rozwój demokratycznej opozycji antysanacyjnej w Polsce w latach 1926–1930* (Poznań: Wydawnictwo Poznańskie, 1963). Czubiński's text is useful despite its overtly ideological character. The trials of those imprisoned at Brześć lasted from October 26, 1931, to January 13, 1932. See Rothschild, *Piłsudski's Coup,* 350–53.

55. Kowalczykowa, *Programy i spory literackie,* 245. Dąbrowska's original statements about Brześć were published as "Rozmowa z przyjaciółmi," *Wiadomości literackie,* no. 3 (January 18, 1931): 2; and in "Na ciężkiej drodze," *Wiadomości literackie,* no. 4 (January 25, 1931): 1.

56. The typical division of the sanacja into three periods (1926–30, 1930–35, 1935–39), is discussed in Andrzej Ajnenkiel et al., "Uwarunkowania zamachu majowego (Dyskusja redakcyjna)," *Kwartalnik historyczny* 93, no. 1 (1986): 124–25 (comments of Zbigniew Landau); Krzysztof Jakubiak, *Wychowanie państwowe jako ideologia wychowawcza sanacji* (Bydgoszcz: Wyższa Szkoła Pedagogiczna w Bydgoszczy, 1994), 44–45.

57. Ajnenkiel et al., "Uwarunkowania zamachu majowego," 118 (comments of Andrzej Paczkowski).

58. Two major biographies of Piłsudski cover the whole of his life: Jędrzejewicz, *Piłsudski: A Life for Poland;* Garlicki, *Józef Piłsudski.* See also Robert Machray, *The Poland of Piłsudski, 1914–1936* (1936; repr., London: Allen and Unwin, 1962); Adam Suchoński, ed., *Józef Piłsudski i jego współpracownicy* (Opole: Wydawnictwo Uniwersytetu Opolskiego, 1999).

59. On the authenticity of this statement, see Polonsky, *Politics in Independent Poland,* 64n3. For the view that Piłsudski was never really attached to socialist ideas, see Micewski, *W cieniu Marszałka,* 251.

60. Rothschild, *Piłsudski's Coup,* 198; Polonsky, *Politics in Independent Poland,* 172.

61. *Conservatives* referred to the aristocrats, to the landed interests in the republic, and to the industrialists. Many joined the BBWR. For a discussion of the Piłsudski camp's relationship to the conservatives after the May coup, see Władysław Władyka, *Działalność polityczna polskich stronnictw konserwatywnych w latach 1926–1935* (Wrocław: Zakład Narodowy im. Ossolińskich, 1977); Władysław T. Kulesza, "Konserwatyści w obozie sanacyjnym w latach 1926–1935," *Przegląd historyczny* 73, nos. 3–4 (1982): 227–50, esp. 229–34.

62. For socialist criticism of Piłsudski and the sanacja, see, for example, Norbert Barlicki, "Przemówienie na II Zjeździe Związku Robotników Przemysłu Metalowego, wygłoszone 12 grudnia 1926 r," in *Norbert Barlicki: Wybór przemówień i artykułów z lat 1918–1939,* ed. Jan Tomicki (Warsaw: Książka i Wiedza, 1964), 163; Mieczysław Niedziałkowski, *Demokracja parlamentarna w Polsce* (Warsaw: Nakładem Księgarni Robotniczej, 1930), 38–42. Niedziałkowski (1893–1940) was editor of the socialist newspaper the *Worker (Robotnik)* from 1927 to 1939.

63. Micewski, *W cieniu Marszałka,* 202; Śliwa, *Polska myśl polityczna,* 98–100.

64. Gombrowicz, *Diary,* 1:151.

Chapter 1

1. Stanisław Kozicki, "Walka z młodem pokoleniem," *Myśl narodowa,* no. 48 (November 6, 1932): 702.

2. On moral panic, see Sonya O. Rose, "Cultural Analysis and Moral Discourses: Episodes, Continuities, and Transformations," in *Beyond the Cultural Turn: New Directions in the Study of Society and Culture,* ed. and intro. by Victoria E. Bonnell and Lynn Hunt (Berkeley: University of California Press, 1999), 218–19, 231; Rose, "Sex, Citizenship, and the Nation in World War II Britain," *American Historical Review* 103, no. 4 (October 1998): 1148.

3. Rose, "Cultural Analysis," 218–19; Rose, "Sex, Citizenship," 1148.

4. Joan Scott, "Rewriting History," in *Behind the Lines: Gender and the Two World Wars,* ed. Margaret Randolph Higonnet et al. (New Haven: Yale University Press, 1987), 27; Rose, "Cultural Analysis," 221–23, 227, 230.

5. For analyses of postwar cultural renderings and remembrances of the Great War, see Paul Fussell, *The Great War and Modern Memory* (New York: Oxford University Press, 1975); Modris Eksteins, *Rites of Spring: The Great War and the Birth of the Modern Age* (New York: Anchor Books, 1989); Jay Winter, *Sites of Memory, Sites of Mourning: The Great War in European Cultural History* (Cambridge: Cambridge University Press, 1995).

6. Mary Louis Roberts, *Civilization without Sexes: Reconstructing Gender in Postwar France, 1917–1927* (Chicago: University of Chicago Press, 1994), 3–4.

7. Angela Woollacott, "'Khaki Fever' and Its Control: Gender, Class, Age and Sexual Morality on the British Homefront in the First World War," *Journal of Contemporary History* 29, no. 2 (April 1994): 325–48.

8. Adelheid von Saldern, "Modernization as Challenge: Perceptions and Reactions of German Social Democratic Women," in *Women and Socialism, Socialism and Women: Europe between the Two World Wars,* ed. Helmut Gruber and Pamela Graves (New York: Berghahn Books, 1998), 117–19.

9. Atina Grossmann, "*Girlkultur* or Thoroughly Rationalized Female: A New Woman in Weimar Germany?" in *Women in Culture and Politics: A Century of Change,* ed. Judith Friedlander et al. (Bloomington: Indiana University Press, 1986), 64–65, 69.

10. On these debates in the postwar American context, see Nancy Cott, *The Grounding of American Feminism* (New Haven: Yale University Press, 1987). For Canada, see Mariana Valverde, *The Age of Light, Soap, and Water: Moral Reform in English Canada, 1885–1925* (1991; repr., Toronto: McClelland and Stewart, 1993).

11. Preliminary analyses of these themes have been most convincingly argued for the Romanian context. On Romania, see Irina Livezeanu, *Cultural Politics in Greater Romania: Regionalism, Nation Building, and Ethnic Struggle, 1918–1930* (Ithaca, NY: Cornell University Press, 1995); Maria Bucur, *Eugenics and Modernization in Interwar Romania* (Pittsburgh: University of Pittsburgh Press, 2002).

12. For literary analyses of the effects of the Great War on Poland, see Eugenia Łoch and Krzysztof Stępnik, eds., *Pierwsza wojna światowa w literaturze polskiej i*

obcej: Wybrane zagadnienia (Lublin: Wydawnictwo Uniwersytetu Marii Curie-Skłodowskiej, 1999); Maria Janion, *Płacz generała: Eseje o wojnie* (Warsaw: Wydawnictwo Sic! 1998).

13. This idea of citizenship as a moral category comes from Rose, "Sex, Citizenship," 168.

14. See Sławomira Walczewska, *Damy, rycerze i feministiki: Kobiecy dyskurs emancypacyjny w Polsce* (Kraków: eFKa, 1999), 41–43; Barbara Jedynak, "Dom i kobieta w kulturze niewoli," in *Kobieta w kulturze i społeczeństwie* (Lublin: Wydawnictwo Uniwersytetu Marii Curie-Skłodowskiej, 1990), 70–105; Anna Żarnowska, "Family and Public Life: Barriers and Interpenetration: Women in Poland at the Turn of the Century," *Women's History Review* 5, no. 4 (1996): 469–86.

15. AAN, Naczelne Dowództwo Wojska Polskiego, file 296/I, vol. 56, 126.

16. On the links between nationalism and (sexual) respectability in western Europe, see George L. Mosse, *Nationalism and Sexuality: Middle-Class Morality and Sexual Norms in Modern Europe* (Madison: University of Wisconsin Press, 1985), ch. 1.

17. Andrzej Paczkowski, *Prasa polska w latach, 1918–1938* (Warsaw: Państwowe Wydawnictwo Naukowe, 1980). In 1928, in Warsaw alone, 715 periodicals were published (about 30 percent of the total in Poland), making Warsaw the indisputable center of the market. See Paczkowski, "Prasa w życiu politycznym Drugiej Rzeczypospolitej," *Dzieje najnowsze* 10, no. 3 (1978): 39; Stefan Żółkiewski, "Kultura literacka—Warunki modernizacji i początki umasowienia," in *Literatura polska, 1918–1932*, vol. 1 of *Literatura polska, 1918–1975*, ed. Alina Brodzka, Helena Zaworska, and Stefan Żółkiewski (Warsaw: Wiedza Powszechna, 1975), 14–15. The average life span for periodicals was three years. See Maria Czarnowska, *Ilościowy rozwój polskiego ruchu wydawniczego, 1501–1965* (Warsaw: Biblioteka Narodowa, 1967), 118.

18. John M. Bates, "Freedom of the Press in Inter-War Poland: The System of Control," in *Poland between the Wars, 1918–1939*, ed. Peter D. Stachura (London: Macmillan, 1998), 99; Urszula Jakubowska, *Oblicze ideowo-polityczne "Gazety Warszawskiej" i "Warszawskiego Dziennika Narodowego" w latach 1918–1939* (Warsaw: Państwowe Wydawnictwo Naukowe, 1984), 30–31, 34.

19. Ludwik Hass, "U socjalnych źródeł przewrotu majowego (Inteligencja-Piłsudczycy)," *Kwartalnik historyczny* 77, no. 2 (1970): 368–91.

20. Nałęcz, *Nie szablą;* Andrzej Ajnenkiel et al., "Uwarunkowania zamachu majowego (Dyskusja Redakcyjna)," *Kwartalnik historyczny* 93, no. 1 (1986): 120 (comments of Andrzej Paczkowski).

21. Kajot., "Polska ma być rodziną," *Świat i prawda*, no. 24 (1925): 115. The journal was established in 1923 in Grudziądz, though it was available in all parts of Poland.

22. Zenon Gątkowski, "Dla kobiet," *Świat i prawda*, no. 24 (1925): 114.

23. Zetgie., "O strojach," *Świat i prawda*, no. 24 (1925): 114.

24. J. K., "Zmierzch publicznej przyzwoitości," *Świat i prawda*, no. 15 (October 1924): 11.

25. Ludwik Życka, "O polski typ kobiety," *Prąd*, no. 4 (April 1926): 181, 183–84; italics in original. This paper was formed in 1913 and, in the period that concerns us, was edited and published by Antoni Chaciński in Warsaw. See Andrzej Notkowski, *Polska prasa prowincjonalna Drugiej Rzeczypospolitej, 1918–1939* (Warsaw: Państwowe Wydawnictwo Naukowe, 1982), 294; Paczkowski, *Prasa polska,* 185.

26. See "O *Myśli narodowej*," *Myśl narodowa*, no. 56 (November 29, 1931): 329.

27. "O *Myśli narodowej*," 329.

28. See "Oznaki odrodzenia Warszawy," *Myśl narodowa*, no. 10 (March 6, 1926): 154–55. For more on the National Democratic press generally, see Jakubowska, *Oblicze ideowo-polityczne,* 7–10.

29. Andrzej Friszke, "Naród, państwo, system władzy w myśli politycznej Związku Ludowo-Narodowego w latach 1919–1926," *Przegląd historyczny* 72, no. 1 (1981): 69. The Dmowski quote is taken from *Wewnętrzna polityka*; reprinted in Krzysztof Kawalec, ed., *Roman Dmowski o ustroju politycznym państwa* (Warsaw: Wydawnictwo Sejmowe, 1996), 43. On the links between politics and morality, see Zygmunt Wasilewski, *O życiu i katastrofach cywilizacji narodowej: Wstęp do rozważań nad programowemi zagadnieniami doby obecnej* (Warsaw: Nakładem Księgarni i Składu Perzyński, 1921).

30. For Dmowski's views on women, see Izabela Wolikowska, *Roman Dmowski: Człowiek, polak, przyjaciel* (Chicago: Nakładem Komitetu Wydawniczego, 1961), 157–60; Andrzej Chojnowski, "Aktywność kobiet w życiu politycznym," in *Równe prawa i nierówne szanse: Kobiety w Polsce międzywojennej*, ed. Anna Żarnowska and Andrzej Szwarc (Warsaw: Wydawnictwo DiG, 2000), 38; Dobrochna Kałwa, "Poland," in *Women, Gender and Fascism in Europe, 1919–1945*, ed. Kevin Passmore (New Brunswick, NJ: Rutgers University Press, 2003), 162–63.

31. On Świętochowski's politics, see Tadeusz Stegner, "Przyczynek do ewolucji ideowo-politycznej Aleksandra Świętochowskiego," *Dzieje najnowsze* 17, no. 3–4 (1985): 27–40. Also on Świętochowski, see Samuel Sandler, introduction to Aleksander Świętochowski, *Wspomnienia,* ed. Samuel Sandler (Wrocław: Zakład Narodowy im. Ossolińskich, 1966), v–xxxviii; Samuel Sandler, *Ze studiów nad Świętochowskim* (Warsaw: Państwowy Instytut Wydawniczy, 1967); Maria Brykalska, *Aleksander Świętochowski redaktor "Prawdy"* (Wrocław: Polska Akademia Nauk/Ossolineum, 1974); Aleksandra Brykalska, *Aleksander Świętochowski: Biografia,* 2 vols. (Warsaw: Państwowy Instytut Wydawniczy, 1987).

32. The name seems to have its roots in a 1922 article by Iza Moszczeńska, "Poseł prawdy—'reakcjonistą.'" *Tydzień polski,* no. 29 (1922). See Brykalska, *Aleksander Świętochowski: Biografia,* 2:279.

33. *Liberum veto* was also the name of a paper that Jan Rembieliński had co-founded with Adolf Nowaczyński in 1918. See *Liberum veto,* no. 1 (December 2, 1918).

For more on the philosophy behind *Liberum veto,* see "Od wydawnictwa," *Liberum veto,* no. 1 (December 2, 1918): 1–2. For a discussion of the historic veto, see Jan Rembieliński, "Czem było 'Liberum veto,'" *Liberum veto,* no. 19 (May 10, 1919): 12.

34. Aleksander Świętochowski, "Liberum veto," *Myśl narodowa,* no. 6 (February 6, 1926): 89.

35. For Świętochowski's views on women, see his collection of aphorisms: *Aleksander Świętochowski: Aforyzmy,* ed. Maria Brykalska (Warsaw: Państwowy Instytut Wydawniczy, 1979), 185–86, 199.

36. On Wasilewski, see Paczkowski, *Prasa polska,* 34–35, 40; Paczkowski, *Prasa codzienna Warszawy,* 100–102; Jakubowska, *Oblicze ideowo-polityczne,* 7; Piotr Stasiński, *Poetyka i pragmatyka felietonu: Z dziejów form artystycznych w literaturze polskiej* (Wrocław: Ossolineum, 1982), 55; Jan Emil Skiwski, "Zygmunt Wasilewski," in *Na przełaj oraz inne szkice o literaturze i kulturze,* ed. Maciej Urbanowski (Kraków: Wydawnictwo Literackie, 1999), 95–103; Friszke, "Naród, państwo," 54–56.

37. Zygmunt Wasilewski, "Likwidowanie obyczaju," *Myśl narodowa,* no. 17 (April 24, 1926): 257.

38. Ibid., 258.

39. Ibid.

40. Friszke, "Naród, państwo," 70.

41. Zygmunt Wasilewski, "Moralne podstawy twórczości," *Myśl narodowa,* no. 11 (March 13, 1926): 162.

42. Jerzy Jedlicki, "Jesteśmy w Polsce, a nie gdzie indziej," *Nowa res publica* 2, no. 77 (February 1995): 3.

43. Andrzej Garlicki, *Józef Piłsudski, 1867–1935* (Warsaw: Czytelnik, 1989), 456n723. The phrase comes from Adam Skwarczyński, "Przegląd polityczny," *Droga,* no. 9 (1923).

44. Using *sanacja* to refer to economic reforms was common. For example, see "Praca," *Świat i prawda,* no. 15 (October 1924): 13. The page number provided here is an archival page number. The article was found in the papers of Władysław Grabski, AAN, file 17. The link between the terms *sanacja finansowa* and *sanacja moralna* is also evident in National Library, Warsaw, Manuscript Collection (hereafter BN), mf. 47163, Ossolineum Manuscript 13260/II, Stanisław Głąbiński, "Wspomnienia polityczne: Część IV. Rządy Sanacji w Polsce, 1926–1939," 14–15. For a similar usage of sanacja, see Kcz., "11:-owa 'Sanacja' Zdziechowskiego," *Robotnik,* no. 8 (January 8, 1926): 1; "Sanacja cen," *Myśl niepodległa,* no. 933 (September 1, 1928): 557.

45. "Rewolucja duchu," *Głos prawdy,* no. 140 (May 15, 1926): 293. The *Voice of Truth* (*Głos prawdy*) was edited and published since 1923 by Wojciech Stpiczyński. See Paczkowski, *Prasa polska,* 92–93.

46. "Rewolucja duchu," *Głos prawdy,* no. 140 (May 15, 1926): 294. Straw mulch or a straw man (*chochoł*) was often used in Polish literature as a metaphor for a slumber-

ing Polish nation; it symbolized stagnation and despair, but also the potential for hope and rebirth. See "Chochoł i jo-jo," *Gazeta warszawska,* no. 7 (January 7, 1933): 3.

47. "Sanacja," *Ster zagłębia,* no. 3 (July 18, 1926): 1. The journal was established as a weekly in Sosnowiec in July 1926 and was edited by Andrzej Kula. The Political-Social Club included members of the Riflemen's Association and the Legionnaires' Union. See "Od redakcji," *Ster zagłębia,* no. 1 (July 4, 1926): 1. The *Helm* established "good relations" with the Union for the Reform of the Republic, which will be discussed in chapter 4. See "Z działalności Klubu Polityczno-Społecznego im. Marszałka J.," *Ster zagłębia,* no. 5 (August 1, 1926): 4.

48. Zbik., "Czem jesteśmy?" *Ster zagłębia,* no. 8 (August 22, 1926): 2.

49. See Władysław Kołodziej, "Przez rewolucję moralną do rewolucji duchowej," *Odrodzenie,* no. 8 (August 1926): 7–8. The journal was published by Józef Chobot and edited by Aleksander Borys between 1926 and 1928. The brotherhood's interests included vegetarianism, international mysticism, universal ethics, and reincarnation.

50. Władysław Kołodziej, "Odrodzenie narodu," *Odrodzenie,* no. 9 (September 1926): 11.

51. Ibid., 12.

52. Władysław Buchner, "Najnowsza choroba," *Mucha,* no. 24 (June 11, 1926): 2. The *Fly* was edited and published by Władysław Buchner. See Paczkowski, *Prasa polska,* 286–87.

53. The first issue of the *Helm,* published on May 3, 1926, carried the subtitle *A weekly devoted to matters of state and nation* (*Tygodnik poświęcony sprawom państwa i narodu*). The first editor was Tadeusz Nowacki, followed in December by Witold Giełżyński, who was associated with the Work Club (Klub Pracy).

54. C. Kalinka, "Hasła wyborcze," *Ster,* no. 25 (October 23, 1926): 3.

55. C. [Czesław Peche], "Na posterunku," *Ster,* no. 4 (May 28, 1926): 8.

56. Zenon Gątkowski, "Kto będzie silną ręką?" *Świat i prawda,* no. 35 (June 1926): 780; "Tak się stać musiało . . . ," *Świat i prawda,* no. 36 (July 1, 1926): 10–16. The reference to cancer comes from page 10.

57. R. A., "Miażdżąca dłoń nałogu," *Świat i prawda,* no. 36 (July 1, 1926): 1–3.

58. One commentator in the pro-Piłsudskiite paper the *Helm of Zagłębia* referred to what he called the many "ironic" ways in which critics used the term. He compared these usages of the term to the slogan that Jews placed on Jesus' cross: "J. N., King of the Jews." See Dr. J. B., "Sanacja moralna," *Ster zagłębia,* no. 9 (August 29, 1926): 2.

59. Roman Dmowski, "Kościół, naród i państwo" (1927), in *Wybór pism,* 4:99, as quoted in Andrzej Walicki, "The Troubling Legacy of Roman Dmowski," *East European Politics and Societies* 14, no. 1 (Winter 2000): 32; italics in original. The entire text appears in *Wybór pism,* 90–115.

60. On the camp, see AAN, Zbiór Druków Ulotnych, file 3, Deklaracja ideowa Obozu Wielkiej Polski. The group's declaration is reprinted in "Głosy," *Myśl narodowa*, no. 47 (October 30, 1932): 694, and in Szymon Rudnicki and Piotr Wróbel, eds., *Druga Rzeczpospolita: Wybór tekstów źródłowych* (Warsaw: Wydawnictwa Uniwersytetu Warszawskiego, 1990), 196–97. The National Democrats claimed between two hundred fifty thousand and four hundred thousand members for the Camp of Great Poland, though some have doubted that membership figures even reached two hundred thousand. The camp was declared illegal by the sanacja government on March 28, 1933. On the Camp of Great Poland, see Roman Wapiński, *Roman Dmowski* (Lublin: Wydawnictwo Lubelskie, 1988), ch. 7; Zygmunt Kaczmarek, "Obóz Wielkiej Polski w latach 1931–1933," *Kwartalnik historyczny* 91, no. 4 (1984): 884; Bogumił Grott, "Geneza i początek formowania się poglądów 'młodych' obozu narodowego na zagadnienia ustrojowe: Okres działalności Obozu Wielkiej Polski," *Dzieje najnowsze* 16, no. 1 (1984): 115–26; Michał Śliwa, *Polska myśl polityczna w I połowie XX wieku* (Wrocław: Ossolineum, 1993, 106–14); Jerzy Holzer, *Mozaika polityczna Drugiej Rzeczypospolitej* (Warsaw: Książka i Wiedza, 1974), ch. 8. On the formation of the National Party, see Andrzej Garlicki, *Od maja do Brześcia* (Warsaw: Czytelnik, 1981), 227–35. For a discussion of the Camp's fascist aspects, see Antony Polonsky, "Roman Dmowski and Italian Fascism," in *Ideas into Politics: Aspects of European History 1880–1950*, ed. R. J. Bullen, H. Pogge von Strandmann, and A. B. Polonsky (London: Croom Helm, 1984), 141–43.

61. Piłsudski had guaranteed the Catholic Church that it would have its basic interests secured, and in return the Vatican promised to favor the sanacja government and to discourage separatism among the Catholic national minorities in Poland. See Neal Pease, "Poland and the Holy See, 1918–1939," *Slavic Review* 50, no. 3 (Fall 1991): 524; Joseph Rothschild, *Piłsudski's Coup d'État* (New York: Columbia University Press, 1966), 249–50; Ronald Modras, *The Catholic Church and Antisemitism: Poland, 1933–1939* (Jerusalem: Hebrew University of Jerusalem/Harwood Academic Publishers, 1994), 30–31, 36–39.

62. Primate of Poland, August Hlond, "Orędzie N. X. Prymasa Polski," *Liga katolicka*, no. 11–12 (November–December 1926). Hlond continued with these themes in a pastoral letter dated April 23, 1932, and found in AAN, Zbiór Paderewskiego, file 3041.

63. Hlond, "Orędzie N. X. Prymasa Polski," 4.

64. Founded in 1922 by Maximilian Kolbe, the *Knight* had print runs that regularly reached four hundred thousand in the later 1920s and 1930s. It was especially popular in the provinces and in rural areas. See Krystyna Sierocka, "Czasopisma literackie—charakterystyka ogólna," in Brodzka, Zaworska, and Żółkiewski, *Literatura polska*, 87; Paczkowski, *Prasa polska*, 242–45; Modras, *Catholic Church*, 41–42. An early 1932 issue of the journal states that its print run was 515,000. *Rycerz niepokalanej*, no. 1 (January 1932).

65. "Z ostatniej chwili," *Rycerz niepokalanej*, no. 7 (July 1926): 193–95.

66. A. K., "Nie wolno milczeć," *Rycerz niepokalanej*, no. 1 (January 1927): 10.

67. The *Knight's* support for Roman Dmowski is established clearly in "Roman Dmowski o protestantyźmie," *Rycerz niepokalanej*, no. 1 (January 1927): 14.

68. Ibid., 11.

69. "U progu zamagań," *Prąd*, no. 6 (June 1926): 289.

70. Rembieliński was associated with the more radical wing of the nationalist right. Early in 1928 he and nineteen other members of the All-Poland Youth (Młodzież Wszechpolska), received revolvers for their personal protection from the main headquarters of the People's National Union. The action seems to have been provoked by the recent attacks on the nationalist right by the sanacja. See "Związek Ludowo-Narodowy," *Poufny Komunikat Informacyjny*, no. 76 (Warsaw, February 28, 1928), in Ministerstwo Spraw Wewnętrznych, *Komunikaty informacyjne Komisariatu Rządu na m. st. Warszawę II: 1 (3 stycznia 1928–26 czerwca 1928)* (Warsaw: Centralne Archiwum Ministerstwa Spraw Wewnętrznych, 1992), 113. Rembieliński was also associated with a secret organization called the Guard (Straż) or Polish Guard (Straż Polska), organized by Roman Dmowski in 1928. The Guard worked with both the National Party (Stronnictwo Narodowe) and the Camp of Great Poland. See Garlicki, *Od maja do Brześcia*, 230–32.

71. Jan Rembieliński, "Po zamachu," *Myśl narodowa*, nos. 20–21 (May 22, 1926): 305.

72. Ibid.

73. Wasilewski's first response to the coup appeared as Zygmunt Wasilewski, "Jaki był motyw zamachu?" *Myśl narodowa*, nos. 20–21 (May 22, 1926): 306. A brief examination of *National Thought's* published responses to the coup (and especially of Świętochowski's reactions) is found in Brykalska, *Aleksander Świętochowski: Biografia*, 2:337–38.

74. Zygmunt Wasilewski, "Kłamstwo," *Myśl narodowa*, no. 23 (May 29, 1926): 322. The phrase "apostles of morality" is used on p. 321.

75. AAN, Zbiór Druków Ulotnych, file 73, poster addressed to "Compatriots," Warsaw, May 21, 1926, published by the Parliamentary Club of the ZLN.

76. Wasilewski, "Kłamstwo," 321.

77. Zygmunt Wasilewski, "Bunt przeciwko cywilizacji," *Myśl narodowa*, no. 36 (October 15, 1926): 141–42. Wasilewski took up these same themes in "Na widowni," *Myśl narodowa*, no. 7 (February 7, 1932): 90.

78. Wasilewski, *O życiu*, 3, 10–11

79. Roman Dmowski, "Wschód i zachód w Polsce," *Myśl narodowa*, no. 39 (November 15, 1926): 184.

80. Jan Rembieliński reviewed Piłsudski's involvement in the Polish Socialist Party in "Odwet ojczyzny," *Myśl narodowa*, no. 52 (December 1, 1929): 337.

81. Wasilewski, "Kłamstwo," 322. The description of the sanacja as a "war over culture" is also used in J. E. S., "Głosy: W obronie sanacji," *Myśl narodowa*, no. 25 (December 1, 1927): 472. See also Stefan Sacha, "Ciemności sanacyjne," *Myśl narodowa*, no. 36 (August 18, 1929): 99.

82. Victoria de Grazia, *How Fascism Ruled Women: Italy, 1922–1945* (Berkeley: University of California Press, 1992), 9.

83. Henryk Glass, "Przewroty w umysłach," *Myśl narodowa*, no. 56 (December 25, 1932): 814–15.

84. "O *Myśli narodowej*," 329. For a similar sentiment, see [Aleksander Świętochowski], "Na marginesie," *Myśl narodowa*, no. 5 (January 25, 1931): 63. Świętochowski left Warsaw and moved to the estate of Gołotczyzna in 1929. At this time, he stopped contributing regularly to the press and ended his position with *National Thought*, where he had been since 1925. (By the early 1930s, Świętochowski was in his eighties.)

85. Aleksander Świętochowski, "Liberum veto," *Myśl narodowa*, no. 15 (April 14, 1929): 234.

86. Aleksander Świętochowski, "Liberum veto," *Myśl narodowa*, no. 33 (July 28, 1929): 58. A similar sentiment is expressed in Jan Rembieliński, "Narodowe … Państwowe," *Myśl narodowa*, no. 3 (January 19, 1930): 33. Brykalska offers an excellent discussion of the role that morality played in Świętochowski's thinking. Brykalska, *Aleksander Świętochowski: Biografia*, 2:517–18.

87. On Nowaczyński's literary output, see Henryk Izydor Rogacki, "Nowaczyński o teatrze," in Adolf Nowaczyński, *Porachunki i projekty: Teksty o teatrze z lat 1900–1938*, ed. Rogacki (Wrocław: Wiedza i Kultura, 1993), 7–9.

88. For a discussion of Nowaczyński as a literary critic, see Anna Kieżuń, *Spór z tradycją romantyczną: O działalności pisarskiej Adolfa Nowaczyńskiego* (Białystok: Uniwersytet Warszawski w Białymstoku, 1993). For a discussion of the role of *National Thought* as an antiromanticist journal, see Leszek Kamiński, *Romantyzm a ideologia: Główne ugrupowania polityczne Drugiej Rzeczypospolitej wobec tradycji romantycznej* (Wrocław: Zakład Narodowy im. Ossolińskich/Wydawnictwo Polskiej Akademii Nauk, 1980), 12–13, and esp. ch. 3.

89. Nowaczyński also contributed regularly to the *Warsaw Gazette* (*Gazeta warszawska*) (1921–22; 1924–35), *ABC* (1927–39), and the *Republic* (*Rzeczpospolita*) (1920–25). See Stasiński, *Poetyka i pragmatyka felietonu*, 55. Nowaczyński wrote under the following pseudonyms: (a.n.), A N, Ad. Now, nów, Adolf Nów, Przyjaciel, Adolf Przyjaciel, Halban, Clarus, Iunius, A. Nuewert. See Artur Hutnikiewicz, "Adolf Nowaczyński," in *Polski słownik biograficzny*, ed. Władysław Konopczyński et al. (Kraków: Polska Akademia Umiętności, 1932–present), 23:249.

90. Adolf Nowaczyński, "Ofensywa: 'Przestępcy' i przestępczość," *Myśl narodowa*, no. 21 (May 25, 1930): 335. This article is reprinted in Nowaczyński, *Porachunki*

i projekty, 172–75. A later version of this article is printed as "Sekty a przestępczość," *Gazeta warszawska,* no. 28 (January 26, 1932): 4.

91. Nowaczyński, "Ofensywa," 335.

92. Kazimierz Bartel had served as premier from May to September 1926 and from June 1928 to April 1929. In April 1929, Piłsudski replaced Bartel with the comparatively hard-line Kazimierz Świtaliski, who formed a cabinet that lasted to December 1929. Bartel became premier again from December 1929 to March 1930. See Ryszard Świętek, "Kazimierz Świtalski, premier Rzeczypospolitej 14.IV–7.XII.1929," in *Prezydenci i premierzy Drugiej Rzeczypospolitej,* ed. Andrzej Chojnowski and Piotr Wróbel (Wrocław: Ossolineum, 1992), 261–83.

93. Antoni Czubiński, *Centrolew: Kształtowanie się i rozwój demokratycznej opozycji antysanacyjnej w Polsce w latach 1926–1930* (Poznań: Wydawnictwo Poznańskie, 1963).

94. For a description of the first attack on Nowaczyński, see Kazimierz Koźniewski, *Historia co tydzień: Szkice o tygodnikach społeczno-kulturalnych* (Warsaw: Czytelnik, 1976), 45; Aleksander Świętochowski, "Liberum veto," *Myśl narodowa,* no. 2 (January 15, 1928): 31. The right-wing journalist and novelist Tadeusz Dołęga-Mostowicz also suffered an attack of this sort. See Daria Nałęcz and Tomasz Nałęcz, *Józef Piłsudski: Legendy i fakty* (Warsaw: Młodzieżowa Agencja Wydawnicza, 1986), 66–67; Zbigniew Mitzner, "Wstęp," in Tadeusz Dołęga-Mostowicz, *Kariera Nikodema Dyzmy* (1932; repr., Warsaw: Czytelnik, 1955), 5. The *Career* (*Kariera*) is considered Dołęga-Mostowicz's revenge on the sanacja and on his attackers.

95. "Głosy: Napad na Nowaczyńskiego," *Myśl narodowa,* no. 26 (May 31, 1931): 347.

96. Adolf Nowaczyński, "Ofensywa: Morga," *Myśl narodowa,* no. 49 (October 18, 1931): 247. For another discussion of the postwar crisis in morality in Poland and western European nations, see Ignotus, "Imponderabilia," *Myśl narodowa,* no. 15 (March 26, 1933): 195–98.

97. Nowaczyński again referred to Poland as "Poland of the First Brigade" in Adolf Nowaczyński, "Ofensywa: Marjanna a Sanator," *Myśl narodowa,* no. 51 (November 1, 1931): 278.

98. Stefan Sacha, "Czy istnieje filozofja polityki sanacyjnej?" *Myśl narodowa,* no. 35 (August 11, 1929): 81–83. These points about what the sanacja was and was not are outlined in Krzysztof Jakubiak, *Wychowanie państwowe jako ideologia wychowawcza sanacji* (Bydgoszcz: Wyższa Szkoła Pedagogiczna, 1994), ch. 1, 17–65.

99. St. Sasorski., "Na tle ostatnich wypadków," *Drogi naprawy,* no. 3 (May 29, 1926): 2–4. A similar exhortation for a more precise definition of the term *sanacja moralna* is offered in Władysław Grabski, "Warunki sanacji moralnej sposobów rządzenia państwem," *Drogi naprawy,* no. 5 (July 1, 1926): 4–7, esp. 6. This journal was formed as a biweekly in Warsaw in April 1926.

100. "Głosy," *Myśl narodowa,* no. 21 (May 19, 1929): 330.

101. The term *moral renaissance* was used in *Głos prawdy,* no. 140 (May 15, 1926) and was quoted in "Głosy," *Myśl narodowa,* no. 21 (May 19, 1929): 330. *Głos prawdy* was edited from 1923 by Wojciech Stpiczyński.

102. Stefan Sacha, "Rozkład i pustka," *Myśl narodowa,* no. 37 (August 25, 1929): 117.

103. See Zbigniew Landau, "Impact of the May 1926 Coup on the State of Polish Economy," *Acta Poloniae Historica* 35 (1977): 169–71, 175; Marian Marek Drozdowski, "Wpływ przewrotu majowego na gospodarkę narodową Polski lat 1926–1929 (Uwagi do dyskusji)," *Kwartalnik historyczny* 93, no. 4 (1986): 1105–13.

104. Andrzej Garlicki and Jerzy Kochanowski, eds., "Obiecanki-cacanki, a Polakom radość," in *Józef Piłsudski w karykaturze* (Warsaw: Wydawnictwo Interpress, 1991), 40.

105. Bates, "Freedom of the Press," 91–92, 94–99. Articles 104 and 105 of the constitution pertained to press freedoms. For a discussion of the controversy surrounding the 1926 decree, see Tadeusz Smoliński, *Rządy Józefa Piłsudskiego w latach 1926–1935: Studium prawne,* Seria Prawo, no. 115 (Poznań: Uniwersytet im. Adama Mickiewicza, 1985), 105–7. See also Michał Pietrzak, *Reglamentacja wolności prasy w Polsce, 1918–1939* (Warsaw: Książka i Wiedza, 1963); Andrzej Notkowski, *Prasa w systemie propagandy rządowej w Polsce, 1926–1939* (Warsaw: Państwowe Wydawnictwo Naukowe, 1987).

106. For one such condemnation of the decree, see Eugenjusz Śmiarowski, "Dekret o niewoli prasy," *Ster,* no. 28 (November 13, 1926): 3–5. Officially, the Polish journalists' organization, the Polish Union of Publishers of Dailies and Periodicals, was not formed until October 22, 1928. See Jakubiak, *Wychowanie państwowe,* 77.

107. The decree was not ratified because the Sejm and the Senate were annulled in December 1926. See Rothschild, *Piłsudski's Coup,* 252.

108. Final decisions regarding the repression of newspapers rested with the courts, but judges who overturned administrative recommendations and decisions were reported to the Interior Ministry and could be "removed." See Bates, "Freedom of the Press," 93–96. The April 1935 constitution deprived freedom of the press of its constitutional status.

109. Rothschild, *Piłsudski's Coup,* 252–53, 274; Antony Polonsky, *Politics in Independent Poland, 1921–1939: The Crisis of Constitutional Government* (Oxford: Clarendon Press, 1972), 226, 257.

110. "Jasno i wyrażnie," *Gazeta bydgoska,* no. 78 (April 3, 1930): 1. This censored article is part of the collection of the Polish Union of Newspaper and Periodical Publishers. See AAN, Zespół Polskiego Związku Wydawnictw Dzienników i Czasopism w Warszawie, file 251, 39.

111. Mocking the moral sanacja was the one and only aim of a satirical paper called the *Moral Sanacja (Sanacja moralna).* It was established in March 1929 in Warsaw by Olaf Słupski and Władysław Włodkowski. The first and only issue, March 28, 1929, was confiscated.

112. An article was left unsigned so that the author would not be held liable for controversial views. See Bates, "Freedom of the Press," 96–97. The government offered attractive economic incentives to those press concerns that were sympathetic to the *sanacja*. Such was the case with Marian Dąbrowski and his mammoth publishing consortium, the *Daily Illustrated Courier* (*Illustrowny kurjer codzienny*). See Eugeniusz Rudziński, "Kształtowanie systemu prasy kontrolowanej w Polsce w latach 1926–1939," *Dzieje najnowsze* 1, no. 1 (1969): 96–97.

113. For a list of confiscations see Jerzy Speina, "*Myśl narodowa*," in *Literatura polska w okresie międzywojennym,* ed. Jerzy Kądziela, Jerzy Kwiatkowski, and Irena Wyczańska (Kraków: Wydawnictwo Literackie, 1979), 1:275. For a general discussion of confiscations, see *Myśl narodowa*, no. 5 (February 17, 1928).

114. Aleksander Świętochowski, "Liberum veto," *Myśl narodowa,* no. 3 (February 1, 1928): 51.

115. Ibid. Translation is from the King James Version.

Chapter 2

1. On letters of denunciation written to authorities in Nazi Germany and the Soviet Union, see *Journal of Modern History* 68, no. 4 (1996) (special issue). On letter writing in the Soviet Union, see Matthew E. Lenoe, "Letter-Writing and the State: Reader Correspondence with Newspapers as a Source for Early Soviet History," *Cahiers du monde russe* 40, nos. 1–2 (January–June 1999): 139–70; Sheila Fitzpatrick, "Supplicants and Citizens: Public Letter-Writing in Soviet Russia in the 1930s," *Slavic Review* 55, no. 1 (Spring 1996): 78–105.

2. Peter Stallybrass and Allon White, *The Politics and Poetics of Transgression* (Ithaca, NY: Cornell University Press, 1986), 196.

3. Iłłakowiczówna won the National Poetry Award in 1935. See "Kazimiera Iłłakowiczówna: Laureatką nagrody państwowej," *Praca obywatelska* 1 (January 15, 1935): 11.

4. On Iłłakowiczówna, see Irena Maciejewska, ed., *Poeci dwudziestolecia międzywojennego* (Warsaw: Wiedza Powszechna, 1982), 1:277–309; Mirosława Oldakowska-Kuflowa, *Chrześcijańskie widzenie świata w poezji Kazimiery Iłłakowiczówny* (Lublin: Catholic University of Lublin, 1993), 8–17; Agnieszka Baranowska, *Perły i potwory: Szkice o literaturze międzywojennej* (Warsaw: Państwowy Instytut Wydawniczy, 1986), 10–11.

5. Stefan Żółkiewski, "Kultura literacka—Warunki modernizacji i początki umasowienia," in *Literatura polska, 1918–1932,* vol. 1 of *Literatura polska, 1918–1975,* ed. Alina Brodzka, Helena Zaworska, and Stefan Żółkiewski (Warsaw: Wiedza Powszechna, 1975), 32–33.

6. Oldakowska-Kuflowa, *Chrześcijańskie widzenie świata,* 10. See specifically Iłłakowiczówna's *Ballady bohaterskie* (Lwów: Wydawnictwo Zakładu Narodowego im. Ossolińskich, 1934). Iłłakowiczówna's poetry devoted to Piłsudski appears in a collection edited by Krzysztof A. Jeżewski: *W blasku legendy: Kronika poetycka życia Józefa Piłsudskiego* (Paris: Editions Spotkania, 1988).

7. Kazimiera Iłłakowiczówna, "W cieniu wielkości," 1928, as quoted in Danuta Zamojska-Hutchins, "Kazimiera Iłłakowiczówna: The Poet as a Witness of History, and of Double National Allegiance," in *Literature and Politics in Eastern Europe: Selected Papers from the Fourth World Congress for Soviet and East European Studies, Harrogate, 1990,* ed. Celia Hawkesworth (London: St. Martin's Press, 1992), 96. The translation is from Zamojska-Hutchins.

8. Kazimiera Iłłakowiczówna, *Ścieżka obok drogi* (1939; repr., Warsaw: Zelpress, 1989), 19–20. In this memoir, whose title means *The Path by the Road,* Iłłakowiczówna is not specific about dates, and it is difficult to determine exactly what she did and where she was at any given point.

9. Ibid., 39–41.

10. Ibid. For a discussion and selected examples of popular wartime poetry, songs, and hymns, see Harold B. Segel, "Culture in Poland during World War I," in *European Culture in the Great War: The Arts, Entertainment, and Propaganda, 1914–1918,* ed. Aviel Roshwald and Richard Stites (Cambridge: Cambridge University Press, 1999), 58–88.

11. Iłłakowiczówna, *Ścieżka obok drogi,* 41. For a very interesting discussion of Piłsudski's views on women, see Jan Lechoń, *Dziennik* (London: Wydawnictwo Wiadomości, 1967), 186. Lechoń raises the idea that Piłsudski regarded Poland itself as a woman, but not an "ideal" woman.

12. Quite surprisingly, Iłłakowiczówna states in her memoir that she joined the Polish spearhead of the Russian army: "Wstąpiłam do służby pielęgniarskiej, a w styczniu 1915 do polskiej czołówki przy armii rosyjskiej." It is not at all clear why a supporter of Piłsudski would have joined the Russian army at this time. The only clue Iłłakowiczówna provides is to write that immediately before entering the war, she was quite ill and that she therefore lost contact with her friends in London, who supported Piłsudski's military efforts. Iłłakowiczówna, *Ścieżka obok drogi,* 47.

13. Ibid., 48.

14. Ibid., 61.

15. Ibid., 61–62.

16. Ibid., 70.

17. Ibid., 89–90. On this period, see also Maria Jehanne Wielopolska, *Pliszka w jaskini lwa: Rozważania nad książką Panny Iłłakowiczówny,* Ścieżka obok drogi (Warsaw: n.p., 1939), 16–17.

18. Iłłakowiczówna, *Ścieżka obok drogi,* 111.

19. Ibid., 112.

20. Ibid., 117, 113.

21. See, for example, Wielopolska, *Pliszka,* 20–24.

22. Iłłakowiczówna, *Ścieżka obok drogi,* 120. Iłłakowiczówna returned to the Ministry of Foreign Affairs in 1936. See also Iłłakowiczówna, *Wspomnienia i reportaże,* ed. Jacek Biesiada and Aleksandra Włoszczyńska (Warsaw: Więź, 1997), 189–93, 239.

23. Piłsudski insisted that Iłłakowiczówna use "Secretary to the Minister of Military Affairs" as her official title. He argued that a public servant can only serve the ministry, and not an individual person. See Iłłakowiczówna, *Ścieżka obok drogi,* 155, 238–39.

24. The text was written in Warsaw and is dated February 1936. See p. 336.

25. Baranowska, *Perły i potwory,* 29–32.

26. Wielopolska, *Pliszka,* 8. On the Iłłakowiczówna-Wielopolska controversy, see also Baranowska, *Perły i potwory,* 45, 48. Chapter 2 of Baranowska's work is entitled "Lady Paradox" and is devoted to Wielopolska. Wielopolska was dubbed Lady Paradox by the *Literary News* (*Wiadomości literackie*), and Witch (*Baba-Jaga*) by trenchant National Democratic publicist Adolf Nowaczyński. See also Stanisława Jarocińska-Malinowska, "Lady paradox des lettres polonaises: Marja Jehanne Wielopolska," *La Pologne littéraire,* no. 13 (October 15, 1927): 1. The Iłłakowiczówna-Wielopolska controversy is also outlined in Włodzimierz Wójcik, *Legenda Piłsudskiego w polskiej literaturze międzywojennej,* 2d ed. (Katowice: Wydawnictwo Śląsk, 1986), 87–91.

27. This phrase is taken from one of Iłłakowiczówna's poems, "Z domu niewoli," written in 1914. The poem was dedicated to Piłsudski and encapsulated Iłłakowiczówna's hopes, and the hopes of many others, that Piłsudski would lead Poland out of the slavery that had marked their existence for over a century. See Zamojska-Hutchins, "Kazimiera Iłłakowiczówna," 95.

28. The comment about the china comes from Wielopolska, *Pliszka,* 8.

29. Ibid., 27.

30. AAN, Zespół Józefa i Aleksandry Piłsudskich, part 2, file 32, "Notatka Pro Domo," 1928, 30–31, 33.

31. AAN, Zespół Piłsudskich, part 2, file 32, Scaevola, "Projektowany wywiad: Nieaprobowany przez Iłłakowiczówną," December 31, 1935, 5. The cover sheet for this interview comes from the Office of the Inspector General of the Armed Forces, E. Rydz-Śmigły, Warsaw. It contains the one following sentence: "I am sending this to you after it was read by the General Inspector of the Armed Forces." See p. 3. This interview contains Iłłakowiczówna's general reflections on her experiences as the secretary of the Ministry of Military Affairs. It is not clear why the project was not approved, but one can speculate that Piłsudski's death may have had some effect. The "Pro Domo Note" and a text written by Scaevola are the two major sources I used to determine who wrote to Piłsudski, in what frequency, and why.

32. AAN, "Notatka Pro Domo," 33. All figures given in the "Notatka Pro Domo" are indicated as being approximate.

33. AAN, Scaevola, "Projektowany wywiad," 4. The same figure is provided in Iłłakowiczówna, *Ścieżka obok drogi,* 191.

34. AAN, Scaevola, "Projektowany wywiad," 4.

35. Ibid., 5.

36. Most of the letters from the general public to Aleksandra Piłsudska (Piłsudski's second wife, with whom he had two girls) were requests for aid. From September 1934 to February 1935, Piłsudska received 3,025 letters—over five hundred each month. The letters continued after Piłsudski's death, which Iłłakowiczówna found to be in very bad taste. See AAN, "Notatka Pro Domo," 33. A large collection of letters to Aleksandra Piłsudska is located in AAN, Zespół Piłsudskich, part 4, file 29. Aleksandra Piłsudska wrote a biography of her husband: *Piłsudski* (New York: Arno Press, 1971).

37. Many letters to Piłsudski from veterans are found in AAN, Zespół Piłsudskich, part 4, file 29. See also Central Military Archives, Rembertów (Centralne Archiwum Wojska Polskiego, hereafter CAW), Gabinet Mininstra Spraw Wojskowych, file I.300.1.327.

38. AAN, "Notatka Pro Domo," 1928, 32.

39. Iłłakowiczówna, *Ścieżka obok drogi,* 148. On Piłsudski's attitudes toward veterans in the post-May period, see Jerzy Halbersztádt, "Józef Piłsudski a mechanizm podejmowania decyzji wojskowych w latach 1926–1935," *Przegląd historyczny* 24, no. 4 (1983): 683.

40. Iłłakowiczówna, *Ścieżka obok drogi,* 191–92.

41. Ibid.

42. For a discussion of Piłsudski's withdrawal from public life, see Maria Jehanne Wielopolska, *Józef Piłsudski w życiu codziennym* (Warsaw: Księgarnia Wojskowa, 1936), 94–95.

43. Iłłakowiczówna, *Ścieżka obok drogi,* 314.

44. AAN, Scaevola, "Projektowany wywiad," 5–6.

45. Ibid., 6.

46. Ibid., 8–9.

47. Iłłakowiczówna, *Ścieżka obok drogi,* 114.

48. Ibid., 315.

49. Ibid., 186–87.

50. CAW, Gabinet Mininstra Spraw Wojskowych, file 483, Stefan [Brzowikowski] to Józef Piłsudski, Warsaw, May 16, 1926, 91–92.

51. Wincenty Rzymowski, "Życiorys," in *Idea i czyn Józefa Piłsudskiego,* ed. Wacław Sieroszewski et al. (Warsaw: Bibljoteka Dzieł Naukowych, 1934), 79.

52. CAW, Gabinet Mininstra Spraw Wojskowych, file I.300.1.327, Jan Wiśniowski to High Chancellery of the Minister of Military Affairs, Warsaw, July 8, 1930, 251. It is

not clear why some letters are archived at the Military Archives and some at the Archive of Recent Documents.

53. AAN, Zespół Piłsudskich, part 2, file 31, Stanisław Przybysz to Józef Piłsudski, Łódź, June 13, 1926.

54. Ibid.

55. Ibid. On women's employment, see Michał Pietrzak, "Sytuacja prawna kobiet w Drugiej Rzeczypospolitej," in *Kobieta i świat polityki w niepodległej Polsce 1918–1939,* ed. Anna Żarnowska and Andrzej Szwarc (Warsaw: Wydawnictwo Sejmowe, 1996), 34, 36–37.

56. "Co trzeba robić?" *Nakazy chwili,* no. 2 (May 24, 1926): 1. See also Andrzej Garlicki, ed., *Herman Lieberman* (Warsaw: Wydawnictwo Sejmowe, 1996), 209. Herman Lieberman was a prominent Socialist and was one of those arrested during the Brześć affair.

57. Andrzej Garlicki, *Przewrót majowy* (Warsaw: Czytelnik, 1978), 290; Andrzej Chojnowski, "Rewolucja moralnego niepokoju," *Gazeta wyborcza,* no. 196 (August 23–24, 1997): 16–18; Kajetan Morawski, *Wczoraj: Pogadanki o niepodległym dwudziestoleciu* (London: Nakładem Polskiej Fundacji Kulturalnej, 1967), 150.

58. Gabriel Czechowicz (1876–1938) resigned from the finance portfolio in March 1929. He was threatened with impeachment over the ways in which state revenue was used to subsidize BBWR electioneering costs during the 1928 election campaign. See Antony Polonsky, *Politics in Independent Poland, 1921–1939: The Crisis of Constitutional Government* (Oxford: Clarendon Press, 1972), 272–77; Joseph Rothschild, *Piłsudski's Coup d'État* (New York: Columbia University Press, 1966), 256, 316, 333–38.

59. AAN, Zespół Piłsudskich, part 2, file 31, Jan Popławski to Józef Piłsudski, Białystok province, June 21, 1926, 310.

60. Ibid., 310a.

61. AAN, Zespół Piłsudskich, part 2, file 31, Andrzej Komorowski to Józef Piłsudski, Warsaw, December 7, 1926, 287–300.

62. Ibid., 294a.

63. Ibid., 287–300.

64. AAN, "Notatka Pro Domo," 32.

65. AAN, Zespół Piłsudskich, part 1, file 29, mf. 23129, Helena Sokołowska to Józef Piłsudski, Warsaw, September 30, 1930, 157–63.

66. Ibid., 159.

67. Ibid., 158–59.

68. Ibid., 162.

69. Ibid., 162–63.

70. Ibid., 159–60.

71. Ibid., 162–63.

72. AAN, Zespół Piłsudskich, part 1, file 29, mf. 23129, "common worker" to Józef Piłsudski, Wilno, 176–78. The only date on the letter has been written by the receiving office: February 20, 1931.

73. Ibid., 176.

74. Ibid.

75. Ibid.

76. Ibid., 177.

77. Ibid.

78. Ibid., 178.

79. Ibid.

80. AAN, Zespół Piłsudskich, part 2, file 32, Knothe to Piłsudski, Poznań, May 22, 1932, 96. The file contains the original handwritten copy of the letter, as well as an identical typed version. The quotations used here are taken directly from the typed copy.

81. Ibid.

82. Ibid.

83. Ibid., 97.

84. AAN, Zespół Piłsudskich, part 2, file 32, Iłłakowiczówna to Knothe and Konopkówna, Warsaw, June 6, 1932, 91–92.

85. AAN, Zespół Piłsudskich, part 2, file 32, Knothe to Iłłakowiczówna, Poznań, n.d., 87. Though the letter is undated, Jola does indicate that she received the book and Iłłakowiczówna's letter on June 24, 1932.

86. Ibid. Jola wrote to secretary Iłłakowiczówna again on May 12 and December 1, 1935, to express her great sadness about Piłsudski's death. See AAN, Zespół Piłsudskich, part 2, file 32, 79–82.

87. Wielopolska, *Józef Piłsudski*, 89–90. The protocol was dated 1 September 1928.

88. See Rothschild, *Piłsudski's Coup*, 168–70.

89. AAN, Zespół Piłsudskich, file 32, Knothe to Piłsudski, May 22, 1932, 96.

90. On the political ideologies prevalent in western Poland, see Tomasz Nodzyński, *"Strażnica Zachodnia," 1922–1939: Źródło do dziejów myśli zachodniej w Polsce* (Zielona Góra: Wyższej Szkoły Pedagogicznej im. Tadeusza Kotarbinskiego, 1997).

91. Włodzimierz Wójcik, *Pisarz i komendant: Literacka legenda Józefa Piłsudskiego* (Katowice: Towarzystwo Zachęty Kultury, 1996), 7. Zegadłowicz was the editor (from 1928) of *Tęcza*, a Poznań-based journal of the Catholic intelligentsia.

92. Alexander J. Groth, "Polish Elections, 1919–1928," *Slavic Review* 24, no. 4 (December 1965): 659. For Piłsudski's views on Poznań, given just a week after the coup, see "Wywiad udzielony korespondentowi *Le Matin*," in Józef Piłsudski, *Pisma wybrane* (London: M. I. Kolin, 1943), 416–17.

93. Roman Dmowski, as quoted in Zygmunt Wasilewski, "Wschód i zachód," *Myśl narodowa*, no. 24 (June 5, 1926): 338.

94. Adolf Nowaczyński, "Ofensywa: Antiwersal," *Myśl narodowa*, no. 28 (July 7, 1929): 15.

95. Zygmunt Wasilewski, "Odsiecz z Poznaniu," *Myśl narodowa*, no. 30 (July 14, 1929): 17. An interesting article contrasting Poznań with Sulejówek is "Tydzień,"

Prawda: Niezależny organ tygodniowy (Łódź), no. 21 (May 23, 1926): 1–2. As used in this context, "Sulejówek" represents, of course, the whole Piłsudski camp. Also on Poznań, see Tadeusz Hołówko, "Pod adresem Poznańskiego," *Robotnik,* no. 140 (May 22, 1926): 1.

96. Wasilewski, "Wschód i zachód," 338.

97. Mieczysław Piszczkowski, "Krytyka obyczajowości współczesnej," *Myśl narodowa,* no. 54 (November 22, 1931): 316.

98. For laudatory texts about Piłsudski, see Juliusz Kaden-Bandrowski, *Piłsudczycy* (1925; repr., Białystok: Krajowa Agencja Wydawnicza, 1990); *Józef Piłsudski, 1867–1935* (Kraków : Spółka Wydawnicza Kurjer, 1935); Julian Woyszwiłło [Władysław Pobóg-Malinowski], *Józef Piłsudski: Życie, idee i czyny, 1867–1935* (1937; repr., Warsaw: Wiedza Powszechna, 1990); Władysław Baranowski, *Rozmowy z Piłsudskim, 1916–1931* (Warsaw: Instytut Wydawniczy "Biblioteka Polska," 1938).

99. Zbigniew Zaporowski, *Józef Piłsudski w kręgu wojska i polityki* (Lublin: Wydawnictwo Uniwersytetu Marii Curie-Skłodowskiej, 1998), 44.

100. See, for example, Jan Starzewski, "Obraz duszy," in *Idea i czyn Józefa Piłsudskiego,* ed. Wacław Sieroszewski et al. (Warsaw: Bibljoteka Dzieł Naukowych, 1934), 82. See also Jan Starzewski, *Józef Piłsudski: Zarys psychologiczny* (Warsaw: Nakł. F. Hoesicka, 1930), 248–50.

101. Anna Borkiewicz-Celińska, "Muzeum Józefa Piłsudskiego w Belwederze (1935–1939)," *Niepodległość* 50 (1999): 257.

102. AAN, Związek Legionistów Polskich, file 49, Odezwa z powodu imienin Komendanta Józefa Piłsudskiego, March 19, 1925, 142.

103. For one such article, see Stanisław Estreicher, "Józef Piłsudski," *Czas* 67 (March 21, 1928), 1.

104. Adam Michnik, "'Kto to ma czelność zwać mnie odszczepieńcem?'" in *Wspomnienia o Antonim Słonimskim,* ed. Paweł Kądziela and Artur Międzyrzecki (Warsaw: Biblioteka Więzi, 1996), 172.

105. Hanna Pohoska, *Wychowanie obywatelsko-państwowe* (Warsaw: Ministerstwo Wyznań Religijnych i Oświecenia Publicznego, 1931), 241.

106. Andrzej Walicki, "Nietzsche in Poland (before 1918)," in *East Europe Reads Nietzsche,* ed. Alice Freifeld, Peter Bergmann, and Bernice Glatzer Rosenthal (Boulder, CO: East European Monographs/Columbia University Press, 1998), 66–67.

107. The polarized opinions on Piłsudski are nicely summed up in Wacław Bitner's memoir, "Dramat Drugiej Rzeczypospolitej," Archiwum Biblioteki Uniwersytetu Warszawskiego (hereafter BUW), file 1767, 123. Bitner was a founding member of the Christian-National Party and was a Sejm member during the sanacja era.

108. Piłsudski as the first Piłsudskiite comes from Marjan Porczak, *Dyktator Józef Piłsudski i "Piłsudczycy"* (Kraków: Nakładem Autora, 1930), 27. Piłsudski as the leader of a mafia comes from Porczak, *Piatiletka sanacyjna w piątą rocznicę zamachu*

majowego 1926 r. (Kraków: Nakładem Tow. Uniwersytetu Robotniczego, oddział im. Adama Mickiewicza w Krakowie, 1931), 14.

109. A perusal of any of the major periodicals tied to the various opposition political groupings reveals this attitude to Piłsudski quite well. See, for example, the *Worker* (*Robotnik*) for the socialist view, and the *Warsaw Gazette* (*Gazeta warszawska*) for the right-nationalist view.

110. Piotr Stasiński, *Poetyka i pragmatyka felietonu: Z dziejów form artystycznych w literaturze polskiej* (Wrocław: Ossolineum, 1982), 69. See also the satirical depiction of Piłsudski by Antoni Wasilewski, "Dyktator: Primo de Madera," in *Józef Piłsudski w karykaturze*, ed. Andrzej Garlicki and Jerzy Kochanowski (Warsaw: Wydawnictwo Interpress, 1991), 146. "Madera" is a reference to the island off the coast of Portugal where Piłsudski vacationed. The political authoritarianism of the day is further reflected in the replacement of *Senator* by *Sanator* as a way of describing the domination of the Polish government by members of the sanacja camp. See, for example, Adolf Nowaczyński, "Sanator o Sanatorach," *Gazeta warszawska*, no. 32 (1927); reprinted in Bolesław Chomicz, ed., *Sanacja czy dezorganizacja: Rzecz o polskiej dyrekcji ubezpieczeń wzajemnych* (Warsaw: Drukarnia Polska, 1927), 12–13. The ironic usages of "Sanator moralny" are discussed in Dr. J. B., "Sanacja moralna," *Ster zagłębia*, no. 9 (August 29, 1926): 2.

111. For a discussion of Piłsudski's views of Italian Fascism and German Nazism, see Władysław Kulesza, *Koncepcje ideowo-polityczne obozu rządącego w Polsce w latach 1926–1935* (Wrocław: Zakład Narodowy im. Ossolinskich, 1985), 233–91.

112. Daria Nałęcz and Tomasz Nałęcz, *Józef Piłsudski: Legendy i fakty* (Warsaw: Młodzieżowa Agencja Wydawnicza, 1986), 46. Pannenkowa outlined her position with respect to Tadeusz Boy Żeleński in "Kłamstwa," *ABC*, no. 1 (January 1, 1932): 3.

113. Jan Lipecki [Irena Pannenkowa], *Legenda Piłsudskiego* (Poznań: Wielkopolska Księgarnia Nakładowa Karola Rzepeckiego, 1922), passim., esp. 33, 83. A segment of this work is reprinted as "Irena Pannenkowa o polityce wschodniej Józefa Piłsudskiego w 1920 r. i o Piłsudczykach," in *Józef Piłsudski o państwie i armii w świetle wspomnień i innych dokumentów*, ed. Jan Borkowski (Warsaw: Państwowy Instytut Wydawniczy, 1985), 89–90.

114. Lipecki, *Legenda Piłsudskiego*, 129.

115. *Myśl narodowa* (date not provided), as quoted in Nałęcz and Nałęcz, *Józef Piłsudski*, 48.

Chapter 3

1. Archiwum PAN-Warsaw, Papiery Towarzystwa Kultury Moralnej w im. Edwarda Abramowskiego (hereafter TKM), file 4, Protokół 1-ego Posiedzenia Komisji, April 29, 1926. The name the Polish Academy of Sciences gives to the society's papers

appears to be a composite of the two different names that the society used at various times during its existence. The society registered itself under the first of these, Society for the Moral Rebirth of the Nation (Towarzystwo Odrodzenia Moralnego Ojczyzny), in May 1927, at which point it also registered its statute. See the registration notice, TKM, file 1. The society changed its name in 1928 to the Edward Abramowski Ethical Society (Towarzystwo etyczne im. Edwarda Abramowskiego). Sometimes this name also appears in the group's records as the Edward Abramowski Society for Ethical Culture (Towarzystwo kultury etycznej im. Edwarda Abramowskiego). In the interests of simplicity and consistency, I will refer to the society only as the Society for Moral Rebirth. In the notes I will use the title accorded to the society by the PAN: Towarzystwo Kultury Moralnej, abbreviated to TKM. The archival collection pertaining to this group consists of fifteen separate files. None of the pages is numbered, and the files are not organized.

2. TKM, file 6, Protokół z Walnego Zebrania T-wa Kultury Etycznej im. Edwarda Abramowskiego, June 17, 1932.

3. In addition, Sławek served in the Polish Legions and helped organize the Polish Military Organization (Polska Organizacja Wojskowa) during the war. After the war he was president of the Legionnaires' Union (Związek Legionistów) (1928–35). On Sławek, see Włodzimierz Suleja, "Walery Sławek," in *Polski słownik biograficzny*, ed. Władysław Konopczyński et al. (Kraków: Polska Akademia Umiętności, 1932–present), 38:586–95.

4. On Jędrzejewicz, see Tadeusz Katelbach, "Janusz Jędrzejewicz—Swej idei do końca wierny," *Zeszyty historyczne* 27 (1972): 228–34; Janusz Jędrzejewicz, *W służbie idei: Fragmenty pamiętnika i pism* (London: Oficyna Poetów i Malarzy, 1972).

5. In 1928 Anusz entered the Sejm on the BBWR ticket. See "Antoni Anusz o stosunku Józefa Piłsudskiego do Sejmu ustawodawczego," in *Józef Piłsudski o państwie i armii w świetle wspomnień i innych dokumentów*, ed. Jan Borkowski (Warsaw: Państwowy Instytut Wydawniczy, 1985), 94–95.

6. Samotyhowa was at the university from 1895 to 1899. Samotyhowa's papers are contained in the Krasiński Palace Manuscript Collection of the National Library (hereafter BNPK). For Samotyhowa's biographical information, see BNPK, Papiery Anieli Samotyhowej, file IV.11.003, Dokumenty Osobiste.

7. A single brief reference to the group is made in Konopczyński et al., *Polski słownik biograficzny*, s.v. Aniela Samotyhowa. The group is also mentioned in passing in Urszula Dobrzycka, *Abramowski* (Warsaw: Wiedza Powszechna, 1992), 10.

8. BNPK, Papiery Samotyhowej, file II.11.006, vol. 2: 1922–1927: Aniela Samotyhowa, *Moja książka*, May 14, 1926, 69–70. *Moja książka* (*My Book*) was a kind of diary.

9. Ibid.

10. BNPK, Samotyhowa, *Moja książka*, May 15, 1926. After May 1926 referring to Piłsudski as a Hercules and describing his acts as herculean became quite common.

See Włodzimierz Wójcik, *Legenda Piłsudskiego w polskiej literaturze międzywojennej,* 2d ed. (Katowice: Wydawnictwo Śląsk, 1986), 16.

11. BNPK, Samotyhowa, *Moja książka,* June 27, 1926, 75.

12. TKM, file 6, Protokół z Walnego Zebrania Towarzystwa Kultury Etycznej im. Edwarda Abramowskiego, June 17, 1932.

13. Those who signed the society's founding statute are Janusz Jędrzejewicz, Jan Pohoski, Helena Sujkowska, Aniela Samotyhowa, Juliusz Poniatowski, and Jadwiga Joteyko. See TKM, file 6, Protokół z Walnego Zebrania, June 17, 1932.

14. TKM, file 2, Deklaracja Programowa Towarzystwa Odrodzenia Moralnego Ojczyzny, 1926. Though there is no date noted on the statement, the declaration was first read to all those present at the society meeting on June 12, 1926. See TKM, file 4, Zebranie Komitetu Odrodzenia Moralnego, June 12, 1926. In the protocol from the meeting on June 30, 1926, Helena Sujkowska referred to the Committee for Moral Rebirth as having drafted the declaration statement and statute in April of that year. The declaration was significantly reworked after the May events. It is not clear how many versions of the declaration existed or how each changed. See TKM, file 4, Protokół. Zebranie Organizacyjne Komitetu Odrodzenia Moralnego, June 30, 1926.

15. TKM, file 2, Deklaracja Programowa Towarzystwa Odrodzenia Moralnego, 1926.

16. Ibid.

17. TKM, file 4, Zebranie Komitetu Odrodzenia Moralnego, June 12, 1926.

18. TKM, file 2, Deklaracja Programowa, 1926.

19. TKM, file 4, Protokół Zebrania, May 22, 1926. The phrase "army of moral action" comes from Capt. Jerzy Radomski.

20. "Co to znaczy rewolucja moralna?" *Nakazy chwili,* no. 3 (May 27, 1926): 1.

21. These (and other) men were associated with the National-State Union (Unia Narodowo-Państwowa), which in 1924 was succeeded by a group called the Confederation of People of Work (Konfederacja Ludzi Pracy). See Krzysztof Jakubiak, *Wychowanie państwowe jako ideologia wychowawcza sanacji: Kształtowanie i upowszechnanie w periodycznych wydawnictwach społeczno-kulturalnych i pedagogicznych* (Bydgoszcz: Wyższa Szkoła Pedagogiczna, 1994), ch. 1.

22. See Stanisław Konarski, "Jan Pohoski," in Konopczyński et al., *Polski słownik biograficzny,* 27:231; Roman Wapiński, *Świadomość polityczna w Drugiej Rzeczypospolitej* (Łódź: Wydawnictwo Łódzkie, 1989), 307–8.

23. The papers of the Society for Moral Rebirth contain one reference to working with the editors of the *Way* in an effort to popularize the goals behind the May coup. See TKM, file 3, Zebranie Zarządu, October 22, 1926.

24. Daria Nałęcz, "*Droga* jako platforma kształtowania się ideologii Piłsudczyków," *Przegląd historyczny* 6, no. 4 (1975): 590–91. The *Way* was published biweekly in 1922 and monthly in 1923. Other contributors to the *Way* included Antoni

Anusz, Jerzy Braun, Tadeusz Hołówko, Janusz Jędrzejewicz, Juliusz Kaden-Bandrowski, Adam Koc, Jan Lechoń, Hanna Pohoska, Jan Pohoski, Wacław Sieroszewski, Walery Sławek, Stefan Starzyński, Andrzej Strug, Kazimierz Świtalski, Julian Tuwim, and Adam Ważyk. See Jakubiak, *Wychowanie państwowe,* 100–116. For a discussion of Skwarczyński, see Andrzej Micewski, *W cieniu Marszałka Piłsudskiego: Szkice z dziejów myśli politycznej II Rzeczypospolitej* (Warsaw: Czytelnik, 1969), 62–95. Skwarczyński sometimes published in the *Way* under the pseudonyms Adam Płomieńczyk and Jan Ogiński.

25. Wójcik, *Legenda Piłsudskiego,* 31. For a discussion of the importance of Skwarczyński to the sanacja camp, see Micewski, *W cieniu Marszałka,* ch. 2.

26. Adam Skwarczyński, *Myśli o nowej Polsce,* 2d ed. (Warsaw: W. Daszewskiego, 1934), 66. Many of the articles in this text first appeared in the *Way.*

27. Ibid., 27. These emphases on work, the collectivity, and moral revolution recall elements of European syndicalism. On syndicalism, see Wojciech Roszkowski, "Syndykalizm polski, 1918–1929," *Niepodległość* 46 (1993): 199–230.

28. Wojciech Stpiczyński, "Pierwsze dziesięć lat ofiary, mozołu i radości," *Głos prawdy,* no. 313 (November 11, 1928); repr. in Daria Nałęcz, ed., *Nie szablą, lecz piórem: Batalie publicystyczne II Rzeczypospolitej* (Warsaw: Instytut Badań Literackich, 1993), 61.

29. Stanislaus A. Blejwas, *Realism in Polish Politics: Warsaw Positivism and National Survival in Nineteenth-Century Poland* (New Haven, CT: Yale University Press, 1984).

30. This argument is also made by Nałęcz, "*Droga,*" 601.

31. See Adam Skwarczyński, "Rewolucja moralna," *Droga,* no. 5 (1926): 1; repr. in *Adam Skwarczyński—od demokracji do autorytaryzmu,* ed. Daria Nałęcz (Warsaw: Wydawnictwo Sejmowe, 1998), 157–60.

32. Only eight issues of the paper, whose subtitle was *A Publication Dedicated to the Moral Revolution in Poland (Pismo poświęcone sprawie rewolucji moralnej w Polsce),* were ever published, in May and June 1926. See Janusz Faryś, *Piłsudski i Piłsudczycy: Z dziejów koncepcji polityczno-ustrojowej, 1918–1939* (Szczecin: Uniwersytet Szczeciński, 1991), 78; Micewski, *W cieniu Marszałka,* 67–68.

33. TKM, file 4, Protokół Zebrania, May 22, 1926.

34. Janusz Jędrzejewicz, n.t., *Nakazy chwili,* no. 1 (May 22, 1926): 1.

35. Ibid.

36. TKM, file 4, Protokół Zebrania, May 22, 1926. Before independence Radomski was associated with the Second Proletariat as well as with the PPS–Revolutionary Faction. See Radomski's entry in Konopczyński et al., *Polski słownik biograficzny,* 29:736–37.

37. TKM, file 4, Protokół Zebrania, May 22, 1926.

38. Ibid.

39. TKM, file 4, Zebranie Komitetu Odrodzenia Moralnego, June 12, 1926.

40. TKM, file 4, Protokół Zebrania, May 22, 1926.

41. Nałęcz, *"Droga,"* 594. See also Jakubiak, *Wychowanie państwowe,* 33–34; Faryś, *Piłsudski i Piłsudczycy,* 100.

42. TKM, file 4, Protokół Zebrania, May 22, 1926.

43. TKM, file 4, Protokół 1-ego posiedzenia Komisji, powołanej przez zebranie w Bibliotece Publicznej, April 29, 1926; PAN Warsaw, TKM, file 13, Listy członków, 1930.

44. TKM, file 4, Zebranie Komitetu Odrodzenia Moralnego, June 12, 1926.

45. BNPK, Samotyhowa, *Moja książka,* November 3, 1923.

46. Ibid., July 20, 1922.

47. TKM, file 4, Zebranie Komitetu Odrodzenia Moralnego, June 12, 1926.

48. See, for example, BNPK, Samotyhowa, *Moja książka,* May 15, 1926. The term *civil war* was often used by contemporaries to describe the May events.

49. BNPK, Samotyhowa, *Moja książka,* May 15, 1926.

50. For Samotyhowa on Słowacki, see BNPK, Samotyhowa, *Moja książka,* June 27, 1927; TKM, file 6, Protokół z walnego zebrania T-wa Kultury Etycznej im. Edwarda Abramowskiego, June 17, 1932.

51. BNPK, Samotyhowa, *Moja książka,* November 11, 1926.

52. Ibid.

53. A fragment of Edward Abramowski's correspondence is located at the National Library in Warsaw, in the Manuscript Division of the Krasiński Palace (BNPK). See BNPK, Papiery Samotyhowej, file III.11.053, Fragment Korespondencji E. Abramowskiego.

54. TKM, file 6, Protokół z Zebrania Zarządu TKE, October 9, 1931.

55. Adam Skwarczyński, "Kryzys demokracji," *Droga* (October 10, 1926); repr. in Daria Nałęcz, ed., *Adam Skwarczyński—od demokracji do autorytaryzmu* (Warsaw: Wydawnictwo Sejmowe, 1998), 169–74.

56. On Abramowski, see Nela Samotyhowa, *Edward Abramowski i jego poglądy na znaczenie dobra i piękna w przebudowie życia: Odczyt, wygłoszony dn. 20 listopada 1928 r. w Kamienicy Ks. Mazowieckich na wieczorze, poświęconym pamięci Edwarda Abramowskiego* (Warsaw: Wydawnictwo Towarzystwa Kultury Etycznej im. Edwarda Abramowskiego, 1931); Bohdan Cywiński, "Myśl polityczna Edwarda Abramowskiego," in *Twórcy polskiej myśli politycznej: Zbiór studiów,* ed. Jan Miś (Wrocław: Nakład Narodowy imienia Ossolińskich/Wydawnictwo Polskiej Akademii Nauk, 1978), 29–105; Andrzej Flis, "Edward Abramowski's Social and Political Thought," in *Masters of Polish Sociology,* ed. Piotr Sztompka (Wrocław: Polish Academy of Arts and Sciences, 1984), 32; Andrzej Walicki, *Stanisław Brzozowski and the Polish Beginnings of "Western Marxism"* (Oxford: Clarendon, 1989), 51, 153.

57. Samotyhowa graduated from the Faculty of Sciences at the University of Geneva in 1897/98. See BNPK, Papiery Samotyhowej, file IV.11.003, Tabela Osobista A. Miłkowska-Samotyhowa, 55.

58. See Maria Dąbrowska, "Pisma Edwarda Abramowskiego," *Wiadomości literackie,* no. 9 (March 2, 1924): 1. See also Samotyhowa, *Edward Abramowski,* 14.

59. Bohdan Cywiński, *Rodowody niepokornych* (Warsaw: Wydawnictwo Krąg, 1984), 53, 56–57.

60. TKM, file 4, Przemówienie Samotyhowej: Działalność Towarzystwa Odrodzenia Moralnego, June 30, 1926.

61. BNPK, Samotyhowa, *Moja książka,* entry dated September 10, 1925.

62. BNPK, Papiery Samotyhowej, file III.11.004, Aniela Samotyhowa, "Myśli, uwagi, obserwacje," vol. 2 (1927–30), entry dated July 15, 1928, 175.

63. BNPK, Papiery Samotyhowej, file IV.11.003, "Uwagi o kulturze," n.d., 32. Samotyhowa paraphrased Piłsudski's original statement.

64. BNPK, Samotyhowa, *Moja książka,* entry dated October 13, 1927.

65. BNPK, Papiery Samotyhowej, file IV.11.026, Aniela Samotyhowa, "Artykuły i notaki o Ed. Abramowskim," n.d. [after 1928], 41–53.

66. TKM, file 14, untitled, n.d.

67. See, for example, TKM, file 4, Zebranie Komitetu Odrodzenia Moralnego, June 12, 1926.

68. TKM, file 3, 4-e Zebranie Zarządu, October 22, 1926.

69. TKM, file 4, Protokół Zebrania, May 22, 1926.

70. TKM, file 4, Zebranie Komitetu Odrodzenia Moralnego, June 12, 1926.

71. Józef Miąso, "Kształcenie dziewcząt w Drugiej Rzeczypospolitej," in *Kobieta i edukacja na ziemiach polskich w XIX i XX w.,* ed. Anna Żarnowska and Andrzej Szwarc (Warsaw: Instytut Historyczny Uniwersytetu Warszawskiego, 1992), 2:76–77.

72. TKM, file 3, 13-e Zebranie Zarządu, April 6, 1927.

73. Hanna Pohoska, *Wychowanie obywatelsko-państwowe* (Warsaw: Ministerstwo Wyznań Religijnych, 1931); Stanisław Konarski, "Hanna Pohoska," in Konopczyński et al., *Polski słownik biograficzny,* 27:228–29.

74. BNPK, Samotyhowa, *Moja książka,* entry dated July 31, 1926.

75. On Jędrzejewicz and school reform, see Micewski, *W cieniu Marszałka,* 372–76; Jędrzejewicz, *W służbie idei,* 113–64.

76. On the sanacja and education, see Władysław Kulesza, *Koncepcje ideowo-polityczne obozu rządącego w Polsce w latach 1926–1935* (Wrocław: Zakład Narodowy im. Ossolinskich, 1985), 207–12; Faryś, *Piłsudski i Piłsudczycy,* 101–2.

77. *Frame (Zrąb)* was formed in the spring of 1929 as a journal for educators. Janusz Jędrzejewicz was involved with establishing and editing it, and from 1931 to 1936, Pohoska served as editor. See Sławomir Czerwiński, *O nowy ideał wychowawczy* (Warsaw: Biblioteka Zrąb, 1932).

78. BNPK, Samotyhowa, "Myśli, uwagi, obserwacje," entry dated August 21, 1927, 60.

79. See TKM, file 4, Zebranie Komitetu Odrodzenia Moralnego, June 12, 1926; BNPK, Samotyhowa, *Moja książka,* entry dated April 13, 1926.

80. Samotyhowa, *Moja książka,* entry dated November 3, 1923.

81. Nałęcz, *"Droga,"* 596–97; Daria Nałęcz, *Sen o władzy: Inteligencja wobec niepodległości* (Warsaw: Państwowy Instytut Wydawniczy, 1994), 150; Borkowski, "Piłsudczykowska koncepcja państwa," *Dzieje najnowsze* 14, no. 1 (1982): 115; Śliwa, *Polska myśl polityczna w I połowie XX wieku* (Wrocław: Ossolineum, 1993), 102–3.

82. TKM, file 4, Protokół Pierwszego Posiedzenia Komisji, powołanej przez zebranie w Bibliotece Publicznej, April 29, 1926.

83. Ibid.

84. TKM, file 4, Instrukcja dla Członków TOM Wyjeżdżących na Prowincję, June 1926.

85. BNPK, Samotyhowa, *Moja książka,* entry dated July 31, 1926.

86. TKM, file 2, Projekt Ankiety, n.d. And see file 2, Sprawozdanie z Działalności Zarządu TOM im. E. A., December 14, 1927–December 1, 1928.

87. BNPK, Samotyhowa, *Moja książka,* entry dated April 13, 1926. Samotyhowa was nominally of the Evangelical-Reform Church. See BNPK, Papiery Samotyhowej, file IV.11.003, Tabela Osobista A. Miłkowska-Samotyhowa, 55.

88. On the concordat, see Jerzy Wisłocki, *Konkordat polski z 1925 roku: Zagadnienia prawno-polityczne* (Poznań: Wydawnictwo Uniwersytetu im. Adama Mickiewicza, 1977); Ronald Modras, *The Catholic Church and Antisemitism: Poland, 1933–1939* (Jerusalem: Hebrew University of Jerusalem/Harwood Academic Publishers, 1994), 36–38.

89. TKM, file 3, Definitywny Tekst Protestu; TKM, file 3, 10-e Zebranie Zarządu, February 22, 1927.

90. TKM, file 3, Definitywny Tekst Protestu; TKM, file 3, 10-e Zebranie Zarządu, February 22, 1927.

91. TKM, file 3, Definitywny Tekst Protestu.

92. TKM, file 3, 10-e Zebranie Zarządu, February 22, 1927.

93. Neal Pease, "Poland and the Holy See, 1918–1939," *Slavic Review* 50, no. 3 (Fall 1991): 525.

94. The concern was expressed in TKM, file 3, 11-e Zebranie Zarządu, March 10, 1927.

95. Sujkowska had been involved with establishing the Women's League in 1913. See Ludwik Hass, "Aktywność wyborcza kobiet w pierwszym dziesięcioleciu Drugiej Rzeczypospolitej," in Żarnowska and Szwarc, *Kobieta i świat polityki,* 70.

96. Name changes are discussed in the following: TKM, file 3, 29-e Zebranie Zarządu, March 5, 1928; TKM, file 3, Zebranie Zarządu, October 23, 1928; TKM, file 4, Protokół Walnego Zebrania Tow. Odr. Mor. im. Edwarda Abramowskiego, December 18, 1928.

97. TKM, file 4, Protokół Zebrania, May 22, 1926. On Budzińska-Tylicka, see Dionizja Wawrzykowska-Wierciochowa, *Nie po kwiatach los je prowadził: Kobiety polskie w ruchu rewolucyjnym* (Warsaw: Iskry, 1987), 297–98. The Polish Society for Freedom was organized in 1922 in Warsaw as a kind of continuation of the wartime underground Polish Military Organization. See BNDŻS, *Komunikat Informacyjno-Polityczny.* Wydawnictwo Okręgu Warszawskiego Polskiej Organizacji Wolności, no. 4 (October 15, 1922).

98. TKM, file 3, 5-e Zebranie Zarządu, October 29, 1926.

99. Samotyhowa often also served as secretary. Loretowa was a member of the Political Club of Progressive Women (Klub Polityczny Kobiet Postępowych). See "Obecny zarząd Klubu Politycznego Kobiet Postępowych," *Kobieta współczesna,* no. 23 (June 8, 1930).

100. TKM, file 6, Protokół z Walnego Zebrania T-wa Kultury Etycznej im. Edwarda Abramowskiego, June 17, 1932.

101. TKM, file 4, Protokół Walnego Zebrania T-wa Odrodzenia Moralnego im. Edw. Abramowskiego, January 27, 1928.

102. TKM, file 7, Marja Jagminowa to "Dear Madam," Warsaw, June 7, 1929.

103. TKM, file 8, Maria Jagminowa to "Dear Madam," Warsaw, January 20, 1930. The handwritten letter bears the reference number L8/30.

104. The modest financial resources available to the society undoubtedly also contributed to the group's desire to raise membership numbers. Society members were required to pay dues, but there were simply not many members, and thus little money was actually collected through dues. See TKM, file 6, Protokół z Walnego Zebrania T-wa Kultury Etycznej im. Edwarda Abramowskiego, June 17, 1932. See also the assorted financial statements in file 11.

105. TKM, file 8, Jadwiga Jahołkowska to Society for Moral Rebirth, Warsaw, January 20, 1930. The letter bears the reference number L9/30. On Jahołkowska, see Dionizja Wawrzykowska-Wierciochowa, "Jadwiga Jahołkowska—postępowa działaczka Ludowego Ruchu Kobiet," *Kultura i społeczeństwo* 20, no. 1 (1976): 61–78. This article contains many references to contemporary sources about Jahołkowska. Jahołkowska's death was mentioned at a 1932 general meeting of the society. See Protokół z Walnego Zebrania, June 17, 1932.

106. TKM, file 5, Protokół Walnego Zebrania TOM im. E. A., February 11, 1930.

107. TKM, file 8, Deklaracja Ideowa Towarzystwa Kultury Etycznej, 1930.

108. Ibid.

109. Ibid.

110. Ibid.

111. See, for example, TKM, file 4, Protokół Walnego Zebrania T-wa Odrodzenia Moralnego im. Edw. Abramowskiego, January 27, 1928.

112. TKM, file 5, Protokół Nadzwyczajnego Walnego Zebrania TOM, March 3, 1930.

113. TKM, file 5, Protokół Walnego Zebrania TOM im. E. A., February 11, 1930.

114. TKM, file 8, n.t., 1930. This statement bears the reference number Lp 57-a/30.

115. TKM, file 13, Listy Członków, 1930.

116. TKM, file 13, Listy Członków, 1930. Dąbrowska came to a society meeting once, when her book *Dom kobiet* (*The House of Women*) was the subject of the evening's discussion. See file 2, Sprawozdanie z Działalności Kultury Etycznej im. E. A., March 3, 1930–February 13, 1931.

117. TKM, file 13, Listy Członków, 1930. See TKM, file 2, Sprawozdanie z Działalności Kultury Etycznej im. E. A., March 3, 1930–February 13, 1931.

118. On Marian Godecki, see Konopczyński et al., *Polski słownik biograficzny*, 8:169.

119. On Radomski, see ibid., 29:737.

120. TKM, file 6, Protokół z Walnego Zebrania T-wa Kultury Etycznej im. Edwarda Abramowskiego, June 17, 1932.

121. Ibid.

122. TKM, file 13, Listy Członków, 1930.

123. Nela Samotyhowa, "W rocznicę," *Praca obywatelska* 1 (November 10, 1928): 1

124. AAN, Zbiór Druków Ulotnych, Demokratyczny Komitet Wyborczy [1926], file 92.

125. TKM, file 4, Protokół. Zebranie Organizacyjne Komitetu Odrodzenia Moralnego, June 30, 1926.

126. On these subjects, see TKM, file 5, Protokół Posiedzenia TKE, April 28, 1930; TKM, file 6, Sprawozdanie z Zebrania Zarządu TKE, April 24, 1931.

127. On links to *Contemporary Woman* (*Kobieta współczesna*), see TKM, file 5, Protokół Zebrania Tow. Kult. Etycznej, April 14, 1930.

128. BNPK, Papiery Anieli Samotyhowej, file IV.11.003, Praca na tle biograficznym Neli/Anieli z Miłkowskich Samotyhowej.

129. See BNPK, Papiery Samotyhowej, file III.11.004, Aniela Samotyhowa, "O miłości, małżeństwie, rodzinie i wolności osobistej," August 1930–November 1930.

130. BNPK, Samotyhowa, "II.1931 r. 1932 r. 1933 r. 1934 r.," entry dated June 7, 1931, 141–42.

131. Ibid. Samotyhowa did not refer to a specific church.

132. TKM, file 5, Protokół Zebrania Zarządu TOM, January 13, 1930. Antoni Anusz defended Brześć. See Iwo Werschler, *Z dziejów obozu belwederskiego: Tadeusz Hołówko, życie i działalność* (Warsaw: Państwowe Wydawnictwo Naukowe, 1984), 282n75.

133. TKM, file 5, Protokół TKE, December 19, 1930. See also file 5, Protokół Zebrania TKE, June 2, 1930.

134. TKM, file 8, letter dated December 22, 1930. The letter, which bears the reference number L81/30, was published in the *Morning Courier* (*Kurier poranny*), December 23, 1930.

135. TKM, file 9, Stanisław Małkowski to the society, Warsaw, November 28, 1931. The letter bears the reference number L136/31.

136. TKM file 3, 4-e Zebranie Zarządu, October 22, 1926; TKM, file 3, 5-e Zebranie Zarządu, October 29, 1926.

137. TKM, file 9, Małkowski to the society, November 28, 1931.

138. The Commissariat of Warsaw was notified of the liquidation by a letter dated March 3, 1933. See TKM, file 12.

139. Ibid.

140. BNPK, Papiery Samotyhowej, file IV.11.003, Praca na tle biograficznym Neli/Anieli/z Miłkowskich Samotyhowej, 61.

141. Samotyhowa, *Edward Abramowski,* 28–31.

Chapter 4

1. National Library, Warsaw, Krasiński Palace Manuscript Collection, Listy Zofii Moraczewskiej do Heleny Kozickiej, file 52, vol. 6, Korespondencja 1926–28, Moraczewska to Kozicka, May 16, 1926, 27. The Moraczewski collection is split between the Archive for Recent Documents (AAN) and the National Library's Manuscript Collection at the Krasiński Palace (BNPK), both in Warsaw. In Norse mythology the Valkyries were the warrior maidens who selected the men that would be slain in battle and took them to Valhalla.

2. On the use of the straw man metaphor in Stanisław Wyspiański's 1901 play *The Wedding,* see Aniela Łempicka, *Wyspiański, pisarz dramatyczny: Idee i formy* (Kraków: Wydawnictwo Literackie, 1973), 339.

3. Moraczewska to Kozicka, May 25, 1926, 32.

4. Archiwum Akt Nowych (hereafter AAN), Zespół Jędrzeja i Zofii Moraczewskich, file 71/III-9, Zofia Moraczewska, *Wspomnienia o moich pracach społecznych,* ca. 1943–45, 28.

5. Moraczewska to Kozicka, June 3, 1926, 39.

6. AAN, Zespół Jędrzeja i Zofii Moraczewskich, file 71/III-6, mf. 1855/6, Zofia Moraczewska, *Demokratyczny Komitet Wyborczy Kobiet i jego praca w r. 1928 i Związek Pracy Obywatelskiej Kobiet, Rozdział II: Założenie Związku Pracy Obywatelskiej Kobiet.*

7. AAN, Moraczewska, *Wspomnienia o moich pracach społecznych,* 29. For an elaboration of a similar point, see BNPK, Zbiór Moraczewskich, file 36, Zarząd Główny, ZPOK/Z. M., *Związek Pracy Obywatelskiej Kobiet* (Warsaw: ZPOK, Dział Prasowy, 1932), 101. ZPOK stands for Women's Union for Citizenship Work (Związek Pracy Obywatelskiej Kobiet) and appears often in the papers of Moraczewska and of the organization generally.

8. AAN, Moraczewska, *Wspomnienia;* emphasis in original.

9. On maternal feminism in the Western context, see, for example, Mariana Valverde, *The Age of Light, Soap, and Water: Moral Reform in English Canada, 1885–1925* (1991; repr., Toronto: McClelland and Stewart, 1993).

10. Sławomira Walczewska, *Damy, rycerze i feministki: Kobiecy dyskurs emancypacyjny w Polsce* (Kraków: eFKa, 1999), 44–46. See also Maria Janion, *Kobieta i duch inności* (Warsaw: Wydawnictwo Sic! 1996), 97; Brian Porter, "*Hetmanka* and Mother: Representing the Virgin Mary in Modern Poland," *Contemporary European History* 14, no. 2 (2005): 159–60.

11. On the meaning of suffrage rights in the Polish context, see Walczewska, *Damy, rycerze,* 53, 60–64. Articles 12, 13, and 96 of the March 1921 constitution guaranteed women's political rights. These rights were renewed in 1928 and 1931. See Zofia Chyra-Rolicz, "Kościół katolicki a ruch kobiecy przed 1939 rokiem," in *Społeczno-kulturalna działalność Kościoła katolickiego w Polsce XIX i XX wieku,* ed. Regina Renz and Marta Meducka (Kielce: Kieleckie Towarzystwo Naukowe, 1994), 154.

12. BNPK, Zespół Jędrzeja i Zofii Moraczewskich, file 36, "Przemówienie Z. Moraczewskiej na zjeździe delegatek Komitetu Wyborczego Kobiecych," March 25, 1927, 31.

13. On Moraczewska, see Dionizja Wawrzykowska-Wierciochowa, *Nie po kwiatach los je prowadził: Kobiety polskie w ruchu rewolucyjnym* (Warsaw: Iskry, 1987); Wiesław Bieńkowski, "Zofia Moraczewska," in *Polski słownik biograficzny,* ed. Władysław Konopczyński et al. (Kraków: Polska Akademia Umiętności, 1932–present), 21:677–79. Notable exceptions to the lacuna in the historiography are Andrzej Chojnowski, "Moralność i polityka. Kobiece Lobby w Bezpartyjnym Bloku Współpracy z Rządem," in *Kobieta i świat polityki w niepodległej Polsce, 1918–1939,* ed. Anna Żarnowska and Andrzej Szwarc (Warsaw: Wydawnictwo Sejmowe, 1996), 161–76.

14. On interwar women's history in Poland, see Dobrochna Kałwa, *Kobieta aktywna w Polsce międzywojennej,* 2 vols. (Kraków: Uniwersytet Jagielloński, 2001). The multivolume collection edited by Anna Żarnowska and Andrzej Szwarc on selected aspects of the history of women in Poland is also extremely important. See especially the following titles: *Kobieta i świat polityki* (1996); *Kobieta i kultura życia codziennego: wiek XIX i XX* (1997); *Kobieta i praca* (2000); *Kobieta i kultura czasu wolnego* (2001); *Kobieta i małżeństwo* (2004). Some of the research in the Żarnowska and Szwarc volumes has been condensed for and summarized in Anna Żarnowska and Andrzej Szwarc, eds., *Równe prawa i nierówne szanse: Kobiety w Polsce Międzywojennej* (Warsaw: Wydawnictwo DiG, 2000). See also Elżbieta Pakszys, "The State of Research on Polish Women in the Last Two Decades," *Journal of Women's History* 3, no. 3 (Winter 1992): 118–25. For an overview of women's activism during the first decade of independence, see Ludwik Hass, "Aktywność wyborcza kobiet w pierwszym

dziesięcioleciu Drugiej Rzeczypospolitej," in Żarnowska and Szwarc, *Kobieta i świat polityki,* 70–99. A good introduction to the political rights of women in the Second Republic is offered in Michał Śliwa, "Kobiety w parlamencie Drugiej Rzeczypospolitej," in *Kobieta i świat polityki w niepodległej Polsce, 1918–1939,* ed. Anna Żarnowska and Andrzej Szwarc (Warsaw: Wydawnictwo Sejmowe, 1996), 53–69.

15. During the war, the Women's League was a branch of the Main National Committee (Naczelny Komitet Narodowy, NKN). The NKN and the Women's League ran into conflict with one another: Moraczewska and the league opposed Polish participation in the Austro-German side of the war; the NKN supported it. See AAN, Moraczewska, *Wspomnienia o moich pracach społecznych,* 26. See also AAN, Zespół Ligi Kobiet Polskich, files 30, 63. Also on this period, see Robert M. Ponichtera, "Feminists, Nationalists, and Soldiers: Women in the Fight for Polish Independence," *International History Review* 19, no. 1 (February 1997): 16–31.

16. Moraczewska's own history of the league was written in the autumn of 1939 and the winter of 1940 in Sulejówek and is entitled *Liga Kobiet z epoki Legjonów Polskich i O. W. Józefa Piłsudskiego walczących o odrodzenie niepodległego państwa polskiego od 1/8 1914 do 1/11 1918.* See AAN, Zespół Jędrzeja i Zofii Moraczewskich, mf. 1855/6.

17. Moraczewska often wrote to her sister about the daily household grind and about the very real economic concerns she and her husband faced. See BNPK, Zbiór Moraczewskich, file 52, vol. 5: letters from Zofia Moraczewska to Helena Kozicka, 1923–25, letter dated January 10, 1923, 9.

18. On women and left politics, see Jerzy Myśliński, "Kobiety w polskich ugrupowaniach lewicowych, 1918–1939," in Żarnowska and Szwarc, *Równe prawa,* 61–76.

19. For an introduction to Moraczewski's biography, see Janusz Gołota, "Ewolucja ideowo-polityczna Jędrzeja Moraczewskiego 1920–1939," *Dzieje najnowsze* 27, no. 3 (1995): 13–29; Gołota, "Jędrzej Moraczewski w latach 1919–1926," *Dzieje najnowsze* 25, no. 2 (1993): 35–51; Bieńkowski, "Jędrzej Moraczewski," in *Polski słownik biograficzny,* 21:684–89.

20. Moraczewska's commitment to socialism was typical of her generation. See Adam Próchnik, *Kobieta w polskim ruchu socjalistycznym* (Warsaw: Spółdzielnia Wydawnicza Wiedza, 1949). Both Moraczewska and her husband, Jędrzej, left the Polish Socialist Party in 1927, when it came out against Piłsudski and the May coup. In October 1928, ten out of sixty-three PPS Sejm deputies split from the main PPS party and formed the PPS–Revolutionary Faction, which supported the BBWR. Moraczewski supported this breakaway party. See Joseph Rothschild, *Piłsudski's Coup d'État* (New York: Columbia University Press, 1966), 255–56, 268.

21. AAN, Moraczewska, *Wspomnienia o moich pracach społecznych,* 27.

22. Pietrzak, "Sytuacja prawna kobiet," 36.

23. For more on the Political Club of Progressive Women, see BNPK, Papiery Teodory Męczkowskiej, file II.10.302, *50 lat pracy w organizacjach kobiecych w Warszawie: Wspomnienia osobiste,* 134–46, esp. 138.

24. AAN, Moraczewska, *Wspomnienia o moich pracach społecznych,* 27.

25. BNPK, Zespół Jędrzeja i Zofii Moraczewskich, file 36, "Przemówienie Z. Moraczewskiej na zjeździe delegatek Komitetu Wyborczego Kobiecych, który powołał do życia ZPOK," Warsaw, March 25, 1927, 30.

26. BNPK, Zespół Jędrzeja i Zofii Moraczewskich, file 131, "Regulamin Demokratycznego Komitetu Wyborczego Kobiet Polskich," 35; BNPK, Zespół Jędrzeja i Zofii Moraczewskich, file 131, Demokratyczny Komitet Wyborczy Kobiet, "Deklaracja ideowa," 32; see also 35/6c. An earlier version of the declaration statement is contained in BNPK, Zespół Jędrzeja i Zofii Moraczewskich, file 127, "Deklaracja."

27. The committee's founding members included Moraczewska (president), Sylwia Bujak Boguska, Dr. Zofja Daszyńska-Golińska, Dr. Bronisława Dłuska, Hanna Hubicka, Halina Chełmicka-Jaroszewiczowa, Teodora Męczkowska, Henryka Pawlewska, Leonja Sas-Kulczycka, Natalja Steinowa, Irena Szydłowska, Eugenja Waśniewska, Dora Wisznicka, and Dr. Kazimiera Żuławska. See BNPK, Demokratyczny Komitet Wyborczy Kobiet, "Deklaracja ideowa," 32. For biographical information on each of these women, see Wawrzykowska-Wierciochowa, *Nie po kwiatach.*

28. These sixteen persons were the chairwoman, four vice-chairwomen, four secretaries, one treasurer, three clerks of the propaganda division, and three clerks of the technical division. See BNPK, Zespół Jędrzeja i Zofii Moraczewskich, file 131, "Regulamin Demokratycznego Komitetu Wyborczego Kobiet Polskich," 35.

29. AAN, Zespół Ligi Kobiet Polskich, file 27, Protokół, December 8, 1927, Warsaw, n.p. On the BBWR, see Jerzy Halbersztadt, "Józef Piłsudski i jego współpracownicy wobec wyborów parlamentarnych w latach 1926–1928: Z badań nad genezą BBWR," *Dzieje najnowsze* 16, no. 1 (1984): 3–34; Andrzej Chojnowski, *Piłsudczycy u władzy: Dzieje Bezpartyjnego Bloku Współpracy z Rządem* (Wrocław: Ossolineum, 1986), 245–52.

30. AAN, Zespół Jędrzeja i Zofii Moraczewskich, file 71/I-81, mf. 2314/9, "Z założeń programowych BB[WR]. Wyjątki z mowy Płk. Sławka na posiedzeniu Klubu BB," June 23, 1928.

31. BNPK, Demokratyczny Komitet Wyborczy Kobiet, "Deklaracja ideowa," 32.

32. AAN, Zespół Jędrzeja i Zofii Moraczewskich, file 71/III-6, mf. 1855/6, Zofia Moraczewska, *Demokratyczny Komitet Wyborczy Kobiet i jego praca w r. 1928 i Związek Pracy Obywatelskiej Kobiet, Rozdział I: Demokratyczny Komitet i jego praca w r. 1928.*

33. Articles in the press were filled with analyses of constitutional reform. See, for example, Kazimierz Dagnan, "Majowe przewroty w Polsce. Podobieństwa i róznice," *Nowa sprawa robotnicza,* no. 4 (June 20, 1926): 2–3.

34. Specifically, the August Amendment allowed the president to dissolve the legislature upon the recommendation of the cabinet and to use a suspensive veto over legislation. See Rothschild, *Piłsudski's Coup*, 223–26; AAN, Zespół Bezpartyjnego Bloku Współpracy z Rządem (hereafter BBWR), file 24, poster for the BBWR addressed to "Poles," February 22, 1929, 2.

35. BNPK, Demokratyczny Komitet Wyborczy Kobiet, "Deklaracja ideowa," 32. Once the permanent constitution was passed in 1935, the Women's Union collected all the articles which pertained to women and published them as Grażyna Szmurłowa, Halina Siemieńska, and Halina Alchimowicz, *Kobieta w prawie publicznym i prywatnym: Zbiór przepisów obowiązujących w Polsce* (Warsaw: Związek Pracy Obywatelskiej Kobiet, Wydział Spraw Kobiecych, Sekcja Prawna, 1937).

36. BNPK, Demokratyczny Komitet Wyborczy Kobiet, "Deklaracja ideowa," 32.

37. BNPK, "Regulamin Demokratycznego Komitetu Wyborczego Kobiet Polskich," 35.

38. For an excellent discussion of discriminatory civil statutes in effect in the Second Republic, see Kałwa, *Kobieta aktywna*, 34–37.

39. AAN, Moraczewska, *Demokratyczny Komitet Wyborczy Kobiet*. See also BNPK, Demokratyczny Komitet Wyborczy Kobiet, "Deklaracja ideowa," 32. On women's employment, see Anna Żarnowska and Andrzej Szwarc, eds., *Kobieta i praca: Wiek XIX i XX* (Warsaw: DiG, 2000).

40. BNPK, Zespół Jędrzeja i Zofii Moraczewskich, file 36, "Przemówienie Z. Moraczewskiej na zjeździe delegatek Komitetu Wyborczego Kobiecych," March 25, 1927, 31.

41. BNPK, Zespół Moraczewskich, file 136, "Odezwy Wyborcze Demokratycznego Komitetu Wyborczego Kobiet Polskich," 1928, 52. More posters from the 1928 elections are found in AAN, Zespół Bezpartyjnego Bloku Współpracy z Rządem, file 33, mf. 31084.

42. BNPK, "Odezwy Wyborcze Demokratycznego Komitetu Wyborczego Kobiet Polskich," 52. On Piłsudski and women's suffrage, see Walczewska, *Damy, rycerze*, 53, 60–64. For a review of suffrage and feminism in other parts of Europe, see Karen Offen, *European Feminisms, 1700–1950: A Political History* (Palo Alto, CA: Stanford University Press, 2000).

43. Ibid., 3. For a poster from Warsaw that raises similar points, see p. 40.

44. Ibid., 24.

45. Ibid., 37; emphasis in original.

46. See, for example, a poster published by the Women's League and addressed to "Female Polish Citizens." The poster is dated 1927. See AAN, Zespół Ligi Kobiet Polskich, file 29.

47. AAN, Zbiór Druków Ulotnych, file 199, "Wybory do Sejmu, 1928."

48. The Catholic-national bloc was composed of the People's National Union, the Christian Nationalists, and some Christian Democrats.

49. On the National Organization of Women, see AAN, Zbiór Druków Ulotnych, file 291, Narodowa Organizacja Kobiet [1922]. On the differences between this group and the Women's Union, see Marja Jaworska, "Narodowa Organizacja Kobiet—a my!" *Praca obywatelska* 2 (December 28, 1928): 2–3. See also Dobrochna Kałwa, "Poland," in *Women, Gender, and Fascism in Europe, 1919–1945,* ed. Kevin Passmore (New Brunswick, NJ: Rutgers University Press, 2003), 161–67. On Catholic women's movements generally, see Zofia Chyra-Rolicz, "Kościół katolicki," 157.

50. National Library, Documents from Social Life (hereafter BNDŻS), Narodowa Organizacja Kobiet, Warsaw, file I, Okólnik no. 14, December 1929.

51. S. W., "O wychowanie religijne i narodowe," *Hasło polki,* no. 9 (October 25, 1937): 1.

52. AAN, Zbiór Druków Ulotnych, file 205, Narodowa Organizacja Kobiet, Chełm, election poster, 1928.

53. AAN, Zbiór Druków Ulotnych, file 103, Komitet Katolicko-Narodowy, 1928, n.

54. Odezwy Wyborcze Demokratycznego Komitetu Wyborczego Kobiet Polskich, 1928, 10.

55. Ibid., 8.

56. AAN, Zespół Bezpartyjnego Bloku Współpracy z Rządem, file 33, mf.31084, Poster addressed to "Catholic Polish Women!" 1928.

57. Odezwy Wyborcze Demokratycznego Komitetu Wyborczego Kobiet Polskich, 1928. An Election Committee poster from Warsaw, contained in the same collection, also makes reference to the fact that Piłsudski had been blessed by the pope. See also BNDŻS, file IA6c1, n.a., "W imię prawdy," *Biuletyn Okręgowego Komitetu Wybor. BBWR Marszałka Piłsudskiego,* no. 2 (February 14, 1928): 1 for a statement about how completely the pope trusted that Piłsudski was committed to a Catholic Poland.

58. AAN, Zespół Bezpartyjnego Bloku Współpracy z Rządem, file 33, mf.31084, election poster, untitled, produced by Democratic Election Committee of Lublin, February 1928.

59. "Odezwy Wyborcze Demokratycznego Komitetu Wyborczego Kobiet Polskich," 17.

60. The BBWR won 122 seats in the Sejm and 46 in the Senate, out of a total of 444 and 111 respectively. The parties of the left won just under 25 percent of the votes for the Sejm and almost 22 percent for the Senate. The elections were a significant defeat for the parties of the Right, most notably for National Democracy. See Chojnowski, *Piłsudczycy u władzy,* 44–63; Jan Tomicki, *II Rzeczpospolita: Oczekiwania i rzeczywistość* (Warsaw: Młodzieżowa Agencja Wydawnicza, 1986), 170–72.

61. Chojnowski, *Piłsudczycy u władzy,* 73.

62. For a brief biography of Jaworska, see the entry by Michalina Grekowicz-Hausnerowa in Konopczyński et al., *Polski słownik biograficzny* 11:103–4. Jaworska headed the Sejm's Education Commission from 1930 to 1935. Waśniewska also served as general secretary of the Polish Eugenics Society. See "Nasze posłanki," *Praca obywatelska* 18 (December 10, 1930): 1–2. See also Śliwa, "Kobiety w parlamencie," 56.

63. BNPK, Męczkowska, *50 lat pracy w organizacjach kobiecych,* 146–47.

64. Kosmowska was minister of social affairs in the 1918 government. See Kałwa, "Poland," 155.

65. Anna Żarnowska, "Women's Political Participation in Inter-War Poland: Opportunities and Limitations," *Women's History Review* 13, no. 1 (2004): 59; Śliwa, "Kobiety w parlamencie," 54–56.

66. AAN, Moraczewska, *Demokratyczny Komitet Wyborczy Kobiet.*

67. Ibid. For a discussion of the Women's Union in the broader context of women's activism in the Second Republic, see Kałwa, *Kobieta aktywna,* ch. 7.

68. Moraczewska herself claimed the group had over forty thousand members. See BNPK, Zespół Jędrzeja i Zofii Moraczewskich, file 36, "Przemówienie wygłaszane przez radjo w Warszawie," November 6, 1930, 88. Chojnowski provides different figures, drawn from Moraczewska's memoirs: thirty-one thousand members grouped in 360 branches in 1930, and ninety thousand members grouped in 900 branches in 1935. See Chojnowski, "Moralność i polityka," 167.

69. BNPK, Zespół Moraczewskich, file 36, "Przemówienie Z. Moraczewskiej na zjeździe delegatek Komitetu Wyborczego Kobiecych, który powołał do życia ZPOK," Warsaw, March 25, 1927, 31.

70. AAN, Zespół Moraczewskich, file 71/III-6, mf. 1855/6, Zofia Moraczewska, *DKWK i jego praca w r. 1928 i ZPOK, Rozdział III: Rozwój Związku,* n.d., n.p.

71. AAN, Moraczewska, *DKWK i jego praca w r. 1928 i ZPOK, Rozdział II: Założenie ZPOK,* n.p.

72. The group also provided material and moral aid to its members. See AAN, Zespół Związku Legionistek Polskich (ZLP), file 1, "Statut ZLP," Warsaw, 1929, 3–10. In 1933 the Legion Women joined the Intra-Associational Committee for Women's Issues (Komitet Międzystowarzyszeniowy do Spraw Kobiecych), an umbrella organization established to coordinate the activities of prosanacja women's organizations. It included the Women's Union for Citizenship Work, among other groups. See AAN, ZLP, file 61, December 2, 1933, 3.

73. This group established the journal *For the Future* (*Dla przyszłości: Wydawnictwo Komitetu Społecznego Przysposobienia Kobiet do Obrony Kraju*) in Warsaw in 1927.

74. On Reform, see Ludwik Hass, "Związek Patriotyczny, 1918–1926: Z dziejów infrastruktury życia politycznego Drugiej Rzeczypospolitej," *Kwartalnik historyczny* 85, no. 4 (1978): 913–42. Members of Reform joined with the Party of Work

(Partia Pracy) (which had evolved from left-wing peasant party PSL-Liberation) to form the Union of Labor in Town and Village (Zjednoczenie Pracy Wsi i Miast) in June 1928. The Union of Labor in turn formed a core block within the BBWR until 1930. On the Union of Labor, see AAN, Zespół Zjednoczenia Pracy Wsi i Miast (ZPWiM), file 1, Rezolucje Zarządu Głównego ZPWiM, October 1, 1929, 19–20; Statut ZPWiM, 1930.

75. Janina Strzelecka, "Jak rozumiemy feminizm," *Praca Obywatelska* 2 (February 28, 1929): 4–5. On the meaning and use of the term *feminist* during this period, see Kałwa, *Kobieta akywna*, 144–45.

76. AAN, Moraczewska, *Demokratyczny Komitet Wyborczy Kobiet i Jego Praca w r. 1928 i Związek Pracy Obywatelskiej Kobiet, Rozdział II: Założenie Związku Pracy Obywatelskiej Kobiet*, n.p.

77. BNDŻS, file ID 1933, "Sprawozdanie ZOK, Poznańskie Zrzeszenie Wojewódzkie, z Działalności za czas 15 stycznia 1931 do 1 maja 1933," Poznań, May 1933, 6.

78. Ibid., 6–7.

79. BNPK, Zespół Jędrzeja i Zofii Moraczewskich, file 125, Natalia Greniewska, "Kobieta w polityce," 1930, 34; see also 31–33.

80. BNDŻS, "Sprawozdanie ZOK," 6.

81. Zarząd Główny, ZPOK/Z. M., *Związek Pracy Obywatelskiej Kobiet*, 104.

82. BNPK, Zespół Jędrzeja i Zofii Moraczewskich, file 36, "Przemówienie Z. Moraczewskiej na Zjeździe Delegatek Komitetu Wyborczego Kobiecych, który powołał do życia ZPOK," Warsaw, March 25, 1927, 32.

83. BNPK, Zespół Moraczewskich, file 137, Zofia Moraczewska to "Dear Madam," October 19, 1932, 34a; copy.

84. Positivist writer Eliza Orzeszkowa described the distance that separated Poles and Jews as a "Chinese wall." Moraczewska was a devoted fan of Orzeszkowa. See AAN, Moraczewska, *Wspomnienia o moich pracach społecznych*, 17.

85. BNPK, Moraczewska to "Dear Madam," October 19, 1932, 34a.

86. AAN, Moraczewska, *Wspomnienia o moich pracach społecznych*, 31.

87. BNPK, Zespół Jędrzeja i Zofii Moraczewskich, file 118, Wydział Wychowania Obywatelskiego, Zarząd Pełny, September 22, 1929, 3.

88. BNPK, Zarząd Główny, ZPOK/Z. M., *Związek Pracy Obywatelskiej Kobiet*, 104.

89. BNPK, Zespół Jędrzeja i Zofii Moraczewskich, file 125, Hanna Hubicka, "Ideologia Obozu Marszałka Piłsudskiego," 1930 lecture given to the Women's Union, 50–52.

90. Ibid.; AAN, Moraczewska, *Wspomnienia o moich pracach społecznych*, 30.

91. BNPK, Zespół Moraczewskich, file 118, "Projekt pracy i regulamin Wyd. Uświadomienia Obywatelskiego," n.d.; BNPK, Zespół Moraczewskich, file 118, ZPOK, Wychow. Obywatel., "Tematy na odczyty," n.d., 92.

92. For a voice in support of the new marriage and divorce law proposals, see BNPK, Zespół Moraczewskich, file 121, Regina Zyndram-Kościałkowska, "Opinja w sprawie nowego prawa małżeńskiego," January 29, 1932, 45.

93. For a collection of papers pertaining to women's rights and the Codification Commission, see AAN, Zespół Moraczewskich, file 71/1–91, mf. 2314/10, esp. 27–33.

94. BNPK, Zespół Jędrzeja i Zofii Moraczewskich, file 106, "Uwagi I. Szydłowskiej w sprawie Policji Kobiecej," n.d. [ca. 1929], 22.

95. BNPK, Zespół Moraczewskich, file 106, "Uwagi I. Szydłowskiej," 22.

96. There were 159 in Germany in 1931 and 294 in Austria in 1932. On the Women's Police, see AAN, Zespół Ministerstwa Opieki Społecznej, file 236; BNPK, Zespół Moraczewskich, file 106, ZPOK, Spraw Kobiecych, c. 1929; Helena Ceysingerówa [Ceysingerówna], "Nasze postulaty w sprawie policji kobiecej," *Kobieta współczesna*, no. 36 (December 4, 1927): 2–3. The statistic comes from AAN, Zespół Komendy Głównej Policji Państwowej, file 147, *Referat Belgijskiego Komitetu Narodowego na X Międzynarodowy Kongres Komitetów Zwalczania Handlu Kobiet i Dzieci w Paryżu*, Paris, n.d [after 1936].

97. BNPK, Zespół Jędrzeja i Zofii Moraczewskich, file 106, ZPOK, Spraw Kobiecych, ca. 1929.

98. BNPK, Moraczewska to "Dear Madam," October 19, 1932, 34b; copy.

99. BNPK, Zespół Jędrzeja i Zofii Moraczewskich, file 106, Sekcja Spraw Kobiecych, ca. 1929.

100. BNPK, Moraczewska to "Dear Madam," October 19, 1932, 34b; and see BNPK, Męczkowska, *50 lat pracy w organizacjach kobiecych w Warszawie*, 158.

101. BNPK, Zespół Jędrzeja i Zofii Moraczewskich, file 121, Zarząd Główny, ZPOK, Warsaw, to Marshal of the Senate, Professor Julian Szymański, March 28, 1930, 15.

102. Ibid.

103. BNPK, Zespół Jędrzeja i Zofii Moraczewskich, file 48. Zofia Moraczewska, *Historia rozłamu w ZPOK w latach 1933, 1934, i 1935*, 10.

104. AAN, Moraczewska, *Wspomnienia o moich pracach społecznych*, 33. See also Chojnowski, "Moralność i polityka," 168.

105. BNPK, Zespół Jędrzeja i Zofii Moraczewskich, file 7626/IX, Zofia Moraczewska to H. Kozicka, December 21, 1932.

106. AAN, Zespół Jędrzeja i Zofii Moraczewskich, file 71/III-9, Zofia Moraczewska, "Moje wspomnienia osobiste o Wielkim Marszałku," Sulejówek, May 1943.

107. AAN, Zespół Jędrzeja i Zofii Moraczewskich, file 71/III-6, mf. 1855/6, Rozdiał VI: "Stosunek ZPOK do BBWR."

108. AAN, Zespół Moraczewskich, file 71/III-6, mf. 1855/6, Rozdział VI: "Stosunek ZPOK do BBWR," n.d., n.p.

109. On the BBWR, see Chojnowski, *Piłsudczycy u władzy*.

110. AAN, Moraczewska, *Wspomnienia o moich pracach społecznych*, 28.

111. BNPK, Zespół Moraczewskich, file 126, Komitet Wyborczy Organizacji Kobiecych, 1930, 12–16.

112. Chojnowski, "Moralność i polityka," 168.

113. The eight women elected to the Sejm were Maria Bałłabanówna, Kazimiera Marczyńska, Halina Jaroszewiczowa, Eugenia Waśniewska, Zofia Berbecka, Maria Jaworska, Janina Kirtiklisowa, and Moraczewska. Hanna Hubicka entered the Senate. See Kałwa, *Kobieta aktywna*, 122.

114. Stanisława Woszczyńska, "Naiwność, obłuda czy poprostu czynizm?" *Robotnik*, January 13, 1931, 1. Woszczyńska's views concern a piece by Moraczewska published in the *Polish Gazette* (*Gazeta polska*).

115. BNPK, Zespół Moraczewskich, file 137, Zofia Moraczewska to Walery Sławek, Warsaw, March 19, 1932, 77, 77a; copy.

116. A collection of local press clippings about this scandal is in AAN, Zespół BBWR, file 107.

117. B. S., "'Wojna domowa,'" *Robotnik*, no. 383 (November 4, 1931).

118. For Jabłońska's side of the story, see AAN, Zespół BBWR, file 107, Jabłońska to Women's Union, May 2, 1931, 1–2. See also B. S., "'Wojna domowa.'"

119. AAN, Zespół BBWR, file 107, Ruling of the Presidium of the Main Branch of the Women's Union, signed by Zofia Moraczewska, Maria Jaworska, and Wanda Drzewiecka, June 5, 1931; copy.

120. AAN, Zespół BBWR, file 107, J. Kirtiklisowa to H. Jabłońska, June 16, 1931; copy.

121. AAN, Zespół BBWR, file 107, Findings of the BBWR in the Matter of J. Kirtiklisowa, September 22, 1931, 104–5.

122. Chojnowski, "Moralność i polityka," 169.

123. AAN, Zespół BBWR, file 107, Z. Moraczewska to H. Jabłońska, December 12, 1931.

124. In December 1932, Jaworska attacked the Education Section of the Women's Union and especially the section's leader, Leokadja Sliwińska. Moraczewska sided with Sliwińska over Jaworska, and already at this point contending camps formed. See BNPK, Moraczewska, Zespół Jędrzeja i Zofii Moraczewskich, file 48, *Historia rozłamu w ZPOK*, 12.

125. Ibid., 36; emphasis in original; see also 35–40.

126. Ibid., 24, 77; BNPK, Zespół Moraczewskich, file 36, Zofia Moraczewska, "Do członkiń ZPOK," April 25, 1934, 181.

127. Zofia Moraczewska to Walery Sławek, Warsaw, March 19, 1932; copy. See also Listy Zofii Moraczewskiej do Heleny Kozickiej, file 52, vol. 9: Korespondencja 1931, Moraczewska to Kozicka, January 28 and 30, 1931.

128. BNPK, Moraczewskich, file 114, "Wycinek z Protokółu, 12/9/1933," 11.

129. BNPK, Moraczewska, *Historia rozłamu w ZPOK*, 78; BNPK, Moraczewska, "Do członkiń Z-P-O-K.," 180–83.

130. In 1934, for example, the Women's Union submitted a protest to the BBWR about the frequent confiscations of opposition papers. See BNPK, Zespół Jędrzeja i Zofii Moraczewskich, file 121, "Protest," 83.

131. AAN, Moraczewska, *Wspomnienia o moich pracach społecznych*, 33–34.

132. AAN, Zespół Samopomocy Społecznej Kobiet (SSK), file 7, "Protokół," October 6, 1935, 19.

133. AAN, Zespół SSK, file 7, Credo Ideowe SSK, October 4, 1936.

134. AAN, Zespół SSK, file 3, Protokół, October 4, 1936.

135. Moraczewska, *Historia rozłamu w ZPOK*, 39. Emphasis in original.

Chapter 5

1. The term *cultural sanacja* appears in Czesław Lechicki, "Wstęp," in *Prawda o Boyu-Żeleńskim: Głosy krytyczne,* ed. Czesław Lechicki (Warsaw: Dom Książki Polskiej, 1933), 5. A reference to Boy leading "a sanacja of culture and of social relations" was made in "Zielony Balonik," *Myśl narodowa,* no. 8 (February 24, 1929): 123 and in "*Myśl narodowa* na marginesie *Dziewic konsystorskich,*" in Lechicki, *Prawda o Boyu-Żeleńskim,* 181; repr. from *Myśl narodowa,* no. 8 (1929).

2. The name is taken from the English *boy,* as in "young man." For a negative analysis of the name Boy, see Stanisław Cywiński, "Dekadencja Boya," in Lechicki, *Prawda o Boyu-Żeleńskim,* 52; repr. from *Dziennik Wileński* (1929–31). Boy signed many of his feuilletons "Boy, the sage" (*Boy-mędrzec*). His critics also called Boy a sage, but out of sarcasm. For one example, see Jan Rembieliński, "Gdzie obowiązek?" *Myśl narodowa,* no. 10 (March 9, 1930): 145.

3. For a reference to Boy as a "social doctor," see Franck L. Schoell, "Enfant terrible de la Pologne" part 2, *L'Europe centrale,* July 4, 1931, 587.

4. Boy also contributed regular pieces to the *Republic (Rzeczpospolita)* (1920–22), *Daily Illustrated Courier (Illustrowany kurjer codzienny)* (1931–34), and *Literary-Scholarly Courier (Kurjer literacko-naukowy)* (1925–39). For a discussion of Boy's association with various journals, see Barbara Winklowa, *Tadeusz Żeleński (Boy): Twórczość i życie* (Warsaw: Państwowy Instytut Wydawniczy, 1967). Boy's articles in support of the right to civil marriage and to divorce were published as *Consistory Virgins (Dziewice konsystorskie)* (1929). *Women's Hell (Piekło kobiet)* and *How to End Women's Hell (Jak skończyć z piekłem kobiet)* (1930) constituted a defense of a woman's right to birth control and to safe and legal abortions. *Our Occupiers (Nasi okupanci)* (1932) condemned what Boy believed was an oppressive and narrow-minded clericalism.

5. Key individuals involved in establishing the clinic include Dr. J. Budzińska-Tylicka, H. Kłuszyński, Dr. H. Rubinraut, Dr. Lorentowicz, W. Melcer, Hulka-Laskowski, H. Krahelska, I. Krzywicka, Z. Nałkowska, H. Boguszewska, J. Wasowski, and Dr. Z. Radliński. See Magda Gawin, "Planowanie rodziny—hasła i rzeczywistość," in *Równe prawa i nierówne szanse: Kobiety w Polsce Międzywojennej,* ed. Anna Żarnowska and Andrzej Szwarc (Warsaw: Wydawnictwo DiG, 2000), 221–42.

6. See, for example, "Z Ligi Reformy Obyczajów," *Epoka,* no. 24 (June 11, 1933): 6–7.

7. Mieczysław Piszczkowski, "O trzech Boy'ach i jednym Żeleńskim," *Myśl narodowa,* no. 1 (January 3, 1932): 6; repr. in Lechicki, *Prawda o Boyu-Żeleńskim,* 79–86. The phrase comes from p. 79.

8. The term *Boy's sanacja* is used in Czesław Lechicki, *W walce z demoralizacją: Szkice literacko-społeczne* (Miejsce Piastowe: Wydawnictwo Towarzystwa Św. Michała Archanioła, 1932–33), 1:65.

9. In 1958 the Polish Publishing Institute issued a twenty-eight volume collection of Boy's works under the title *Żeleński, Pisma* (Writings), ed. Henryk Markiewicz (Warsaw: Państwowy Instytut Wydawniczy, 1958). A number of Boy's prominent feuilletons have been reprinted in Daria Nałęcz, ed., *Nie szablą, lecz piórem: Batalie publicystyczne II Rzeczypospolitej* (Warsaw: Instytut Badań Literackich, 1993), 163–85. See also Barbara Winklowa's biographical bibliography of Boy's works, *Tadeusz Żeleński (Boy): Twórczość i życie* (1967). There are many biographies of Boy. See, for instance, Andrzej Stawar, *Tadeusz Żeleński (Boy)* (Warsaw: Państwowy Instytut Wydawniczy, 1958); Wojciech Natanson, *Boy-Żeleński: Opowieść biograficzna* (Warsaw: Ludowa Spółdzielnia Wydawnicza, 1977); Barbara Winklowa, *Nad Wisłą i nad Sekwaną: Biografia Tadeusza Boya-Żeleńskiego* (Warsaw: Iskry, 1998), x.

10. Karol Ludwik Koniński, "Dwie misje Boya," *Myśl narodowa,* no. 5 (January 25, 1931): 54.

11. Karol Ludwik Koniński, "Boy," *Myśl narodowa,* no. 55 (December 18, 1932): 804. See also Ignotus, "Imponderabilia," *Myśl narodowa,* no. 15 (March 26, 1933): 195–98.

12. Adolf Nowaczyński, "Reformacja seksualna," in Lechicki, *Prawda o Boyu-Żeleńskim,* 121; repr. from *ABC,* June 24, 1932. *ABC* had been established in 1926 by the Camp of Great Poland. On *ABC,* see Andrzej Notkowski, *Polska prasa prowincjonalna Drugiej Rzeczypospolitej, 1918–1939* (Warsaw: Państwowe Wydawnictwo Naukowe, 1982), 279–82.

13. Adolf Nowaczyński, "Ofensywa: Tragedja Boya," *Myśl narodowa,* no. 4 (January 27, 1929): 63. The ellipsis between "under" and "Belvedere" occurs in the original.

14. Adolf Nowaczyński, "Boyszewizm," in Lechicki, *Prawda o Boyu-Żeleńskim,* 104–5; repr. from *Gazeta warszawska,* no. 389 (December 24, 1931): 17–18.

15. Adolf Nowaczyński, "Ofensywa," *Myśl narodowa,* no. 16 (April 21, 1929): 255; italics in original.

16. Lechicki also wrote under the pseudonyms Catholicus and Verus Catholicus. See National Library, mf. 60364, from the Manuscripts of the Jagiellonian University Library 8976 III, vol. 6, *Korespondencja Kazimierza Czachowskiego z lat 1912–1942:* Lechicki to Czachowski, May 2, 1933, 5–6 and August 25, 1933, 8–9. Czachowski was the editor of *Czas* (*Time*). Brief mention is made of Lechicki in Józef Hen, *Błazen—wielki mąż: Opowieść o Tadeuszu Boyu-Żeleńskim* (Warsaw: Iskry, 1998), 252; Winklowa, *Nad Wisłą*, x.

17. Lechicki, *W walce z demoralizacją,* 1:65.

18. Lechicki, "Wstęp," lxxxvii. See also Czesław Lechicki, *Boy-Żeleński we wklęsłem zwierciadle* (Lwów: Nakładem Autora, 1933), 87. In *The Truth about Boy* (*Prawda o Boyu*), Lechicki reprinted some of the most important articles (which first appeared in the press of the period) criticizing Boy. For this reason, that work constitutes an especially valuable source for Boy scholars.

19. Lechicki, *W walce z demoralizacją,* 2:433.

20. Lechicki, "Wstęp," lxxxix.

21. Ibid. In 1933 Lechicki published three books : *The Truth about Boy-Żeleński: Critical Voices* (*Prawda o Boyu-Żeleńskim*); *Boy-Żeleński in the Concave Mirror* (*Boy-Żeleński we wklęsłem zwierciadle*); and *A Guide to Belles Lettres* (*Przewodnik po beletrystyce*) (Poznań: Akcja Katolicka). He also published *In a Battle with Depravity: Literary-Social Sketches* (*W walce z demoralizacją: Szkice literacko-społeczne*) (2 vols.; 1932–33).

22. The term *half-intelligentsia* is used, for example, in Aleksander Bocheński, "Taczka do gnoju i złota tarcza," *Wiadomości literackie,* no. 45 (November 8, 1931): 1.

23. For a text that is simultaneously a defense of Boy and a critique of Boy's staunchest critic, Nowaczyński, see Aleksander Świętorzecki, *Handlarz językiem: Rzecz o Adolfie Neuwert-Nowaczyńskim i spółce w sprawie "Boy'szewizmu"* (Warsaw: n.p, 1932).

24. Nowaczyński, "Boyszewizm," 110–11, 115. For a similar view that Boy popularized base tastes and appealed to the lowest common denominator, see Jerzy Braun, "Atakujemy Boya," in Lechicki, *Prawda o Boyu-Żeleńskim,* 5; repr. from *Zet,* nos. 16–17 (November 15, 1932).

25. Nowaczyński, "Reformacja seksualna," 121–22. In this article, Nowaczyński discussed specifically the frivolity of early modern Sarmatian (noble) culture.

26. Mieczysław Piszczkowski, "Krytyka obyczajowości współczesnej," *Myśl narodowa,* no. 54 (November 22, 1931): 316. The term *pansexualism* is also used by Lechicki in "Wstęp," xxxvii.

27. Piszczkowski, "Krytyka obyczajowości," 316. For Nowaczyński's critique of the Americanization of Polish culture, see Adolf Nowaczynski, "Kryzys teatru w Polsce," in Nowaczyński, *Porachunki i projekty: Teksty o teatrze z lat 1900–1938,* ed. Henryk Izydor Rogacki (Wrocław: Wiedza i Kultura, 1993), 160; repr. from *Prawda,* no. 72 (March 28, 1926).

28. According to Czesław Lechicki, Stanisław Przybyszewski was one of the first to "morally deprave" the Polish nation, and as such, he deserved the distinction of being named "the archpriest of the cult of the phallus." Boy, Lechicki continued, was Przybyszewski's moral and intellectual heir in the modern, postpartition period. See Lechicki, *Boy-Żeleński*, 17; Lechicki, *W walce z demoralizacją*, 2:369.

29. Andrzej Notkowski, "W kręgu Piłsudczyków: Poglądy ideowo-polityczne 'Gazety Polskiej' (1929–1939)," *Rocznik historii prasy polskiej* 2, no. 2 (1999): 221–32. In one satirical paper entitled the *Moral Sanacja* (*Sanacja moralna*), the pro-Piłsudski *Voice of Truth* (*Głos prawdy*) is described as a quintessential sanacja journal that might more appropriately be called the *Voice from under the Blanket* (*Głos z pod koca*) (*koc* means blanket). Adam Koc was the surname of a key Piłsudskiite politician. See "Zmiana tytułów," *Sanacja moralna*, no. 1 (March 28, 1929): 6.

30. See "Na marginesie," *Myśl narodowa*, no. 12 (March 13, 1932): 175; Jan Rembieliński, "Na widowni," *Myśl narodowa*, no. 25 (June 5, 1932): 361.

31. Adolf Nowaczyński, "Ofensywa: Nieco o . . . repertuarze," *Myśl narodowa*, no. 42 (September 29, 1929): 207; repr. in Nowaczyński, *Porachunki i projekty*, 166.

32. Nowaczyński, "Ofensywa: Tragedja Boya," *Myśl narodowa*, no. 4 (January 27, 1929): 63.

33. Adolf Nowaczyński, *Plewy i perły* (1934; repr., Warsaw: Presspol, 1991), 183. The *Republic's Tomorrow* was established in Warsaw in 1931, was edited by Adam Uziembło, and was published by Stanisław Wieczorkiewicz. Throughout 1932, it printed many articles in support of civil marriages and divorce.

34. W. Z. [Father Jan Piwowarczyk], "Minister WRO i 'Minister Oświecenia,'" in Lechicki, *Prawda o Boyu-Żeleńskim*, 175; repr. from *Głos narodu* (March 1932).

35. Some commentators decided to publish guide books to help readers wade through the choices. See, for example, Father Marjan Pirożyński, *Co czytać? Poradnik dla czytających książki: Beletrystyka* (Kraków: Wydawnictwo Księży Jezuitów, 1932), 5–6. Pirożyński called Boy's writings especially harmful to the moral health of the nation. For his part, Boy dismissed Pirożyński's guide as a pathetic display of Polish provincialism and proclaimed that the name Pirożyński should be inserted into the Polish lexicon as a synonym for obscurity, backwardness, and buffoonery. Boy published two reviews of Pirożyński's work: "Ku czemu Polska idzie . . ." and "Moralnie obojętnie" in Żeleński, *Pisma*, 15:320–30, 341–47. For a discussion of Pirożyński's book, see Mirosława Dołęgowska-Wysocka, *Poboyowisko* (Warsaw: BWG, 1992), 59–64. Lechicki published a similar guide book entitled *Literary Guide* (*Przewodnik po beletrystyce*) (1935). He included 1,092 authors and commented on several thousand titles, categorizing these works as either traditional, psychopathic, or morally insane. See Lechicki, comp., *Przewodnik po beletrystyce* (Poznań: Akcja Katolicka, 1935).

36. For the *News*'s mandate, see editors, *Wiadomości literackie* no. 1 (January 6, 1924): 1. See also Widz., "Refleksja," *Kurier polski*, no. 5 (January 5, 1924): 5. At the end

of 1926, Grydzewski established what would become a very successful French version of *Wiadomości literackie* called *La Pologne littéraire.* See Jan Błoński, "Le double miroir: *La Pologne littéraire, 1926–1936,*" in *La presse polonaise en France, 1918–1984,* ed. Daniel Beauvois (Lille: Revue du Nord, 1988), 152.

37. On Grydzewski, see Mirosław A. Supruniuk, "Mieczysław Jerzy Grydzewski," in *"Wiadomości" i okolice: Szkice i wspomnienia,* ed. Mirosław A. Supruniuk (Toruń: Uniwersytet Mikołaja Kopernika, 1995), 239.

38. The circulation figures come from "Prospekt na rok 1925," *Wiadomości literackie,* no. 1 (January 4, 1925): 1. On the *News,* see Janusz Stradecki, *W kręgu Skamandra* (Warsaw: Państwowy Instytut Wydawniczy, 1977), 192–207; Andrzej Paczkowski, *Prasa polska w latach 1918–1939* (Warsaw: Państwowe Wydawnictwo Naukowe, 1980), 259–65; Magdalena M. Opalski, "*Wiadomości literackie:* Polemics on the Jewish Question, 1924–1939," in *The Jews of Poland between Two World Wars,* ed. Yisrael Gutman et al. (Hanover, NH: University Press of New England, 1989), 434–49; Magdalena Marcinkowska-Gawin, "'Boyownicy i Boyowniczki.' Środowisko *Wiadomości literackich* wobec problemu regulacji urodzeń," in *Kobieta i kultura życia codziennego,* ed. Anna Żarnowska and Andrzej Szwarc (Warsaw: Wydawnictwo DiG, 1997), 133–47.

39. Nowaczyński, for example, wrote for the *News* in 1924, 1926–29, 1931, and 1933–38. At the same time, the *News* was criticized by militantly left journals like *Literary Monthly* (*Miesięcznik literacki*). The socialists of the PPS also often condemned the *News* for its elitism. For a brief discussion of the relationship between the *News* and the PPS, see Kazimierz Koźniewski, *Historia co tydzień* (Warsaw: Czytelnik, 1976), 42, 46–48.

40. It was not until the establishment of *Straight from the Hip* (*Prosto z mostu*) in January 1935 that Poland's nationalist right wing could boast a real competitor to *Wiadomości literackie.* See Paczkowski, *Prasa polska,* 35, 265. For more on *Prosto z mostu,* see Koźniewski, *Historia co tydzień,* 241–308.

41. On the impact of this column on a number of key personalities from the period, see Paweł Kądziela and Artur Międzyrzecki, eds., *Wspomnienia o Antonim Słonimskim* (Warsaw: Biblioteka Więzi, 1996). Among foreign authors published in *Wiadomości literackie* were Bertrand Russell, G. B. Shaw, Anatole France, G. K. Chesterton, Marcel Proust, and H. G. Wells.

42. For a critique of the *News,* see Jadwiga Kosicka and Daniel Gerould, eds., *A Life of Solitude: Stanisława Przybyszewska: A Biographical Study with Selected Letters* (London: Quartet Books, 1986), 188–89. Przybyszewska was the daughter of Stanisław Przybyszewski.

43. For Krzywicka's recollections of the Ziemiańska, see Irena Krzywicka, *Wyznania gorszycielki,* ed. Agata Tuszyńska (Warsaw: Czytelnik, 1995), 196–97. The popular expression *military Ziemiańska* (*wojskowa Ziemiańska*) referred to the presence of a number of Piłsudskiite military men within the café circle. For an additional discussion of the café, see Stradecki, *W kręgu Skamandra,* 141, 171–74.

44. See, for instance, Józef Stanisław Czarnecki, "Drygał uwieńczony," *Antena*, no. 1 (May 7, 1933): 1.

45. Adolf Nowaczyński, "Ofensywa: Donna Krzywicka, 'The Devils Disciple,'" *Myśl Narodowa*, no. 31 (July 17, 1932): 458.

46. Father Charczewski, as quoted in Dołęgowska-Wysocka, *Poboyowisko*, 64; Lechicki, *W walce z demoralizacją*, 2:554. Lechicki used the *Gynecological-Venereal News* as the subtitle to a section of the appendix. In this section, he commented on and reprinted an article by Jan N. Miller entitled, "Rozkład wewnętrzny *Wiadomości literackich*," which first appeared in *Robotnik*, nos. 2–3 (September 1932).

47. Paczkowski, *Prasa polska*, 260, 263.

48. Aniela Mieczysławska, "Antoni," in Paweł Kądziela and Artur Międzyrzecki, eds., *Wspomnienia o Antonim Słonimskim* (Warsaw: Biblioteka Więzi, 1996), 204.

49. Koźniewski, *Historia co tydzień*, 43. On Brześć, see Antoni Słonimski, "List otwarty do Wacława Sieroszewskiego and J. Kadena-Bandrowskiego," *Robotnik*, December 21, 1930. Słonimski wrote about Brześć in his *Weekly Chronicle* (*Kronika tygodniowa*). See *Wiadomości literackie*, no. 1 (January 4, 1931): 5; no. 34 (August 23, 1931): 4. Boy, Julian Tuwim, and Kazimierz Wierzyński, among others, expressed their criticisms of Brześć in "Pisarze o Brześciu," *Wiadomości literackie*, no. 2 (January 11, 1931): 3. Nowaczyński offered his support of the writers who protested Brześć in "Korespondencja," *Wiadomości literackie*, no. 7 (February 15, 1931): 4.

50. The reference to Kaden as "the little Piłsudski" is made in Karol Irzykowski, "Przewrót majowy w literaturze," *Wiadomości literackie*, no. 44 (October 20, 1927): 1. The main character in Kaden-Bandrowski's *Generał Barcz* (1922) is modeled on Piłsudski, and the novel constitutes a critical reflection on contemporary political realities and on the quality of Polish independence more broadly. See Anna Nasiłowska, *Trzydziestolecie, 1914–1944* (Warsaw: Wydawnictwo Naukowe PKW, 1997), 26–29. For an analysis of Kaden-Bandrowski as a political writer and propagandist, see Włodzimierz Suleja, "Propagandowe powieści politycznych Juliusza Kadena-Bandrowskiego," *Dzieje najnowsze* 13, no. 3 (1981): 93–113.

51. Natan Gross, "Przyjmują do *Wiadomości*," in Supruniuk, *"Wiadomości" i okolice*, 227.

52. The *News*'s earliest reference to the May coup came in 1927 in the form of an article by eminent literary critic Karol Irzykowski (1873–1944). See Irzykowski, "Przewrót majowy w literaturze," *Wiadomości literackie*, no. 44 (October 30, 1927):1.

53. Endek was the pejorative form of Endecja, which referred to National Democracy. See Adam Michnik, "'Kto to ma czelność zwać mnie odszczepieńcem?'" in Kądziela and Międzyrzecki, *Wspomnienia o Antonim Słonimskim*, 178.

54. BNPK, Listy Boya do M. H. Staniewskich, file III 11.143, Boy to Staniewska, June 16, 1926, 31. A fragment of Boy's letter is reprinted in Winklowa, *Tadeusz Żeleński*, 214–15 and in Żeleński, *Tadeusz Żeleński Boy: Listy* (Warsaw: Państwowy

Instytut Wydawniczy, 1972), 250–51. The same quote is also used in Hen, *Błazen*, 196 and in Winklowa, *Nad Wisłą*, 121. In 1933, Staniewska was involved in setting up a family planning clinic in Kalisz. See Boy to Helena Staniewska, March 12, 1934, as reprinted in Żeleński, *Listy*, 411.

55. For a description of the interwar feuilleton, see Piotr Stasiński, *Poetyka i pragmatyka felietonu: Z dziejów form artystycznych w literaturze polskiej* (Wrocław: Ossolineum, 1982), ch. 1, esp. p. 14.

56. Lechicki, *Boy-Żeleński*, 38–39. For a laudatory analysis of Boy's feuilleton writings, see Irena Krzywicka, "Nieznany pisarz," *Wiadomości literackie*, no. 11 (March 16, 1930): 2.

57. Jalu Kurek, "Legenda Boya," in Lechicki, *Prawda o Boyu-Żeleńskim*, 14; repr. from *Głos narodu* (February 1930). For a discussion of Kurek in the context of the interwar Polish avant-garde, see Bogdana Carpenter, *The Poetic Avant-Garde in Poland, 1918–1939* (Seattle: University of Washington Press, 1983).

58. Lechicki, "Wstęp," li.

59. Lechicki, *Boy-Żeleński*, 52.

60. Karol Irzykowski, *Beniaminek: Walka o treść* (1933; repr., Kraków: Wydawnictwo Literackie, 1976). For a discussion of the terms of the disagreement between Boy and Irzykowski, see Tomasz Burek, "Krytyka literacka—odmiany i rozbieżności wielkiej krytyki," in *Literatura polska, 1918–1932*, vol. 1 of *Literatura polska, 1918–1975*, ed. Alina Brodzka, Helena Zaworska, and Stefan Żółkiewski (Warsaw: Wiedza Powszechna, 1975), 174–86. For a discussion of the falling-out between Boy and Irzykowski that the publication of *Beniaminek* generated, see Krzywicka, *Wyznania gorszycielki*, 243–44.

61. Theodor Fontane, *Politik und Gesellschaft* (Munich: 1969), as quoted in Peter Fritzsche, *Reading Berlin 1900* (Cambridge, MA: Harvard University Press, 1996), 43–44.

62. The term *moral prostitution* comes from Stanisław Miłaszewski, "Blaski i nędze Boya Żeleńskiego," in Lechicki, *Prawda o Boyu-Żeleńskim*, 35; repr. from *Rzeczpospolita*, nos. 44, 47, 54, 61, 68 (1929).

63. Nowaczyński, "Ofensywa: Tragedja Boya," *Myśl narodowa*, no. 4 (January 27, 1929): 63.

64. Nowaczyński, "Boyszewizm," 108; see also 104.

65. In addition to the real minister of education appointed by the president, Janusz Jędrzejewicz, Poland had a second minister not appointed by the president, and that was Boy. W. Z. "Minister WRO," 173–74.

66. Ibid., 174.

67. Nowaczyński, "Boyszewizm," 109.

68. Karol Ludwik Koniński, "Boy," *Myśl narodowa*, no. 55 (December 18, 1932): 804. See also W. Z. [Father Jan Piwowarczyk], "Przeciw poniżeniu macierzyństwa,"

in Lechicki, *Prawda o Boyu-Żeleńskim,* 154; repr. from *Głos narodu,* no. 245 (September 10, 1932). The same article is repr. in Nałęcz, *Nie szablą,* 201. Piwowarczyk further made the point that women (and "not just Jewish women," he added) were especially frequent contributors to the *Literary News.*

69. See Nowaczyński, "Boyszewizm," 110, 113. Nowaczyński was particularly fond of using the English term Play-Boy.

70. Kurek, "Legenda Boya," 14.

71. Mieczysław Piszczkowski, "Krytyka obyczajowości współczesnej," *Myśl narodowa,* no. 54 (November 22, 1931): 316. Abortion was a frequent subject of satirical cartoons of the period. See, for example: "BB: BOY contra BOCIAN czyli . . . BOY— ORĘDOWNIKIEM DZIEWIC," *Bocian,* no. 18 (September 15, 1932): 1; Maja Berezowska, "Życie świadome," *Cyrulik warszawski,* no. 44 (October 22, 1932): 8.

72. W. Z., "Przeciw poniżeniu macierzyństwa," 155.

73. Boy, as quoted in Miłaszewski, "Blaski i nędze Boya-Żeleńskiego," 41.

74. Boy, "Przedmowa," *Nasi okupanci,* as quoted in Dołęgowska-Wysocka, *Poboyowisko,* 51.

75. Boy to Izabela Moszczeńska, October 12, 1928; reprinted in Żeleński, *Listy,* 277 and in Żeleński, *Pisma,* 16:327–31.

76. Boy, as quoted in Dr. K. M. Morawski, "Na marginesie polemiki z Boyem," in Lechicki, *Prawda o Boyu-Żeleńskim,* 29; repr. from *Przegląd katolicki,* no. 3 (1929). Boy's statement was first published in *Kurier poranny,* September 1, 1928.

77. Izabela Moszczeńska-Rzepecka, "Przedwojenne matki," in Lechicki, *Prawda o Boyu-Żeleńskim,* 149; repr. from *Kurier warszawski,* no. 278 (October 7, 1928). The same article is reprinted in Nałęcz, *Nie szablą,* 196–99. Moszczeńska had been a women's rights advocate and self-described anticlerical before World War I but by the interwar period had become, according to Lechicki, a "repentant free thinker." See Lechicki, *Przewodnik po beletrystyce,* 288.

78. Moszczeńska-Rzepecka, "Przedwojenne matki," 146–57. Another interesting article on those themes by Moszczeńska is "Sursum corda!" *Tęcza,* no. 25 (June 23, 1928): 1–2.

79. Aleksander Świętochowski, "Liberum veto," *Myśl narodowa,* no. 8 (February 24, 1929): 121.

80. Marja Sucheni, "Wyższe aspiracje," *Myśl narodowa,* no. 38 (September 3, 1933): 560. See also Adolf Nowaczyński, "Ofensywa: Marjanna a Sanator," *Myśl Narodowa,* no. 51 (November 1, 1931): 278; W. Z., "Przeciw poniżeniu macierzyństwa," 153. Margueritte and the influence of this novel in French debates about morality is analyzed extensively by Mary Louis Roberts, *Civilization without Sexes: Reconstructing Gender in Postwar France, 1917–1927* (Chicago: University of Chicago Press, 1994).

81. Lechicki, *W walce z demoralizacją,* 11:499; Lechicki, *Boy-Żeleński,* 80; Lechicki, "Wstęp," lxxxi, xxviii–xxxi; Lechicki, *Przewodnik po beletrystyce,* 14–15.

82. Nowaczyński, "Boyszewizm," 111. For a discussion of the perceived effects of women's emancipation, see Lechicki, *W walce z demoralizacją*, vol. 1, ch. 2.

83. Adolf Nowaczyński, "Miss 'Sanacja,'" *Myśl narodowa*, no. 9 (March 3, 1929): 143. This article concerns theater in Warsaw.

84. An interesting depiction of a kind of Miss Sanacja is offered in Magdalena Samozwaniec, *Kartki z pamiętnika młodej mężatki* (Warsaw: E. Wende i Ska, [1926]). This short memoir is a satire simultaneously of the May coup and of modern femininity. The story concerns a Polish woman who has been living in France with her wealthy husband for many years. She arrives in Warsaw just as the coup is beginning and, from her vantage at Warsaw's tony Hotel Bristol, observes the unfolding of events. The woman has absolutely no idea what is going on or why and is annoyed by such things as the fact that streets littered with bullets might damage her delicate French shoes (30). With a little help, she finally understands that what she has witnessed is a civil war. She concludes glibly, "Everything that is homemade is healthy" ("To była wojna domowa, a co domowe—to zawsze zdrowe") (39). Immediately after the coup, she turns her attention to thinking about how nice it will be to see all the extravagant funerals and all the people dressed up in their pretty clothes (41). Samozwaniec (1899–1972) was the sister of poet Maria Pawlikowska-Jasnorzewska and a friend of satirical cartoonist and illustrator Maja Berezowska. See Samozwaniec, *Maria i Magdalena* (Kraków: Wydawnictwo Literackie, 1956).

85. Thomas Milton Kemnitz, "The Cartoon as a Historical Source," *Journal of Interdisciplinary History* 4, no. 1 (Summer 1973): 81.

86. On Skamander, see Stradecki, *W kręgu Skamandra*, esp. 178–92; see also 134–63.

87. Maja Berezowska, "Częste wypadki majowe," *Cyrulik warszawski*, no. 20 (May 14, 1932): 8.

88. One could also suggest another meaning. In its reference to the month of May, the cartoon recalled the recent May Day demonstrations and the worker and peasant unrest that was a part of those. In doing so, it condemned the government's Depression-era social and economic policies.

89. Other cartoons from the *Warsaw Barber* played with the idea that morality had indeed fallen in sanacja-era Poland and that women were at the heart of that cultural decline. In one such cartoon, two very fashionable young and modern women are lying together on a bed, reading Boy's *Women's Hell* (*Piekło kobiet*), which presents arguments in favor of easily available contraception and discusses the benefits of access to safe and legal abortions. The smoke from one of the women's cigarettes leads up to a cloud where two baby angels look down and say to the women: "For you this is a game; for us it is about life." See Maja Berezowska, "Bajeczka Jachowicza o 'świadomem macierzyństwie,'" *Cyrulik warszawski*, no. 3 (January 6, 1932): 8.

90. Maja Berezowska, "Ciało dyplomatyczne," *Cyrulik warszawski*, 1932, 8. An interesting collection of similar cartoons is found in 1929 issues of *Stork* (*Bocian*).

91. Nowaczyński, "Boyszewizm," 105.

92. Anna Landau-Czajka, "Elementy światopoglądu prawicy nacjonalistycznej 1926–1939," *Przegląd historyczny* 79, no. 1 (1988): 84; Landau-Czajka, "Królestwo bez Żydów: Sprawa żydowska w myśli polskich monarchistów okresu międzywojennego," *Kultura i społeczeństwo* 43, no. 1 (January–March 1999): 48. For a review of the National Democrats' views on Jews, see Wapiński, *Świadomość polityczna w Drugiej Rzeczypospolitej* (Łódź: Wydawnictwo Łódzkie, 1989) 424–30; Roman Dmowski, "Wschód i zachód w Polsce," in Dmowski, *Wybór pism* (New York: Instytut Romana Dmowskiego), 10:87–90.

93. Virtually any opinion that was not consistent with Roman Catholic teachings and a narrowly circumscribed definition of nation could be branded with the label Masonic. See, for example: "Na marginesie," *Myśl narodowa*, no. 2 (January 13, 1929): 31. On the Masons generally, see Ludwik Hass, *Masoneria polska XX wieku: Losy, loże, ludzie* (Warsaw: Wydawnictwo KOPIA, 1996). The newspaper *Liberum veto* was especially keen on linking Jews to Masons and to the so-called "barbarity of the East" and thus to the problems that the newly independent state faced. See *Liberum veto*, no. 1 (December 2, 1918): 1–2.

94. Leon Chajn, *Polskie wolnomularstwo, 1920–1938,* 2d ed. (Warsaw: Czytelnik, 1984), 110–11. For a brief history of Freemasonry and a discussion of the evolution of a "Judeo-Masonic alliance," see Modras, *The Catholic Church and Antisemitism: Poland, 1933–1939* (Jerusalem: Hebrew University of Jerusalem/Harwood Academic Publishers, 1994), ch. 2.

95. See Żeleński, "Rozerwalna nierozerwalność," in Żeleński, *Pisma,* 15:48–49. For a discussion of Boy's claims that he was not a member of any Masonic organization, see S. Cywiński, "Dekadencja Boya," 57. See also Dołęgowska-Wysocka, *Poboyowisko,* 32–33.

96. "Z ostatniej chwili," *Rycerz niepokalanej*, no. 7 (July 1926): 193–94. For a scathing critique of *Rycerz*, see W. Rulikowski, "Pomnik zdziczenia umysłowego w Polsce," *Wolnomyśliciel polski*, no. 42 (December 1, 1933): 1057–62. For another expression of the links between the Masons and the *sanacja*, see Jan Rembieliński, "Odwet ojczyzny," *Myśl narodowa*, no. 52 (December 1, 1929): 337.

97. Modras, *Catholic Church*, 64–65, 243–44.

98. Followers of Jakub Frank (1726–91), Frankists were Jews who converted to Roman Catholicism.

99. Lechicki, *Boy-Żeleński*, 10–11, 87; Lechicki, "Wstęp," x–xi; Świecki., "Pamflet antyklerykalny," in Lechicki, *Prawda o Boyu-Żeleńskim*, 168; repr. from *Gazeta kościelna*, no. 40 (1932). Another author described Boy's journalism as pervaded by freethinking Nalewkiite (*wolnomyślicielstwem Nalewkowskiem*) ideas. Nalewki was a main street in Warsaw's Jewish district. See "Zielony balonik," *Myśl narodowa*, no. 8 (February 24, 1929): 123.

100. Morawski, "Na marginesie polemiki z Boyem," in Lechicki, *Prawda o Boyu-Żeleńskim*, 26.

101. Es., "Nie może braknąć polskiej inteligencji w szeregach w imie idei odżydzenia Polski," *Hasło podwawelskie*, no. 5 (January 31, 1931): 1. *Hasło podwawelskie* was a Kraków paper established in 1929 as a "nonparty weekly." Edited by Jan Kozicki and published by Ludwik Gronuś, it expressed clear antisemitic views.

102. "Dyskusja o małżeństwie," *Jutro rzeczypospolitej*, no. 1 (January 3, 1932): 6.

103. George L. Mosse, *Nationalism and Sexuality: Middle-Class Morality and Sexual Norms in Modern Europe* (Madison: University of Wisconsin Press, 1985), ch. 2, esp. p. 36. For an interesting discussion of the Jewish question and the rise of antisemitism in interwar Romania, see Irina Livezeanu, *Cultural Politics in Greater Romania: Regionalism, Nation Building, and Ethnic Struggle, 1918–1930* (Ithaca, NY: Cornell University Press, 1995), esp. 11–13, ch. 5.

104. For a discussion of the National Democrats' approach to the Jewish question after the May coup, see Miezcysław Sobczak, *Stosunek Narodowej Demokracji do kwestii żydowskiej w Polsce w latach 1918–1939* (Wrocław: Wydawnictwo Akademii Ekonomicznej im. Oskara Langego, 1998), 338–64. See also William W. Hagen, "Before the 'Final Solution': Toward a Comparative Analysis of Political Anti-Semitism in Interwar Germany and Poland," *Journal of Modern History* 68, no. 2 (1996): 351–81, esp. 368–39.

105. See, for example, Ignacy Oksza Grabowski, "Przeciwko małpim obyczajom," *Gazeta poranna*, no. 13 (January 14, 1925): 4. *Gazeta poranna* supported the Christian Democrats. The association of Jews with "liberalism" is also touched on in Antoni Gronowicz, *Antysemityzm rujnuje moją ojczyznę* (Lwów: Nakładem Dobrego Polaka, 1938). For a general, wide-view exploration of these themes, see Magdalena Opalski and Israel Bartal, *Poles and Jews: A Failed Brotherhood* (Hanover, NH: University Press of New England, 1992).

106. X. [Ignacy] Charszewski, *Niebezpieczeństwo kobiece* (Warsaw: Druk. Społeczna, 1929).

107. Dmowski elaborated his views on the Jewish question in the *Warsaw Gazette*. For a collection of some of these articles, see BUW, file 1770, Roman Dmowski, Wycinki z prasy z lat 1924–1933.

108. "Sanacyjno-żydowskie czułości," *Kurier poznański*, no. 518 (November 10, 1931): 2.

109. The English term *moral insanity* is used in a number of places in journalism of the period. See, for example, Stefan Rayski, "O banicję czarnych charakterów," *Straż polska*, no. 8 (August 1926): 2; Lechicki, *W walce z demoralizacją*, 1:187; Lechicki, *W walce z demoralizacją*, 2:285; Lechicki, "Wstęp," xx.

110. "Moral-in-semity," *Gazeta warszawska*, no. 75 (March 12, 1933): 13.

111. Adolf Nowaczyński, "Ofensywa," *Myśl narodowa*, no. 16 (April 21, 1929): 255. A similar view is expressed in Nowaczyński, "Boyszewizm," 104, 107. The assumption

that Jews were the most avid supporters of the sanacja regime is made time and again. See, for example, Tadeusz Bielicki, "Pozory siły," *Myśl narodowa,* no. 51 (November 20, 1932): 733.

112. "Nie da się dłużej przemilczać," *Gazeta warszawska,* no. 84 (March 18, 1933): 3.

113. A representative sample of sanacja-era election posters that singled out Jews in this way can be found at AAN, Zbiór Druków Ulotnych, files 73, 103, 199.

114. AAN, Zbiór Druków Ulotnych, file 103, Komitet Katolicko-Narodowy, 1928. No page numbers are provided in this file.

115. "Pod gazową osłoną moralności," *Myśl narodowa,* no. 26 (June 19, 1926): 368.

116. Stefan Sacha, "Ciemności sanacyjne," *Myśl narodowa,* no. 36 (August 18, 1929): 98.

117. Ibid., 97–99.

118. Stefan Sacha, "Rozkład i pustka," *Myśl narodowa,* no. 37 (August 25, 1929): 115.

119. Aleksander Świętochowski, "Liberum veto," *Myśl narodowa,* no. 3 (February 1, 1928): 52.

120. E. T., "O rehabilitację polskości," *Hasło podwawelskie,* no. 27 (September 13, 1936): 1.

121. "Żydzi i ustawa małżeńska," *Gazeta warszawska,* no. 387 (December 22, 1931): 3.

122. Lechicki, *W walce z demoralizacją,* 2:391.

123. Słonimski was well known for his 1924 attacks in the *News* on Jewish nationalism, separatism, and chauvinism. For a discussion of the *News's* views on the Jewish question, see Opalski, "*Wiadomości literackie,*" 434–49.

124. The first translation comes from Jan Błoński, "*Wiadomości literackie, 1924–1933:* A Problem for the Poles, a Problem for the Jews," *Gal-Ed* 14 (1995): 42. The latter translation comes from Opalski, "*Wiadomości literackie,*" 436.

125. Lechicki, *W walce z demoralizacją,* 2:285.

126. Jan Błoński believes that the special issue of the *News* was the work of Tuwim. See Błoński, "*Wiadomości literackie,*" 42. See also Gross, "Przyjmują do *Wiadomości,*" 227. In this special issue, Julian Tuwim was referred to as Tertuljan Juwim, Jan Lechoń as Jan Lichoń, and Antoni Słonimski as Frantoni Słorymski. See Koźniewski, *Historia co tydzień,* 49–51. Koźniewski states that copies of this issue are quite rare and extremely difficult to locate; I have not been able to locate one.

127. For a discussion of "Judeo-Communism," see Modras, *Catholic Church,* ch. 4.

128. For a discussion of how the *News* treated Soviet topics, see Koźniewski, *Historia co tydzień,* 74–78. A special issue of the *News* regarding all matters Soviet appeared on October 29, 1933.

129. See, for example, Adolf Nowaczyński, "Ofensywa: Antiwersal," *Myśl narodowa,* no. 28 (July 7, 1929): 15; Nowaczyński, "Ofensywa: 'Sanacja' i Sowieci," *Myśl*

narodowa, no. 28 (June 7, 1931): 367. See also "Ku czemu idziemy?" *Sygnały,* no. 3 (January 1934): 1–2. The author of this last article states that anyone who thinks "differently" is castigated as a "Bolshevik, Mason, Jew, communist."

130. "Na Marginesie," *Myśl narodowa,* no. 2 (January 11, 1931): 31.

131. Ibid. Nowaczyński issued a defense of Kaden-Bandrowski in "Boyszewizm," 105.

132. As Irena Krzywicka—author and at one time Boy's lover—pointed out in an article in the *News,* Boy was himself a master of invention in this regard. Krzywicka noted that many new terms in the Second Republic—like consistory virgin (*dziewica konsystorska*; see below)—concerned the sexual revolution, of which Boy was said to be the undisputed leader. See Irena Krzywicka, "Nieznany pisarz," *Wiadomości literackie,* no. 11 (March 16, 1930): 2.

133. Nowaczyński, "Boyszewizm," 116. The term Boyshevism was used by a variety of authors, but according to Father Piwowarczyk, it was coined by Nowaczyński himself. See W. Z. [Father Jan Piwowarczyk], "Minister WRO," 174. For other examples of the use of the term Boyshevism, see Lechicki, "Wstęp," lxxv, lxxxvii, lxxxix; Świecki., "Pamflet antyklerykalny," 170; Nowaczyński, "Reformacja seksualna," 3. Its use is also mentioned in Koźniewski, *Historia co tydzień,* 70.

134. Nowaczyński, "Boyszewizm," 115.

135. Lechicki, "Wstęp," lxxxvii. See also Lechicki, *Przewodnik po beletrystyce,* 369. This same quote is used in Dołęgowska-Wysocka, *Poboyowisko,* 8. Dołęgowska-Wysocka further takes up the connections between Boy and Bolshevism on pp. 52–53.

136. Lechicki, *Przewodnik po beletrystyce,* 369.

137. Świecki., "Pamflet antyklerykalny," 205.

138. Lechicki, *W walce z demoralizacją,* 2:551.

139. Żeleński, "Niebezpieczna fikcja," in *Pisma,* 15:292.

140. For an introduction to the controversy surrounding civil marriages and divorces, see Pietrzak, "Sytuacja prawna kobiet," 33–52.

141. Dolegowska-Wysocka, *Poboyowisko,* 12–15.

142. On the commission, see Dołęgowska-Wysocka, *Poboyowisko,* 34, 48. See also Komisja Kodyfikacyjna RP, Podsekcja i Prawa Cywilnego, vol. 1, no. 1, *Projekt Prawa Małżeńskiego uchwalony przez Komisję Kodyfikacyjną RP w dniu 28 maja 1929* (Warsaw: Wydawnictwo Urzędowe Komisji Kodyfikacyjnej, 1931); Komisja Kodyfikacyjna RP, Podsekcja i Prawa Cywilnego, vol. 1, no. 3, *Zasady Projektu Prawa Małżeńskiego uchwalonego przez Komisję Kodyfikacyjną w dniu 28 maja 1929* (Warsaw: Wydawnictwo Urzędowe Komisji Kodyfikacyjnej, 1931).

143. Żeleński, "Rozerwalna nierozerwalność," in *Pisma,* 15:49. See also Żeleński, *Dziewice konsystorskie,* February 1929, repr. in Nałęcz, *Nie szablą,* 169; Żeleński, "Nowa ustawa małżeńska," *Wiadomości literackie,* no. 43 (October 25, 1931): 1.

144. Hlond's condemnation of the commission's proposal was published in letter form in *Gazeta warszawska,* November 29, 1931. See Dolegowska-Wysocka, *Poboyowisko,* 22–23.

145. Czytelnik, "Katolicy, na szańce!" *Rycerz niepokalanej,* no. 1 (January 1932): 7. See also editors, "Przyjdź królestwo twoje!" *Rycerz niepokalanej,* no. 6 (June 1934): 162. Boy engaged with the Polish bishops' response to the proposals for civil marriage and divorce in Boy-Zeleński, "Nasi okupanci," *Wiadomości literackie,* no. 50 (December 13, 1931): 1.

146. Nowaczyński, "Reformacja seksualna," 126.

147. "List pasterski episkopatu Polski. Kościół potępia sanacyjny komunizm," *Sztafeta: Pismo narodowo-radykalne* (Warsaw), no. 8 (March 11, 1934): 3. The episcopal letter was reprinted in a variety of different journals from the period. See, for instance, "List pasterski biskupów polskich," *Gazeta świąteczna* (Warsaw), no. 9 (March 4, 1934): 1–2. The letter was signed by twenty-six bishops, including Aleksander Kakowski, the archbishop of Warsaw, August Hlond, the archbishop of Gniezno and Poznań, and Adam Sapieha, the archbishop of Kraków.

148. Lechicki, *W walce z demoralizacją,* 2:532–33; Lechicki, "Wstęp," lx.

149. See Dolegowska-Wysocka, *Poboyowisko,* 16; see also 42–44.

150. BN, mf. 52720, Ossolineum Manuscripts no. 13533/II, Maria Bobrzyńska, "Życie zmiennym jest," vol. 2, 1919–39, 54.

151. W. Z. [Father Jan Piwowarczyk], "Wystąpienie red. Haeckera," in Lechicki, *Prawda o Boyu-Zeleńskim,* 132; repr. from *Głos narodu* (January 1932).

152. W. Z., "Minister WRO," 173–74.

153. Ibid., 175. For Boy on Mussolini, see "Co mówi Mussolini?" in Żeleński, *Pisma,* 15:211–13.

154. Emil Haecker, "Słówka do Boya," in Lechicki, *Prawda o Boyu-Żeleńskim,* 131; repr. from *Naprzód,* no. 13 (January 17, 1932). The same article is reprinted in Nałęcz, *Nie szablą,* 191–93. For a review of Haecker's years as editor of *Forward,* see Alfred Toczek, *Krakowski* Naprzód *i jego polityczne oblicze, 1919–1934* (Kraków: Wydawnictwo Naukowe WSP, 1997), 23–24, 151. After the *Worker, Forward* was the most popular socialist journal of the period.

155. Kazimierz Świtalski, Józef Beck, Janusz Jędrzejewicz, Ignacy Matuszewski, and Bogusław Miedziński were said to have converted to Protestantism for this reason. See Zbigniew Zaporowski, *Józef Piłsudski w kręgu wojska i polityki* (Lublin: Wydawnictwo Uniwersytetu Marii Curie-Skłodowskiej, 1998), 46.

156. Haecker, "Słówka do Boya," 131.

Chapter 6

1. Anna Nasiłowska, *Trzydziestolecie, 1914–1944* (Warsaw: Wydawnictwo Naukowe PKW, 1997), 159–69.

2. Irena Krzywicka, "Ankieta *Epoki* o współczesnym kryzysie duchowym," *Epoka*, no. 14 (April 2, 1933): 5.

3. Others, like Wanda Melcer, reported in *Warsaw, Black Land (Czarny ląd Warszawa)* (Warsaw: Dom Książki Polskiej, 1936), about the economic devastation that marked the Jewish district in Warsaw. For a brief discussion of these social reports, and of the tendency for women to dominate in this kind of writing, see Koźniewski, *Historia co tydzień,* 63–69.

4. Andrzej Chojnowski, "'Wobec Boga i historii,'" *Nowa res publica* 11 (November 1996): 27–30.

5. BN, mf. 83263, Ossolineum Manuscripts no. 15346/II, Wincenty Bryja, "Wincenty Witos w mojej pamięci. Wspomnienia z lat 1923–1939," 49.

6. Ron Landau, *Piłsudski and Poland,* trans. Geoffrey Dunlop (New York: Lincoln MacVeagh/Dial Press, 1929), v.

Bibliography

Abbreviations of Archives

AAN–Archiwum Akt Nowych
BN–Biblioteka Narodowa
BNDŻS–Biblioteka Narodowa, Dokumenty z Życia Społecznego
BNPK–Biblioteka Narodowa, Pałac Krasińskich
BUW–Archiwum Biblioteki Uniwersytetu Warszawskiego
CAW–Centralne Archiwum Wojskowe
MSWW–Archiwum Miasta Stołecznego i Województwa Warszawskiego w Warszawie
PAN–Archiwum Polskiej Akademii Nauk

Primary Sources

Archives

AAN
Archive of Recent Documents (Archiwum Akt Nowych), Warsaw

Akta Instytucji Wojskowych, Naczelne Dowództwo Wojska Polskiego
    files 296/I, vol. 56; 296/II, vol. 1
Zbiór Druków Ulotnych
    files 3, 39, 73, 92, 99, 103, 154, 192, 199, 205, 225, 232, 278, 291
Zespół Bezpartyjnego Bloku Współpracy z Rządem
    files 11, 29, 31, 41, 49, 73–74, 92, 107; file 1, mf. 31068; file 3, mf. 31070; file 23, mf. 31076;
        file 25, mf. 31078; file 32, mf. 31083; file 33, mf. 31084; file 34, mf. 31085; file 35, mf.
        31086
Zespół Józefa i Aleksandry Piłsudskich
    part 1, file 29, mf. 23129; part 2, files 31, 32; part 4, file 22
Zespół Komendy Głównej Policji Państwowej
    files 8, 147, 149, 152, 155, 156
Zespół Ligi Kobiet Polskich
    files 4, 14, 24, 26, 27, 29, 30, 63
Zespół Ligi Obrony Praw Człowieka i Obywatela w Polsce
    files 180/I, nos. 1–6; 180/II, nos. 1–4

Zespół Ministerstwa Opieki Społecznej
files 76, 174–76, 178, 183, 187–88, 195–96, 205, 209, 216, 230, 236, 239, 244, 248, 254, 309, 532–33, 549, 575, 641, 642, 650, 672, 734, 862, 1577–79, 1581, 1582, 1584, 1585, 1604, 1643, 1646
Zespół Ministerstwa Spraw Wewnętrznych
files 18, 667, 832, 849, 1297, 1305, 1543, 1545; file 19, mf. 23119; file 112, mf. 20177
Zespół Ministerstwa Wyznań Religijnych i Oświecenia Publicznego
files 220, 388, 431, 641, 650–51, 655, 920, 951–52, 957, 1508–9, 2165, 7110
Zespół Moraczewskich
file 71/I-60, mf. 2314/7; file 71/I-81, mf. 2314/9; file 71/I-91, mf. 2314/10; file 71/I-92, mf. 2314/10; file 71/I-96, mf. 2314/11; file 71/I-97, mf. 2314/11; file 71/I-98, mf. 2314/11; file 71/I-101, mf. 2314/12; file 71/I-104, mf. 2314/12; file 71/III-5; file 71/III-6, mf. 1855/6; file 71/III-9
Zespół Obozu Zjednoczenia Narodowego
files 1, 12, 34, 49
Zespół Ignacego Jana Paderewskiego
file 3041
Zespół Polskiego Związku Wydawnictw Dzienników i Czasopism w Warszawie
files 2–5, 98, 183, 250–51, 506
Zespół Samopomocy Społecznej Kobiet
files 1–16
Zespół Stowarzyszenia Wolnomyślicieli Polskich
file 183/I-1, 183/II-1
Zespół Walerego Sławka
file 11, mf. 27898–27907
Zespół Władysława Grabskiego
files 12, 15, 19
Zespół Zjednoczenia Pracy Wsi i Miast
files 1–5, 13, 19, 24, 26, 28, 30
Zespół Związku Legionistek Polskich
files 1–3, 13, 24, 48, 51, 54, 56, 58, 60–61
Zespół Związku Legionistów Polskich
files 47, 49, 138, 140, 144, 145

BN
National Library Microfilms (Biblioteka Narodowa), Warsaw

Archiwum Ligi Kobiet Naczelnego Komitetu Narodowego we Lwówie 1915–38
Ossolineum Manuscripts 14035/III, BN mf. 60706; 14030/III, BN mf. 60701
Fragment Archiwum Naczelnego Zarządu Ligi Kobiet Naczelnego Komitetu Narodowego 1915–17, Ligi Kobiet Polskich 1917–18
Jagiellonian University Library files 8836 IV, BN mf. 50126

Henryk Dzendzel, "Moje wspomnienia, rok 1926. Cz. 2: miesiąc luty"
    Ossolineum Manuscripts 14448/II, vols. 2–3, BN mf. 64621
Jan Bobrzyński, "Zwierciadło 'gasnącego świata.' Pamiętnik z ćwierćwiecza na służ-
    bie ojczyzny"
    Ossolineum Manuscripts 13531/II, BN mf. 52717
Józef Błoński, "Pamiętnik 1891–1969," vols. 1–2 (1952–69)
    Ossolineum Manuscripts 15381/II, BN mf 83332
Korespondencja Kazimiera Czachowskiego, 1912–45
    Jagiellonian University Manuscripts, files 8974 III, BN mf. 60350; 8975 III, vol. 5,
        BN mf. 60363; 8976 III, vol. 6, BN mf. 60364
Maria Bobrzyńska, "Życie zmiennym jest. Pamiętnik z lat 1900–1958"
    Ossolineum Manuscripts 13533/II, BN mf. 52720
Odezwy, zarządzenia, komunikaty polityczne, pisma ulotne różnych organizacji
    politycznych z lat 1914–29
    Ossolineum Manuscripts 13491/III, BN mf. 52665
Papiery różne Sekcji Kobiet Polskiej Partii Socjalistycznej we Lwowie za lata 1927–36
    Ossolineum Manuscripts 13511/II, III, BN mf. 52694
Stanisław Głąbiński, "Wspomnienia polityczne: Część IV. Rządy Sanacji w Polsce,
    1926–1939"
    Ossolineum Manuscripts 13260/II, mf. 47163
Wincenty Bryja, "Wincenty Witos w mojej pamięci. Wspomnienia z lat 1923–1939"
    Ossolineum Manuscripts 15346/II, BN mf. 83263

BNDŻS
National Library Special Collection: Documents from Social Life (Dokumenty z
    Życia Społecznego), Warsaw
Bezpartyjny Blok Współpracy z Rządem
    BNDŻS-IA6c1, IB 1935
Komunikat Informacyjno-Polityczny; Wydawnictwo Okręgu Warszawskiego Pol-
    skiej Organizacji Wolności–POW, no. 4 (October 15, 1922)
    BNDŻS-IB, 1922, Warsaw
Narodowa Organizacja Kobiet
    BNDŻS-IO
Piąta Rada Naczelna Koło Polek
    BNDŻS-IO, 1923, Warsaw
Polska Organizacja Wolności i Związek Legjonistów
    BNDŻS-IB, 1926, Warsaw
Sprawozdanie Sodalicji Pań w Poznaniu
    BNDŻS XX B11, 1928–30
Sprawozdanie Zarządu Związek Sodalicji Marjańskich Inteligencji Męskiej w Polsce
    BNDŻS XX B11 1926, Kraków, 1926–34

Sprawozdanie ZPOK, Poznańskie Zrzeszenie Wojewódzkie [1931–33]
  BNDŻS-ID, 1933, Poznań

BNPK
National Library Manuscript Collection, Krasiński Palace (Biblioteka Narodowa,
  Pałac Krasińskich), Warsaw
Listy Boya do M. H. Staniewskich
  file III.11.143
Papiery Anieli Samotyhowej
  files II.11.006, II.11.017, II.11.016, II.11.045, III.11.004, III.11.006, III.11.013, III.11.018,
  III.11.021, III.11.045, III.11.052, III.11.053, IV.11.003, IV.11.026
Papiery Teodory Męczkowskiej
  files II.10.303, II.10.302, III.10.304
Zespół Jędrzeja i Zofii Moraczewskich
  files 30, 36, 48, 52, 71, 81, 94, 99, 101, 106, 114, 116, 118, 121, 122, 125–27, 131, 136, 137, 138, 144

BUW
Archive of the University of Warsaw Library (Archiwum Biblioteki Uniwersytetu
  Warszawskiego)
Artykuły Romana Dmowskiego i Wycinki z Prasy z lat 1924–33
  file 1770
Materiały dotyczące działalności kobiecych organizacji ziemiańskich
  file 2937, vols. 1–2
Papiery Antoniego Słonimskiego
  file 1482
Papiery i Listy Mieczysława Rettingera
  file 1476
Wacław Bitner, "Dramat Drugiej Rzeczypospolitej"
  file 1767
Wycinki z Prasy. Zbiór Stanisława Stempowskiego
  files 1578, 1582

CAW
Central Military Archives (Centralne Archiwum Wojskowe), Rembertów

Gabinet Mininstra Spraw Wojskowych
  files I.300.1.327, I.300.1.483

MSWW
State Archives of the Capital City and the Voivodship of Warsaw (Archiwum
  Państwowe Miasta Stołecznego i Województwa Warszawskiego w Warszawie)

Papiery Konrada Olchowicza: "Wspomnienia i Refleksje Dziennikarza, 1914–1939"
    (Kraków, 1963–64), file 273
Towarzystwo Wydawnicze Bluszcz, 1936

PAN
Archives of the Polish Academy of Sciences in Warsaw (Archiwum Polskiej Aka-
    demii Nauk w Warszawie)
Papiery Witolda Chodźko
    files 16, 20, 22, 131, 145, 155, 156
Zespół Towarzystwa Kultury Moralnej im. E. Abramowskiego
    files 1–15

Periodicals

ABC (Warsaw) 1932
Antena (Warsaw)
Bocian (Kraków)
Cyrulik warszawski (Warsaw) 1926–34
Czas (Kraków) 1926, 1928
Dla przyszłości (Warsaw) 1927–28, 1929–31,1933, 1936, 1939
Droga (Warsaw) 1924–28
Drogi naprawy (Warsaw) 1926
Dwór Marji (Kraków) 1926–37
Epoka (Warsaw) 1932–33, 1936
Express poranny (Warsaw) 1928
Gazeta polska (Warsaw) 1929
Gazeta poranna (Warsaw) 1925
Gazeta świąteczna (Warsaw) 1934
Gazeta warszawska (Warsaw) 1924, 1931–33
Gazeta warszawska poranna (Warsaw) 1926
Głos kobiet (Warsaw) 1928–30
Głos monarchisty (Częstochowa/Warsaw) 1926–34
Głos prawdy (Warsaw) 1926
Hasło podwawelski (Kraków) 1929–32, 1935–36
Hasło polski (Łódź) 1926–27
Illustrowany kurjer codzienny (Kraków) 1931
Jutro rzeczypospolitej (Warsaw) 1931–32
Kobieta w Sejmie (Warsaw) 1919
Kobieta współczesna (Warsaw) 1927–34
Kurier poranny (Warsaw) 1926, 1929, 1935
Kurier poznański (Poznań) 1931
Kurier warszawski (Warsaw) 1924–25, 1929

Liberum veto (Warsaw) 1918–19
Mucha (Warsaw) 1926–28
Myśl (Warsaw) 1927, 1929
Myśl narodowa (Warsaw) 1926–33
Myśl niepodległa (Warsaw) 1926–28
Nakazy chwili (Warsaw) 1926
Nakazy dnia (Warsaw) 1935
Naprzód (Kraków) 1931
Nasz przegląd (Warsaw) 1929–35
Odrodzenie (Katowice) 1926
Polska odrodzona (Kraków) 1923–24, 1926–28, 1930
Praca obywatelska (Warsaw) 1930–35
Prawda (Łódź) 1926
Prąd (Lublin/Warsaw) 1926
Pro fide, rege et lege (Warsaw) 1926–28
Pro patria (Warsaw) 1924–29
Przyszłość (Bielsko-Biała) 1928
Rakieta (Warsaw) 1925
Robotnik (Warsaw) 1926–27
Rozwój (Warsaw) 1919–20, 1922
Rycerz niepokalanej (Grodno) 1926–27, 1929, 1932–34
Rzeczpospolita (Warsaw) 1926
Sanacja moralna (Warsaw) 1929
Słowo 1929, 1935
Ster zagłębia (Sosnowiec) 1926
Straż polska (Lwów) 1926
Szaniec (Warsaw) 1927, 1929–30
Świat (Warsaw) 1932
Świat i prawda (Grudziądz) 1924–26
Tęcza (Poznań) 1927–29, 1931
Wiadomości kobiece (Warsaw) 1931, 1933
Wiadomości literackie (Warsaw) 1924–35
Życie świadome (Warsaw) 1936–37

Government Publications

Główny Urząd Statystyczny Rzeczypospolitej Polskiej. *Mały rocznik statystyczny 1937*. Warsaw: Nakładem Głównego Urzędu Statystycznego, 1937.
Komisja Kodyfikacyjna RP. Podsekcja i Prawa Cywilnego. Vol. 1, no. 1: *Projekt Prawa Małżeńskiego uchwalony przez Komisję Kodyfikacyjną RP w dniu 28 maja 1929*. Warsaw: Wydawnictwo Urzędowe Komisji Kodyfikacyjnej, 1931.

————. Vol. 1, no. 3: *Zasady Projektu Prawa Małżeńskiego uchwalonego przez Komisję Kodyfikacyjną w dniu 28 maja 1929*. Warsaw: Wydawnictwo Urzędowe Komisji Kodyfikacyjnej, 1931.

Ministerstwo Spraw Wewnętrznych. *Komunikaty informacyjne Komisariatu Rządu na m. st. Warszawę I: 1 (6 grudnia 1926–23 czerwca 1927)*. Ed. Bernadetta Gronek and Irena Marczak. Warsaw: Centralne Archiwum Ministerstwa Spraw Wewnętrznych, 1991.

————. *Komunikaty informacyjne Komisariatu Rządu na m. st. Warszawę I: 2 (4 lipca 1927–30 grudnia 1927)*. Ed. Bernadetta Gronek and Irena Marczak. Warsaw: Centralne Archiwum Ministerstwa Spraw Wewnętrznych, 1992.

————. *Komunikaty informacyjne Komisariatu Rządu na m. st. Warszawę II: 1 (3 stycznia 1928–26 czerwca 1928)*. Ed. Bernadetta Gronek and Irena Marczak. Warsaw: Centralne Archiwum Ministerstwa Spraw Wewnętrznych, 1992.

————. *Komunikaty informacyjne Komisariatu Rządu na m. st. Warszawę III: 1 (29 stycznia 1929–28 marca 1929)*. Ed. Bernadetta Gronek and Irena Marczak. Warsaw: Centralne Archiwum Ministerstwa Spraw Wewnętrznych, 1993.

Published Primary Sources

Abramowski, Edward. *Filozofia społeczna: Wybor pism*. Warsaw: Państwowe Wydawnictwo Naukowe, 1965.

————. *Rzeczpospolita przyjaciół: Wybór pism społecznych i politycznych*. Ed. Damian Kalbarczyk. Warsaw: Instytut Wydawniczy Pax, 1986.

Anusz, Antoni. *Podstawy wychowania obywatelskiego*. Warsaw: Wydawnictwo Związku Strzeleckiego, 1930.

————. *Rola Józefa Piłsudskiego w życiu narodu i państwa*. Warsaw: Biblioteka Wydawnictwa "Głosu Prawdy," 1927.

Baranowski, Władysław. *Rozmowy z Piłsudskim, 1916–1931*. Warsaw: Instytut Wydawniczy "Biblioteka Polska," 1938.

Bełcikowska, Alicja. *Walki majowe w Warszawie, 11 maj–16 maj 1926*. Warsaw: Nakładem Drukarni W. Maślankiewicz i F. Jabczyński, 1926.

Charszewski, X. [Ignacy]. *Niebezpieczeństwo żydowskie w niebezpieczeństwo kobiecem*. Warsaw: Druk. Społeczna, 1929.

Chomicz, Bolesław, ed. *Sanacja czy dezorganizacja: Rzecz o polskiej dyrekcji ubezpieczeń wzajemnych*. Warsaw: Drukarnia Polska, 1927.

Chodźko, Witold. *Handel kobietami*. 2d ed. Warsaw: Polski Związek Walki z Handlem Kobietami i Dziećmi, 1938.

Cywiński, Stanisław. "Dekadencja Boya." In *Prawda o Boyu-Żeleńskim: Głosy krytyczne*, ed. Czesław Lechicki. Warsaw: Dom Książki Polskiej, 1933.

Czerwiński, Sławomir. *O nowy ideał wychowawczy*. Warsaw: Biblioteka Zrąb, 1932.

Dąbrowska, Maria. *Dzienniki, 1914–1932.* Ed. Tadeusz Drewnowski. Warsaw: Czytelnik, 1988.

———. *Życie i dzieło Edwarda Abramowskiego.* Warsaw: Wydawnictwo Związku Polskich Stowarzyszeń Spożywców, 1925.

Dmowski, Roman. *Wybór pism.* Ed. Antonina Bogdan. 4 vols. New York: Instytut Romana Dmowskiego, 1988.

Dołęga-Mostowicz, Tadeusz. *Kariera Nikodema Dyzmy.* 1932. Reprint, Warsaw: Czytelnik, 1955.

Etchegoyen, Olivier, comte d'. *The Comedy of Poland.* Trans. Nora Bickley. 1925. Reprint, London: Allen and Unwin, 1927.

Gronowicz, Antoni. *Antysemityzm rujnuje moją ojczyznę.* Lwów: Nakładem Dobrego Polaka, 1938.

Iłłakowiczówna, Kazimiera. *Ballady bohaterskie.* Lwów: Wydawnictwo Zakładu Narodowego im. Ossolińskich, 1934.

———. *Ścieżka obok drogi.* 1939. Reprint, Warsaw: Zelpress, 1989.

———. *Wspomnienia i reportaże.* Ed. Jacek Biesiada and Aleksandra Włoszczyńska. Warsaw: Więź, 1997.

Irzykowski, Karol. *Beniaminek: Walka o treść.* 1933. Reprint, Kraków: Wydawnictwo Literackie, 1976.

Józef Piłsudski, 1867–1935. Kraków: Małopolska Oficyna Wydawnicza, 1935.

Kaden-Bandrowski. Juliusz. *Piłsudczycy.* 1925. Reprint, Białystok: Krajowa Agencja Wydawnicza, 1990.

Krzyżanowski, Adam. *Dlaczego kandyduję z listy nr. 1, Bezpartyjnego Bloku Współpracy z Rządem?* Kraków: BBWR, n.d.

Kutrzeba, Stanisław. *Polska odrodzona, 1914–1928.* 3d ed. Warsaw: Gebethner and Wolff, 1928.

Kwiatkowski, Eugeniusz. *Dysproporcje: Rzecz o Polsce przeszłej i obecnej.* Ed. Andrzej Garlicki. 1931. Reprint, Warsaw: Czytelnik, 1989.

Landau, Ron. *Piłsudski and Poland.* Trans. Geoffrey Dunlop. New York: Lincoln MacVeagh/Dial Press, 1929.

Lechicki, Czesław. *Boy-Żeleński we wklęsłem zwierciadle.* Lwów: Nakładem Autora, 1933.

———, ed. *Prawda o Boyu-Żeleńskim: Głosy krytyczne.* Warsaw: Dom Książki Polskiej, 1933.

———, comp. *Przewodnik po beletrystyce.* Poznań: Akcja Katolicka, 1935.

———. *W walce z demoralizacją: Szkice literacko-społeczne.* 2 vols. Miejsce Piastowe: Wydawnictwo Towarzystwa Św. Michała Archanioła, 1932–33.

———. "Wstęp." In *Prawda o Boyu-Żeleńskim: Głosy krytyczne,* ed. Czesław Lechicki. Warsaw: Dom Książki Polskiej, 1933.

Lipecki, Jan [Irena Pannenkowa]. *Legenda Piłsudskiego*. Poznań: Wielkopolska Księgarnia Nakładowa Karola Rzepeckiego, 1922.

Machray, Robert. *The Poland of Piłsudski, 1914–1936*. 1936. Reprint, London: Allen and Unwin, 1962.

Melcer, Wanda. *Czarny ląd Warszawa*. Warsaw: Dom Książki Polskiej, 1936.

Męczkowska, Teodora. *Szkoły mieszane: Koedukacja*. Warsaw: M. Arcta, 1920.

———. *Wychowanie seksualne dzieci i młodzieży*. Warsaw: Nakładem "Naszej Księgarni," Spółki Akc./Związku Nauczycielstwa Polskiego, 1934.

Męczkowska, Teodora, et al. *Polskie Stowarzyszenie Kobiet z Wyższem Wykształceniem w latach 1926–1936*. Warsaw: Nakładem Polskiego Stowarzyszenia Kobiet z Wyższem Wykształceniem, 1936.

Niedziałkowski, Mieczysław. *Demokracja parlamentarna w Polsce*. Warsaw: Nakładem Księgarni Robotniczej, 1930.

Niewiadomski, Eligiusz. *Kartki z więzienia*. Poznań: Wielkopolska Księgarnia Nakł. K. Rzepeckiego, 1923.

Nowaczyński, Adolf. "Boyszewizm." In *Prawda o Boyu-Żeleńskim: Głosy krytyczne*, ed. Czesław Lechicki. Warsaw: Dom Książki Polskiej, 1933. Reprinted from *Gazeta warszawska*, no. 389 (December 24, 1931): 17–18.

———. *Plewy i perły*. 1934. Reprint, Warsaw: Presspol, 1991.

———. *Porachunki i projekty: Teksty o teatrze z lat 1900–1938*. Ed. Henryk Izydor Rogacki. Wrocław: Wiedza i Kultura, 1993.

———. "Reformacja seksualna." In Lechicki, *Prawda o Boyu-Żeleńskim*. Reprinted from *ABC*, June 24, 1932.

Piłsudski, Józef. *Pisma wybrane*. London: M. I. Kolin, 1943.

———. *Pisma zbiorowe: Wydanie prac dotychczas drukiem ogłoszonych*. 10 vols. Ed. Kazimierz Świtalski. 1937. Reprint, Warsaw: Krajowa Agencja Wydawnicza, 1991.

Pirożyński, Marjan. *Co czytać? Poradnik dla czytających książki: Beletrystyka*. Kraków: Wydawnictwo Księży Jezuitów, 1932.

Podoleński, Stanisław T. J. *Podręcznik pedagogiczny: Wskazówki dla rodziców i wychowawców*. Kraków: Wydawnictwo Księży Jezuitów, 1921.

Pohoska, Hanna. *Wychowanie obywatelsko-państwowe*. Warsaw: Ministerstwo Wyznań Religijnych i Oświecenia Publicznego, 1931.

Polska Partia Socjalistyczna. *Kobiety, stańcie w szeregu!* Warsaw: Centralny Wydział Kobiecy P.P.S., 1928.

Porczak, Marjan. *Dyktator Józef Piłsudski i "Piłsudczycy."* Kraków: Nakładem Autora, 1930.

———. *Piatiletka sanacyjna w piątą rocznicę zamachu majowego 1926 r.* Kraków: Nakładem Tow. Uniwersytetu Robotniczego, Oddział im. Adama Mickiewicza w Krakowie, 1931.

———. *Rewolucja majowa 1926 i jej skutki.* Kraków: Nakładem Autora, 1927.

Rataj, Maciej. *Pamiętniki, 1918–1927.* Ed. Jan Dębski. Warsaw: Ludowa Spółdzielnia Wydawnicza, 1965.

———. *Wskazania obywatelskie i polityczne: Wybór pism i przemówień z lat 1919–1938.* Ed. Stanisław Lato. Warsaw: Ludowa Spółdzielnia Wydawnicza, 1987.

Rychliński, Stanisław. *Warszawa jako stolica polski.* Warsaw: Wydawnictwo Biura Ekonomicznego Zarzadu Miejskiego, 1936.

Rymkiewicz, Władysław. *Prawo do miłości: Powieść.* Warsaw: Wydawnictwo J. Mortkowicza, 1931.

Rzętkowska, Marja. *Kobieta w Obozie Wielkiej Polski.* n.p.: Nakładem Akademika Polskiego, 1933.

Samotyhowa, Nela. *Edward Abramowski i jego poglądy na znaczenie dobra i piękna w przebudowie życia: Odczyt, wygłoszony dn. 20 listopada 1928 r. w Kamienicy Ks. Mazowieckich na wieczorze, poświęconym pamięci Edwarda Abramowskiego.* Warsaw: Wydawnictwo Towarzystwa Kultury Etycznej im. Edwarda Abramowskiego, 1931.

Samozwaniec, Magdalena. *Kartki z pamiętnika młodej mężatki.* Warsaw: E. Wende i Ska, [1926].

Sieroszewski, Wacław, et al., eds. *Idea i czyn Józefa Piłsudskiego.* Warsaw: Bibljoteka Dzieł Naukowych, 1934.

Skwarczyński, Adam. *Myśli o nowej Polsce.* 2d ed. Warsaw: W. Daszewskiego, 1934.

———, ed. *Pod znakiem odpowiedzialności i pracy: Dziesięć wieczorów.* Warsaw: Wydawnictwo Droga, 1933.

Starzewski, Jan. *Józef Piłsudski: Zarys psychologiczny.* Warsaw: Nakł. F. Hoesicka, 1930.

Strumph-Wojtkiewicz, Stanisław. *O własnych siłach: Kartki z prywatnego archiwum, 1921–1939.* Warsaw: Książka i Wiedza, 1967.

Strumph-Wojtkiewicz, Stanisław, Wanda Melcer Rutkowska, and Marja Szpyrkówna. *Moment zwrotny.* Warsaw: Towarzystwo Wyd. Rój, 1926.

Szmurłowa, Grażyna, Halina Siemieńska, and Halina Alchimowicz. *Kobieta w prawie publicznym i prywatnym: Zbiór przepisów obowiązujących w Polsce.* Warsaw: Związek Pracy Obywatelskiej Kobiet, Wydział Spraw Kobiecych, Sekcja Prawna, 1937.

Świecki. "Pamflet antyklerykalny." In *Prawda o Boyu-Żeleńskim: Głosy krytyczne,* ed. Czesław Lechicki. Warsaw: Dom Książki Polskiej, 1933.

Świętochowski, Aleksander. *Aleksander Świętochowski: Aforyzmy.* Ed. Maria Brykalska. Warsaw: Państwowy Instytut Wydawniczy, 1979.

———. *Pisma wybrane.* Ed. Wacław Kubacki. Warsaw: Państwowy Instytut Wydawniczy, 1951.

———. *Wspomnienia.* Ed. Samuel Sandler. Wrocław: Zakład Narodowy im. Ossolińskich, 1966.

Świętorzecki, Aleksander. *Handlarz jęzorem: Rzecz o Adolfie Neuwert-Nowaczyńskim i spółce w sprawie "Boy'szewizmu."* Warsaw: n.p., 1932.

Takiej Polski chce Józef Piłsudski. Warsaw: n.p., 1938.

Wasilewski, Zygmunt. *O życiu i katastrofach cywilizacji narodowej: Wstęp do rozważań nad programowemi zagadnieniami doby obecnej.* Warsaw: Nakładem Księgarni i Składu Perzyński, Niklewicz i Sp., 1921

———. *Pokolenia w służbie narodu.* London: Nakładem Katolickiego Ośrodka Wydawniczego Veritas, 1962.

Wielopolska, Maria Jehanne. *Józef Piłsudski w życiu codziennym.* Warsaw: Księgarnia Wojskowa, 1936.

———. *Pliszka w jaskini lwa: Rozważania nad książką Panny Iłłakowiczówny, Ścieżka Obok Drogi.* Warsaw: [Druk J. Zielony], 1939.

Witos, Wincenty. *Czasy i ludzie.* Tarnów: Józef Pisza, 1926.

———. Dzieła wybrane. Vol. 2, pt. 2: *Moje wspomnienia (lata 1918–1933).* Ed. Eugeniusz Karczewski and Józef Ryszard Szaflik. Warsaw: Ludowa Spółdzielnia Wydawnicza, 1990.

Wojciechowski, Stanisław. *Wspomnienia, orędzia, artykuły.* Ed. Maria Groń-Drozdowska and Marian Marek Drozdowski. Warsaw: Bellona, 1995.

Woyszwiłło [Julian Władysław Pobóg-Malinowski]. *Józef Piłsudski: Życie, idee i czyny, 1867–1935.* 1937. Reprint, Warsaw: Wiedza Powszechna, 1990.

W. Z. [Father Jan Piwowarczyk]. "Minister WRO i 'Minister Oświecenia.'" In *Prawda o Boyu-Żeleńskim: Głosy krytyczne,* ed. Czesław Lechicki. Warsaw: Dom Książki Polskiej, 1933.

———. "Przeciw poniżeniu macierzyństwa." In Lechicki, *Prawda o Boyu-Żeleńskim.*

Zakrzewski, Kazimierz. *Kryzys demokracji.* Warsaw: Bibljoteka *Drogi,* 1930.

Żeleński, Tadeusz (Boy). *Pisma.* Ed. Henryk Markiewicz. 28 vols. Warsaw: Państwowy Instytut Wydawniczy, 1958.

———. *Tadeusz Żeleński Boy: Listy.* Ed. Barbara Winklowa. Warsaw: Państwowy Instytut Wydawniczy, 1972.

Secondary Sources

Adamczyk, Arkadiusz. "Relacja Bogusława Miedzińskiego z wydarzeń majowych 1926 r." *Zeszyty historyczne* 132 (2000): 226–34.

Ajnenkiel, Andrzej. *Od "rządow ludowych" do przewrotu majowego: Zarys dziejów politycznych polski, 1918–1926.* Warsaw: Wiedza Powszechna, 1978.

————. *Parlamentaryzm II Rzeczypospolitej.* Warsaw: Wiedza Powszechna, 1975.

————. *Polska po przewrocie majowym: Zarys dziejów politycznych Polski, 1926–1939.* Warsaw: Wiedza Powszechna, 1980.

————. *Spór o model parlamentaryzmu polskiego do roku 1926.* Warsaw: Książka i Wiedza, 1972.

Ajnenkiel, Andrzej et al. "Uwarunkowania zamachu majowego (Dyskusja redakcyjna)." *Kwartalnik historyczny* 93, no. 1 (1986): 111–32.

Albert, Andrzej. [Wojciech Roszkowski]. *Najnowsza historia Polski, 1918–1980.* 1983. Reprint, London: Polonia, 1989.

Bankowicz, Bożena, Antoni Dudek, and Jacek Majchrowski. *Główne nurty współczesnej polskiej myśli politycznej.* Kraków: Wydawnictwo Uniwersytetu Jagiellońskiego, 1996.

Baranowska, Agnieszka. *Perły i potwory: Szkice o literaturze międzywojennej.* Warsaw: Państwowy Instytut Wydawniczy, 1986.

Barany, George. "Political Culture in the Lands of the Former Habsburg Empire: Authoritarian and Parliamentary Traditions." *Austrian History Yearbook* 29, pt. 1 (1998): 195–248.

Bates, John M. "Freedom of the Press in Inter-War Poland: The System of Control." In *Poland between the Wars, 1918–1939,* ed. Peter D. Stachura. London: Macmillan, 1998.

Bauman, Zygmunt. "Intellectuals in East-Central Europe: Continuity and Change." *East European Politics and Societies* 1, no. 2 (Spring 1987): 162–86.

Beauvois, Daniel, ed. *La presse polonaise en France, 1918–1984.* Lille: Revue du Nord, 1988.

Beck, Józef. *Final Report.* New York: Robert Speller and Sons, 1957.

Benda, Julian. *The Treason of the Intellectuals.* Trans. Richard Aldington. 1928. Reprint, New York: Norton, 1969.

Berend, Iván T. *Decades of Crisis: Central and Eastern Europe before World War Two.* Berkeley: University of California Press, 1998.

Berend, Iván T., and György Ránki. *Economic Development in East-Central Europe in the Nineteenth and Twentieth Centuries.* New York: Columbia University Press, 1974.

Bereza, Tadeusz. "Formacja Boya." *Nowa kultura,* nos. 51–52 (1951): 6.

Bernhard, Michael. "Institutional Choice and the Failure of Democracy: The Case of Interwar Poland." *East European Politics and Societies* 13, no. 1 (Winter 1999): 34–70.

Biskupski, M. B. "The Origins of the Paderewski Government in 1919: A Reconsideration in Light of New Evidence." *Polish Review* 33, no. 2 (1988): 157–66.

Blackwood, Lee. "Czech and Polish National Democracy at the Dawn of Independent Statehood, 1918–1919." *East European Politics and Societies* 4, no. 3 (Fall 1990): 469–88.

Blejwas, Stanislaus A. *Realism in Polish Politics: Warsaw Positivism and National Survival in Nineteenth Century Poland.* New Haven: Yale Concilium on International and Area Studies, 1984.

———. "Warsaw Positivism—Patriotism Misunderstood." *Polish Review* 27, nos. 1–2 (1982): 47–54.

Błoński, Jan. "*Wiadomości literackie*, 1924–1933: A Problem for the Poles, A Problem for the Jews." *Gal-Ed* 14 (1995): 39–48.

Bojanowska, Małgorzata, ed. "Korespondencja Jarosława Iwaszkiewicza z Mieczysławem Grydziewskim, 1922–1967." *Twórczość* 2, no. 579 (February 1994): 122–86.

Borkiewicz-Celińska, Anna. "Muzeum Józefa Piłsudskiego w Belwederze (1935–1939)." *Niepodległość* 50 (1999): 257.

Borkowski, Jan, ed. *Józef Piłsudski o państwie i armii w świetle wspomnień i innych dokumentów.* Warsaw: Państwowy Instytut Wydawniczy, 1985.

———. *Ludowcy w II Rzeczypospolitej.* Warsaw: Ludowa Spółdzielnia Wydawnicza, 1987.

———. "Naprawiacze w latach 1926–1935: Związek Naprawy Rzeczypospolitej i Zjednoczenie Pracy Wsi i Miast." *Dzieje najnowsze* 17, no. 2 (1985): 37–73.

———. "Piłsudczykowska koncepcja państwa." *Dzieje najnowsze* 14, no. 1 (1982): 93–124.

———. "Sprawy społeczno-gospodarcze w *Drodze*, 1922–1937." *Dzieje najnowsze* 11, no. 3 (1979): 51–83.

———. "Wincenty Witos w naszej historiografii i publicystyce: Uwagi krytyczne." *Kwartalnik historyczny* 78, no. 1 (1978): 103–30.

Brodzka, Alina, Helena Zaworska, and Stefan Żółkiewski, eds. *Literatura polska, 1918–1932.* Vol. 1 of *Literatura polska, 1918–1975.* Warsaw: Wiedza Powszechna, 1975.

Bromke, Adam. *Poland's Politics: Idealism vs. Realism.* Cambridge, MA: Harvard University Press, 1967.

Brykalska, Maria. *Aleksander Świętochowski: Biografia.* 2 vols. Warsaw: Państwowy Instytut Wydawniczy, 1987.

———. *Aleksander Świętochowski redaktor "Prawdy."* Wrocław: Polska Akademia Nauk/Ossolineum, 1974.

Brzezinski, Mark. *The Struggle for Constitutionalism in Poland.* Basingstoke, Hampshire: Macmillan, 1998.

Brzoza, Czesław, and Adam Roliński. *Bij Bolszewika! Rok 1920 w przekazie historycznym i literackim.* Kraków: Libertas, 1990.

Carpenter, Bogdana. *The Poetic Avant-Garde in Poland, 1918–1939.* Seattle: University of Washington Press, 1983.

Chajn, Leon. *Polskie Wolnomularstwo, 1920–1938.* 2d ed. Warsaw: Czytelnik, 1984.

Chirot, Daniel. "Ideology, Reality, and Competing Models of Development in Eastern Europe between the Two World Wars." *East European Politics and Societies* 3, no. 3 (Fall 1989): 378–411.

———, ed. *The Origins of Backwardness in Eastern Europe: Economics and Politics from the Middle Ages until the Early Twentieth Century.* Berkeley: University of California Press, 1989.

Chojnowski, Andrzej. "Idee i imponderabilia." *Res publica nowa,* no. 5 (May 1997): 10–16.

———. "Józef Piłsudski przed i po przewrocie majowym." *Przegląd historyczny* 77 (1986): 723–32.

———. "Moralność i polityka: Kobiece lobby w Bezpartyjnym Bloku Współpracy z Rządem." In *Kobieta i świat polityki w niepodległej Polsce, 1918–1939,* ed. Anna Żarnowska and Andrzej Szwarc. Warsaw: Wydawnictwo Sejmowe, 1996.

———. *Piłsudczycy u władzy: Dzieje Bezpartyjnego Bloku Współpracy z Rządem.* Wrocław: Ossolineum, 1986.

———. "Polish National Character, the Sanacja Camp, and the National Democracy." In *National Character and National Ideology in Interwar Eastern Europe,* ed. Ivo Banac and Katherine Verdery. New Haven: Yale Center for International and Area Studies, 1995.

———. "Rewolucja moralnego niepokoju." *Gazeta wyborcza,* no. 196 (August 23–24, 1997): 16–18.

———. "Utopia utracona Walerego Sławka: Projekt Powszechnej Organizacji Społecznej." *Przegląd historyczny* 80, no. 2 (1989): 353–65.

———. "'Wobec Boga i historii.'" *Res publica nowa* 11 (November 1996): 27–30.

Chojnowski, Andrzej, and Piotr Wróbel. *Prezydenci i premierzy Drugiej Rzeczypospolitej.* Wrocław: Ossolineum, 1992.

Chyra-Rolicz, Zofia. "Kościół katolicki a ruch kobiecy przed 1939 rokiem." In *Społeczno-kulturalna działalność kościoła katolickiego w Polsce XIX i XX wieku,* ed. Regina Renz and Marta Meducka. Kielce: Kieleckie Towarzystwo Naukowe, 1994.

Ciborowski, Janusz. *Józef Piłsudski w zbiorach Janusza Ciborowskiego.* Pruszków: Oficyna Wydawnicza "Ajaks," 1996.

Cieślak, Tadeusz. "Badania nad historią Polski od 1914 do 1964—w Polsce Ludowej." *Kwartalnik historyczny* 72, no. 1 (1965): 30–38.

Cywiński, Bohdan. "Myśl polityczna Edwarda Abramowskiego." In *Twórcy polskiej myśli politycznej: Zbiór studiów,* ed. Jan Miś. Wrocław: Nakład Narodowy imienia Ossolińskich/Wydawnictwo Polskiej Akademii Nauk, 1978.

————. *Rodowody niepokornych.* Warsaw: Wydawnictwo Krąg, 1984.

Czajecka, Bogusława. *"Z domu w szeroki świat": Droga kobiet do niezalezności w zaborze Austriackim w latach 1890–1914.* Kraków: Towarzystwo Autorów i Wydawców Naukowych Universitas, 1990.

Czajowski, Jacek, and Jacek M. Majchrowski. *Sylwetki polityków Drugiej Rzeczypospolitej.* Kraków: Wydawnictwo ZNAK, 1987.

Czapliński, Władysław. *Dzieje sejmu polskiego do roku 1939.* Kraków: Wydawnictwo Literackie, 1984.

Czarnik, Oskar Stanisław. *Proza artystyczna a prasa codzienna, 1918–1926.* Wrocław: Ossolineum, 1982.

Czarnowska, Maria. *Ilościowy rozwój polskiego ruchu wydawniczego, 1501–1965.* Warsaw: Biblioteka Narodowa, 1967.

Czubiński, Antoni. *Centrolew: Kształtowanie się i rozwój demokratycznej opozycji antysanacyjnej w Polsce w latach 1926–1930.* Poznań: Wydawnictwo Poznańskie, 1963.

————. *Polska odrodzona: Społeczne i polityczne aspekty rozwoju odrodzonego Państwa Polskiego: Rozprawy i studia.* Poznań: Wydawnictwo Poznański, 1982.

Dobrzycka, Urszula. *Abramowski.* Warsaw: Wiedza Powszechna, 1992.

Dołęgowska-Wysocka, Mirosława. *Poboyowisko.* Warsaw: BWG, 1992.

Drozdowski, Marian. *Sprawy i ludzie II Rzeczypospolitej: Szkice i polemiki.* Kraków: Wydawnictwo Literackie, 1979.

————. *Warszawa w latach 1914–1939.* Warsaw: Państwowe Wydawnictwo Naukowe, 1990.

————. "Wpływ przewrotu majowego na gospodarkę narodową Polski lat 1926–1929 (Uwagi do Dyskusji)." *Kwartalnik historyczny* 93, no. 4 (1986): 1105–13.

Drozdowski, Marian, et al. "Kultura polityczna w II Rzeczypospolitej: Dyskusje i polemiki." *Dzieje najnowsze* 12, no. 1 (1980): 95–118.

Eustachiewicz, Lesław. *Dwudziestolecie, 1919–1939.* Rev. ed. 1982. Reprint, Warsaw: Wydawnictwa Szkolne i Pedagogiczne, 1990.

————. *Między współczesnością a historią.* Warsaw: Pax, 1973.

Faryś, Janusz. *Piłsudski i Piłsudczycy: Z dziejów koncepcji polityczno-ustrojowej, 1918–1939.* Szczecin: Uniwersytet Szczeciński, 1991.

————. *Stanisław Stroński: Biografia polityczna do 1939 roku.* Szczecin: Wydawnictwo Naukowe Uniwersytetu Szczecińskiego, 1990.

Fitzpatrick, Sheila. "Supplicants and Citizens: Public Letter-Writing in Soviet Russia in the 1930s." *Slavic Review* 55, no. 1 (Spring 1996): 78–105.

Flis, Andrzej. "Edward Abramowski's Social and Political Thought." In *Masters of Polish Sociology,* ed. Piotr Sztompka. Wrocław: Polish Academy of Arts and Sciences, 1984.

Friedlander, Judith, et al., eds. *Women in Culture and Politics: A Century of Change.* Bloomington: Indiana University Press, 1986.

Friszke, Andrzej. "Naród, państwo, system władzy w myśli politycznej Związku Ludowo-Narodowego w latach 1919-1926." *Przegląd historyczny* 72, no. 1 (1981): 51-73.

———. *O kształt niepodległej.* Warsaw: Biblioteka Więzi, 1989.

Fritzsche, Peter. *Reading Berlin 1900.* Cambridge, MA: Harvard University Press, 1996.

Garlicki, Andrzej, ed. *Herman Lieberman.* Warsaw: Wydawnictwo Sejmowe, 1996.

———. *Józef Piłsudski, 1867-1935.* Warsaw: Czytelnik, 1989.

———. *Od maja do Brześcia.* Warsaw: Czytelnik, 1981.

———. *Przewrót majowy.* Warsaw: Czytelnik, 1978.

———, ed. *Rok 1918, tradycje i oczekiwania.* Warsaw: Czytelnik, 1978.

———. *U źródeł obozu belwederskiego.* Warsaw: Państwowe Wydawnictwo Naukowe, 1978.

Garlicki, Andrzej, and Aleksandra Garlicka. *Józef Piłsudski: Życie i legenda.* Warsaw: Kancelaria Sejmu, 1993.

Garlicki, Andrzej, and Jerzy Kochanowski, eds. *Józef Piłsudski w karykaturze.* Warsaw: Wydawnictwo Interpress, 1991.

Garlicki, Andrzej, Tomasz Nałęcz, and Wiesław Władyka. "Druga Rzeczpospolita w powojennych badaniach historyków polskich." *Przegląd historyczny* 69, no. 3 (1978): 389-404.

Garlicki, Andrzej, and Piotr Stawecki. "Przewrót wojskowy w Polsce w 1926 r. Wybór dokumentów." *Wojskowy przegląd historyczny* 23, no. 1 (1978): 218-73.

Gawin, Magda. "Dispute over the Sex Education of Children and Young People during the Inter-War Years." *Acta Poloniae Historica* 79 (1999): 185-205.

———. "Liberalizm społeczno-obyczajowy, czyli rzecz o Boyownikach." *Społeczeństwo otwarte,* no. 6 (1997): 22-29.

Gąsiorowski, Zygmunt J. "Joseph Piłsudski in the Light of American Reports, 1919-1922." *Slavonic and East European Review* 49, no. 116 (July 1971): 425-36.

———. "Joseph Piłsudski in the Light of British Reports." *Slavonic and East European Review* 50, no. 121 (October 1972): 558-69.

Gella, Aleksander. "The Life and Death of the Old Polish Intelligentsia." *Slavic Review* 30, no. 1 (March 1971): 1-27.

Geremek, Bronisław, and Antoni Mączak, eds. *Poland at the 14th International Congress of Historical Sciences in San Francisco: Studies in Comparative History.* Wrocław: Polish Academy of Sciences, 1975.

Giełżyński, Wojciech. *Edward Abramowski zwiastun Solidarności.* London: Polonia Books, 1986.

Giertych, Maciej. *Dmowski czy Piłsudski?* Wrocław: Wydawnictwo Norton, 1995.

Glen, Gendzel. "Political Culture: Genealogy of a Concept." *Journal of Interdisciplinary History* 28, no. 2 (Fall 1997): 225–50.

Gołota, Janusz. "Ewolucja ideowo-polityczna Jędrzeja Moraczewskiego, 1920–1939." *Dzieje najnowsze* 27, no. 3 (1995): 13–29.

———. "Jędrzej Moraczewski w latach 1919–1926." *Dzieje najnowsze* 25, no. 2 (1993): 35–51.

Gombrowicz, Witold. *Diary: Volume One, 1953–1956.* Trans. Lillian Vallee. 1957. Reprint, Evanston, IL: Northwestern University Press, 1988.

Gomori, George. "The Cultural Intelligentsia: The Writers." In *Social Groups in Polish Society,* ed. David Lane and George Kolankiewicz. London: Macmillan, 1973.

Gosfeld, Leon. "Czy Anglicy rzeczywiście byli inspiratorami przewrotu majowego?" *Kwartalnik historyczny* 76, no. 3 (1969): 677–81.

Gross, Natan. "Przyjmują do *Wiadomości.*" In *"Wiadomości" i okolice: Szkice i wspomnienia,* ed. Mirosław A. Supruniuk. Toruń: Uniwersytet Mikolaja Kopernika, 1995.

Groth, Alexander J. "Dmowski, Piłsudski and Ethnic Conflict in Pre-1939 Poland." *Canadian Slavic Studies* 3, no. 1 (Spring 1969): 69–91.

———. "The Legacy of Three Crises: Parliament and Ethnic Issues in Prewar Poland." *Slavic Review* 27, no. 3 (September 1968): 564–80.

———. "Polish Elections, 1919–1928." *Slavic Review* 24, no. 4 (December 1965): 653–65.

———. "Proportional Representation in Prewar Poland." *Slavic Review* 1, no. 23 (March 1964): 103–16.

Grott, Bogumił. "Geneza i początek formowania się poglądów 'młodych' obozu narodowego na zagadnienia ustrojowe: Okres działalności Obozu Wielkiej Polski." *Dzieje najnowsze* 16, no. 1 (1984): 115–26.

Gruber, Helmut, and Pamela Graves, eds. *Women and Socialism, Socialism and Women: Europe between the Two World Wars.* New York: Berghahn Books, 1998.

Grydzewski, Mieczysław, and Jarosław Iwaszkiewicz. *Listy: 1922–1967.* Comp. Małgorzata Bojanowska. Warsaw: Czytelnik, 1997.

Grzeloński, Bogdan. "Zamach 1926 r. w raportach attaché wojskowego poselstwa USA w Warszawie." *Kwartalnik historyczny* 91, no. 3 (1984): 515–24.

Grzędziński, January. *Maj 1926.* Paris: Instytut Literacki, 1965.

Gutman, Yisrael, et al., eds. *The Jews of Poland between Two World Wars.* Hanover, NH: University Press of New England, 1989.

Hagen, William W. "Before the 'Final Solution': Toward a Comparative Analysis of Political Anti-Semitism in Interwar Germany and Poland." *Journal of Modern History* 68, no. 2 (1996): 351–81.

Halbersztadt, Jerzy. "Józef Piłsudski a mechanizm podejmowania decyzji wojsko-wych w latach 1926–1935." *Przegląd historyczny* 74, no. 4 (1983): 677–724.

———. "Józef Piłsudski i jego współpracownicy wobec wyborów parlamentarnych w latach 1926–1928: Z badań nad genezą BBWR." *Dzieje najnowsze* 16, no. 1 (1984): 3–34.

Hass, Ludwik. *Masoneria polska XX wieku: Losy, loże, ludzie.* Warsaw: Wydaw-nictwo KOPIA, 1996.

———. "Portret zbiorowy międzywojennego wolnomularza polskiego (Losy pewnej formacji inteligenckiej)." *Kwartalnik historyczny* 101, no. 1 (1994): 91–103.

———. "U socjalnych źródeł przewrotu majowego (Inteligencja-Piłsudczycy)." *Kwartalnik historyczny* 77, no. 2 (1970): 368–91.

———. "Związek Patriotyczny, 1918–1926: Z dziejów infrastruktury życia politycz-nego Drugiej Rzeczypospolitej." *Kwartalnik historyczny* 85, no. 4 (1978): 913–42.

Hen, Józef. *Błazen-wielki mąż: Opowieść o Tadeuszu Boyu-Żeleńskim.* Warsaw: Iskry, 1998.

———. "Kaprys." *Magazyn gazety,* no. 39 (September 25–26, 1998): 48–50.

———. "Tadeusz, Stachu i Dagny." *Magazyn gazety,* no. 25 (June 19–20, 1998): 22–26.

Hertz, Alexander. "The Case of an Eastern European Intelligentsia." *Journal of Central European Affairs* 11, no. 1 (January 1951): 10–26.

Holzer, Jerzy. *Mozaika polityczna Drugiej Rzeczypospolitej.* Warsaw: Książka i Wiedza, 1974.

———. "The Political Right in Poland, 1918–1939." *Journal of Contemporary History* 12, no. 2 (July 1977): 395–412.

———. *Polska Partia Socjalistyczna w latach 1917–1919.* Warsaw: Państwowe Wydaw-nictwo Naukowe, 1962.

Horak, Stephan. *Poland and Her National Minorities, 1919–1939: A Case Study.* New York: Vantage Press, 1961.

Jabłoński, Henryk. "Inteligencja polska w dwudziestoleciu, 1918–1939: Parę Kon-frontacji." *Kwartalnik historyczny* 72, no. 1 (1965): 95–98.

———. "Konserwatyśći przed przewrotem majowym 1926 r." *Przegląd historyczny* 57, no. 4 (1966): 610–33.

———. *Narodziny Drugiej Rzeczypospolitej, 1918–1919.* Warsaw: Wiedza Pow-szechna, 1962.

———. *Polityka Polskiej Partii Socjalistycznej w czasie wojny, 1914–1918.* Warsaw: Państwowe Wydawnictwo Naukowe, 1958.

———. "Przyczynek do dziejów zamachu majowego 1926 r. w Polsce." *Przegląd historyczny* 61, no. 2 (1970): 249–59.

———. *Z rozważań o II Rzeczypospolitej.* Wrocław: Wydawnictwo Polskiej Aka-demii Nauk, 1987.

Jachymek, Jan. *Myśl polityczna PSL Wyzwolenie, 1918–1931.* Lublin: Wydawnictwo Lubelskie, 1983.

Jachymek, Jan, et al., eds. *Chłopi, naród, kultura.* Rzeszów: Wydawnictwo Wyższej Szkoly Pedagogicznej, 1996.

Jakubiak, Krzysztof. *Wychowanie państwowe jako ideologia wychowawcza sanacji: Kształtowanie i upowszechnanie w periodycznych wydawnictwach społeczno-kulturalnych i pedagogicznych.* Bydgoszcz: Wyższa Szkoła Pedagogiczna, 1994.

Jakubowska, Urszula. *Oblicze ideowo-polityczne "Gazety Warszawskiej" i "Warszawskiego Dziennika Narodowego" w latach 1918–1939.* Warsaw: Państwowe Wydawnictwo Naukowe, 1984.

Janion, Maria. *Kobiety i duch inności.* Warsaw: Wydawnictwo Sic! 1996.

———. *Płacz Generała: Eseje o wojnie.* Warsaw: Wydawnictwo Sic! 1998.

Jankowska, Hanna. "Abortion, Church and Politics in Poland." *Feminist Review* 39 (Autumn 1991): 174–81.

———. "The Reproductive Rights Campaign in Poland." *Women's Studies International Forum* 16, no. 3 (1993): 291–96.

Jedlicki, Jerzy. "Historia inteligencji polskiej w kontekście europejskim." *Kultura i społeczeństwo* 44, no. 2 (April–June 2000): 141–62.

———. "Polish Concepts of Native Culture." Trans. Konstanty Gebert. In *National Character and National Ideology in Interwar Eastern Europe,* ed. Ivo Banac and Katherine Verdery. New Haven: Yale Center for International and Area Studies, 1995.

———. *A Suburb of Europe: Nineteenth-Century Polish Approaches to Western Civilization.* 1988. Reprint, trans. Budapest: Central European University Press, 1999.

Jedynak, Barbara, ed. *Kobieta w kulturze i społeczeństwie.* Lublin: Wydawnictwo Uniwersytetu Marii Curie-Skłodowskiej, 1990.

Jezierski, Romuald. *Poglądy etyczne Edwarda Abramowskiego: Studium struktury, genezy i funkcji systemu etycznego.* Poznań: Wydawnictwo Poznańskie, 1970.

Jeżewski, Krzysztof A., ed. *W blasku legendy: Kronika poetycka życia Józefa Piłsudskiego.* Paris: Editions Spotkania, 1988.

Jędruch, Jacek. *Constitutions, Elections, and Legislatures of Poland, 1493–1993: A Guide to Their History.* 1982. Reprint, New York: EJJ Books, 1998.

Jędrzejewicz, Janusz. *W służbie idei: Fragmenty pamiętnika i pism.* London: Oficyna Poetów i Malarzy, 1972.

Jędrzejewicz, Wacław. *Józef Piłsudski, 1867–1935: Życiorys.* London: Polska Fundacja Kulturalna, 1982.

———. *Kronika życia Józefa Piłsudskiego, 1867–1935.* Vol. 2, *1921–1935.* London: Polska Fundacja Kulturalna, 1977.

————. *Piłsudski: A Life for Poland.* New York: Hippocrene Books, 1982.

Jędrzejewicz, Wacław, and Janusz Cisek. *Kalendarium życia Józefa Piłsudskiego.* Vol. 3, *1926–1935.* Wrocław: Ossolineum, 1994.

Jolluck, Katherine R. *Exile and Identity: Polish Women in the Soviet Union during World War II.* Pittsburgh: University of Pittsburgh Press, 2002.

Kaczmarek, Zygmunt. "Obóz Wielkiej Polski w latach 1931–1933." *Kwartalnik historyczny* 91, no. 4 (1984): 863–85.

————. "Obóz Wielkiej Polski w Poznańskim w latach 1926–1932." *Dzieje najnowsze* 6, no. 3 (1974): 21–56

Kaczyński, Andrzej. "Świadectwo Witosa." *Rzeczpospolita,* no. 23 (January 27–28, 1996): 17–18.

Kałwa, Dobrochna. *Kobieta aktywna w Polsce międzywojennej: Dylematy środowisk kobiecych.* Kraków: Uniwersytet Jagielloński, 2001.

————. "Poland." In *Women, Gender, and Fascism in Europe, 1919–1945,* ed. Kevin Passmore. New Brunswick, NJ: Rutgers University Press, 2003.

Kamiński, Leszek. *Romantyzm a ideologia: Główne ugrupowania polityczne Drugiej Rzeczypospolitej wobec tradycji romantycznej.* Wrocław: Zakład Narodowy im. Ossolińskich/Wydawnictwo Polskiej Akademii Nauk, 1980.

Katelbach, Tadeusz. "Janusz Jędrzejewicz—swej idei do końca wierny." *Zeszyty historyczne* 27 (1974): 228–34.

————. *Spowiedź pokolenia.* Lippstadt, Germany: Jutro Pracy, 1948.

Kawalec, Krzysztof. "Myśl polityczna Romana Dmowskiego." *Przegląd zachodni* 60, no. 3 (July–September 1999): 41–58.

————. *Narodowa Demokracja wobec faszyzmu, 1922–1939.* Warsaw: Państwowy Instytut Wydawniczy, 1989.

————. *Roman Dmowski.* Warsaw: Editions Spotkania, 1996.

————, ed. *Roman Dmowski o ustroju politycznym państwa.* Warsaw: Wydawnictwo Sejmowe, 1996.

Kądziela, Jerzy, Jerzy Kwiatkowski, and Irena Wyczańska. *Literatura polska w okresie międzywojennym.* 4 vols. Kraków: Wydawnictwo Literackie, 1979.

Kądziela, Paweł, and Artur Międzyrzecki, eds. *Wspomnienia o Antonim Słonimskim.* Warsaw: Biblioteka Więzi, 1996.

Kemnitz, Thomas Milton. "The Cartoon as a Historical Source." *Journal of Interdisciplinary History* 4, no. 1 (Summer 1973): 81–94.

Kieżuń, Anna. *Spór z tradycją romantyczną: O działalności pisarskiej Adolfa Nowaczyńskiego.* Białystok: Uniwersytet Warszawski w Białymstoku, 1993.

Kłoczowski, Jerzy, and Lidia Müllerowa, "W dwudziestym stuleciu." In *Zarys dziejów kościoła katolickiego w Polsce,* ed. Jerzy Kłoczowski, Lidia Müllerowa, and Jan Skarbek. Kraków: Wydawnictwo Znak, 1986.

Kociowa, Regina. *Irena Kosmowska.* Warsaw: Ludowa Spółdzielnia Wydawnicza, 1960.

Kofman, Jan. *Economic Nationalism and Development: Central and Eastern Europe between the Two World Wars.* Trans. Maria Chmielewska-Szlajfer. Boulder, CO: Westview Press, 1997.

Konefał, Jan. "Lubelski oddział Związku Legionistów Polskich (1922–1926)." *Roczniki humanistyczne* 46 (1998): 187–205.

Konopczyński, Władysław, et al. *Polski słownik biograficzny.* Kraków: Polska Akademia Umiętności, 1932–present.

Kosicka, Jadwiga, and Daniel Gerould, eds. *A Life of Solitude: Stanisława Przybyszewska: A Biographical Study with Selected Letters.* London: Quartet Books, 1986.

Kott, Jan. "Tadeusz Boy-Żeleński." *Nowa kultura* 51/52 (91/92) (1951): 5–6.

Kowalczykowa, Alina. *Programy i spory literackie w dwudziestoleciu, 1918–1939.* Warsaw: Ludowa Spółdzielnia Wydawnicza, 1978.

Koźniewski, Kazimierz. *Historia co tydzień: Szkice o tygodnikach społeczno-kulturalnych.* Warsaw: Czytelnik, 1976.

———. *Przekorni.* Warsaw: Iskry, 2000.

Koźniewski, Kazimierz, and Ewa Sabelanka, eds. *7599 dni Drugiej Rzeczypospolitej.* Warsaw: Iskry, 1983.

Krajewska, Hanna, and Isabel Röskau-Rydel. "Poland." *Austrian History Yearbook* 29, pt. 2: *A Guide to East-Central European Archives* (1998): 83–104.

Krawczyk, Zbigniew. "Długie życie gorszycielki." *Gazeta magazyn,* no. 28 (July 10–11, 1998): 24–29.

———. *Socjologia Edwarda Abramowskiego.* Warsaw: Państwowy Instytut Wydawniczy, 1965.

Krzywicka, Irena. *Wyznania gorszycielki.* Ed. Agata Tuszyńska. Warsaw: Czytelnik, 1995.

Kulesza, Władysław. *Koncepcje ideowo-polityczne obozu rządącego w Polsce w latach 1926–1935.* Wrocław: Zakład Narodowy im. Ossolińskich, 1985.

———. "Konserwatyści w obozie sanacyjnym w latach 1926–1935: Spór o konserwatywną interpretację ideologii obozu rządzącego." *Przegląd historyczyny* 73, nos. 3–4 (1982) 227–50.

Kułakowski, Mariusz. *Roman Dmowski w świetle listów i wspomnień.* 2 vols. London: Gryf Publications, 1972.

Landau, Zbigniew. "Impact of the May 1926 Coup on the State of Polish Economy." *Acta Poloniae Historica* 35 (1977): 169–87.

———. "Przewrót majowy w raportach poselstwa RP w Londynie." *Kwartalnik historyczny* 66 (1959): 155–58.

———. "The Reconstruction of Polish Industry after World War I." *Acta Poloniae Historica* 18 (1968): 238–49.

Landau, Zbigniew, and Jerzy Tomaszewski. "O polityce zagranicznej Polski w latach 1924–1925." *Kwartalnik historyczny* 68, no. 3 (1961): 725–38.

———. *The Polish Economy in the Twentieth Century.* London: Croom Helm, 1985.

Landau-Czajka, Anna. "Królestwo bez żydów: Sprawa żydowska w myśli polskich monarchistów okresu międzywojennego." *Kultura i społeczeństwo* 43, no. 1 (January–March 1999): 43–54.

———. "Wszechobecni wrogowie: Niektóre elementy światopoglądu prawicy nacjonalistycznej, 1926–1939." *Przegląd historyczny* 79, no. 1 (1988): 63–92.

Laroche, Jules. *La Pologne de Piłsudski: Souvenirs d'une ambassade, 1926–1935.* Paris: Flammarion, 1953.

Lato, Stanisław. "Walka ruchu ludowego o demokratyczny charakter państwa polskiego, 1918–1939." In *Ruch ludowy a sprawa niepodległości,* ed. Alicja Więzikowa. Warsaw: Ludowa Spółdzielnia Wydawnicza, 1969.

Lato, Stanisław, and Witold Stankiewicz. *Programy Stronnictw Ludowych: Zbiór dokumentów.* Warsaw: Państwowe Wydawnictwo Naukowe, 1969.

Lechoń, Jan. *Dziennik.* London: Wydawnictwo Wiadomości, 1967.

Leinwand, Artur. *Poseł Herman Lieberman.* Kraków: Wydawnictwo Literackie, 1983.

Lenoe, Matthew E. "Letter-Writing and the State: Reader Correspondence with Newspapers as a Source for Early Soviet History." *Cahiers du monde russe* 40, nos. 1–2 (January–June 1999): 139–70.

Leszczyński, Rafał, ed. *Paweł Hulka-Laskowski (1881–1946): Szkice do portretu.* Żyrardów: Towarzystwo Przyjaciół Żyrardowa, 1995.

Leszkiewicz, Janina. "Jeszcze o polskiej inteligencji XIX w." *Kwartalnik historyczny* 72, no. 1 (1965): 89–93.

Ludwikowski, Rett R. *Continuity and Change in Poland: Conservatism in Polish Political Thought.* Washington, DC: Catholic University of America Press, 1991.

Ładniewska-Blankenheimowa, Wanda. "Z dwu ostatnich lat Boya (Lwów 1939–1941)." *Zeszyty historyczne* 4 (1963): 123–44.

Łempicka, Aniela. *Wyspiański, pisarz dramatyczny: Idee i formy.* Kraków: Wydawnictwo Literackie, 1973.

Łoch, Eugenia, and Krzysztof Stępnik, eds. *Pierwsza wojna światowa w literaturze polskiej i obcej: Wybrane zagadnienia.* Lublin: Wydawnictwo Uniwersytetu Marii Curie-Skłodowskiej, 1999.

Łossowski, Piotr. *Kraje bałtyckie na drodze od demokracji parlamentarnej do dyktatury, 1918–1934.* Wrocław: Zakład Narodowy im. Ossolińskich, 1972.

Łozińska, Maja, and Jan Łoziński. *Życie codzienne i niecodzienne w przedwojennej Polsce.* Warsaw: Wydawnictwa Prószyński i S-ka SA, 1999.

Maciejewska, Irena, ed. *Poeci dwudziestolecia międzywojennego.* 2 vols. Warsaw: Wiedza Powszechna, 1982.

Majchrowski, Jacek M. *Ugrupowania monarchistyczne w latach Drugiej Rzeczypospolitej.* Wrocław: Ossolineum, 1988.

Makowiecki, Andrzej. *Tadeusz Żeleński (Boy).* Warsaw: Wiedza Powszechna, 1974.

Malinowska, Iwona. "Polskie centrum parlamentarne, 1919–1926." *Przegląd historyczny* 81, nos. 3–4 (1990): 581–610.

Markiewicz-Lagneau, Janina. *La formation d'une pensée sociologique: La societé polonaise de l'entre-deux-guerres.* Paris: Editions de la Maison des Sciences de l'Homme, 1982.

Melman, Billie. *Women and the Popular Imagination in the Twenties: Flappers and Nymphs.* London: Macmillan, 1988.

Micewski, Andrzej. "Polish Youth in the Thirties." *Journal of Contemporary History* 4, no. 3 (July 1969): 155–67.

———. *Roman Dmowski.* Warsaw: Wydawnictwo Verum, 1971.

———. *W cieniu Marszałka Piłsudskiego: Szkice z dziejów myśli politycznej II Rzeczypospolitej.* Warsaw: Czytelnik, 1969.

———. *Z geografii politycznej II Rzeczypospolitej.* Kraków: Znak, 1964.

Micgiel, John S., ed. *Wilsonian East Central Europe: Current Perspectives.* New York: Piłsudski Institute, 1995.

Michnik, Adam. "'Kto to ma czelność zwać mnie odszczepieńcem?'" In *Wspomnienia o Antonim Słonimskim,* ed. Paweł Kądziela and Artur Międzyrzecki. Warsaw: Biblioteka Więzi, 1996.

Miłosz, Czesław. *The History of Polish Literature.* 2d ed. Berkeley: University of California Press, 1983.

Modras, Ronald. *The Catholic Church and Antisemitism: Poland, 1933–1939.* Jerusalem: Hebrew University of Jerusalem/Harwood Academic Publishers, 1994.

Morawski, Kajetan. *Wczoraj: Pogadanki o niepodległym dwudziestoleciu.* London: Nakładem Polskiej Fundacji Kulturalnej, 1967.

Morawski, Wojciech. "Town-Country Economic Relations versus Stability of the System of Parliamentary Democracy in Poland of the 1920s." *East European Quarterly* 24, no. 1 (1990): 47–56.

Mosse, George L. *Nationalism and Sexuality: Middle-Class Morality and Sexual Norms in Modern Europe.* Madison: University of Wisconsin Press, 1985.

Mysłek, Wiesław. *Kościół katolicki w Polsce w latach 1918–1939: Zarys historyczny.* Warsaw: Książka i Wiedza, 1966.

Nałęcz, Daria, ed. *Adam Skwarczyński—od demokracji do autorytaryzmu.* Warsaw: Wydawnictwo Sejmowe, 1998.

———. "*Droga* jako platforma kształtowania się ideologii Piłsudczyków." *Przegląd historyczny* 66, no. 4 (1975): 589–606.

———. *Kultura Drugiej Rzeczypospolitej.* Warsaw: Krajowa Agencja Wydawnicza, 1991.

———, ed. *Nie szablą, lecz piórem: Batalie publicystyczne II Rzeczypospolitej.* Warsaw: Instytut Badań Literackich, 1993.

———. *Sen o władzy: Inteligencja wobec niepodległości.* Warsaw: Państwowy Instytut Wydawniczy, 1994.

———. *Zawód dziennikarza w Polsce, 1918–1939.* Warsaw: Państwowe Wydawnictwo Naukowe, 1982.

Nałęcz, Daria, and Tomasz Nałęcz. *Józef Piłsudski: Legendy i fakty.* Warsaw: Młodzieżowa Agencja Wydawnicza, 1986.

Nałęcz, Tomasz. *Irredenta polska.* Warsaw: Książka i Wiedza, 1992.

Nasiłowska, Anna. *Trzydziestolecie, 1914–1944.* Warsaw: Wydawnictwo Naukowe PKW, 1997.

Natanson, Wojciech. *Boy-Żeleński: Opowieść biograficzna.* Warsaw: Ludowa Spółdzielnia Wydawnicza, 1977.

Nodzyński, Tomasz. "*Strażnica Zachodnia,*" *1922–1939: Źródło do dziejów myśli zachodniej w Polsce.* Zielona Góra: Wyższej Szkoly Pedagogicznej im. Tadeusza Kotarbińskiego, 1997.

Notkowski, Andrzej. *Polska prasa prowincjonalna Drugiej Rzeczypospolitej, 1918–1939.* Warsaw: Państwowe Wydawnictwo Naukowe, 1982.

———. *Prasa w systemie propagandy rządowej w Polsce, 1926–1939.* Warsaw: Państwowe Wydawnictwo Naukowe, 1987.

———. "W kręgu Piłsudczyków. Poglądy ideowo-polityczne *Gazety polskiej,* 1929–1939." *Rocznik historii prasy polskiej* 2, no. 2 (1999): 221–32.

Nowak, Andrzej. "Wojna Polsko-Sowiecka 1919–1921 w świetle najnowszych publikacji." *Kwartalnik historyczny* 100, no. 3 (1993): 79–107.

Oldakowska-Kuflowa, Mirosława. *Chrzescijańskie widzenie świata w poezji Kazimiery Iłłakowiczówny.* Lublin: Wydawnictwo Katolickiego Uniwersytetu Lubelskiego, 1993.

Opalski, Magdalena M. "*Wiadomości literackie:* Polemics on the Jewish Question, 1924–1939." In *The Jews of Poland between Two World Wars,* ed. Yisrael Gutman et al. Hanover, NH: University Press of New England, 1989.

Opalski, Magdalena, and Israel Bartal. *Poles and Jews: A Failed Brotherhood.* Hanover, NH: University Press of New England, 1992.

Paczkowski, Andrzej. *Prasa codzienna Warszawy w latach 1918–1939.* Warsaw: Państwowy Instytut Wydawniczy, 1983.

———. *Prasa polska w latach 1918–1939.* Warsaw: Państwowe Wydawnictwo Naukowe, 1980.

———. "Prasa w życiu politycznym Drugiej Rzeczypospolitej." *Dzieje najnowsze* 10, no. 3 (1978): 29–55.

Pajewski, Janusz. *Odbudowa państwa polskiego, 1914–1918.* Warsaw: Państwowe Wydawnictwo Naukowe, 1980.

Pakszys, Elżbieta. "The State of Research on Polish Women in the Last Two Decades." *Journal of Women's History* 3, no. 3 (Winter 1992): 118–25.

Pease, Neal. "Poland and the Holy See, 1918–1939." *Slavic Review* 50, no. 3 (Fall 1991): 521–30.

Pietrzak, Michał. "'Jak doszło do wojny domowej' i 'przewrót majowy'" (Dwa nieopublikowane memoriały). *Kwartalnik historyczny* 66 (1959): 127–54.

———. *Reglamentacja wolności prasy w Polsce, 1918–1939.* Warsaw: Książka i Wiedza, 1963.

———. *Rządy parlamentarne w Polsce w latach 1919–1926.* Warsaw: Książka i Wiedza, 1969.

———. "Sytuacja prawna kobiet w Drugiej Rzeczypospolitej." In *Kobieta i świat polityki w niepodległej Polsce 1918–1939,* ed. Anna Żarnowska and Andrzej Szwarc (Warsaw: Wydawnictwo Sejmowe, 1996).

Piłsudska, Aleksandra. *Memoirs of Madame Piłsudski.* London: Hurst and Blackett, 1940.

———. *Piłsudski.* New York: Arno Press, 1971.

———. *Wspomnienia.* London: Gryf Publications, 1960.

Piotrowicz, Teofil. "Myśl polityczna Związku Naprawy Rzeczypospolitej wobec kwestii ukraińskiej, 1926–1930." *Przegląd historyczny* 70, no. 2 (1979): 285–300.

Pobóg-Malinowski, Władysław. *Najnowsza historia polityczna Polski.* Vol. 2, *1914–1939.* 2d ed. London: B. Świderski, 1967.

Polonsky, Antony. *The Little Dictators: The History of Eastern Europe since 1918.* London: Routledge and Kegan Paul, 1975.

———. *Politics in Independent Poland, 1921–1939: The Crisis of Constitutional Government.* Oxford: Clarendon Press, 1972.

———. "Roman Dmowski and Italian Fascism." In *Ideas into Politics: Aspects of European History, 1880 to 1950,* ed. R. J. Bullen, H. Pogge von Strandmann, and A. B. Polonsky. London: Croom Helm, 1984.

Ponichtera, Robert M. "Feminists, Nationalists, and Soldiers: Women in the Fight for Polish Independence." *International History Review* 19, no. 1 (February 1997): 16–31.

Porter, Brian. "*Hetmanka* and Mother: Representing the Virgin Mary in Modern Poland." *Contemporary European History* 14, no. 2 (2005): 151–70.

Poznańska, Barbara. "Klasy posiadające—burżuazja i ziemiaństwo—wobec przewrotu majowego 1926 r. i jego konsekwencji politycznych i społecznych." *Dzieje najnowsze* 10, no. 2 (1978): 65–75.

Pragier, Adam. *Czas przeszły dokonany.* London: R. Świderski, 1966.

Próchnik, Adam. *Kobieta w polskim ruchu socjalistycznym.* Warsaw: Spółdzielnia Wydawnicza Wiedza, 1949.

Pruska-Carroll, Małgorzata. "The Poetry of Maria Pawlikowska-Jasnorzewska: Femininity and Feminism." *Polish Review* 26, no. 1 (1981): 35–50.

Rakowski, Janusz. "Józef Piłsudski w krzywym zwierciadle historiografii Andrzeja Garlickiego." *Niepodległość* 17 (1984): 224–38.

———. "Ostatnie lata Józefa Piłsudskiego (Artykuł recenzyjny)." *Niepodległość* 21 (1988): 219–34.

———. "Zetowcy i Piłsudczycy." *Zeszyty historyczne* 54 (1980): 3–39.

Reddaway, W. F. *Marshal Piłsudski.* London: Routledge, 1939.

Renz, Regina. *Życie codzienne w miasteczkach województwa kieleckiego, 1918–1939.* Kielce: Kieleckie Towarzystwo Naukowe, 1994.

Roberts, Mary Louis. *Civilization without Sexes: Reconstructing Gender in Postwar France, 1917–1927.* Chicago: University of Chicago Press, 1994.

Rogger, Hans, and Eugen Weber, eds. *The European Right: A Historical Profile.* 1965. Reprint, Berkeley: University of California Press, 1974.

Romeyko, Marian. *Przed i po maju.* Warsaw: Wydawnictwo Ministerstwa Obrony Narodowej, 1967.

Rose, Sonya O. "Cultural Analysis and Moral Discourses: Episodes, Continuities, and Transformations." In *Beyond the Cultural Turn: New Directions in the Study of Society and Culture,* ed. and intro. by Victoria E. Bonnell and Lynn Hunt. Berkeley: University of California Press, 1999.

———. "Sex, Citizenship, and the Nation in World War II Britain." *American Historical Review* 103, no. 4 (October 1998), 1147–76.

Rose, William John. *Poland's Political Parties, 1919–1939.* Liverpool: Tinling, 1947.

Roszkowski, Wojciech. "The Growth of the State Sector in the Polish Economy in the Years 1918–1926." *Journal of European Economic History* 18, no. 1 (Spring 1989): 105–26.

———. "The Reconstruction of the Government and State Apparatus in the Second Polish Republic." In *The Reconstruction of Poland, 1914–1923,* ed. Paul Latawski. London: Macmillan, 1992.

———. "Syndykalizm polski, 1918–1929." *Niepodległość* 46 (1993): 199–230.

Rothschild, Joseph. "A Chapter in Polish Politics of the 1920s." In *Studies in Polish Civilization,* ed. Damian S. Wandycz. New York: Columbia University/Polish Institute of Arts and Sciences in America, 1966.

———. *East Central Europe between the Two World Wars.* Seattle: University of Washington Press, 1974.

———. "The Military Background of Piłsudski's Coup d'État." *Slavic Review* 21, no. 2 (June 1962): 241–60.

————. *Piłsudski's Coup d'État.* New York: Columbia University Press, 1966.

Rudnicki, Szymon. *Działalność polityczna polskich konserwatystów, 1918–1926.* Wrocław: Ossolineum, 1981.

Rudnicki, Szymon, and Piotr Wróbel, eds. *Druga Rzeczpospolita: Wybór tekstów źródłowych.* Warsaw: Wydawnictwa Uniwersytetu Warszawskiego, 1990.

Rudziński, Eugeniusz. "Kształtowanie systemu prasy kontrolowanej w Polsce w latach 1926–1939." *Dzieje najnowsze* 1, no. 1 (1969): 89–111.

Rudzki, Jerzy. *Świętochowski.* Warsaw: Wiedza Powszechna, 1963.

Rybczyński, Mieczysław. "Wypadki majowe 1926 roku." *Zeszyty historyczne* 86 (1988): 63–96.

Ryszka, Franciszek. "Poland: Some Recent Revaluations." *Journal of Contemporary History* 2, no. 1 (January 1967): 107–24.

Sadkowski, Konrad. "From Ethnic Borderland to Catholic Fatherland: The Church, Christian Orthodox, and State Administration in the Chełm Region, 1918–1939." *Slavic Review* 57, no. 4 (Winter 1998): 813–39.

Samozwaniec, Magdalena. *Maria i Magdalena.* Kraków: Wydawnictwo Literackie, 1956.

Sandler, Samuel. *Ze studiów nad Świętochowskim.* Warsaw: Państwowy Instytut Wydawniczy, 1967.

Schaetzel, Tadeusz. *Pułkownik Walery Sławek.* Jerusalem: Hamadpis Liphshitz Press, 1947.

Schwonek, Matthew R. "Kazimierz Sosnkowski and the Foundations of Polish Military Policy, 1918–1926." *Polish Review* 42, no. 1 (1997): 45–76.

Singer, Bernard. *Od Witosa do Sławka.* Paris: Instytut Literacki, 1962.

Słonimski, Antoni. *Alfabet wspomnień.* 1975. Reprint, Warsaw: Państwowy Instytut Wydawniczy, 1989.

————. *Jedna strona medalu: Niektóre felietony, artykuły, recenzje, utwory poważne i niepoważne publikowane w latach 1918–1968.* Warsaw: Czytelnik, 1971.

Smoliński, Tadeusz. *Rządy Józefa Piłsudskiego w latach 1926–1935: Studium prawne.* Seria Prawo, no. 115. Poznań: Uniwersytet im. Adama Mickiewicza, 1985.

Sobczak, Miezcysław. *Stosunek Narodowej Demokracji do kwestii żydowskiej w Polsce w latach 1918–1939.* Wrocław: Wydawnictwo Akademii Ekonomicznej im. Oskara Langego, 1998.

Sokół, Zofia. *Prasa kobieca w Polsce w latach 1945–1995.* Rzeszów: Szkoła Wyższa, 1998.

Soloway, Richard A. "The 'Perfect Contraceptive': Eugenics and Birth Control in Britain and America in the Interwar Years." *Journal of Contemporary History* 30, no. 4 (October 1995): 637–64.

Stallybrass, Peter, and Allon White. *The Politics and Poetics of Transgression.* Ithaca, NY: Cornell University Press, 1986.

Starowieyska-Morstinowa, Zofia. "Zagadnienie Boya." *Tygodnik powszechny* 22 (January 13, 1952): 7–9.

Stasiński, Piotr. *Poetyka i pragmatyka felietonu: Z dziejów form artystycznych w literaturze polskiej.* Wrocław: Ossolineum, 1982.

Stawar, Andrzej. *Tadeusz Żeleński (Boy).* Warsaw: Państwowy Instytut Wydawniczy, 1958.

Stegner, Tadeusz. "Przyczynek do ewolucji ideowo-politycznej Aleksandra Świętochowskiego." *Dzieje najnowsze* 17, no. 3–4 (1985): 27–40.

Sterkowicz, Stanisław. *Tadeusz Boy-Żeleński: Lekarz, pisarz, społecznik.* 1959. Reprint, Warsaw: Państwowy Zakład Wydawnictw Lekarskich, 1974.

Stradecki, Janusz. *W kręgu Skamandra.* Warsaw: Państwowy Instytut Wydawniczy, 1977

Suchoński, Adam, ed. *Józef Piłsudski i jego współpracownicy.* Opole: Wydawnictwo Uniwersytetu Opolskiego, 1999.

Sugar, Peter F., ed. *Native Fascism in the Successor States, 1918–1945.* Santa Barbara, CA: Clio, 1971.

Sugar, Peter F., and Ivo J. Lederer, eds. *Nationalism in Eastern Europe.* Seattle: University of Washington Press, 1969.

Suleja, Włodzimierz. "Propagandowe treści powieści politycznych Juliusza Kadena-Bandrowskiego." *Dzieje najnowsze* 13, no. 3 (1981): 93–113.

Supruniuk, Mirosław A., ed. *"Wiadomości" i okolice: Szkice i wspomnienia.* Toruń: Uniwersytet Mikolaja Kopernika, 1995.

Śliwa, Michał. "Kobiety w parlamencie Drugiej Rzeczypospolitej." In *Kobieta i świat polityki w niepodległej Polsce, 1918–1939,* ed. Anna Żarnowska and Andrzej Szwarc. Warsaw: Wydawnictwo Sejmowe, 1996.

———. *Polska myśl polityczna w I połowie XX wieku.* Wrocław: Ossolineum, 1993.

Tighe, Carl. "Living in Unreality: Politics and Language in the People's Republic of Poland." *Journal of European Studies* 22, no. 86 (1992): 143–74.

Toczek, Alfred. *Krakowski* Naprzód *i jego polityczne oblicze, 1919–1934.* Kraków: Wydawnictwo Naukowe WSP, 1997.

Tomaszewski, Jerzy. "Ogólny wskaźnik produkcji przemysłowej polski, 1928–1938." *Kwartalnik historyczny* 72, no. 2 (1965): 279–99.

———. "Zamach majowy 1926 r. w raportach poselstwa bułgarskiego." *Kwartalnik historyczny* 83, no. 3 (1976): 616–31.

Tomicki, Jan. *II Rzeczpospolita: Oczekiwania i rzeczywistość.* Warsaw: Młodzieżowa Agencja Wydawnicza, 1986.

———, ed. *Norbert Barlicki: Wybór przemówień i artykułów z lat 1918–1939.* Warsaw: Książka i Wiedza, 1964.

———, ed. *Polska odrodzona, 1918–1939: Państwo, społeczeństwo, kultura.* Warsaw: Wiedza Powszechna, 1982.

Tymieniecka, Aleksandra. *Polityka Polskiej Partii Socjalistycznej w latach 1924-1928.* Warsaw: Książka i Wiedza, 1969.

Urbanowski, Maciej, ed. *Na przełaj oraz inne szkice o literaturze i kulturze.* Kraków: Wydawnictwo Literackie, 1999.

Urbańczyk, Tadeusz. "Polska myśl wojskowa i doktryna wojenna na łamach *Bellony.*" *Zeszyty naukowe Uniwersytetu Jagiellońskiego, Prace historyczne* 1142, no. 112 (1994): 33-44.

Walczewska, Sławomira. *Damy, rycerze i feministiki: Kobiecy dyskurs emancypacyjny w Polsce.* Kraków: eFKa, 1999.

Walicki, Andrzej. "Intellectual Elites and the Vicissitudes of 'Imagined Nation' in Poland." *East European Politics and Societies* 11, no. 2 (Fall 1997): 227-53.

———. "Nietzsche in Poland (before 1918)." In *East Europe Reads Nietzsche,* ed. Alice Freifeld, Peter Bergmann, and Bernice Glatzer Rosenthal. Boulder, CO: East European Monographs/Columbia University Press, 1998.

———. *Philosophy and Romantic Nationalism: The Case of Poland.* Oxford: Clarendon Press, 1982.

———. "Poland's Place in Europe in the Concepts of Piłsudski and Dmowski." *East European Politics and Societies* 4, no. 3 (Fall 1990): 451-68.

———. *Stanisław Brzozowski and the Polish Beginnings of "Western Marxism."* Oxford: Clarendon Press, 1989.

———. "The Troubling Legacy of Roman Dmowski." *East European Politics and Societies* 14, no. 1 (Winter 2000): 12-46.

Wandycz, Piotr S. *France and Her Eastern Allies, 1919-1925.* Minneapolis: University of Minnesota Press, 1962.

———. "French Diplomats in Poland, 1919-1926." *Journal of Central European Affairs* 23, no. 4 (1964): 440-50.

———. "Historiographies of the Countries of Eastern Europe: Poland." *American Historical Review* 97, no. 4 (October 1992): 1011-25.

———. "Poland's Place in Europe in the Concepts of Piłsudski and Dmowski." *East European Politics and Societies* 4, no. 3 (Fall 1990): 451-68.

Wapiński, Roman. "Miejsce Narodowej Demokracji w życiu politycznym II Rzeczypospolitej." *Dzieje najnowsze* 1 (1969): 47-62.

———. *Narodowa Demokracja, 1893-1939.* Wrocław: Ossolineum, 1980.

———. "Niektóre problemy ewolucji ideowo-politycznej Endecji w latach 1919-1939." *Kwartalnik Historyczny* 73, no. 4 (1966): 861-77.

———. "Pokolenia Drugiej Rzeczypospolitej." *Kwartalnik historyczny* 90, no. 3 (1983): 483-504.

———. *Pokolenia Drugiej Rzeczypospolitej.* Wrocław: Ossolineum, 1991.

———. *Roman Dmowski.* Lublin: Wydawnictwo Lubelskie, 1988.

————. *Świadomość polityczna w Drugiej Rzeczypospolitej.* Łódź: Wydawnictwo Łódzkie, 1989.

Wapiński, Roman, Andrzej Ajnenkiel, and Jerzy Holzer. "Między Hitlerem a Stalinem." *Magazyn gazety* (November 6–7, 1998): 18–25.

Watt, Richard. *Bitter Glory: Poland and Its Fate, 1918–1939.* 1979. Reprint, New York: Hippocrene Books, 1998.

Wawrzykowska-Wierciochowa, Dionizja. "Jadwiga Jahołkowska—postępowa działaczka Ludowego Ruchu Kobiet." *Kultura i społeczeństwo* 20, no. 1 (1976): 61–78.

————. *Nie po kwiatach los je prowadził: Kobiety polskie w ruchu rewolucyjnym.* Warsaw: Iskry, 1987.

————. *Z dziejów kobiety wiejskiej: Szkice historyczne, 1861–1945.* Warsaw: Ludowa Spółdzielnia Wydawnicza, 1961.

Werschler, Iwo. "Stanowisko Tadeusza Hołówki wobec kwestii mniejszości słowiańskich w Drugiej Rzeczypospolitej (1918–1927)." *Dzieje najnowsze* 12, no. 4 (1980): 41–60.

————. *Z dziejów obozu belwederskiego: Tadeusz Hołówko, życie i działalność.* Warsaw: Państwowe Wydawnictwo Naukowe, 1984.

Wierzbiański, Bolesław. "Stroński-Dziennikarz." In *Stanisław Stroński: W 50-lecie pracy pisarskiej,* ed. Antoni Bogusławski et al. Tunbridge Wells, Kent: Oficyna Poetów i Malarzy na Emigracji w Anglii, 1954.

Wierzbicki, Andrzej. *Naród-państwo w polskiej myśli historycznej dwudziestolecia międzywojennego.* Wrocław: Polska Akademia Nauk, 1978.

————, ed. *O przewrocie majowym 1926: Opinie świadków i uczestników.* Intro by Eugeniusz Kozłowski. Warsaw: Ministerstwo Obrony Narodowej, 1984.

Winklowa, Barbara. *Nad Wisłą i nad Sekwaną: Biografia Tadeusza Boya-Żeleńskiego.* Warsaw: Iskry, 1998.

————. *Tadeusz Żeleński (Boy): Twórczość i życie.* Warsaw: Państwowy Instytut Wydawniczy, 1967.

Wisłocki, Jerzy. *Konkordat polski z 1925 roku: Zagadnienia prawno-polityczne.* Poznań: Wydawnictwo Uniwersytetu im. Adama Mickiewicza, 1977.

Władyka, Władysław. *Działalność polityczna polskich stronnictw konserwatywnych w latach 1926–1935.* Wrocław: Zakład Narodowy im. Ossolińskich, 1977.

————. "Konserwatyści w Bezpartyjnym Bloku Współpracy z Rządem." *Przegląd historyczny* 68, no. 1 (1977): 87–105.

Wolikowska, Izabela. *Roman Dmowski: Człowiek, polak, przyjaciel.* Chicago: Nakładem Komitetu Wydawniczego, 1961.

Woollacott, Angela. "'Khaki Fever' and Its Control: Gender, Class, Age and Sexual Morality on the British Homefront in the First World War." *Journal of Contemporary History* 29, no. 2 (April 1994): 325–48.

Wójcik, Włodzimierz. *Legenda Piłsudskiego w polskiej literaturze międzywojennej.* 2d ed. Katowice: Wydawnictwo Śląsk, 1986.

———. *Pisarz i komendant: Literacka legenda Józefa Piłsudskiego.* Katowice: Towarzystwo Zachęty Kultury, 1996.

Wróbel, Piotr. "Kombatanci kontra politycy: Narodziny i początki działania Związku Legionistów Polskich, 1918-1925." *Przegląd historyczyny* 76, no. 1 (1985): 77-111.

Wyka, Kazimierz. *Modernizm polski.* 2d ed. Kraków: Wydawnictwo Literackie, 1968.

Wynot, Edward D., Jr. *Polish Politics in Transition: The Camp of National Unity and the Struggle for Power, 1935-1939.* Athens: University of Georgia Press, 1974.

———. *Warsaw between the World Wars: Profile of the Capital City in a Developing Land, 1918-1939.* Boulder, CO: East European Monographs; New York: Columbia University Press, 1983.

Zakrzewski, Andrzej. *Wincenty Witos.* Warsaw: Iskry, 1985.

———. "Wincenty Witos—chłopski mąż stanu w latach 1918-1926." *Kwartalnik historyczny* 75, no. 3 (1968): 565-94.

Zaleski, Marek, et al. "Jesteśmy w Polsce, a nie gdzie indziej." *Res publica nowa* 2, no. 77 (February 1995): 3-8.

Zamojska-Hutchins, Danuta. "Kazimiera Iłłakowiczówna: The Poet as a Witness of History, and of Double National Allegiance." In *Literature and Politics in Eastern Europe: Selected Papers from the Fourth World Congress for Soviet and East European Studies, Harrogate, 1990,* ed. Celia Hawkesworth. London: St. Martin's, 1992.

Zaporowski, Zbigniew. *Józef Piłsudski w kręgu wojska i polityki.* Lublin: Wydawnictwo Uniwersytetu Marii Curie-Skłodowskiej, 1998.

Zieliński, Zygmunt. "O konkordacie polskim z 1925 roku." *Kwartalnik historyczny* 87, no. 2 (1980): 471-81.

Zientara, Benedykt, Antoni Mączak, Ireneusz Ihnatowicz, and Zbigniew Landau. *Dzieje gospodarcze polski do roku 1939.* Warsaw: Wiedza Powszechna, 1988.

Żarnowska, Anna. "Family and Public Life: Barriers and Interpenetration: Women in Poland at the Turn of the Century." *Women's History Review* 5, no. 4 (1996): 469-86.

———. "Women's Political Participation in Inter-War Poland: Opportunities and Limitations." *Women's History Review* 13, no. 1 (2004): 57-68.

Żarnowska, Anna, and Andrzej Szwarc, eds. *Kobieta i edukacja na ziemiach polskich w XIX i XX w.* 2 vols. Warsaw: Instytut Historyczny Uniwersytetu Warszawskiego, 1992.

———, eds. *Kobieta i kultura.* Warsaw: Wydawnictwo DiG, 1996.

———, eds. *Kobieta i kultura życia codziennego: Wiek XIX i XX.* Warsaw: Wydawnictwo DiG, 1997.

———, eds. *Kobieta i świat polityki w niepodległej Polsce, 1918–1939.* Warsaw: Wydawnictwo Sejmowe, 1996.

———, eds. *Równe prawa i nierówne szanse: Kobiety w Polsce międzywojennej.* Warsaw: Wydawnictwo DiG, 2000.

Żarnowski, Janusz, ed. *Dictatorships in East-Central Europe, 1918–1939: Anthologies.* Warsaw: Polish Academy of Sciences, 1983.

———. "East-Central European Societies, 1918–1939: The Polish Example." Trans. Charles E. Railsback. In *Poland at the 14th International Congress of Historical Sciences in San Francisco. Studies in Comparative History,* ed. Bronisław Geremek and Antoni Mączak. Wrocław: Polish Academy of Sciences, 1975.

———, ed. *Metamorfozy społeczne: Badania nad dziejami społeczeństwa polskiego XIX i XX Wieku.* Warsaw: Instytut Historii PAN, 1997.

———. "Odbudowa niepodległości w 1918 r. w historiografii polskiej." *Kwartalnik historyczny* 85, no. 4 (1978): 818–30.

———. "Państwo Polskie, a rozwój społeczeństwa polskiego, 1918–1939." In *Odrodzenie państwowości i przemiany struktur społecznych w Polsce i Czechosłowacji, 1918–1945: Materiały XXVI posiedzenia komisji historyków Polskich, Czeskich i Słowackich, Warszawa 20–23 listopada 1988 r.* ed. Maria Bogucka. Warsaw: Polska Akademia Nauk, Instytut Historii, 1991.

———. *Społeczeństwo Drugiej Rzeczypospolitej, 1918–1939.* Warsaw: Państwowe Wydawnictwo Naukowe, 1973.

———. "Społeczeństwo i kultura II Rzeczypospolitej." In *Z dziejów Drugiej Rzeczypospolitej,* ed. Andrzej Garlicki. Warsaw: Wydawnictwa Szkolne i Pedagogiczne, 1986.

———. *Struktura społeczna inteligencji w Polsce w latach 1918–1939.* Warsaw: Polskie Wydawnictwo Naukowe, 1964.

———, ed. *Życie polityczne w Polsce, 1918–1939.* Wrocław: Ossolineum, 1985.

Żebrowski, Rafał, ed. *Dzieje Żydów w Polsce: Wybór tekstów źródłowych, 1918–1939.* Warsaw: Żydowski Instytut Historyczny w Polsce, 1993.

Żółkiewski, Stefan. "Kultura literacka—Warunki modernizacji i początki umasowienia." In *Literatura polska, 1918–1932,* ed. Alina Brodzka, Helena Zaworska, and Stefan Żółkiewski. Warsaw: Wiedza Powszechna, 1975.

Żurowski, Maciej, et al., ed. *Les cahiers de Varsovie: Boy Żeleński (1874–1974).* Cieszyn: Cieszyńska Drukarnia Wydawnicza, 1976.

Index